Gardening with Ed Hume

Gardening with Ed Hume

Northwest Gardening Made Easy

Ed Hume

with photographs by James Hume

SASQUATCH BOOKS
SEATTLE

To my wife, Myrna, who for the past forty-four years has been a wonderful mother to our sons, a great supportive force for me, and my creative partner in the garden and all things.

Printed in Hong Kong
Published by Sasquatch Books
Distributed by Publishers Group West
09 08 07 06 05 04 03 6 5 4 3 2 1

Cover and interior design: Kate Basart
Cover and interior photographs: James Hume
Copy editor: Kris Fulsaas
Proofreader: Sigrid Asmus

Library of Congress Cataloging in Publication Data
Hume, Ed.
Gardening with Ed Hume : Northwest gardening made easy / by Ed Hume ; photographs by James Hume.
p. cm.
ISBN 1-57061-328-1
1. Gardening—Northwestern States. I. Title.
SB453.2N82 H86 2003
635'.09795—dc21 2002029412

Sasquatch Books
119 South Main Street, Suite 400
Seattle, Washington 98104
206/467-4300
www.sasquatchbooks.com
books@sasquatchbooks.com

Contents

Acknowledgments

It's been a great challenge to write this book, because there are so many aspects to gardening in the Northwest. Just consider trees and shrubs alone—we are so fortunate to be able to grow such a wide range of plant material. So which do I recommend and, because of page limitations, which do I have to omit? It's a tough decision! I've had a few sleepless nights, but in the long run it's been fun, and this book is my answer to that challenge.

Staff members have worked tirelessly, revising my scrambled words and making sense of what I was trying to say. There are not enough ways to say thank you to them. They have weathered the original copy, the revisions, and the rewrites with flying colors.

My wife, Myrna, has been most supportive and understanding of the countless hours and time I have had to devote to writing, revising, and rewriting. She has offered suggestions and has been very dedicated to working with Sasquatch on giving the book just the right title.

James Hume, our younger son, the director of *Gardening in America,* my television show, has been busy taking pictures for this book for the past two seasons. Jeff Hume, our older son, has been helping solve our many computer woes. So you can see, in many ways this has been a family project.

I have received invaluable help from Phil Edmunds and Rich Baer of Edmunds Roses in Wilsonville, Oregon. These two rosarians have advised me on the latest and best roses for the region. Sam Benowitz of Raintree Nursery in Morton, Washington, has also provided me with invaluable information on the proven varieties of fruit and berries that grow and mature here. The cooperation, knowledge, and assistance I've received from all three of these professionals are priceless.

Over the years, I have been fortunate to meet and get to know some of the really outstanding horticulturists, botanists, and gardening authorities of this era. I dare say, each of them in some way (even though they don't know it) has participated in helping me write this book. The knowledge and tips they have passed along are invaluable. People such as the late Gordon Baker Lloyd, Ed Woods, Claude Mills, Paul Brown, and Bruce Briggs, just to name a few. My Canadian friends Brian Minter and Bev and

Helen Hadley and many others have been a rich source of gardening information. To all of you, and countless others, thank you!

One always saves the best for last. My special thanks to you for being so supportive for the past thirty-eight years of my television and radio programs, newspaper columns, lectures, and public appearances. The staff at Ed Hume Seeds also joins me in thanking you for being so supportive of our products. This book has been written especially for you. It is my sincere hope that the information is valuable to you, and that it makes your gardening a lot easier, more productive, and really enjoyable. Happy gardening!

Special Thanks

Edmunds Roses / 6235 Southwest Kahle Road / Wilsonville, OR 97070

Raintree Nursery / 391 Butts Road / Morton, WA 98356

Introduction

The first question that I am frequently asked is, "How did you get interested in gardening?" and the next question is, "Why don't you write a book on Northwest gardening?" Well, the answers are simple, and the following few paragraphs will give you a quick rundown on how my gardening career started. This book is the answer to the second question. There really isn't a gardening handbook for Northwest homeowners, so this book is my "answer" to solving garden problems, sharing ideas, and making it fun and easy to garden in the Northwest!

Both of my parents were from farming families in Canada. They met and married in Vulcan, Alberta, then later moved to the Seattle area. Dad had six fruit trees and three nut trees, and was a beekeeper in his spare time. Mom was a great flower gardener; she could grow just about anything. I am the youngest of six kids (two brothers, three sisters), and we all helped out around the property. We raised chickens, rabbits, ducks, and even a couple of goats. Mowing our lawn, trimming the privet hedge out front, and shoveling the sawdust that we used for heating fuel became my jobs during my elementary school days, because both older brothers were off fighting in World War II.

During the summer I had a lawn-mowing route. For a couple of years during the war, my folks leased 5 acres of farmland in Seattle's north end. My sister Nina and I worked with Dad growing beans, corn, and other vegetables on that land, and sold them at a roadside stand to the defense workers from the Sand Point Naval Air Station. In high school, I worked two summers planting and gathering bulbs for University Flower and Bulb Company. They grew bulbs and flowers of gladiolus and the Dutch and English iris. That job is what really piqued my interest in gardening.

As a high school graduation present, my folks gave me a suit, because they thought I should be a banker like my oldest brother. But much to their surprise, I applied for a job at Malmo Nursery—a family-owned nursery—in Seattle. I got the job, started immediately, and have been in the garden field ever since (more than fifty years now), except for a couple of years in the U.S. Army during the Korean conflict. By the way, I only wore that suit one time!

One incident that really helped me gain gardening experience happened during my first year at Malmo's. I was chosen (nobody else would do it!) to inventory the nursery. That was before the advent of growing plants in containers, so everything was grown in the ground. They had approximately one million plants, all labeled by botanical name. In December, this twenty-year-old kid, with the help of an old-time nurseryman, started inventorying the nursery. It was a cold, miserable December, so after just a few days my partner quit, leaving me alone to finish the job. Well, needless to say, one learns plants and botanical names in a hurry under those conditions.

I worked for them for two years, then moved on to a management position with Wight's nursery and had eleven wonderful years with Chauncey Wight and his staff. In 1963, I joined Richmond Nursery as their general manager and spent a challenging two years there before beginning my career in television, radio, and writing. At that time, I also took on the job of executive secretary for the Washington State Nurserymen's Association and remained with them for a couple of years.

The last thirty-seven years have been spent talking and writing about, and showing and doing garden-related projects. In addition, Myrna and our two sons have joined me in conducting tours and cruises to more than seventy countries, giving us an opportunity to visit some of the most beautiful gardens in the world. In 1977, Myrna and I started a seed company, which now covers all of the Pacific Northwest. Both of our sons are involved in our seed and TV production businesses.

During the past thirty-seven years, we have had the honor of being invited twice to the White House to view the gardens, once by a first lady and once by a president's brother. In the sixties, along with Lt. Governor John Cherberg and members of the Washington State Nurserymen's Association, I had the honor of presenting King Olaf of Norway with a western hemlock (the Washington State tree) and with a rhododendron (the Washington State flower) named for him. My family and I have met governors, college presidents, corporate heads, and some of the world's leading botanists and horticulturists. But most of all I have had the opportunity to meet and share gardening ideas with thousands of people in the Northwest, and that's the real frosting on the cake.

Myrna, a native of Everett, Washington, and I have been married for forty-four years. During that time, we have had fun designing, planting, and enjoying gardens in six different homes from Edmonds, Lakewood, and Auburn to Kent.

In this book, with the help of family, I have attempted to make just about every section stand on its own. Hopefully, this will make it really easy for you to find what you want to know. For example, if you want to know something about feeding, pruning, or planting, you won't have to read the whole chapter—you can find it quickly under those section headings. This is a handbook, intended to be a hands-on book that you can take right into the garden with you. It's designed to put the answers right at your fingertips, so hopefully it will become one of your favorite gardening tools. My answers and comments are based on my fifty-plus years in the gardening field here in the Northwest.

Keep in mind there are a dozen different ways to do most garden projects. I have attempted to give you the quickest, easiest, and most successful methods I know. That doesn't mean that other methods won't work; in fact, you may have already found tricks of your own, and I encourage you to experiment.

Weather plays an important part in gardening, and what works one year may not another, so experiment a little. If you live in an area where conditions are a bit different, such as near the ocean or in the foothills, and don't know what to grow, here's my suggestion to you: Get in the car, drive around your neighborhood, observe, and make a list of what is successfully growing around the older homes in the area. It's a surefire way of knowing which plants are the survivors!

It's my belief that all of gardening is based on common sense. Don't waste your time worrying about what to do; just use common sense, and you will develop your own green thumb. Mother Nature plays tricks on us all the time! So if something isn't working out the way you think it should, just change your strategy and rethink how to go about solving the problem.

Whatever you do, enjoy your garden—don't become a slave to it! That's the aim of this book: to make your gardening experience easy, fun, and rewarding!

1 LANDSCAPING

One of the best investments you can make when you buy your new home is to immediately begin your landscaping. A well-planned landscape can increase the value of your home anywhere from 12 to 21 percent, depending upon the extent of the landscaping. This is especially important when you think about the other investments in your home and lifestyle. For example, when you put carpeting on the floors, it immediately decreases in value; when you hang drapes and install your window dressings, they immediately decrease in value. When you drive your new car into the driveway, it immediately decreases in value.

Landscaping, on the other hand, automatically increases the value of your home, and yet it is often the last thing done. I can't stress to you enough what a valuable investment you make when you put a few dollars, some thought, and a little time into your landscape. Each time Myrna and I have sold a house, we have been pleasantly reminded of this fact.

Facing page: Pink dogwood and tulips welcome you to the Hume residence in springtime. *Below:* Leaf texture, foliage color, flowers, and plant shapes combine to create a pleasant landscape planting.

One of the wonderful things about living in the Pacific Northwest is the tremendous variety of plants we can grow. Not to mention the dollar value, satisfaction, and enjoyment you will get from beautifying your home landscape.

I could write an entire book on landscaping. It is impossible to give you a well-rounded presentation of the subject in a single chapter, but hopefully this chapter will give you a few ideas of how to get started.

Choosing a Landscape Style

Architecture, location, and terrain may play a part in determining the most attractive type of landscape style for you. For example, the type and scale of a landscape around a two-story Tudor will very likely be different from the design/style used when landscaping a one-story rambler. You may need to decide whether your landscape should be informal, semi-formal, or formal. Or maybe your tastes favor a specialty cottage, Mediterranean, European, Chinese, Japanese, or tropical-style garden. It's really up to you!

Some of the best landscaping I've seen doesn't fit into any rigid category, but is an expression of the homeowner's personal taste, imagination, and sense of style. I encourage you to start simple and become more creative as you feel more confident with your design, the various types of plants, and their placement in your garden.

Northwest Style

Each area of the country has its own style, and we're in an enviable situation because we have so many choices of plant material. West of the Cascade Mountains, it's lush and green throughout the year. In this area, there's a mix of native evergreens and maples, dogwood, and other deciduous trees, which create the framework and are usually underplanted with rhododendrons, azaleas, heather, ferns, and other evergreen plants. Mix in some fine-foliage conifers, a few more flowering broadleaf evergreens, then add some perennials and a few summer flowering annuals, and you have created a landscape setting unequaled in practically any other part of the world.

East of the Cascade Mountains, the warm summers and cold winters challenge the home gardener to come up with a selection of hardier evergreen trees and shrubs. But by combining texture, leaf color, and flowering plants; using shapes effectively; and incorporating fragrance, a Midwestern landscape style emerges.

The Ed Hume Style

My style is a Northwest-English cottage garden hybrid. This involves a little more maintenance maybe, but a lot more color from annuals and perennials, casual winding paths, mixed borders, and plenty of flowering broadleaf evergreens. I like to round a bend on a path and walk into a new and different landscape setting, so the garden actually becomes several small gardens in one. All the borders in my garden are on raised soil *(berms)*, for better drainage and because I feel the plants show off better. We feature about three dozen hanging baskets and a dozen container plantings to add seasonal color and interest. Our garden is designed for us—nobody else—and that's what I hope you'll do too! I encourage you to develop your landscape to fit your needs and lifestyle.

Sketching Your Property

Make a rough sketch of your property and the dimensions of your property. You can do this on a piece of paper or small blackboard/erase board. I like the blackboard/erase board, because you can easily erase and re-sketch as you change your mind. Roughly sketch in your home, driveway, sidewalks, patio, fire hydrant, mailboxes, and any large trees or shrubs already on the property.

Draw in your first idea of where the flowerbeds should be and what shapes you think would look nice. Don't worry about exact dimensions or fret about your drawing skills. This is just a working idea on paper/blackboard/erase board. If you have no idea where to go from here . . . I have some ideas for you!

Assessing the Site

Walk and visually observe your entire property to assess what needs to be done. Make a checklist and look for any possible problems. Here's what I suggest you include on your list:

Drainage/Contour

List any problem areas. Can the problem be corrected by simply changing the contour (slope) in that part of the garden? Be certain the soil (contour) slopes away from the home. Likewise, be certain the soil is contoured on the entire property so the surface water runs off and does not gather in any low spots. If this cannot be accomplished then it may be necessary to consider providing an underground drainage system.

Utilities

Make sure you find out where all above- and belowground utility lines are located. Otherwise, you take a chance of cutting into these utility lines when planting or doing any type of construction. You can find out this information from your builder or local utility companies. In addition there are utility locator companies that provide that service for a fee.

Existing Plants

Can you use them in your new landscape design? Do the plants need to be moved? When and how?

Determining Your Landscape Needs

The best place for you to start planning is to consider your needs and desires. The first thing for you to do is to make a list of what needs to be done to your property and your family's desires for the landscape. Here are a few things to consider:

- Do you need privacy or a planting to screen out an eyesore?
- Do you need a play area for the children? A sandbox, swingset, etc.
- Do you need a special parking area for a boat or RV?
- Do you want a spot to grow a few fruit trees, roses, or a vegetable garden?
- Do you want to add a water feature, swimming pool, hot tub, firepit, etc.?

Do You Need Fencing?

Does the yard need to be fenced for privacy or to aid in protecting children or pets? Which part of the property needs fencing? What materials are going to be used? What is the priority of this project? If you have small children, this may be the first item on your list of things to do.

Do You Want to Add New Features and Structures?

Plan right from the beginning where and when new features will become a part of the landscape. If you want to include night lighting and/or a sprinkler system, you may need to install them before you do anything else. Other features you might consider adding:

- more parking space
- sprinkler system
- retaining walls
- family areas

These items may not fit into your budget right now, but if you plan to have them eventually, decide now where they will be situated. A little planning at the beginning will make the job a lot easier when you're ready to do the construction. Here's a list of a few new structures you might want to eventually include in your outdoor living area:

- swimming pool
- greenhouse
- hot tub/spa
- tool shed/storage unit
- firepit/barbecue
- waterfall/pond/water feature

How Much Time Do You Have to Spend on Your Garden?

If time is a factor or if you're not particularly interested in gardening, consider a few of the ways you can make your garden low maintenance.

- One is to use ground covers in your flower and shrub beds to cover the soil and help crowd out weeds and nuisance grasses.
- Another method is to mulch the landscape beds with bark, sawdust, or compost to help choke out nuisance weeds and grasses.
- You can use natural preemergent herbicides (such as gluten of cornmeal) to help keep weed and grass seed from germinating.

Below: Our entry garden includes our favorite annuals, perennials, trees, and shrubs, selected for year-round color.

Getting Landscape Ideas

There are several places you can go to get ideas for your landscape.

From Friends and Neighbors

As you drive around the neighborhood and surrounding areas, observe what other people have done. Commercial plantings also offer some great ideas, especially on low-maintenance gardening. You can copy the ones

Need Help? Here Are Some Ideas.

- Totally baffled about what to plant, where to plant, and how to plant it? Seeking the advice of a landscape contractor, designer, or architect may be your best solution. Ask for references from friends and neighbors or contact licensed members of a trade organization.
- Take time to plan your garden, keeping in mind the needs of your family. Allot areas of the garden for different uses, such as a play or family area, entry, outdoor or patio area, and parking, and determine whether you want a space for a vegetable garden, fruit trees, and/or berries. A little planning will save you a lot of time, money, and energy in the long run.
- When it comes to hardscapes (walks, walls, patios), I am not very construction savvy. However, I've found a couple of ways to overcome my inexperience:
- Simply observe what others have done to solve a construction problem and copy their ideas.
- Thumb through handbooks on the particular subject and get ideas from the pictures. Then you can simply copy the idea, or better yet, add your personal touch to the project, and you will usually come up with something even better looking and more useful.
- Have a limited budget? Start with the lawn, for the kids and pets. Next, plant your trees and your privacy plantings. The entry and family areas are next. Then the rest of the garden can be done as the budget permits. With a limited budget, plant small trees and shrubs, they'll grow (some quite quickly).
- Ever heard the saying "curb appeal"? That's a term the real estate industry uses a lot to describe the appearance of a home from the street. It's of utmost importance when you are buying or selling your home. Approximately 85 percent of people get an impression of your home before they ever step inside the front door. So it's important to give special consideration to designing and planting the entry area of your home.

you like, or take the idea and change it to fit your needs. Some of the prettiest landscapes I have ever seen are from such gardens, where the homeowner has taken someone else's idea and added their own personal touch.

From Landscape Books

Many books feature plans, construction ideas, planting combinations, and landscape styles, and most include a lot of pictures of finished projects. These pictures often stir your creative juices, and you can transform the ideas into a beautiful landscape setting in your own garden.

From Photographs

Take snapshots of each area of your garden. Then take these photos to your local garden center/nursery and ask the certified nursery or landscape person on staff to give you some suggestions for the particular area you are working on. Don't do this on the weekend or during busy hours; take it to them at a time when they are not busy and can devote some time to showing you what plants would do best in that particular area of your garden. That way, you can see the plants, even though you may not be familiar with them, and see if you like their attributes.

From Landscape Consultants

You can get a consultation from many landscape contractors, designers, or landscape architects. This is a great way to get your landscape project underway. It will cost some well-spent money. You might want to get a reference from your local nursery, garden center, or a neighbor. With a landscape consultation, these professionals will not make a plan, so you need a pencil and piece of paper to make notes of their many suggestions.

Making a Landscape Plan

If it's within your budget and you like the ideas of your landscape consultant, you may decide to have the landscape architect, designer, or contractor go ahead and draw up a finished landscape plan. Landscape contractors can even complete the installation if you desire and if the costs are within your budget.

Here are just a few simple ideas you should keep in mind when starting (or planning) your own landscape:

Screen Any Problem Areas

Unsightly telephone poles, utility boxes, fire hydrants, or neighboring unkempt yards can easily be screened by the simple use of evergreen shrubs or trees.

Provide Privacy

Providing privacy is easy: just choose the right plant for that spot. Here again, you might want to seek some advice from a professional. There usually is more than one type of plant that will provide the privacy you desire. See my listings of privacy plants throughout this book, especially in Chapter 4, Shrubs.

Below: Total privacy can be created by using evergreen or flowering trees and shrubs.

Plant the Trees

Remember that trees take the longest to grow and are responsible for providing shade, privacy, structure, and scale to the landscape. Landscape architects refer to the trees as the "bones" of the landscape, so start by planting the trees you want.

Shape Flower and Shrub Beds

If you're working with your own ideas or from a plan, you may need some help in actually shaping the outline of the beds. Here's my suggestion: just take your garden hose, lay it out on the ground, and move it around until you have formed the actual shape you desire. Then take a straight-edge spade and cut right along the edge of the hose. Now you have the exact bed shape you like!

I suggest you mound your soil beds, creating berms, which have several advantages:

- Plants show off better.
- Raised soil provides better drainage for plants.
- Soils warm up faster, so plants grow better and often flower more.

Selecting Plants

Avoid making the big mistake that many homeowners make: buying a plant because you like the flower or leaf color, then getting home and not having the slightest idea of where to plant it. I see this happen all the time. People buy plants because they like the flowers, leaves, or berries; then they have no idea where to plant them. First thing you know, the garden begins to take on a hodgepodge look and it becomes a discouraging mess. You can lose interest in a hurry if there is no advance planning and no sign of a landscape taking shape.

Work new plants into your overall plan; don't just plunk them anywhere in the ground. Keep in mind exposure to sunlight, soil conditions, the plant's need for moisture, the amount of time you will have to spend maintaining the plant, and, most important, what it will look like all year long.

Plan Year-Round Color and Interest

It's wonderful to have spots of color and interest in the garden all twelve months of the year. Use the plant lists in the chapters on trees, shrubs, and perennials to help you choose plants that will provide a staggered blooming season in your garden.

Look for These Features

Below are the five basic characteristics that in my opinion will make or break a good landscape. Actually, with just the first two—leaf color and texture—you can create an absolutely beautiful garden, and the other three features are the frosting on the cake!

Right: The textures and colors of a variegated elaegenus, *Viburnum davidii,* and dusty miller create a pleasant contrast.

Below: Curved walkways, attractive fencelines, and a variety of plant fragrances, shapes, and colors lead to the back of the Hume residence.

Leaf Color

Select plants with attractive leaf colors. Some of the best trees and shrubs have leaves that are in shades of green, variegated gold and green, reds, grays, or blues.

Leaf Texture

Choose plants with various leaf textures. A combination of fine, medium, and bold textures are very attractive in the landscape. For example, junipers and heathers have fine leaf textures, while evergreen azaleas and lily-of-the-valley shrubs have medium textures, and rhododendrons and camellias have larger, bolder textures.

Flower Color

Flower color is a bonus because you can create the most beautiful landscape setting by simply using leaf color and leaf texture. Adding flower color creates a whole new dimension for the garden.

Shape

You can create interest and a very exciting landscape style by simply using plants that have unusual shapes. There are many plant shapes: pyramidal, oval, spreading, round, vase-shaped, and countless others. Use them wisely to highlight sections of your garden.

Fragrance

This adds another element to any garden. Use fragrant plants near the entry area, on the patio, or wherever foot traffic is heavy, so the fragrance can be fully enjoyed. You can plan your landscape so you have fragrance in some part of the garden all twelve months of the year.

Landscaping for a Pre-Owned House

Where do you start when you buy a pre-owned house and want to landscape it? Do exactly the same things already mentioned, seeing how many of the existing plants you can work into your plans. Some of the older overgrown plants may need to either be pruned back to fit your landscape plan or transplanted to a new, more suitable location. If they don't fit at all, offer to let relatives, friends, or neighbors dig and transplant them for use in their gardens.

2 LANDSCAPING WITH CONTAINERS

CONTAINERS

One of the most interesting parts of your garden can be the landscaping on your patio, deck, or lanai. Because these are frequently used areas, you may want to use a combination of containers and hanging baskets to provide a pleasant, tranquil setting. By gardening in containers, you can grow flowers, vegetables, shrubs, even small trees, and create a private, colorful extension of your home. Of course, the types of plants you use in any container will depend on the season you will use that container planting and whether the container will be placed in the sun or shade.

Facing page: I used a variety of foliage and flower shapes and colors in this container to create a bright spot in our landscape beds.

Below: Nasturtiums combine nicely with other annuals in this planting created at Minter Gardens (Chilliwack, B.C.).

CHOOSING TYPES OF CONTAINERS

What you use is up to you! Keep in mind that it's not necessary to use the same kind of container throughout the landscape. A mixture of wood, ceramic, clay, or plastic containers can be quite appealing and functional. However, in a formal setting, containers made of the same material (and size) would be more attractive.

What Size of Containers Should You Use?

Be certain to choose a large enough container for the plants you want to use. As a rule, the tallest plant should never be more than three times higher than the greatest height or width of the container. If you have a container that's 2 feet high and 2 feet wide, the tallest plant should not exceed 6 feet in height. Even then, be careful not to use a large-spreading plant, which would tend to make the container top-heavy and susceptible to being blown over in a strong windstorm.

What About Moss Hanging Baskets?

In recent years, the wire baskets lined with green moss have become very popular. These are quite easy to make. Simply line a wire basket with green sphagnum moss, fill with soil, and plant. You can also pull the wire and moss apart on the sides and add plants to create a wonderful mass effect. Always wear gloves when handling the moss, especially if you have any cuts on your hands. Otherwise you take a chance of picking up a disease, *Sporotrichum schenckii,* from the green sphagnum moss.

Can You Reuse Containers?

If you have an empty container left over from last year and you intend to use it again this season, be certain to clean it up first. One of the best ways to do this is to mix up a solution of 90 percent water and 10 percent bleach. Put on a pair of waterproof gloves, use a coarse rag or soft brush, and clean the container thoroughly with the solution. Let it dry, or dry it with a cloth, and plant!

Choosing a Location for Containers

Whether you have a large or small space in which to grow your vegetables or flowers, you'll find it fun and useful to grow a few things in containers. Shrubs, small trees, flowers, or even vegetables can very easily be grown in containers on the average patio, deck, or lanai.

Looking for a really spectacular hanging basket plant? Take a look at the new million bells, *Calibrachoa.* Of all the different types of plants for hanging baskets, this and the lavender-blue flowering scaevola are by far our favorites. Our million bells hanging basket flowers prolifically all summer and into the fall. The flowers look a lot like miniature petunias. The plants trail about 3 feet in a single year. This plant likes full sun and well-drained soil, and it's easy to grow!

Create Privacy with Containers

Yes, you can create considerable privacy simply by placing the larger-growing container plants in strategically chosen spots on your patio, deck, or lanai. Use evergreens for year-round privacy and deciduous flowering shrubs or small trees for seasonal summer privacy.

Make Your Containers Portable

Give your containers wheels! My wife, Myrna, has purchased inexpensive plant coasters (several different kinds are available) to put under our containers. Now we can very easily wheel our planters from one area of the deck to another, or even turn them occasionally, so the plants get equal light and do not grow lopsided. If there is inclement weather, the containers can easily be wheeled to a more protected area.

Planting in Containers

What Soil Should You Use in Containers?

I recommend using a high-quality potting soil, one that you buy from a garden store or greenhouse grower. Commercial potting or planting mixes are sterilized and usually contain a balance of organic humus and nutrients. When planting containers, I do not recommend using soil from the garden, because you are apt to introduce poor-quality soil, insects, weed seed, and other problems.

Also, there is no need to place any rocks or broken pots in the bottom of the containers. In the past, this was done thinking it would aid in drainage, and instead it does just the opposite.

Can You Use Soil from Last Year's Container?

One of the questions I am most often asked is, "I still have the soil in last year's hanging basket; can I use it again this year?" My answer is, "Yes and no!" If you add at least 50 percent new potting soil, it is OK to use it again. However, for the few cents it costs, the addition of all new soil is sure worth it! That doesn't mean you have to throw the old soil away; simply spread and mix it with your soil in the vegetable or flower garden.

Left: This planter of variegated hebe, fuchsia 'Gartenmeister', coleus, and impatiens would work well in shade or part shade.

Tips on Planting and Transplanting

Dig the Planting Hole

As a rule, I suggest that you make the new planting (or transplanting) hole twice as wide and twice as deep as the actual size of the root ball of the plant you are planting. Downsize the new planting hole if you are transplanting big garden shrubs. Otherwise you're apt to dig up half the garden just to plant one tree or shrub. In those cases, just make the new planting hole about 1 foot wider and about 6 inches deeper than the existing root system of the plant.

Check for Adequate Drainage

You can check the drainage of the planting site by pouring a gallon or two of water into the planting hole, then watching to see how long it takes to drain away. If water sits for any length of time, that indicates you need to provide additional drainage before planting. This can be done by digging a sump hole next to the planting hole, or by using drain tile to direct excess water away from the hole. Sometimes you can eliminate a drainage problem by simply recontouring the soil grade in the planting area, or by planting on raised soil.

Prepare the Soil for Planting

For the past fifty years, I have found that proper soil preparation is the key to developing healthy, vigorous-growing plants. If the plant is given an organic-rich soil in which to become established, the roots will continue to develop into the surrounding unprepared soil and flourish with minimal care. Remember, the only time you can get nutrients and organic matter down into the root zone is at planting time, so take the time and spend the money to properly prepare the planting soil. Here's the way to start:

Add Organic Matter to the Soil

Now here's the really important step. Using two-thirds of the existing soil, add organic matter in the form of compost, peat moss, processed manure (the bagged stuff), or well-rotted manure; use enough to replace the other one-third of the existing soil that you will not be using. Never use fresh manure, because the gases it creates might burn the roots and cause more damage than good. Mix the organic matter thoroughly with the existing soil. Add some of this mixed soil to the bottom of the planting hole and use the rest to fill in around the plant as you finish planting.

Set the Plant at the Right Depth

Again, this is a very important factor in properly setting out new plants. Try to place the plant right at ground level (that's the same level at which it was previously planted). As a rule, there will be a soil mark on the stem or trunk of the plant that indicates the proper planting depth. If you are planting a tree or shrub that has been growing in a container, be sure to set it so the surface roots are right at the same ground level as they were in the container.

As a final step, make a small recessed area around the stem or trunk to collect rainwater. This recessed area also makes it easier to water the plant, plus it will help conserve on the amount of water you use. This recessed area is often referred to as a *well*.

Stake Plants After Planting

It's best to let plants become established on their own whenever you can. However, if the plant is top-heavy or tends to be unsteady in the soil, staking is probably necessary. You will need to stabilize the plant with stakes or guywires. Supporting materials that come in contact with the trunk of the plant or tree must have a covering so they do not cut into the bark and damage the stem or trunk. On trees, a piece of old rubber hose is great for this job. Place the guywire or rope right through the center of the piece of cut hose. For smaller plants, use soft materials such as rags or pantyhose to wrap the stem.

If possible, the staking support should be removed within six months to a year at most. This is necessary because the plant needs to build up its own resistance to wind, snow, and the elements.

Below: Pots of 'Lime' sweet potato, impatiens, heliotrope, and lobelia brighten this Northwest patio.

Watering Plants in Containers

The watering needs of plants grown in containers and hanging baskets are much greater than those of plants grown in the landscape. This is due in large part to the limited soil space in containers, plus the fact that they are exposed to air, wind, and the sun; consequently, the soil dries out much quicker. It is very important to check watering needs regularly and experiment a little to determine how often it's necessary to water.

Water thoroughly when you water, allowing just a little water to run out the drainage hole in the bottom of the container or hanging basket. Then you know the pot has been thoroughly soaked.

Feeding Plants in Containers

Plants grown in containers and hanging baskets are usually crowded for space and competing with one another for needed nutrients. They need to be fertilized about once every other week during the spring, summer, and early autumn growing seasons in order to keep them in a good, healthy growing condition. (Evergreens growing in containers will need to be fed only once or twice a year.)

Protecting Containers from Cold Weather

Containers are exposed to air on all four sides, plus the top and the bottom, so they can freeze very easily. One of the easiest ways to give containers winter protection is to simply take them into an unheated basement or garage during a cold spell (avoid putting them into a heated room). Use a hand truck or some other means to move them. Then, once the weather improves, put them right back outside. Do not leave the planted containers inside all winter unless you have a greenhouse or sun porch for them.

If the planted container is too large to move into a basement or garage during cold weather, you can leave it outside and mulch around the sides of the container. Simply mound bark or sawdust up around the sides of the pot, or wrap the container with blankets or packing material. These are not very attractive solutions, but they will get your large containers through a cold spell if you can't move them inside.

Choosing Plants for Containers

Besides the information in this section, in each chapter I recommend types and varieties of plants I think will do best in containers. Please check out the chapters on shrubs, ornamental grasses, annual flowers, herbs, etc., for more information for those particular types of plants.

For Seasonal Color

You can vary the color in containers from season to season. Here are just a few of the plants that offer seasonal color:

Spring

Tulips, daffodils, hyacinths, and crocus bulbs are great for sunny locations. Pansies, primroses, and some spring-blooming perennials (see Chapter 9, Perennials) are ideal for shaded areas. Azaleas, dwarf rhododendrons, and heather are wonderful evergreen shrubs.

Summer

Impatiens, fuchsias, coleus, begonias, and pansies are great in the shade. In sunny spots, use marigolds, petunias, geraniums, lobelia, zinnias, stock, and other summer annuals. Summer-flowering heather, hebe, and abelia are a few evergreens to consider.

Fall and Winter

Flowering kale and cabbage, winter pansies, 'Bright Lights' Swiss chard, fall chrysanthemums, and Michaelmas daisies are quite showy in bright light. Winter-flowering heather and any berried plants like cotoneaster, pernettya, or wintergreen are attractive evergreens.

Left: Many new varieties of petunias provide outstanding summer color in containers and hanging baskets. 'Wave' petunias are one of my favorites.

3 · TREES

A well-designed landscape includes a combination of trees, shrubs, and flowers that offers color and interest at all times of the year. Trees provide the framework for the home and landscape, with their interesting shapes, foliage color, leaf textures, flowers, berries, and/or seed pods. Plus they provide shade, privacy, and structure for the yard. Here are some hints on how to select, grow, care for, and enjoy trees in the home garden.

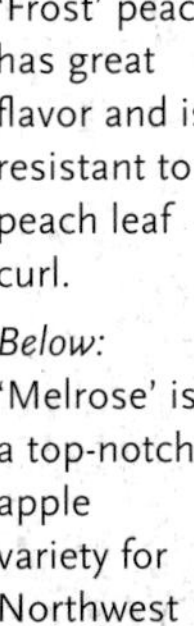

Facing page: 'Frost' peach has great flavor and is resistant to peach leaf curl.

Below: 'Melrose' is a top-notch apple variety for Northwest gardens.

DETERMINING THE RIGHT TREES FOR YOUR GARDEN

There's a type or variety of tree to fit just about any landscape need, from small trees to huge ones, from some that lose their leaves over winter to others that are evergreen. The right tree in the right location is invaluable for beauty and year-round interest. Give some serious consideration to these eight questions before choosing a tree for your garden:

- How small a tree will do the job?
- What shape is needed (oval, vase-shaped, pyramidal, spreading)?
- Should it have foliage year-round? Should it be evergreen or deciduous?
- Do you want the tree to have flowers, berries or seedpods, and/or autumn leaf color?
- What color should the foliage be?
- Do you want a low-maintenance tree?
- Do you want a messy tree? Does it self-seed, drop pods or fruit, or continually drop leaves?
- Are the roots apt to create problems with sewer lines, sidewalks, or other paved surfaces?

How Tall Do You Want Your Tree to Grow?

One of the biggest mistakes people make is selecting a fast-growing tree. Remember, a "fast-growing tree" is quickly going to become a "big tree," and the average-size lot is too small to support a large tree; there's just not enough space. Size, variety, and shape should be your main concerns.

Fruit Trees

If you want to include fruit trees in your landscape, keep in mind that most fruit tree varieties come in dwarf, semi-dwarf, and standard trees. For example, here's a rundown on approximate sizes of apple trees. (Actual heights vary, depending upon the variety and the rootstock on which they are grafted. Researchers have developed specialty rootstocks that actually will determine the ultimate height of a tree.)

Mini-dwarf: 4 to 6 feet, EMLA-27 rootstock
Dwarf: 8 to 12 feet, M-26 rootstock
Semi-dwarf: 12 to 16 feet, EMLA-7 or MM-106
Standard: 20 to 35 feet (few standard trees are offered now)
Columnar: narrow, upright growth habit to about 8 to 12 feet. These are an excellent size of tree to grow in containers and are ideal for small yards and/or for children to grow. My columnar crabapple is now about 3 feet in width, and it should grow only a foot wider with age.

Choosing the Location

There are several things to consider before you actually plant a tree in your garden:

- Avoid planting near underground water lines, electrical cables, sewer lines, etc. In addition, stay away from overhead wires (telephone and electrical).
- Choose a spot where the tree will not grow over into a neighbor's property, restrict their view, or exceed any height restrictions.
- Consider whether the tree's roots will lift up sidewalks, driveways, patios, or other surfaces if it is planted too close to them. The roots of big trees planted too close to the foundation of the house can also create possible damage to the home's foundation.
- Never plant a berried tree near a walkway or patio. Messy fruit dropping creates a mess and sometimes stains wood or concrete surfaces.

For Fruit Trees

When selecting a spot for your fruit tree, here are a few points to keep in mind:

- Choose a bright, sunny spot in the garden.
- Make sure the soil is well drained. Avoid overly wet planting soils. If the soil tends to be quite moist, consider mounding the soil in the planting area.
- Avoid frost pockets. Many gardens have microclimates within the garden, such as low spots that tend to be a bit colder or places where there is poor air circulation. Avoid planting in those places.

Buying a Tree

Choose the Right Size for Easy Transplanting

Generally we want the biggest tree, so it can give us immediate privacy, screening, or shade. But is that really wise? Often the larger the tree, the more transplanting shock it suffers, and the longer it takes to recover. However, that's not to say that there are no advantages to planting large trees. In fact, here are a few advantages:

- A large tree has already reached the height needed to provide immediate privacy/screening.
- A large tree's height might be needed to keep the rest of the landscape in scale.
- A large tree could be what is needed to replace an old diseased or dead tree.
- A large tree is important for providing instant shade.

Professional orchardists start with one-year-old fruit trees (called *whips*) because they are easier to shape and they go through less transplanting shock; as a result, they catch up in size with older trees within a relatively short period. Plus they cost less. However, most garden/nursery centers offer two-year-old trees, which are easy to plant and already have the beginning of a branching structure.

Choose a Well-Shaped Tree

Shape is the key in selecting any tree for your garden. You want the tree to have uniform branches in tiers all the way around the trunk. The only reason you would select a one-sided tree is if you plan to place it near a fence or wall and are only concerned about it facing one way. Basically, what you want to do is use good common sense in selecting a well-shaped tree. If you feel unqualified or confused, ask the nurseryperson on staff for their advice.

Select a tree that has a sturdy, straight, upright growth habit and three to four (or more) branches extending out from the trunk evenly in different directions. In other words, you want a tree that has a nice, even, uniform growth habit. Because most trees sold are two-year-old trees, the first tier of branches should already have formed on the tree. If you choose a one-year-old tree, it will simply be an upright whip with few if any signs of branching.

Check for Damage

Before buying a prospective tree, check it for broken branches, scars on the trunk or branches, and, if it is a bare-root tree, broken or damaged roots. (A *bare-root* tree does not have soil around the roots.)

Planting a Tree

Once you have selected and purchased a new tree, get it into the ground as soon as possible. This is especially the case if the tree is bare-root because the exposure to air will dry out the roots very quickly. But even container-grown trees should be planted right away. The reason is simple: the sooner you get it into the ground, the sooner it will begin establishing a new root system and begin to grow.

When to Plant or Transplant Trees

Nursery-grown trees in containers can be safely planted at most any time throughout the year. However, avoid planting when temperatures are below freezing and when temperatures are in excess of 90 degrees Fahrenheit.

The best time for transplanting is during the winter dormant season of November, December, January, and February. Transplanting should take place at a time when the ground is not frozen and when temperatures are above freezing. The main reason for this is so that the roots are not exposed to cold temperatures or drying wind. Plus this is the time when local nurseries, garden centers, and mail-order firms begin shipping their new trees, so you have the pick of the lot.

However, if that's not a convenient time for you, most garden outlets do pot up their surplus trees and have them available for sale during the late spring and summer months. Because the roots of these containerized trees have not become established, I suggest you plant them pot and all. Then in late October to December, dig up the tree, take it out of the container, and permanently replant it.

Bare-Root Deciduous Trees

Fruit, flowering, and shade trees are often planted bare-root during their dormant season. Bare-root planting or transplanting is done during the winter months of November, December, January, and February. The ideal time to plant fruit trees is during the winter dormant season, when the trees can be dug and transplanted bare-root (in other words, during the winter months of December through early March). Planting in the winter gives new roots a chance to become established over winter. I do not recommend digging and transplanting established fruit trees in your garden during the spring or summer months; wait until winter.

Deciduous Trees That Cannot Be Planted Bare-Root

It is important to note that some deciduous trees are sensitive to root disturbance so they cannot be transplanted bare-root at any time. Therefore, they must have soil attached to the roots when they are either planted or transplanted. Examples of this are dogwood, Japanese maples, and magnolias. Others that need soil attached to the root system include beech, sourwood, stewartia, and sweetgum. When in doubt, check with the certified nurseryperson at your local garden outlet.

How to Dig Up Trees for Transplanting

If you are going to move a tree in your garden, where do you start digging? As a guideline, you can start digging the root ball at a distance halfway between the drip line of the tree and its trunk. Be certain the soil is moist, so the dirt will cling to the roots, lessening transplanting shock. Some of the larger roots can be cut, or you can try to save part of them by extending the digging a little farther away from the trunk. In most all cases, it's almost impossible to dig any plant without cutting some of the roots.

If possible, immediately enclose the roots in burlap or dark polyethylene so exposure to the air does not dry them out. Then get the tree into the new planting soil immediately.

Moving Established Trees

In the case of moving extra-large trees, look for a commercial firm that has tree-digging equipment for moving large, established trees up to 35 feet high. You will find them listed under "Tree Services" or "Landscaping" in the yellow pages.

Below: The crimson foliage and unusual flowers of 'Royal Purple' smoke tree add interest and color to the garden.

Transplanting Seedling Trees

Madrona, hemlock, fir, pines, conifers, holly, and other seedlings that appear in the garden are best transplanted when they are 6 to 18 inches tall. Since they have not developed a very vast root system, it is important to move them during the autumn, winter, or earliest spring when the small plants are dormant. Try to get as much soil with the roots as you can, and take some of the surrounding soil to add into the new transplanting hole.

Transplanting Suckers

The small 6- to 12-inch sucker growth that appears around the base of some trees (such as lilacs and sumac) can sometimes be separated and started as a new tree. Simply dig them up, separate them, and replant the suckers. The best time to do this is during the winter dormant months of November through February. *Note:* If the tree is grafted, the sucker growth will not be the same variety as the parent tree from which it is growing.

Dig the Planting Hole

I recommend digging the planting hole about twice the width of the root ball of the tree, and approximately 6 to 12 inches deeper than the present depth of the existing root ball. When planting or transplanting fruit and nut trees, prepare the new planting hole about twice the width and depth of the size of the roots of your new tree.

Check for Adequate Drainage

Check to be certain the soil is well drained. One way to do this is to take a bucket of water, pour it into the planting hole, and see that it drains away in a relatively short time. If the water remains for an hour or more, then you must figure out a way to provide better drainage. This might mean growing the tree on raised soil (a berm), drain-tiling away excess water, or digging a sump hole next to where you are going to plant the tree. You make a sump hole by digging a hole next to the planting hole, making it deeper than the planting hole, and filling it with drainage material such as rocks or gravel. This provides a place where the excess water in the bottom of the planting hole can go.

Prepare the Soil for Planting

Planting time is the only time you'll have a chance to get organic humus and nutrients directly into the root zone of your new tree. And remember, the better the root system, the better the top growth and eventual health and vigor of the tree. When I plant a tree, I use one-sixth part peat moss or processed manure (the bagged stuff), one-sixth part compost (either homemade or purchased), and two-thirds existing soil. Mix them thoroughly together. I also add a small amount of a nonburning transplanting or organic fertilizer.

Fruit and Nut Trees

For fruit and nut trees, into the planting soil mix one-third to one-half part organic humus with your existing soil. Compost, peat moss, and/or processed manure (the bagged stuff) are all excellent forms of organic humus. Add the correct amount of an all-purpose transplanting fertilizer with the planting soil (see Ed's Method of Feeding Trees later in this chapter). Use a manure fork, pitchfork, or spade to mix the organic humus and fertilizer with your existing soil.

Set the Tree at the Proper Planting Depth

Set the tree at the same depth as it was previously growing. Generally you will see a soil mark on the trunk indicating the depth that it had previously been planted. If the tree has been grafted, be sure the *graft* (the knob on the trunk) is an inch or two above soil level.

For fruit trees, this is essential; if you plant your tree too deep, it could revert to a different size. So be certain the *bud union* (the swelling at the base of the trunk) is 2 to 3 inches above ground level. Often nursery people will recommend that fruit trees be planted at the depth of the soil mark on the tree trunk, indicating where the tree was planted in the field. However, a few words of caution: Sometimes the trees are heeled-in too deep at the retail nursery, which marks the stem with an incorrect soil mark. It's best to go by my recommendation of keeping the bud union 2 to 3 inches aboveground.

Make a cone in the center of the planting hole, then spread the roots over the cone and carefully pull the soil in over the roots. Make certain the tree is standing straight upright, then firm the surrounding soil around the roots. Leave a well—a recessed soil area—at the base for watering, and then water in until the surrounding soil is completely moist. It's that easy!

Stake a Newly Planted Tree

If the tree tends to be top-heavy, it will probably require staking for the first six months or so. I prefer not to stake trees, because they establish their own resistance to wind and become established on their own much quicker. But sometimes it is necessary, especially with larger, older trees or if you live in a windy area.

A single stake placed near the trunk is often all that is needed to support small trees. Larger trees may need to be staked on three or four sides. Place the stakes 2 to 4 feet away, then use small-diameter rope, wire, or hose to provide the support the tree needs. Be certain to use some kind of protection on the trunk of the tree where the supporting material comes into contact with the trunk, so there is no chance of damaging the tree's bark. A piece of cut garden hose or flexible heavy plastic can be used for this. If possible, remove the staking support within six months, twelve months at most.

Fruit Trees

Generally, one- or two-year-old fruit trees do not need staking. Avoid staking, unless the tree seems unsteady or is situated in a very windy spot. If staking is required, use a piece of nylon stocking or something soft to tie the tree to the stake. Don't tie it too tight; allow for a little movement, so the tree has a better chance of becoming established on its own. Only leave it staked for six months or up to one year if needed.

Pruning Trees

When to Prune

This is the number-one question asked by home gardeners. Here's my answer: "Wondering when to prune a plant? You can do it anytime you have a sharp, clean pair of pruning shears in your hand." There really are no exceptions to this rule.

Deciduous/Shade Trees

I was always taught that the best time to prune maples is in December or January. However, I know a great bonsai gardener who prunes his outdoor maples, including the laceleaf varieties, in June. By experimenting, I have found they can be pruned at any time.

Flowering Trees

Flowering trees can be pruned at any time; however, you can see the branching pattern easiest in the autumn or winter after the leaves have fallen. So the months of November through February are my favorites for pruning these.

Tips on Pruning

What to Prune

A word to the wise: *Never prune for the sake of pruning!* Prune only plants that need to be pruned. Just because someone says a plant needs to be pruned yearly doesn't mean it needs to be pruned at all. Use good common sense; you are the judge of whether the plant needs pruning or not. Many plants will go an entire lifetime without the need of any kind of pruning.

When to Prune

This is the number-one question asked by home gardeners. You can do it any time you have a sharp, clean pair of pruning shears in your hand. There really are no exceptions to this rule.

How Much to Prune

This is a tough question to answer. How much needs to be removed? How will it affect the appearance of the plant? Why are you pruning? Less is easier on the plant, usually results in a better-looking plant, and doesn't affect the overall growth of the plant as much. However, sometimes a plant has just been allowed to grow too big for its location and steps need to be taken to bring it back into shape. My recommendation is to never remove more than one-third of the total growth. Otherwise you take a big chance of ruining the shape of any tree or shrub forever. In cases in which the plant is severely overgrown, the best solution may be to dig and replace the plant with a more suitable choice.

How to Prune

Always make your pruning cut just above an outside bud. This forces the new growth outward. Otherwise the plant becomes a tangled mess of inside growth. Cuts larger than the diameter of your thumb should be treated with a pruning paint. This is especially important here in the West where moisture could aid in the development of moss, algae, and lichens, which could eventually create a dieback on the cut surface. Make your pruning cut at a slight angle so moisture runs off the cut. On a flat cut, the moisture would sit, and then during cold weather the moisture could freeze and cause damage or possibly dieback.

One more time: Never prune for the sake of pruning! Only prune trees and shrubs if they need to be pruned, then prune to enhance their shape and beauty.

Evergreens

This group includes the tall-growing evergreen trees, cypress, and conifers. I prefer to prune these plants during their growing season, so the new growth quickly covers up the new pruning cuts. I also think it's a good idea to prune evergreens in spring rather than in the fall . . . the reason is simple common sense: plants pruned in fall will looked pruned all winter, because no new growth occurs that would conceal the pruning cuts. Consequently, you look at an ugly pruned evergreen for six months. If you wait until springtime, the plant's new growth soon covers the pruning cuts. But it doesn't really make any difference when you prune the plant!

Fruit Trees

Pruning fruit trees is done during the winter dormant-season months, November through February. If leggy or spindly growth develops during the growing season, prune it off—don't wait until winter. For additional pruning tips, see the Tips on Pruning sidebar. If you are looking for one best time to prune fruit trees, here are some suggestions.

- *Stone fruits:* Cherries, prunes, peaches, apricots, and any fruit that has a pit within the fruit (hence the name *stone fruit)* can be pruned in the autumn.
- *Apple, pears, and nonstone fruits:* The early winter months of January and February are the best. When is the best time to prune pears? The months of January and February are considered the best for pruning European pears. Asian pears, in the wet Pacific Northwest, are subject to a bacterial disease if pruned in cold weather; wait until at least late May to prune them. Water sprouts can be removed as they appear during the growing season. (*Water sprouts* are like suckers—they are the extra-long, straight-up new growth that develops at the tops of trees.)

Some Pruning Guidelines

Flowering Trees

Nothing special needs to be done unless the tree has an irregular shape. Then, using good common sense, prune to enhance the shape. You can use the same guidelines used in pruning fruit trees, if you want to. Simply thin out the weak, thin branches to allow for good air circulation and better sunlight exposure into the center of the tree. With a flowering tree, you want to encourage a bushy growth habit, because this results in more flowering branches. However, if the tree becomes too entangled with branches, simply thin them out. Thinning—not pruning!

> Select trees for height, spread, texture, flower or leaf color, and their value for beauty and as shade or privacy trees. Fortunately, in the Northwest we have many deciduous and evergreen trees that answer almost all of these specifications.

Fruit Trees

The most important thing to remember about pruning fruit trees is to spend the first two or three years shaping the tree. After that, it's just a matter of thinning the tree yearly to open it up for best air circulation and sunlight exposure. Probably the first three or four years are the most important in shaping and training a fruit tree.

A German fruit-tree grower once told me you should prune off between one-third and one-half of the current season's growth. He said to prune back to an outside growth bud and prune all branches so they create a balanced structure. Then thin out the weak, leggy, damaged branches; if two branches rub together, remove the weaker of the two.

Topping Trees

This is one of the most controversial pruning subjects. The argument against pruning that is set forth by so-called specialists is that the tree's roots are affected by topping. This is utter nonsense. Take just one example: the tallest redwood in the world, in Yosemite National Park, has been hit by lightning numerous times and the tops have been lost several times, yet the tree stands in all its majesty.

A second example: my wife's family topped trees for a living during the Depression and into the early '50s. Recently I asked Myrna's uncle if they ever had to go back to cut down a topped tree, or had clients call and say they had lost the tree afterward. The answer: "Not once!"

Recently, two noted horticulturists have joined me in saying it's all right to top a tree in at least some cases; for example, a beautiful evergreen that's 40 or 50 feet tall and is outgrowing the garden or is a threat in case of a windstorm. Then it makes sense to me to reduce the height, because at that stage of growth you cannot replace the tree and by reducing its height you can still enjoy its shade, privacy, or value as a windbreak.

However, if the job is not going to be done properly, then I would agree: don't do it. When you top a tree, you must keep a couple of things in mind:

First, make the pruning cut just above a set of branches, so they help hide the pruning cut.

Second, shorten the tips of the upper branches, so they are tapered back to provide a typical tree shape.

Third, be on the lookout for any new growth that may develop new tops and remove them immediately, so the tree does not become top-heavy and even more of a hazard.

Fourth, thin out some of the lower branches to allow the wind to pass through the tree more freely.

Ed's Method for Feeding Trees

I have my own method of feeding trees and here it is: Fertilize trees by making holes with a pipe, crowbar, or root feeder at the drip line of the tree. Make the holes 8 to 10 inches deep, and space them 12 to 18 inches apart. Put the fertilizer down the holes; if you use a dry-type fertilizer (see Chapter 16, Composting and Fertilizing), don't forget to water it in thoroughly. This method gets the fertilizer down to the roots, where it will do the most good. Avoid applying fertilizer on the surface of the soil because it encourages the roots to grow to the surface. Surface tree roots do not anchor the tree, can buckle the concrete or asphalt of walkways and driveways, and can get in the way of mowing.

When to Feed Trees

The big questions are "What do we use to fertilize trees?" and "When should it be done?" The best time to feed trees is as new growth starts in spring or just after the new growth has begun; in the Pacific Northwest, this is from mid- to late March. If off-color leaves or poor growth persist, a second feeding can be made in late May.

One of the biggest mistakes we make in landscaping is choosing fast-growing trees, because we want privacy or shade in a hurry. The problem is simple. Fast-growing trees become too large for the average size landscape. Take time to select trees and shrubs that will fulfill your needs but remain manageable and in scale with the surroundings.

Fruit Trees

Feed fruit trees in mid-February, if needed.

What to Feed Trees

Deciduous Trees

Plants that lose their leaves over winter are called *deciduous.* A rose or all-purpose garden fertilizer (vegetable fertilizer too) can be used to feed deciduous plants; for example, fruit, flowering, and shade trees.

Evergreen Trees

As a general rule, a rhododendron or evergreen-type fertilizer is used to feed those plants that maintain green foliage all twelve months of the year; for example, camellias, conifers, and most other evergreen trees.

Choosing Deciduous Shade and Flowering Trees

By Size

Small-Growing

Here are a few of my favorite small trees that are ideal for small gardens, in areas where there is limited space, or to use where they will not obstruct views:

dogwood, *Cornus florida* or *C. kousa*
glorybower, *Clerodendrum trichotomum*
goldenchain tree, *Laburnum watereri*

Japanese maple, *Acer palmatum* (many varieties)
Japanese snowbell, *Styrax japonicus*
lilac, *Syringa vulgaris* (most varieties)
Persian parrotia, *Parrotia persica*
smoke tree, *Cotinus coggygria*
sourwood, *Oxydendrum arboreum*
vine maple, *Acer circinatum*

Small to Medium-Sized

These make nice trees for larger lots where more privacy or additional shade is needed. In some areas, height covenants may restrict the use of these trees, so be sure to check the requirements in your community. Here are just a few of my favorites:

crabapple, *Malus* (several varieties)
Eastern redbud, *Cercis canadensis*
flowering ash, *Fraxinus ornus*
flowering cherry, *Prunus serrulata*
flowering pear, *Pyrus calleryana*
hawthorn, *Crataegus laevigata* (several varieties)
magnolia (tree varieties)
mountain ash, *Sorbus aucuparia*
silk tree, *Albizzia julibrissin*
stewartia, *S. koreana*

Large (Shade)

Need a big tree to provide shade or privacy or screen out an eyesore? These are a few of the ones I think are relatively easy to grow and care for:

beech, *Fagus sylvatica* (European beech)
birch, *Betula* (several species)
crimson king maple, *Acer platanoides* 'Crimson King'
dove tree (handkerchief tree), *Davidia involucrata*
empress tree, *Paulownia tomentosa*
oak, *Quercus* (many varieties)
sweetgum, *Liquidambar styraciflua*
tulip tree, *Liriodendron tulipifera*
weeping willow, *Salix alba tristis* 'Niobe'

By Particular Features

With Colorful Leaves

There's so much green in the garden, it's always nice to add a new dimension by including a tree that has colorful leaves. Here are eight showy ones:

box elder, *Acer negundo*

copper beech, *Fagus sylvatica* 'Atropunicea'
crimson king maple, *Acer platanoides* 'Crimson King'
purple-leaf plum, *Prunus cerasifera* 'Atropurpurea'
sunburst locust, *Robinia pseudoacacia*
tricolor beech, *Fagus sylvaticus* 'Tricolor'
tricolor dogwood, *Cornus florida* 'Welchii'
variegated sweetgum, *Liquidambar styraciflua* 'Variegata'

With Fragrance

Anytime you add a tree or shrub to the garden that provides fragrance, you've got a winner. Find a planting location that is close to the entry, patio, or areas of heavy foot traffic so you can thoroughly enjoy the beauty of the tree and its fragrance. Here are six nice ones:

American linden, *Tilia americana*
cherry (Japanese), *Prunus serrulata* varieties
empress tree, *Paulownia tomentosa*
glorybower, *Clerodendrum trichotomum*
Japanese snowbell, *Styrax japonicus*
southern magnolia, *M. grandiflora*

With Unusual Bark

There are some really attractive trees that have very interesting bark, some with color, others that peel to reveal combinations of bark colors and shapes. All add interest during the winter. Here are eight I find most interesting:

coral bark maple, *Acer palmatum* 'Sango Kaku'
corkscrew willow, *Salix matsudana* 'Tortuosa'
crape myrtle, *Lagerstroemia indica*
paperbark maple, *Acer griseum*
redtwig dogwood, *Cornus sanguinea*
sycamore, *Platanus acerifolia*
weeping (golden) willow, *Salix alba tristis* 'Niobe'
white birch, *Betula papyrifera* varieties

Flowering Trees

Whether you are selecting a tree for privacy, shade, or screening, it's a bonus if you can choose one that also flowers. Here are eight of my favorite flowering trees:

crabapple, *Malus* varieties
dogwood, *Cornus* varieties
flowering cherry, *Prunus serrulata*
flowering plum, *Prunus cerasifera*
goldenchain, *Laburnum watereri* 'Vossii'
hawthorn, *Crataegus laevigata* varieties

magnolia species
silk tree, *Albizzia julibrissin*

Weeping Trees of Interest

All weeping trees have a purpose in the landscape. The weeping branches draw the eye downward, so there should be some point of interest at the base of the tree. For example, weeping trees are often used around a pool or waterfall to draw the eye to the water below:

weeping beech, *Fagus sylvatica* 'Pendula'
weeping birch, *Betula pendula*
weeping Camperdown elm, *Ulmus glabra* 'Camperdownii'
weeping flowering cherry, *Prunus serrulata* 'Pendula'
weeping goldenchain tree, *Laburnum anagyroides* 'Pendulum'
weeping pussy willow, *Salix caprea* 'Pendula'

With Showy Autumn Leaf Color

One of the most overlooked features of using trees in the landscape is choosing those that have attractive autumn leaf color. Here are six of my favorite trees with colorful autumn leaves:

dogwood, *Cornus* varieties
maple, especially vine maple, *Acer circinatum*
oak, *Quercus* species
smoke tree, *Cotinus coggygria*
sourwood, *Oxydendrum arboreum*
sweetgum, *Liquidambar styraciflua*

When is the best time to add a new tree to the garden? Because many trees are now sold container grown, they can be planted year-round, unless the ground is frozen or the weather is excessively hot.

For Specific Sites

In Wet Soil

If you need to plant a tree in soil that is quite wet, or tends to be wet during the rainy season, be sure to choose a tree that will tolerate moist soil. Maple (some varieties), willow, birch, and ash are among the best to use.

In Dry Soils

If there is an area in your garden that remains quite dry and is difficult to get water to, consider planting one of the trees that thrives on a certain amount of neglect. Hawthorn, ash, locust, sumac, and elm are a few of the best.

In Containers

Looking for a tree to grow in a large container, such as a whiskey barrel? There are several small trees that you can grow in containers to help provide shade, screening, or height. Here are a few of the best (see also the listing in Small-Growing, above):

Camperdown elm, *Ulmus glabra* 'Camperdownii'

dogwood, Eastern, *Cornus florida*
flowering plum, *Prunus cerasifera*
glorybower, *Clerodendrum trichotomum*
holly, English, *Ilex aquifolium*
sourwood, *Oxydendrum arboreum*

Trees to Avoid Near Pavement and Foundations

If you're choosing a tree to use near walkways, driveways, or the foundation of buildings, remember that big tree roots can create problems. You should shy away from these trees: bigleaf maple species, ash, large cherry tree varieties, locust, and willow.

Choosing Evergreen Trees

For year-round privacy, screening, or windbreaks, it's hard to beat evergreen trees. The blue, gray, and green needles or leaves often add another pleasing aspect to the landscape. Most are very hardy and easy to grow, with a minimum amount of maintenance. One thing we must always keep in mind is that many of these evergreen trees will eventually grow very tall, so their use on a small city lot is not practical. Here are a few of my favorites:

With Broad Leaves

bamboo, *Bambusa* species
Chinese photinia, *Photinia serrulata*
English laurel, *Prunus laurocerasus*
holly, English, *Ilex aquifolium*
madrona, *Arbutus menziesii*
monkey puzzle tree, *Araucaria araucana*
southern magnolia, *Magnolia grandiflora*

With Needles or Fine Foliage

Alaska cedar, *Chamaecyparis nootkatensis*
Atlantic cedar, *Cedrus atlantica*
fir, *Abies* species
hemlock, *Tsuga* species
Japanese black pine, *Pinus thunbergiana*
Leyland cypress, *Cupressocyparis leylandii*
pine, *Pinus* species
redwood, *Sequoiadendron giganteum*
spruce, *Picea* species
western cedar, *Thuja plicata*

Shade, Flowering, and Evergreen Tree Encyclopedia

Alaska cedar *(Chamaecyparis nootkatensis).* This is one of my favorite evergreen trees. The dark, glossy green, hanging foliage is attractive. It's not unusual for this tree to develop more than one trunk (which I really like), or it can be maintained with just one tree trunk. Ultimate height is up to 60 feet, less if it is multi-trunk. Plant in rich, well-drained soil.

Albizia *(Albizzia julibrissin).* This beautiful spreading tree is commonly called the silk tree. It has fine, fernlike leaves that fold up at night. Umbrellalike growth to 35 feet, with up to twice the spread. Can be shaped and kept smaller. Pink pincushion-like summer flowers. Must have good drainage. Plant in rich garden soil. May need staking at first.

American linden *(Tilia americana).* Grows up to 35–50 feet tall and half as wide. Green, heart-shaped leaves are 5–6 inches. Often used as a shade or street tree. Paperlike seed bracts follow small clusters of whitish late-spring flowers. Plant in moist, fertile, well-drained soil.

Atlantic cedar *(Cedrus atlantica).* Commonly called the atlas cedar. When the tree is young, it has an open growth habit. Probably the outstanding feature of the tree is its attractive, short, bluish-green needles. When they form, the cones are upright and quite showy. Slow growth to 50 feet or more. They become deep rooted, so plant them in rich, well-drained garden soil.

Bamboo (*Bambusa* species). This is a broad family of mostly evergreen plants. They range from dwarf (as low as 1 foot) to intermediate to tall species (timber bamboo up to 35–60 feet). It is important to confine the roots of most varieties. This can be done by encircling the root system at planting time with a heavy grade of 32-mil polyethylene. Put it in to a depth of about 24 inches. Bamboo is a great plant to use for providing privacy or to screen a part of the garden. Nurseries often carry two or three varieties, specialty bamboo growers stock dozens of choice varieties. My three favorites are commonly called *Phyllostachys aurea* 'Gold Stem', *P. nigra* 'Black Stem', and *P. bambusoides* 'Timber Bamboo'. Our gold and black stem bamboos are about 10–15 feet and the timber bamboo I see around the area are about 35–60 feet. These are popular ones to use to provide privacy and garden interest.

Beech *(Fagus sylvatica).* This is a big tree that is used so effectively in the British Isles and parts of Europe. It's a large, broad-shaped tree to 80 feet or more. Myrna and I really like the variety 'Tricolor', which has green, pink, and white leaves. It grows much smaller, 25–35 feet, and can be kept even lower.

Copper beech (*F. s.* 'Atropunicea'). With its copper leaves, 40–45 feet, it is very attractive among the large trees. The leaves are up to 4 inches long. Needs well-drained soil; go light on feeding. Plant in full sun or part sun and shade.

Weeping copper beech (*F. s.* 'Purpurpea Pendula'). With its copper leaves it is also a nice one to use around a pool or pond or wherever a weeping tree is needed.

Birch (*Betula,* several species). These trees are best known for their attractive white bark. Most grow on single or multiple trunks. Eventual growing height is about 35–40 feet. Deciduous. The cutleaf and pyramidal forms are also popular. Bright green leaves are a nice contrast to the white bark. Watch for aphids. Plant in a sunny spot in moist, humus-rich soil.

European white birch *(B. pendula).* Varieties are probably the most popular ones here.

White birch *(B. papyrifera).* This tree is commonly called the canoe or paper-bark birch. It is similar to the European birch, but has a more distinctive white bark and grows 50–75 feet, or about twice the height. The showy white bark peels off in layers. Plant in a sunny spot in humus-rich soil.

Young's weeping birch (*B. p.* 'Youngii'). Another popular birch, this is a true weeping variety, one that would be good planted by a pool or pond.

Black locust. See sunburst locust.

Box elder *(Acer negundo)* The trees grow about 30–40 feet high and almost as wide. Colorful, large, maplelike leaves are 6–10 inches wide. Excellent shade tree. Plant in full sun, in ordinary garden soil.

A. negundo 'Variegatum'. The variegated variety is a very colorful tree. Leaves are green and creamy white and really provide quite a show in a large garden.

Camperdown elm (*Ulmus glabra* 'Camperdownii'). This is by far Myrna's favorite weeping tree. We have one in our garden and really like its growth habit and colorful new chartreuse growth and flowers in springtime. The weeping growth habit forms a tree about 10–15 feet high, with weeping branches that we train into an umbrella shape. My uncle called this deciduous tree the "upside-down tree," because the branching pattern during the winter truly does look like a tree's root system.

Canoe birch. See birch, white.

Cherry, Japanese flowering *(Prunus serrulata).* These Japanese flowering cherries are really showy, prolific flowering trees. Many varieties merit a place in the home garden. Grafted on 6-foot standards, weeping-type cherries grow 10–12 feet high and about the same width, with branches that hang to the ground. Over the

Left: There are not many yellow-flowering trees, so the golden-chain tree, *Laburnum* 'Vossii', is a favorite here in the Northwest.

years, Myrna and I have enjoyed all of them in one of our gardens. Here are just a few of my favorites:

P. s. 'Pendula'. Japanese weeping cherries come in both single and double pink-flowering varieties.

P. s. 'Shirotae'. The double white-flowering 'Mt. Fuji'. This one spreads 25 feet but only grows about 20 feet high.

P. s. 'Whitcombii'. Also a spreading (30 feet wide, 25 feet high) variety with very early-flowering, single pink flowers.

P. subhirtella 'Autumnalis'. Fall- and winter-flowering with pinkish-white flowers. Same size as Whitcomb cherry.

P. yedoensis 'Akebono'. Early, bright pink flowers fade to soft pink. Tree is 25 feet by 25 feet.

Chinese photinia *(P. serrulata).* Not to be confused with the lower-growing *P. fraseri,* which is often grown as a hedge or screen. This one can be grown as a large shrub or small 18- to 20-foot tree. The evergreen leaves open reddish, then mature to a bright dark green. Best leaf color when planted in full sun. Plant in organic-enriched, well-drained garden soil.

Copper beech (*Fagus s.* 'Atropunicea'). See beech.

Corkscrew willow (*Salix matsudana* 'Tortuosa'). As the name implies, this fascinating tree has branches that are twisted. It has an upright pyramidal growth habit that creates a tree about 30–35 feet high and 15–20 feet wide. We have one and Myrna loves to use the unusual-shaped branches in floral arrangements. I find the tree a little brittle and messy, but a nice tree for a wet area. Plant in organic-rich, moist garden soil.

Crabapples (*Malus,* several varieties). This is a large family of the flowering types of crabapples. Most crabapples range from 15–20 feet, some taller, a few lower growing. Here are a few of my favorite varieties; keep in mind there are many others, some of which you might like better. Plus there are several weeping varieties. (See page 65 for fruiting varieties.) Plant in rich, well-drained garden soil.

'Donald Wyman'. Pink buds, white flowers.

'Maypole'. A pyramidal variety we currently have in our garden that we really like. It only grows about 2–4 feet wide and about 8–10 feet high. Showy carmine red flowers and deep bronze-green leaves. Fruit is dark crimson.

'Oekonomierat Echtermeyer'. Still my favorite because of its dark purplish-red flowers and reddish-purple leaves that turn bronze-green with age.

'Prairifire'. Rose-red flowers with maroon foliage.

'Profusion'. Foliage red, fading to bronze-green. Flowers are red, fading to pink.

M. sargentii. White fragrant flowers, dark green leaves.

Crape myrtle (*Lagerstroemia indica* and hybrids). A most interesting flowering tree. Some varieties are large shrubs, others small to medium-sized 25- to 30-foot trees. It has been my experience that the new hybrids are hardiest in this region. Flowers, growth habit, and unusual peeling bark combine to make these trees fascinating. Flowers come in shades of pink, red, lavender, and white. Bark peels back to expose smooth pink inner bark. Some varieties have showy autumn leaf color. Plant in full sun in organic-rich, well-drained garden soil. You'll have to check to see which varieties your local garden outlet stocks.

Dogwood (*Cornus* varieties). Probably one of the most popular of all flowering trees. There are the old ones and many new varieties. Several have outstanding variegated leaf color. I am not going to name varieties, because we just bought two new ones that are spectacular, better than the usual ones, yet at this writing they are not readily available (so I know anything I mention here would be outdated by the time you read this chapter). Check with your local nurseryperson to see which trees they feature, and don't overlook some of the variegated ones; I think you'll really like them. Provide shade at the base of the tree, so as to shade the trunk from sun, wind, and cold weather. The bark of dogwoods is very thin and susceptible to cracking from exposure to the elements if protection is not provided. Plant dogwoods in full sun or part shade, in organic-rich, well-drained soil.

Bloodtwig dogwood *(C. sanguinea).* The red bark of this variety is not as brilliant as the red-osier dogwood, but it grows taller and can be trained into a multiple-trunk, 12-foot small tree. Allowed to grow on its own, it will develop many stems. Plant in full or part sun in moist, ordinary, enriched garden soil.

Eastern dogwood *(C. florida).* Of the tree type, probably the most popular. The eastern dogwood comes in many different named varieties with flowers in pink, rosy red, and white. However, you should know the eastern dogwoods (pink-, red-, and white-flowering) have a lower-spreading growth habit and are prolific flowering trees. They will usually grow 35–40 feet tall with a spread of 20–25 feet.

Kousa dogwood *(C. kousa).* The Kousa dogwood may be one of the best of them all, because it is less susceptible to anthracnose than the others. (*Anthracnose,* or dogwood leaf blotch, creates blotches on the leaves and may cause premature leaf drop; it spoils the appearance of the tree.) It is later flowering, and the trees have a more upright, 20- to 30-foot growth habit. The creamy-white flowers cover the tree, but appear after the tree has leafed out.

Tricolor dogwood (*C. f.* 'Welchii'). Leaves are a showy combination of green, pink, and creamy white throughout the growing season. Tree grows 20–25 feet high. Plant in filtered shade for best color and to keep the leaves from sunburning. Plant in organic, enriched, well-drained garden soil.

Western dogwood *(C. nuttallii).* The native tree dogwood, sometimes called the Pacific or western dogwood, 45–50 feet, is not the best landscape tree for the home garden because it does not like the water, fertilizer, or cultural conditions of home gardens. However, that's not to say it cannot be used in a naturalized landscape setting.

Dove tree *(Davidia involucrata).* Occasionally called the handkerchief tree. The large white flowers come out after the leaves, and as you look up into the tree, it looks somewhat like doves sitting in the tree. Others see the flowers as white handkerchiefs. The first fully mature tree I ever saw in full bloom was at Leonardslee Gardens in England, home of the Loderi rhododendrons. The dove tree was the most talked-about plant in the entire garden. Leaves are heart-shaped, 4–6 inches, and dark green. Place it in a spot in the landscape where you can look up into the tree, so you can fully enjoy the beauty of the large flowers. Trees grow 40–50 feet high and 20–35 feet wide. Plant in full sun or part shade, in fertile, well-drained soil.

Eastern redbud *(Cercis canadensis).* A very attractive tree that needs a warm, sunny spot in the garden. It will not tolerate wet feet. In spring, small sweetpea-shaped flowers hug the branches. There are magenta-, pink-, pinkish purple–, or white-flowering varieties. Small leaves are heart-shaped. It is not unusual for this tree to have more than one trunk. Trees grow to 20–30 feet in height and width. Plant in full sun, in enriched, well-drained garden soil.

Empress tree *(Paulownia tomentosa).* Best known for its showy lavender, fragrant flowers. This deciduous tree has rather large leaves, often 6–12 inches long and 4–6 inches wide. Colorful spring clusters of 2-inch deep-lavender fragrant flowers are followed by seedpods. Branches may be a bit brittle if exposed to strong winds. Surface roots make it hard to garden under this tree. Plant in full sun, in well-drained, organic-rich garden soil.

English laurel *(Prunus laurocerasus).* This plant is most often grown as a trimmed hedge plant (see Chapter 4, Shrubs), but if allowed to grow, it becomes a nice 20- to 25-foot evergreen tree. The dark, glossy green, 4- to 6-inch leaves cover the tree. Late-spring, early-summer fragrant flower spikes (4–6 inches) are somewhat hidden by the new foliage. As a tree, it is as wide as it is tall, but can easily be shaped to fit practically any spot in the sunny or partially shady garden. Plant in ordinary, well-drained garden soil.

Fir (*Abies,* many species). There are several evergreen fir trees that are ideal to use in the Northwest landscape. The greatest advantage of the various species is that the evergreen foliage provides year-round privacy, shade, and beauty. These are all large evergreens (80 feet or more) and need a large area in which to grow, so they are not really suitable for a small garden space.

Above: A close-up of gorgeous pink dogwood.

Left: A dense stand of trees provides an ideal backdrop for the bright colors of rhododendrons and azaleas.

Alpine fir *(A. lasiocarpa).* A species that is often used as a rock garden, container, or low-growing (dwarf) specimen tree.

Fraser fir (*A. balsamea* 'Fraseri'). Popular cut Christmas trees; often containerized and offered as live Christmas trees, so they make their way into the landscape.

Grand fir *(A. grandis).* Also sometimes used in the landscape.

Noble fir *(A. procera).* Popular cut Christmas trees; often containerized and offered as live Christmas trees.

White fir *(A. concolor).* Popular cut Christmas trees.

Flowering ash *(Fraxinus ornus).* This is one of the best-known ash trees because of its 3- to 5-inch spring clusters of white to chartreuse fragrant flowers. This medium-sized tree grows approximately 40 feet or more, with a broad, rounded growth habit to 25 feet wide. Leaves are 8–10 inches long, but divided into several leaflets. Plant in organic-rich, well-drained soil.

Flowering cherry *(Prunus serrulata).* See cherry, Japanese flowering.

Flowering pear *(Pyrus calleryana).* Many of the named varieties have the typical pyramidal form of the fruiting types of pears. These flowering pears have very attractive late-winter and early-spring white flowers. The autumn leaf color on some varieties is very showy. Recently in local nurseries, I have seen the white-flowering varieties 'Cleveland Select', 'Redspire', and 'Aristocrat'. Plant in full sun, in ordinary garden soil.

Flowering plum (*Prunus cerasifera* 'Glabra'). One of my favorite flowering trees because of the profusion of flowers, nice growing habits, and the many varieties that have distinctive leaf color. Plant in organic-enriched, well-drained soil. Here are the ones I would suggest you consider:

P. c. 'Atropurpurea'. 25–30 feet. I know it as 'Pissardii', with single white flowers and dark purple-red leaves.

P. c. 'Hollywood'. 30–35 feet, single light pink flowers, with reddish green leaves. Often produces 2- to 2½-inch red plums.

P. c. 'Newport'. 15–18 feet. Single light-pink flowers have a light fragrance. Leaf color is dark reddish-purple.

P. x 'Blireiana'. 20–25 feet. Early double, bright rose-pink flowers have a light fragrance. Leaves are reddish-purple, turning bronze by early summer.

French pussy willow. See willow, weeping pussy willow.

Glorybower *(Clerodendrum trichotomum).* This tree is best known for its late-summer fragrant flowers. I've got to find space in my garden for one, because of its unusual, late flowering period and intense fragrance. It would be great near the entry area! The clusters of white tubular flowers sit on top of the branches. Bright blue berries with crimson calyxes follow them. Leaves are large, 4–8 inches long. This small tree only grows 15–18 feet high. Plant it a warm, sunny spot, in enriched, well-drained garden soil.

Golden weeping willow. See willow, weeping (golden).

Goldenchain tree *(Laburnum x watereri).* There are not many yellow flowering trees, and this is a popular one. There are upright and weeping varieties, but probably the most popular is 'Vossii'. Its yellow clusters of pea-shaped flowers hang from the tree much like a wisteria blossom. They are about 18 inches long, providing quite a show in springtime. Trunk and branches are bright green. This small tree only grows about 15–25 feet, less for the weeping varieties. Please pick off the seed pods, as they are toxic. They look like pea pods and are really tempting to kids, so it is very important to pick and discard them. I know because one of our sons and a neighbor kid ate some, and ended up in the hospital emergency room! Plant in full or partial sun, in organic-enriched, well-drained garden soil.

Weeping goldenchain tree (*L. anagyroides* 'Pendulum'). Green stems and bright green leaves really show off the long wisterialike yellow flowers. Tree has a definite weeping growth habit. Main trunk is usually 6–8 feet high and weeping branches eventually will touch the ground. Please see goldenchain tree (above) for important information about the toxic seedpods. Plant in full or partial sun, in organic-enriched, well-drained garden soil.

Hawthorn (*Crataegus laevigata* varieties). Flowers and berries attract birds and bees. Make nice small trees because they only grow about 15 feet high.

'Crimson Cloud'. Has large single red flowers with a white, star-shaped center.

'Paul's Scarlet'. Has clusters of double, brilliant rose-red flowers in late spring.

Carriere hawthorn *(C. x lavallei).* 18–24 feet. White flowers and orange-red berries. We had the variety preplanted when we lived in the Lakewood area. It was a nice tree and a wonderful source of food for the birds in the fall and winter. But boy, did we learn a lesson: don't plant berried trees near a sidewalk.

Hemlock (*Tsuga* species). These graceful evergreen trees are wonderful for a semi-shady spot.

Canadian hemlock *(T. canadensis).* 40–60 feet. Has many uses in the garden as a specimen tree, trimmed as a large hedge or privacy screen, or for shade. Limbs have graceful drooping branches. Some dwarf varieties and a weeping form are also available.

Mountain hemlock *(T. mertensiana).* These are often collected by specialty collectors, brought down from high elevation, and used in landscapes as alpine hemlocks. They are very slow growing and are often twisted or have artistic growth shapes. These plants are usually used in rock gardens or in outcroppings of rocks, as specimen plants. They must be planted at the same depth as they were in the mountains, or the plant is apt to die within a few years.

Western hemlock *(T. heterophylla).* Is faster growing and about twice as tall. It's a large tree that needs space, so it is not suitable for a small city lot garden. Limbs have graceful drooping branches.

Holly, English *(Ilex aquifolium).* There are many varieties of these beautiful broadleaf evergreen trees and shrubs. I will not attempt to name varieties, because there are hundreds, and most garden outlets only carry one or two of them. But do look at some of the variegated-leaf forms, as they provide a great contrast in leaf color with other trees and shrubs. Plus they are wonderful to use as cut greens during the holidays. With most varieties, you need a female plant for berries and a male plant to provide the pollen. Most holly trees are slow growing to about 35–40 feet, but are usually kept lower because of so many branches being cut as Christmas greens. The holiday season is the best time of the year to prune them. Holly trees make excellent hedges or privacy screens or are nice individual evergreen trees. Plant in full sun or part sun and shade, in enriched, well-drained garden soil. See also Chapter 4, Shrubs.

Japanese black pine. See pine.

Japanese maple. See maple.

Japanese snowbell *(Styrax japonicus).* Attractive small tree with spring clusters of white bell-shaped flowers. Lightly fragrant, the June flowers hang from the somewhat horizontal branches. The small green leaves make an attractive background for the showy flowers. Autumn leaf color is bright yellow. Flowers, growth habit, and fall color make this a superb small 25- to 30-foot tree for the landscape. Plant in organic-enriched, well-drained garden soil.

Leyland cypress (x *Cupressocyparis leylandii).* Tall evergreen tree that is often used for privacy screening. Can be sheared and kept 20–40 feet or less. It has a pyramidal growth habit, with attractive blue-green foliage. Plant in rich, well-drained garden soil. Grows well in full or partial sun.

Lilac (*Syringa vulgaris* varieties). Grow these as small trees or large shrubs. See Chapter 4, Shrubs.

London plane tree. See sycamore.

Madrona *(Arbutus menziesii).* One of the truly beautiful broadleaf native trees of this region. Shiny, coarse, bold evergreen leaves. If there is one complaint about this tree, it's that it loses leaves practically all year long. Red berries follow white (sometimes fragrant) flowers. The bark is an attractive, rich, brownish red color. Mature trees grow up to 75 feet. Nursery-grown plants are hard to find, and only tiny 12- to 15-inch seedlings will transplant. Often found growing near water, the tree nevertheless needs good drainage and grows in rather sandy to poor soil. Plant in full sun.

Magnolia *(Magnolia* spp.). Many of the deciduous species make nice small trees. Both saucer and star manolias are deciduous. Plus there are several other species that merit a place in the garden (see southern magnolia), but I think saucer and star magnolias are the best for the beginner. Plant them in a bright, sunny to partly sunny location in enriched, well-drained soil.

Saucer magnolia *(M.* x *soulangiana).* Grows 10–30 feet depending upon variety and whether they are grown on a single trunk or multiple stems. Flowers of some are fragrant. The 4- to 6-inch flowers are shaped like a large tulip; that's why first-time homeowners will often refer to the tree as the tulip tree. Flowers range in shades of pink, purplish red, or white.

Southern magnolia *(M. grandiflora).* These large-leaf evergreen trees can grow to 90 feet in the South, but considerably less here. The large, glossy green, 6- to 8-inch leaves make an excellent background for the pure-white, 8- to 10-inch, fragrant summer flowers. These are just a few of the named varieties. Evergreen leaves, bold texture, summer fragrant flowers, and various growing heights combine to make this a nice landscape tree. Protect from cold winds. Plant in full or part sun in enriched, well-drained garden soil.

'Little Gem'. 20–25 feet. A slower-growing, pyramidal variety, with smaller leaves and flowers. Darkest green leaves have brownish undersides.

'St. Mary'. 20–25 feet (maybe higher with age). Also a slow-growing variety. However, it has larger flowers and bold leaves.

Star magnolia *(M. stellata).* Grows 10–15 feet depending upon variety and how it is grown. This is an early-flowering variety that has either white or pink flowers. Each flower consists of about 12–18 straplike petals.

Maple.

Coral bark maple *(Acer palmatum* 'Sango Kaku'). A favorite because of its showy red bark. Dark green leaves have red margins in springtime, which turn green as the leaves mature. Grows up to 25 feet. Autumn leaf color is bright yellow with some shades of orange and red. Plant in organic-enriched soil. Provide good drainage. Grows best in full sun or part shade.

Crimson king maple (*A. platanoides* 'Crimson King'). A wonderful tree because of its crimson leaves and round growth habit. The deep-colored leaves hold their color right up until the leaves drop in the late autumn. Bold leaves are five-lobed and 5 inches or more across. The biggest ones I have seen here in the Northwest are about 40 feet high. Plant in a sunny location in organic-rich, well-drained garden soil.

Japanese maple *(A. palmatum).* Attractive cut-leaf varieties of small-growing maple trees. The coral bark maple (see above) is one of these. Plus there are countless other varieties and seedlings that merit a place where a small tree is needed. Plant in full sun for best color, protected from strong winds, and avoid wet feet. Enrich the soil with organic matter, and plant in well-drained soil.

Laceleaf maple. See Chapter 4, Shrubs.

Red Japanese maple (*A. p.* 'Atropurpureum'). Grows upright to about 12–15 feet. Leaf color varies between plants from bronze to reddish purple.

A. p. 'Bloodgood'. 12–15 feet. Has wonderful red leaf color and scarlet autumn leaf color.

A. p. 'Burgundy Lace'. 12–15 feet. Burgundy leaf color and deeply cut leaves.

Paperbark maple *(A. griseum).* The two outstanding features of this maple are the cinnamon bark and the attractive, fine leaf texture. This small maple, 25–30 feet, is a wonderful specimen tree for the landscape. The cinnamon bark peels off, creating an interesting effect on the trunk and branches. The leaves have three parts, are finely textured, and have brilliant red autumn leaf color. Plant in enriched, well-drained garden soil.

Vine maple *(A. circinatum).* A nice native landscape tree. Often grown as single- or multiple-trunk trees. Single-stem trees usually grow 35–40 feet; the multiple ones usually 25–30 feet. They have a more round shape in the sun and a more open shape in the shade. Autumn leaf color is brilliant scarlet, yellow, and orange. Plant in sun or shade, in moist, enriched, well-drained soil.

Monkey puzzle tree *(Araucaria araucana).* The dark-green, sharp-pointed leaves encircle the branches. It is said that it is the only tree a monkey cannot climb. (Once you see the sharp-pointed leaves, you'll know why!) We had a small one in our garden when I was growing up, and it seemed like it took forever to grow, then after about six or seven years it took off, and today is probably 40–50 feet high. At maturity the trees may grow to 75–90 feet and 25–30 feet at the base. Once established, they pretty well take care of themselves. Plant them in full sun, in enriched, well-drained garden soil.

Mountain ash *(Sorbus aucuparia).* As kids we had more fun having berry-throwing contests with this one. The rather flat clusters of spring flowers are followed by midsummer orange-red cluster of berries. Birds love the berries, but the tree can be a bit messy when the berries drop, so don't plant it near a walkway or driveway. It will grow about 30–40 feet, making it a nice small to medium-sized tree for the landscape. The one we have in our garden now is at the back of a rhododendron planting, and the berries fall unnoticed because of the underplanting. Round to oval in shape. Good autumn leaf color in shades of yellow, orange, and red. Plant in full to part sun in well-drained, ordinary garden soil.

Oak *(Quercus* species). There are over 500 species of oaks. The native *garryana* oak is evergreen, but seldom used in the home garden because it is so slow in becoming established. Here are a few of the most popular deciduous varieties used in home gardens. As you can see, these are big trees, but beautiful ones, so if you have a large area to cover, these varieties may be just right for you. Oaks need good drainage, so plant them in well-drained, ordinary garden soil.

Pin oak *(Q. palustris).* Grows up to 75–100 feet. Its deeply cut leaves are very attractive and the autumn leaf color ranges in shades of pink, yellow, gold, and red.

Red oak *(Q. rubra).* Grows 65–75 feet with bright red autumn leaf color.

Scarlet oak *(Q. coccinea).* Grows up to 75 feet with scarlet red autumn leaf color.

Oxydendrum. See sourwood.

Paperbark birch. See birch.

Persian parrotia *(Parrotia persica).* A very nice, small, 15- to 25-foot deciduous tree. March flowers are dull red and similar to those of the Chinese witch hazels. Wide spreading, sometimes with several trunks. Attractive dark green leaves, turning brilliant yellow, orange, and scarlet in the autumn. Bark flakes off, leaving an attractive cream and brown spotted pattern on the trunk. Plant in full to partial sun, in enriched, well-drained garden soil.

Pine (*Pinus* species). Several varieties of pines offering interesting shapes and varying needle color. Of course, these are only some of many. Plant in full sun, in most any ordinary garden soil.

Austrian pine *(P. nigra).* Long 3- to 6-inch, dark green needles. Large tree to 80–90 feet. Dense, pyramidal shape. A nice specimen pine.

Japanese black pine *(P. thunbergiana).* This is a fast-growing pine that is often trained and shaped into a specimen, irregular, 10- to 15-foot bonsai. Otherwise, it will grow up to 80–100 feet. Dark green needles 3–4 inches, with 3-inch cones. Dense when young; spreads out with age. Plant in full sun in most any ordinary garden soil.

Japanese red pine *(P. densiflora).* Horizontal branching habit up to 80–100 feet high.

Mugho pine. See Chapter 4, Shrubs.

Shore pine *(P. contorta).* Rather slow growth to 30 feet. Needles are dark green and twisted.

Weeping Japanese red pine. See Chapter 4, Shrubs.

Purple-leaf plum *(Prunus cerasifera* 'Atropurpurea'). See flowering plum.

Redwood *(Sequoiadendron giganteum).* This is truly a big tree, 250–300 feet, and not suitable for anything but large gardens. Although we think of this as a California tree, it is amazing how often you will find them in large Northwest gardens.

Dense pyramidal growth habit, with deep green foliage. Requires ample moisture. Plant in organic-enriched, ordinary garden soil

Coastal redwood *(Sequoia sempervirens).* Likewise is a large tree and not quite as hardy.

Silk tree. See albizia *(Albizzia julibrissin).*

Smoke tree *(Cotinus coggygria).* Can be grown as a small 15-foot tree. We grew one as a small tree in the '70s and thoroughly enjoyed the midsummer clusters of grayish-flowering panicles, which (if you use your imagination) look a bit like a puff of smoke. The variety 'Royal Purple' has gorgeous reddish-purple leaves and darker flower clusters. Must have good drainage, and will grow just fine in most ordinary garden soils.

Sourwood *(Oxydendrum arboreum).* This is a slow-growing deciduous tree (15–25 feet). It has attractive, small, creamy-white, 8- to 10-inch clusters of lightly fragrant flowers that hang at the tips of the branches. Its unusual late-summer flowering period and brilliant autumn leaf color make this a top-notch choice for a small tree. Plant in full sun, in enriched, well-drained garden soil.

Southern magnolia. See magnolia.

Spruce (*Picea* species). There are some beautiful evergreen species of spruce trees. Needless to say, these are only a few of the most popular ones. Plant spruce trees in full sun or very light shade, in ordinary, well-drained garden soil.

Colorado blue spruce (*Picea pungens* 'Glauca'). These varieties are the most popular trees. 'Fat Albert' is 12 feet by 12 feet with bright bluish needles and is becoming quite popular. 'Koster' and 'Moerheimii', 30–40 feet, are maybe the two most popular bluish silver spruces.

Norway spruce *(P. abies).* 100 feet or more. A popular living Christmas tree, so it is often used as a landscape tree. Short, dark green needles on a somewhat pyramidal tree.

Weeping blue spruce (*P. p.* 'Pendula'). Can be staked and trained as a small 6- to 10-foot weeping tree. See also Chapter 4, Shrubs.

Stewartia *(S. koreana* and *S. pseudocamellia).* Maybe one of the most overlooked summer-flowering deciduous trees. Camellia-like 3-inch single white flowers in July have brilliant yellow-orange stamens. Autumn leaf color is bright orange-red. Trees grow about 35–45 feet high. Plant in full or part sun, in enriched, well-drained garden soil.

Sumac (*Rhus* species). See Chapter 4, Shrubs.

Sunburst locust *(Robinia pseudoacacia).* Gorgeous bright yellow leaves. Tree grows to about 40 feet by 30 feet wide in 30 years. It has an upright, open and arching branching habit. Plant in full sun, in enriched, well-drained garden soil.

Above: Select the right size trees for the various areas of your garden—and don't plant the trees too close to the house.

Left: A Japanese flowering cherry in splendid bloom.

Sweetgum *(Liquidambar styraciflua).* Corklike bark, brilliant leaf color, and pyramidal growth habit combine to make this an interesting deciduous shade tree. Five-pointed, maplelike leaves turn yellow to bright red in the autumn. Grows about 50–60 feet high. The variety 'Variegata' has green leaves with contrasting yellow markings. The autumn leaf color on this variety includes pinks, yellow, and red. Plant either type in full sun, in organic-rich, well-drained soil.

Sycamore *(Platanus acerifolia).* Common name for this tree is London plane tree. Large, 5- to 10-inch-wide, maplelike leaves. This large, 80- to 100-foot tree has an open habit, with wide-spreading branches. A popular, fast-growing, large shade tree. Fall fruits hang in ball-like clusters. Plant in full sun, in ordinary, well-drained garden soil.

Tricolor beech. See beech.

Tulip tree *(Liriodendron tulipifera).* The small 2-inch flowers are greenish yellow, marked orange, and somewhat cup-shaped like a tulip. They are rather inconspicuous because of the bright green, 4- to 6-inch leaves. It's hard to describe the shape of the leaves other than to say they look a bit like a four-pointed (tulip-shaped) maple leaf. It makes a very nice shade tree. Plant full sun, in rich, well-drained garden soil.

Variegated sweetgum (*Liquidambar s.* 'Variegata'). See sweetgum.

Weeping beech (*Fagus sylvatica* 'Pendula'). See beech.

Weeping birch *(Betula pendula).* See birch.

Weeping Camperdown elm (*Ulmus glabra* 'Camperdownii'). See Camperdown elm.

Weeping flowering cherry (*Prunus serrulata* 'Pendula'). See cherry, Japanese flowering.

Weeping goldenchain tree. See goldenchain tree.

Weeping (golden) willow. See willow.

Weeping pussy willow. See willow.

Western cedar *(Thuja plicata).* These trees have a nice pyramidal growth habit. The tree has dark green foliage and red bark. It becomes a large 100- to 200-foot tree in its native setting, but considerably less (50–100 feet) in the home garden. Can be trained into a large hedge or privacy screen. Plant in full sun or partial shade, in ordinary, well-drained garden soil.

White birch. See birch.

Willow.

Pussy willow. See Chapter 4, Shrubs.

Weeping (golden) willow (*Salix alba tristis* 'Niobe'). The golden weeping willow will grow 50–60 feet high and even wider. New growth is yellow, turning a light bright green. Narrow 2- to 4-inch leaves turn yellow in the autumn. This tree needs plenty of space and is hard to garden under because of the surface roots. Trees will grow next to water, but probably will not survive if they sit in water continually. Grows in full sun or part shade in moist, well-drained, ordinary garden soil.

Weeping pussy willow (*S. caprea* 'Pendula'). Commonly called French pussy willow. The weeping variety is usually grown on a 6- or 8-foot standard. My neighbors have a tree planted on their hillside and it looks great in springtime. The weeping branches and grayish white catkins really show off as you look up at them from street level. Plant in ordinary garden soil.

Choosing Fruit Trees

Every garden should have at least one fruit tree, two if a pollinator is needed. There's nothing like picking fresh, mouth-watering fruit from your own tree. So why, as homeowners, don't we include more fruit trees in our landscape? That's a good question when you think of all the attributes of fruit trees. They create shade, furnish privacy, have attractive showy flowers, and then provide us with colorful, fresh, tasty, nutritious fruit. What more can you ask for? It's too bad that we tend to overlook the potential value of fruit trees as landscape trees. If you're looking for a tree to add to the landscape, consider using a fruit tree.

> Wondering how to determine if the pears on your tree are ripe? Lift the fruit upward, and if the stem breaks, it's ready to be picked. Some varieties may need additional ripening time. Place them on the kitchen counter for a few days. If they are late varieties, you will need to store them in a dark place for up to a month or more, then place them on the kitchen counter for a few days to fully ripen.

We have a peach, a cherry, and an apple tree in our front garden. You cannot believe how much enjoyment they give us. During harvest time, it's a daily check to see what's ready, and a challenge to see if the ripe fruit makes it to the dinner table before being devoured on site. The trees are very attractive and take minimal care. Both Myrna and I are sure glad we planted fruit trees instead of nonfruiting flowering trees!

Today, with the smaller trees available and a better selection of varieties, it is easy to find a size, type, and variety that meets the needs of the average family. And if you're limited in space, there are some interesting new extra-small fruit trees that make excellent container plants. Fruit trees come in dwarf, semi-dwarf, and standard trees, so there is a size to fit even a small piece of property and just about any planting situation.

The confusion begins when it's time to select the variety. We are accustomed to buying fruit from the produce counter in the supermarket and are familiar with the varieties being featured there. But are they really the varieties that grow in the Northwest? Or are they shipped in from somewhere else? Below we'll take a look at the best varieties to grow here.

Allow Time for the Tree to Bear Fruit

With most two-year-old fruit trees, you can count on them to start bearing fruit within two to five years after planting, depending upon the variety. In my garden, I find that new fruit trees will often bear a few fruits the first year after planting. Older trees are often available, but keep in mind the older trees may experience a bit of transplanting shock, and it may set the tree back to the point where there is no fruiting advantage. However, it would give you an advantage of having a larger tree sooner.

Provide for Pollination

Most varieties of fruit trees need a second variety in order to set pollen and bear fruit. Look later in this chapter under each type of fruit tree to see their individual pollinating needs.

Using Native Bees for Pollination

Even if you have two varieties of fruit trees, you still need a means for spreading the pollen. That's where orchard bees (also known as mason bees or blue bees) come in. These are bees naturally here, so all you have to do is capture them and they will do a great job of pollinating your fruit trees.

These bees are better at pollinating than regular honeybees. Because orchard bees are smaller than honeybees, they can go deeper into the blossom and do a better job of pollination. In fact, it is estimated that they are about seventeen times more successful in pollination than honeybees. Another benefit is that they work at lower temperatures than most honeybees. Their life cycle is only about six weeks, but they hatch out at about the same time as most fruit trees flower.

Making an Orchard Bee Hive

Simply take a 4-by-4 piece of wood about 8 to 10 inches long. Drill holes into it on 1-inch centers using a 5⁄16-inch drill bit. Don't drill quite all the way through the 4-by-4. Next, nail this hive under the eaves of the house or an outbuilding near your fruit trees. Use old weathered wood for the hive, if possible.

The orchard bees will find the hive and lay about seven eggs in each hole. They seal the hole with gray matter that looks a lot like a masonry substance. When it's time to emerge from the holes, the baby bees make a small hole in the covering and leave. At the end of their six-week cycle, they lay new layers of eggs and the cycle is repeated for another year.

The same hive can be used year after year. Be certain to set the hive in place before the trees bloom, in order to attract the orchard bees for the following year. Incidentally, some garden outlets are now selling these hives already full of eggs. They are generally available at nurseries and garden centers during late winter.

Limited in space? Grow your fruit tree on a trellis, or as an espaliered tree. Dwarf-sized trees can also be grown in containers on the patio, deck, or lanai.

Control Insect and Disease Problems with Dormant Spraying

Spraying trees during the winter dormant season *(dormant spraying)* helps control overwintering scale, aphid, mildew, and other insects and diseases. It's best to make three spray applications: the first in November, the second in December, and the third in January.

Usually a combination of lime-sulfur and oil is used for this treatment. Be careful how it is sprayed because the lime-sulfur can burn the foliage of evergreens and will stain painted surfaces. Be sure to cover evergreens and put up paper or plastic to protect painted surfaces. Lime-sulfur should not be used on apricots; use a copper spray instead, following label instructions.

Renovate Old Fruit Trees

What do you do with that old fruit tree that has been neglected for years? Maybe when you bought the property, it was struggling but alive. It's full of old tangled growth, and some of the branches are even dead or dying. The first thing you need to do is ask yourself these questions:

- Is it worth saving? Does the tree have any value as a shade tree, fruit tree, or landscape tree?
- Does it bear fruit? Will it ever produce a quality crop?
- Is it diseased and not in the best of health?
- Would it be best to replace it with a new young tree?

If it is worth saving, start by cutting out the old dead or dying branches. Next, thin out the weaker growth, branches that rub together, crisscrossing branches, and other limbs to open up the tree for best possible air circulation and sunlight exposure. Then in late winter, feed the tree as outlined earlier in this chapter.

Apples

This region is one of the best-known areas of the entire world for growing apples. A wide selection of varieties grow and produce exceptionally well here. In addition to the old favorites, a lot of new varieties have become proven winners in gardens here. It's hard to beat the fresh flavor and taste of an apple picked off your own tree. Apples have almost unlimited uses in pies, apple crisp, sauces, cider, breads, butters, and wine, as well as baked, dried, and even a chocolate-covered fruit delicacy. With the mini-dwarf, dwarf, semi-dwarf, and standard trees, there's a size to fit any garden. Relatively easy to grow, apples are a colorful flowering and fruiting tree and make an ideal landscape tree.

Cultivation

Choose disease-resistant varieties. You need two trees of different varieties in order to set fruit. Plant apple trees in full sun in well-drained soil. Expect them to bear fruit about two to three years after planting. Harvest by taste, or you can pick them by whether they are early (summer), mid-season (fall), or late (winter keepers) varieties.

Varieties

If you have enough space, you may want to plant varieties that bear at different times. Here are a few of the proven ones with a note of when they bear:

'Akane' (September)
'Chehalis' (September)
'Enterprise' (October)
'Gravenstein' (September)
'Honeycrisp' (September)
'Jonagold' (October)
'Liberty' (October)
'Melrose' (October
'Pristine' (August)
'William's Pride' (August)

Crabapples

An old-time favorite gains popularity again. Give them the same care as apples. Though most crabapples are purely ornamental, some varieties have small apples that are prized for their rather tart taste. The attractive flowers, bright foliage, and fine form make crabapple trees colorful in the landscape. If the flowering periods overlap, crabapples are also excellent pollinators for apple trees. Here are a couple of the varieties that are often recommended because of their fruit:

'Centennial'
'Dolgo'
'Evereste'
'John Downie'

Questions I Am Often Asked About Apples

Bitter pit: These are round, slightly sunken, brown, spongy spots that develop toward the bottom of the fruit. This indicates a calcium deficiency. Best control is to spray with calcium chloride as fruit begins to enlarge. Use at the rate of 6 milliliters to 1 liter of water. Also apply dolomite lime around the tree during the winter or in earliest spring.

Apple scab: This disease shows up in the form of black spots on the leaves and spotting of the fruit. It requires special spraying with a fruit-tree fungicide (look for one that lists scab on the label). Apply when flower buds are pink, again as soon as flower petals fall, and a third time two weeks later. (You can avoid this problem by simply selecting varieties that have resistance to scab.)

Cherries

Cherries are another delicious fruit that is hard to beat when picked fresh off the tree. They are used in jams and canned for winter use. The sour cherries are the ones used to make cherry pies. Cherries have become even more popular in recent years due to the development of dwarfing rootstock, which produces trees that are easily maintained at 8 to 10 feet tall. We have one in our yard that we think is super. It produces fruit early and is low-growing, making it easier to pick and to keep the birds away. Cherry trees have very attractive flowers and some have a pleasant fragrance. The new dwarf varieties make excellent landscape trees.

> Now you can keep the birds out of your cherry trees (and other fruit trees) with Birdscare Flash Tape. It's also effective in the berry patch, or wherever you want to discourage birds. It will not harm the birds, and it is environmentally safe, effective, and easy to use.

Cultivation

Most sweet cherry varieties need a second pollinating variety in order to set fruit. Plant the trees in full sun. Cherries will not tolerate wet soils, so plant them in well-drained soils. Birds love cherries, so steps should be taken to protect your crop. Products like BirdScare Flash Tape, Scare-A-Way Flash Tape, or netting can be used to help protect your crop. New dwarf trees usually begin bearing cherries two to three years after planting.

Varieties

These are a few of the proven varieties that merit a place in the home garden:

'Angela'
'Early Burlat'
'Hardy Giant'
'Lapins'
'Montmorency' (tart; pie cherry)
'Stella'

Questions I Am Often Asked About Cherries

Why is there premature fruit drop? When fruit gets about the size of your little fingernail and starts dropping off the tree, it is an indication that the flowers were not properly pollinated, so you need a second pollinating variety, or you need bees to distribute the pollen. See Provide for Pollination earlier in this chapter.

What causes blossom rot? This occurs during wet spring weather. The blossom clusters remain on the tree and a mold forms over the top of them. Some of the developing fruit may show rot spots or be mummified and remain on the tree. Pick off this fruit and affected blossom clusters and discard them. During wet springs, spray with a fruit-tree fungicide at the pink flower bud stage, and again at flower petal drop.

Peaches, Nectarines, and Apricots

These are naturally low-growing trees with attractive flowers and large, colorful fruit with a juicy, fresh taste that's unbeatable. I group these three together here even though apricots need extra care. Many new varieties of peaches are resistant to peach leaf curl (see Questions I Am Often Asked About Peaches, Nectarines, and Apricots, below). Eat any of them fresh off the tree (you may need a bib), slice them over a little ice cream, use them in a cobbler, pie, or dried, or can them for winter use. The new miniature peach varieties (genetic dwarf; 5–6 feet) are ideal to grow in containers or in the landscape, but need special care.

Cultivation

The only significant difference between peaches and nectarines is that they have a little different flavor, and the skin of the nectarine is smoother than that of a peach. Their cultural requirements are the same. Plant both in full sun in soil that is well drained. They bear fruit on new growth, so it is important to prune and shape them every year. Both are self-fruitful, so a second pollinating tree is not necessary.

The care of apricots is somewhat similar, except they are very early-flowering trees and the blossoms are apt to be touched by frost in some areas, so try to plant them in the warmest, most protected part of the garden. I recommend varieties that flower a little later and tend to tolerate a bit more cold weather.

Varieties

'Frost' (peach)
'Harken' (peach)
'Hardired' (nectarine)
'Harglow' (apricot)
'Puget Gold' (apricot)

Questions I Am Often Asked About Peaches, Nectarines, and Apricots

How do I control peach leaf curl? Curling and deformed leaves indicate *peach leaf curl*. To help control peach leaf curl, simply cover the tree with polyethylene from late December through the first week of February. This keeps the rain from spreading the fungus. Spraying should not be necessary. Any affected leaves should be picked off and destroyed. My neighbor espaliered his peach trees under the eaves of the house and has never experienced leaf curl.

How do I keep squirrels out of my apricots? Squirrels love to nibble on all three of these fruits, so netting or some other control may be necessary if squirrels are around. Live traps can also be used to catch the squirrels and move them to a different location. Check with your state's Department of Fish and Wildlife for advice on this subject.

Pears

Maybe one of the most overlooked of fruit trees, pears have an interesting vertical growth habit, attractive flowers (to people, but not to bees), and delicious fruit. Easy to grow, pears are a very popular fruit to eat fresh, dried, or canned. They are a good breakfast fruit and dessert fruit, and can be used as jams and preserves. Pears make an attractive landscape tree. There are two types: European and Asian pears.

Cultivation

This is another type of fruit that needs a second tree of a different variety for pollination. Pears do best if they are given a spot in the garden with at least a half day or more of sunshine. Pears are tolerant of many soils, but do best in moderate to well-drained soils, rich in organic humus. Most varieties of pears ripen best after being picked. The best way to determine when they are ready to be harvested is to simply lift the fruit up and to the side. If the stem separates from the tree, it's ready for harvesting. Trees usually bear about two to three years after planting.

Varieties

This fruit is becoming more popular because of its many culinary uses. Here are a few of the best European pear varieties:

'Bosc'
'Comice'
'Highland' (keeper)
'Orcas'
'Rescue'

Asian Pears

These are sometimes referred to as apple pears or pear apples, because many are shaped somewhat like an apple. The fruit of the Asian pear is crispy, sweet, and quite juicy. It grows well in this region, in moist to moderately well-drained soils. Place in a spot where they get more than half a day of sunshine. These trees often bear very heavily, and should be thinned to one pear per cluster if larger, juicier fruit is desired. Trees are usually maintained at a height of 12 to 14 feet. Asian pears ripen on the tree.

These Asian pear varieties have gained in popularity over the past decade due in part to the introduction of many new varieties. Here are three varieties to consider:

'Chojuro'
'Ichiban'
'Shinseiki'

Questions I Am Often Asked About Pears

How do you know when pears are ripe after picking them? The early pears ripen in a few days after being picked. Later varieties may need to be stored for up to a month or more before ripening takes place. You can tell if they are ripe by smell, color, feel, or taste testing.

What are the small slugs on the leaves of my pear tree? That's an insect commonly called the pear slug because it looks like a small slug. It is controlled with natural sprays like Rotenone or neem oil. Apply the spray at the first sign of insect infestation.

Do you need more than one variety of Asian pears to set fruit? Yes, and they should have the same blooming period: early, midseason, or late.

Plums (Prunes)

Two types of plums are most commonly planted in our region: European and Japanese. The Japanese varieties flower first and bear fruit earlier in the summer, while the European varieties bear fruit in late summer and early autumn. Plums are ideal for eating fresh or using in jams and jellies. Standard trees tend to be smaller than standard apples or pears, so they make nice landscape trees for average-sized gardens.

If you're pruning large trees or shrubs, you need two people to do the job right! One person should be on the ground circling the plant, advising which branches need pruning and which do not. The other person is on a ladder or has climbed the tree, and does the actual pruning.

Cultivation

Semi-dwarf trees grow to about 10 to 15 feet. Plums grow and produce best when planted in full sun. The European varieties will tolerate heavy soils, while the Japanese varieties will do best in lighter (sandy) soils. Thin dense growth of Japanese varieties for better air circulation and sun exposure. Japanese plums usually start bearing fruit about two to three years after planting. European plums can take three to five years.

Varieties

Here are a few of the best plum varieties for this region:

'Beauty' (Japanese)
'Damson' (European)
'Gage' (European)
'Italian' (European)
'Methley' (Japanese cross)
'Seneca' (European)
'Shiro' (Japanese)
'Valor' (European)
'Yellow Egg' (European)

Questions I Am Often Asked About Plums

What's a prune? A dull or otherwise unpleasant person, or a variety of plum that can be dried.

Why does the fruit drop prematurely? Two possible reasons that I know of are (1) some varieties need a pollinating, second variety, and (2) it could be a natural thinning of fruit due to a heavy fruit set.

Right: It's hard to beat the crisp fresh flavor of an apple picked from your own tree.

❶ color
❷ uses
❸ bearing time
❹ comments

Apple. There are so many varieties of really fine, top-quality apples. In this listing I have tried to share with you ten of the top-rated ones. But that's not to say that varieties like 'Braeburn', 'Fuji', 'King', 'Lodi', 'Northern Spy', 'Spartan', 'Summerred', 'Yellow Transparent', and many other old favorites aren't good too! If you have a favorite variety, by all means grow and enjoy it! (Keep in mind the ones I have listed have outperformed them all.)

'Akane'. ❶ Red. ❷ Excellent eating apple. ❸ Ripens in mid-September. ❹ Scab- and mildew-resistant. Very productive, bears fruit every year. One of our favorites.

'Chehalis'. ❶ Yellow. ❷ Crisp eating and pie apple. ❸ September. ❹ Resembles golden delicious but larger and highly scab- and somewhat mildew-resistant. Highly productive and reliable.

'Enterprise'. ❶ Red. ❷ Good keeper. All-round apple. ❸ Ripens in October. ❹ Flavor improves in storage. Resistant to fireblight and mildew and immune to scab. Productive, vigorous, and spreading. Researchers like this one!

'Gravenstein'/'Red Gravenstein'. ❶ Red or striped. ❷ Eat fresh or use for applesauce or apple cider. ❸ Ripens in early September. ❹ Bears every other year. This old-time favorite has wonderful flavor. We have found it slow to begin bearing fruit, but once it does, it's worth it.

'Honeycrisp'. ❶ Red. ❷ Good keeper. Excellent for pies, applesauce, and cobblers. ❸ Ripens in September, but has best flavor if picked in mid-October. ❹ Developed at the University of Minnesota and is very hardy to minus 40 degrees Fahrenheit. Big, crispy, juicy, aromatic-flavored variety of superior quality. Somewhat scab resistant.

'Jonagold'. ❶ Red and yellow color. ❷ Good keeper. All-round apple. ❸ Ripens early to mid-October. ❹ This one has won numerous taste tests, and is considered one of the top varieties here and throughout the country. Firm, crisp, sweet-flavored variety.

'Liberty'. ❶ Red of medium size. ❷ All-round apple. ❸ Ripens in early October. ❹ Excellent flavor and highly productive. It has high resistance to scab and mildew. Medium-sized, elongated apple.

'Melrose'. ❶ Red. ❷ Excellent keeper. All-round apple. ❸ Ripens in late October. ❹ A tart, flavorful apple. Top-rated for keeping qualities and reliability. Ours bears heavily every year.

'Pristine'. ❶ Yellow. ❷ Summer eating, baking, and sauce variety. ❸ Ripens in August. ❹ Highly resistant to scab and rust and somewhat resistant to mildew and fireblight. Crisp, tasty, mildly tart flavor.

'William's Pride'. ❶ Large red. ❷ Eating, baking, and applesauce variety. ❸ Ripens in early August. ❹ Sweet, rich, spicy flavor. Highly rated variety, very productive and immune to apple scab and resistant to rust and fireblight.

Apricot

'Harglow'. ❶ Deep orange with a yellow blush. ❷ Use them dried, canned, or in preserves, or eat them fresh. ❸ Ripens in August. ❹ A Canadian introduction that has proven itself in Northwest home gardens. Medium to large, firm, sweet fruit. It is self-fruitful and shows some resistance to brown rot and other diseases.

'Puget Gold'. ❶ Gold with an orange blush; elongated fruit. ❷ Very good eating flavor. Also ideal for using in preserves, canning, or drying. ❸ Ripens in early August. ❹ This one was introduced by Washington State University and does very well in the maritime Pacific Northwest. Tree has a natural semi-dwarf growth habit, making it ideal for the home garden.

Asian pear

'Chojuro'. ❶ Brown russetted skin. ❷ Very tasty for eating fresh and drying, and a good keeper. ❸ Ripens in mid-September. ❹ Good-sized fruit with a distinctive aromatic flavor. Bears prolifically.

'Ichiban'. ❶ Brownish skinned. ❷ Excellent eating variety; also good for drying and in salads. ❸ Ripens in mid-August. ❹ Among the best in field tests at Mount Vernon. Mellow butterscotch flavor. This is an excellent, productive, fine-textured variety.

'Shinseiki'. ❶ Yellow skin with white flesh. ❷ Sweet flavor, ideal for eating fresh or in salads, or drying. ❸ Ripens in late August. ❹ Bears heavy crop of sweet, fine-quality, large-sized fruit. A popular variety with Northwest home gardeners. Performs better than the more popular 'Nijiseiki' variety.

Cherry. Needless to say, the old-time favorites like 'Sam', 'Van', 'Royal Ann', 'Bing', and 'Lambert' still have a place in the garden, but why not try some of these newer varieties that are superior in many ways to the old ones? When they see these recommendations, my kids will never understand why I didn't include their favorite 'Rainier' cherry. So before anyone starts throwing darts, just let it be known that 'Rainier' tends to crack some years, due to the wetter climate west of the Cascades. However, it is an excellent variety in the drier climates.

'Angela'. ❶ Glossy black fruit. ❷ Tasty when eaten fresh or canned. ❸ Ripens in mid-July. ❹ Among the best in tests at Mount Vernon. Heavy producer; you may have to thin some fruit or sacrifice size. Excellent flavor and fruit resists cracking.

'Early Burlat'. ❶ Dark red fruit. ❷ Early eating or canning variety. ❸ Ripens in late June. ❹ One of the first cherries to ripen. Large, sweet, tasty fruit. Very productive and consistent-bearing. Resistant to cracking. Becoming very popular as a home garden variety.

'Hardy Giant'. ❶ Black, medium-size fruit. ❷ Excellent eating and canning variety. ❸ Ripens in mid-July. ❹ Fruit ripens over a longer period than most cherry varieties. Excellent flavor.

'Lapins'. ❶ Black fruit. ❷ Fine eating and canning variety. ❸ Ripens in early to mid-July. ❹ This one is self-fertile (it does not need a pollinizer to bear fruit). The crack-resistant cherries have very good flavor.

'Montmorency'. ❶ Bright red, tart fruit. ❷ This is the pie-cherry variety. ❸ Ripens in late July. ❹ This is a self-pollinating variety. It is naturally a small tree and each spring is covered with white flowers, making it a showy landscape tree.

'Stella'. ❶ Black, heart-shaped fruit. ❷ Excellent eating and canning variety. ❸ Ripens in early July. ❹ A Canadian introduction that is productive and produces fruit of excellent quality.

Crabapple. See page 40 for flowering varieties.

'Centennial'. ❶ Bright orange-red. ❷ Excellent flavor for eating fresh, for canning, or for jelly. ❸ Ripens in mid-August. ❹ Dwarf tree to only 8 feet. 1- to 1½-inch oval fruit. Crisp, sweet, with juicy white flesh. Good producer and excellent pollinizer for all apple varieties. Highly scab resistant.

'Dolgo'. ❶ Crimson fruit. ❷ Excellent all-purpose variety. ❸ Ripens in early September. ❹ Large 1½-inch tart fruit make a bright ruby-red jelly. Excellent for eating and canning too! Tree grows approximately 10 feet tall. Very pretty white spring flowers.

'Evereste'. ❶ Red 1-inch tart fruit. ❷ Use in jellies or pickled apples, or add to cider. ❸ Ripens late summer into fall; fruit remains on tree until midwinter. ❹ White flowers cover tree in springtime, followed by thousands of colorful small 1-inch crabapples. A very pretty landscape tree. Unpicked fruit is a good source of food for birds. The folks at Raintree Nursery say, "Of the many dozens of varieties in the disease-resistant crabapple trials, 'Evereste' was the most resistant, easiest to care for, and the most beautiful."

'John Downie'. ❶ Red-orange fruit. ❷ Eat fresh or use in jellies. ❸ Ripens late summer into fall. ❹ Prolific flowering, producing large quantities of flavorful conical fruit. This English variety produces at an early age.

European plums *(Prunus domestica).*

'Damson'. ❶ Blue, small round fruit. ❷ Can be eaten fresh, canned, or used in jams and jellies. ❸ Ripens in early September. ❹ Used to make the famous Damson preserves. Vigorous grower, heavy producer. (Damson is a type of plum. There are many good varieties.)

'Gage'. ❶ Greenish yellow/yellow-amber flesh. ❷ Excellent for eating, canning, and making preserves. ❸ Ripens in August. ❹ Good sweet flavor. (Gage is a type of plum. There are many good varieties.)

'Italian' ❶ Purple-blue with yellow-green flesh. ❷ Excellent for eating fresh, canning, making preserves, and drying. ❸ Several strains; most ripen in August. ❹ Probably the most popular old-time prune variety. Popular because of its reliability and heavy fruit set. It is self-fruitful.

'Seneca'. ❶ Red skin, yellow flesh. ❷ Eat fresh, canned, or dried. ❸ Ripens in early September. ❹ A sweet, delicious, freestone variety. A New York introduction that has proven itself to be one of the best in Northwest test gardens.

'Valor'. ❶ Purple skin, yellow flesh. ❷ Delicious fresh or dried. ❸ Ripens in September. ❹ Fruit is much larger than the Italian prune. It does not need a pollinizer. Very sweet, with wonderful flavor. Another very productive variety.

'Yellow Egg'. ❶ Yellow, oblong-shaped fruit. ❷ Tasty as a fresh plum, canned, or when used for making preserves. ❸ Ripens in late August. ❹ Large egg-shaped fruit has good flavor and is quite productive.

Japanese plums *(Prunus salicina).*

'Beauty'. ❶ Bright red skin, amber-streaked red flesh. ❷ Rich-flavored eating plum. ❸ Ripens in early August. ❹ Does not need a pollinizing tree. Melt-in-your-mouth, medium-sized fruit.

'Methley'. ❶ Reddish-purple, medium-sized. ❷ Tasty eating plums. ❸ Is one of the earliest to ripen in July. ❹ Self-pollinating. Produces thousands of fruit over a ten-day period, but like other Japanese plums they don't last, so enjoy and share.

'Shiro'. ❶ Yellow, large round size. ❷ Very juicy eating variety. ❸ Ripens in mid-August. ❹ Sweet flavor, juicy, yellow flesh. Heavy-bearing, self-pollinating variety.

Nectarine (*Prunus persica nucipersica* 'Hardired'). ❶ Red skin, yellow flesh. ❷ Ideal for eating fresh, canned, dried, or in pies. (We like ours with cream or ice cream or just sliced with a little sugar.) ❸ Ripens in early August. ❹ This hardy Canadian introduction is considered one of the best nectarines for this region. Spring pink flowers are large and showy. It is tolerant of bacterial spot and brown rot. (This variety needs to be covered in January or sprayed for leaf curl.)

Peach *(Prunus persica).*

'Frost'. ❶ Yellow-fleshed peach. ❷ Excellent eating and canning variety. Great in cobblers too! ❸ Ripens in mid-August. ❹ Some years our tree is so loaded with delicious fruit that we have to prop up the branches or the limbs would all break off. Ours is resistant to peach leaf curl. (Oh, we might get a few, but nothing to worry about.) Specialists recommend that the tree be sprayed for peach leaf curl (if needed) the first couple of years. Semi-freestone.

'Harken'. ❶ Yellow-fleshed peach. ❷ Pick fruit before table ripe for canning. Pick ripe for eating. ❸ Ripens in early August. ❹ An introduction from Canada, this variety is hardy and considered one of the best-flavored peaches for our area. It produces large freestone peaches. (This variety needs to be covered or sprayed for leaf curl.)

Pear *(Pyrus communis).*

'Bosc'. ❶ Brownish russetted skin. ❷ Excellent sliced as fresh fruit, or use for canning or making preserves. ❸ Ripens in October. Tastes better after storing for a month. ❹ Very sweet, juicy, firm-textured pear. A favorite variety for home gardens.

'Comice'. ❶ Large yellow pears. ❷ Sweet, juicy eating variety; also excellent for making preserves or for canning. ❸ Ripens in early October. ❹ One of the most flavorful of all Northwest pears. Fire blight resistant. Tastes better when stored for a month.

'Highland'. ❶ Yellow with some russetting. ❷ Considered one of the best dessert pears. Also used in preserves and canning. ❸ Ripens in early October. ❹ High-quality keeper pear. Best flavor if it is stored for about a month. Trees produce large, smooth-textured pears that are rich in flavor.

'Orcas'. ❶ Yellow with a carmine blush. ❷ Ideal for drying, canning, or eating fresh. ❸ Ripens in early September. ❹ Discovered by horticulturist Joe Long on his property on Orcas Island in the San Juan Islands. Large, flavorful fruit is scab resistant. This is an excellent variety for home gardens.

'Rescue'. ❶ Yellow with bright red blush. ❷ Excellent eating, dessert, and canning pear. ❸ Ripens in September. ❹ Sweet, smooth, and juicy fruit. Trees are loaded with large, scab-resistant fruit every year. Another good Northwest garden variety.

4 SHRUBS

There are very few places in the world that grow as many different types of shrubs as the Pacific Northwest. You'll find an amazing range of plants with fascinating leaf textures, foliage color, and unusual growing shapes. Plus there are both evergreen and deciduous shrubs that grow in a wide range of sizes, from miniatures to large forms. In this chapter, I will share with you a few of my favorites for specific uses and locations in the garden.

Whereas roses are the most popular garden plants nationwide, here in the Pacific Northwest, rhododendrons and azaleas are number one. Select the right spot for them, give them the drainage they need, and you will find that both are easy-to-grow, attractive landscape subjects.

DETERMINING WHAT SHRUBS ARE RIGHT FOR YOUR LANDSCAPE

It is important not only to select plants for the right location, but equally important to be certain that they are hardy in your specific area. Always keep in mind that microclimates can occur in your garden, in places where the elevation is even 500 or 1,000 feet higher, or where wind, drying sun exposure, and/or sun reflection exist. A plant that is hardy at sea level or 500 feet may not be hardy at 750 or 1,000 feet elevation.

So how can you determine whether a shrub is hardy or not? One of the best ways is to simply drive through established neighborhoods where you live and see what is growing. Another way is to ask the certified nurseryperson at your local garden center or nursery. A third way is to ask a neighbor who has a nice garden. Often the local Master Gardener can advise you of which plants are the most suitable in your neighborhood. The garden columns in your local newspaper (if written by a local columnist) can also be a good source of gardening information.

Facing page: Pieris japonica, commonly called lily-of-the-valley, provides both early spring color and brilliant new leaf color.

Above: The colorful butterfly bush attracts hummingbirds, butterflies, and bees.

Newer Introductions

Growers and hybridizers are constantly introducing new and exciting shrubs that merit use in the landscape. One that has been a real show-stopper in our garden is fringe flower (*Loropetalum chinense* 'Burgundy'). The purplish-colored leaves and spreading growth habit make it a very nice, low-growing border shrub. Also, take a look at the new lower-growing varieties of hydrangeas, lily-of-the-valley shrub *(Pieris japonica),* laurustinus *(Viburnum tinus),* and butterfly bush. There are countless other new introductions. Garden magazines, books, and catalogs are the best source for obtaining the most current information on plant introductions.

Choosing the Location

One of the biggest mistakes I see novice gardeners make is buying shrubs because they think the flower is pretty, the shape is nice, or it has a pleasant fragrance. Then they get the plant home and plunk it in the ground, unaware of where it should be planted or how large it will get. If you don't have experience with shrubs, see Chapter 1, Landscaping, to help you avoid this pitfall. Proper landscape planning is a no-brainer once you have the basic information, and need not be costly if you follow a few of my ideas.

Best Location for Planting Rhododendrons

For years we were told you can only grow rhododendrons in the shade! Now we know that isn't true; most varieties do exceptionally well in part sun and shade where they are protected from the hot midday sun. Others will take just about full sun. One grower told me to always feel the leaf: if it is coarse and the flower is medium to dark in color, that variety will grow in the sun. Another grower said to always look to the smaller-leaf varieties; they will tolerate the most sun. I think both are right!

For the majority of varieties, look for a spot with partial shade where the soil has good drainage and the plant will be protected from cold, strong winds. Avoid planting all varieties in a spot where they will get full sun, and reflected sunlight as well. An example of this exposure would be the south side of a house or fence. Few if any varieties will tolerate this exposure.

Good drainage is *a must* because rhododendrons will not tolerate wet soil. They are subject to root rot (if the soil is too wet), which can affect one branch at a time and could eventually kill the plant.

Buying a Shrub

The lists later in this chapter will make it easier for you to choose the right plant for the right location. Now comes another challenge: choosing the best plant of those on display. Look for the bushiest, well-proportioned plant that has good leaf color and is obviously free of insect or disease problems. The best way to do this is to simply pick up the plant and set it in the aisle where you can inspect the individual plant and evaluate its merit. Compare it with one or two others, so you are sure you're getting the best one. Check for broken branches and be certain it is sturdy in the pot. If you have never chosen a new plant before, don't hesitate to ask another customer or the clerk for their opinion. Let them know this is your first experience in choosing plants, and that you value their opinion.

Planting a Shrub

When to Plant Shrubs

Nursery-grown plants in containers can be safely planted at most any time throughout the year. However, avoid planting when temperatures are below freezing and if temperatures are in excess of 90 degrees Fahrenheit. Late autumn or earliest spring are the two best times for transplanting rhododendron plants. I like to do it in the fall, so the roots have a chance to become reestablished over winter.

Bare-Root Deciduous Shrubs

Many flowering shrubs such as forsythia, quince, lilac, etc. are often planted *bare-root* during their dormant season. This term means the plants do not have soil around the roots. Bare-root planting or transplanting is done during the winter months of November, December, January, and February.

Deciduous Shrubs That Cannot Be Planted Bare-Root

It is important to note that some deciduous shrubs are sensitive to root disturbance so they cannot be transplanted bare-root at any time; therefore, they must have soil attached to the roots when you are either planting or transplanting them. When in doubt, check with the certified nursery person at your local garden outlet.

Dig the Planting Hole

Dig a large planting hole. As a rule, I suggest that you prepare the planting hole twice as wide and twice as deep as the size of the root ball of the shrub you are planting.

Check for Drainage

Once the hole is dug, check its drainage by pouring a gallon of water into the hole and see how long it takes for the water to drain away. If the water remains in the hole for any length of time (if it takes several hours), that will let you know that additional drainage is needed and steps must be taken to improve the drainage. This can be done by installing drain tile, by digging a sump hole next to the planting hole, or by mounding the soil and planting plants in that area on raised soil.

Prepare the Soil for Planting

Soil preparation is the key to having success with any plant. Be certain that the planting hole will provide good drainage, fertile soil, and ample root-growing area. Planting time is the only chance you will have to get nutrients and organic matter directly into the root zone. Take the time to add and mix about 33 percent organic humus with your existing soil. Peat moss, compost, and processed manure are all excellent sources of organic humus. If possible, use more than one of these. Next, add a nonburning organic transplanting fertilizer, mixing it into the transplanting hole and surrounding soil. Read and follow label instructions as to how much to use and whether it needs to be watered in after application.

For Rhododendrons

These are acid-loving plants, so mix peat moss and compost, plus a little processed manure, into the planting soil. Add the correct amount of a nonburning transplanting fertilizer, mixing it with the prepared soil, and water in thoroughly.

Remove the Shrub from Its Container

First, water the plant so the soil will cling to the roots as the plant is being removed from the pot. If the soil is dry, the dirt is apt to fall away from the roots. Second, put the fingers of one hand over the soil area, turn the plant upside down, then gently tap the lip of the pot on the edge of a hard raised surface (like a wheelbarrow) so the plant's root will slowly slide out of the pot. Once the plant is out of the pot, put your hand on the bottom of the root ball; never hold the plant by its stem, because the weight of the root ball could cause it to break off.

Set the Shrub into the Planting Hole

Practically every plant has a front side and a back side, so take the time to determine which side (the best one) faces forward. Set the plant in the planting hole, making certain that the top of the root ball is level with the surface of the soil. Planting too deeply can result in limited flowering and can restrict the development of new growth. Then gently fill in the surrounding soil and firm gently, so the plant sits upright. Make a recessed basin (well) around the base of the plant to hold water. Pour water into the recessed area around the plant. It's that easy.

I can't tell you how many times people say to me, "My rhododendron doesn't bloom." Nine times out of ten, it's because they planted it too deep. This is one plant where the top of the root ball must be at ground level or even ½ inch above. After you set the plant at the right depth and firm the soil in around the root ball, go light on mulching, or it is apt to cover the root ball too much, and again, the plant won't bloom.

How to Transplant a Shrub

An Established Rhododendron

Prepare the new planting soil as you would when planting out a new plant (see above). Have the new planting hole ready before you dig the plant, so it is out of the ground (and exposed to drying air) for the

Below: There are thousands of varieties of rhododendrons. Choose them when they're in bloom, so you get the flower form, color, and size you desire.

> Have a plant that isn't doing well? There's a tendency to look up at the branches, leaves, and new growth when maybe you should be looking down at the soil and conditions below the ground. Drainage, soil moisture, soil insects, and lack of (or improper) feeding are often the problem. If you cannot determine what's causing the condition, take a sample of leaves (good and bad) into your local garden outlet, and have the certified nurseryperson on staff make an on-the-spot diagnosis for you.

shortest possible time. When you dig the plant, be certain to dig a root ball with soil attached. With large plants, I usually start digging the root ball out about half to two-thirds of the distance between the trunk of the plant and the drip line.

Extra-Large Plants

The ideal solution to moving well-established or large shrubs is to use a tractor with a front-loader or backhoe. It can just scoop up the plant with little or no damage to the roots. Dig down under the root ball and simply lift the plant with soil attached, and move it to the new location. With the tractor, dig the new transplanting hole first, then carefully place the plant into the new planting hole.

Seedling Shrubs

Cotoneasters and other seedlings that appear in the garden are best transplanted when they are 6 to 18 inches tall. Since they have not developed a very extensive root system, it is important to move them during the autumn, winter, or earliest spring when the small plants are dormant. Try to get as much soil with the roots as you can, and take some of the surrounding soil to place in the new transplanting hole.

Suckers

The small 6- to 12-inch sucker growths that appear around the base of some plants can sometimes be separated and started as new plants. Lilacs, quince, and forsythia are perfect examples. Simply dig, separate, and replant the suckers. The best time to do this is during the winter dormant months of November through February. *Note:* If the plant is grafted, the sucker growth will not be the same variety as the upper part of the shrub on which it is growing.

Watering Shrubs

Newly Planted Shrubs

Water thoroughly at planting, then check the plant every two or three days to see if the soil is dry and in need of additional water. Temperature, wind, and location will determine the frequency of watering. Do not make the mistake of watering the plant every single day; overwatering cuts off air to the roots and the plant can drown and die.

Established Shrubs

Once a shrub is established, it should require less frequent watering. If the leaves look wilted or lose their luster, then it's probably time to water the plant again. The basic tips above also apply to established shrubs.

Rhododendrons

Once established, rhododendrons' watering requirements are minimal. Again, just look at the ones growing in a native setting. Who waters *them?* At the same time, if rainfall is low and temperatures high, they will need watering attention in the home garden, especially right after flowering, when the new growth begins.

FEEDING SHRUBS

Plants will show you when they need to be fed. Poor growth, discolored leaves, and limited flowering or fruit development are often indicators that a plant needs feeding. (See also Chapter 16, Composting and Fertilizing.)

What to Feed Shrubs

Rhododendron Fertilizer for Evergreens

As a general rule, a rhododendron or evergreen-type fertilizer is used to feed those plants that maintain green foliage all twelve months of the year; for example, rhododendrons, camellias, azaleas, junipers, conifers, and most other evergreen shrubs.

Rose Food for Deciduous Shrubs

Plants that lose their leaves over winter are called *deciduous.* A rose or all-purpose garden fertilizer (vegetable fertilizer too) can be used to feed deciduous plants; for example, lilacs, roses, forsythia, and butterfly bush.

When and How to Feed Rhododendrons

Over the years, I have found that rhododendrons are not really heavy feeders. In fact, if we examine the areas where they grow native, we have to ask, who feeds *them?* Yet they have nice leaf color and flower regularly.

If the leaves are off-color, an application of a rhododendron or evergreen-type fertilizer can be made from mid-February to the end of April. If they need additional feeding, a second application can be made immediately after flowering. Always apply the fertilizer at the drip line and be certain to water it in after application. If yellow leaves persist, give the plant an application of sulfate of magnesium (Epsom salts) around April 15. Mix it in the liquid form, about 1 tablespoon per gallon of water.

Use 1 gallon around small plants, 2 to 3 gallons around larger plants.

I do not recommend feeding rhododendrons during the summer months. However, if you are experiencing poor leaf color, weak growth, or poor bud-set, I advise making an application of liquid 0-10-10 fertilizer (see Chapter 16, Composting and Fertilizing) in late July, a second application in August, and again in September and/or October. This type of feeding, with no nitrogen, tends to harden plants for winter, improve vigor, and help in bud-set. Spray the liquid 0-10-10 right onto the rhododendron leaves during the coolest part of the day.

Pruning Shrubs

At planting time, any irregular tip growth can be pinched off to create a bushier, neater-appearing plant. Refer to the Tips on Pruning sidebar, on page 29, for the best time to do other types of pruning.

When to Prune

Flowering Shrubs

Without exception, prune them after they finish flowering. Some of the prolific-flowering shrubs such as forsythia, quince, beauty bush, and others will benefit from having up to one-third of the oldest growth removed completely. This type of pruning revitalizes the shrub and promotes a younger, healthier, more prolific-flowering plant. The new growth that develops after flowering is the growth that will produce next year's flowers.

> For seasonal fragrance, it's pretty hard to beat daphnes. The low-growing rose daphne *(D. cneorum)* is especially nice to use in sunny rock gardens, containers, or on berms where the soil is well drained. The winter daphne *(D. odora)* needs good drainage too, but likes to be protected from the hot midday sun. Both like a little lime in the soil.

Hydrangeas

I prefer to prune them in mid-February. They can be pruned earlier or even after flowering, but they tend to be a little tender and if any freeze damage occurs over winter, there should be enough growth left to prune back. Many home gardeners tend to overprune them, which results in loss of flowers for up to a year or more. My rule: never prune more than 50 percent; for example, if the plant is 6 feet tall, do not prune below 3 feet in height.

Lilacs

Best to prune these after blooming. This is often done during the dormant season; however, you take a chance of removing some of next spring's flowers.

Broadleaf Evergreens

This group includes rhododendrons, camellias, daphne, andromeda, photinia, and all other plants that maintain their leaves all twelve months of the year. The best time to prune is during the growing season, or in the case of those that flower, right after they have finished blooming, in mid- to late spring. (Actually they can be pruned anytime you have a sharp pair of pruning shears in your hands.) Keep in mind that pruning will result in the loss of flowers for at least one season. Severe pruning may result in the loss of flowers for two or three years.

How to Prune Rhododendrons

Here's the number-one question about the care of rhododendrons: "Can they be pruned?" Yes, they sure can. However, the majority of them have such a nice, neat growth habit they will never need pruning.

Where to Make a Pruning Cut

The best place to make your pruning cut is just above where a previous season's growth took place. The best way to determine such a spot is to look for a series of rings around the stem, or a point where the branch has developed several new branches. Make the pruning cut just above either of those points.

Pruning Over a Three-Year Period

If you have to do severe pruning, it may be best to prune the plant over a three-year period. To do this, simply (at random) cut back one-third of the plant one year, then cut back another third the next year, and finish

Left: Need a barrier plant? The barberry, with its large thorns, will keep animals at bay.

the pruning the third year. By using this method, you are reducing the height of your plant, but at the same time it will have some flowers each year. And by the third year, the new growth following where you cut the first year should be ready to flower again.

Removing (Deadheading) Old Flowers

When your plant has finished flowering, it is a good idea to pick off the old spent flowers. If you leave them on the plant, they not only look ratty, they also take strength away from the plant, often affecting the next year's flowering. You may want to wear gloves when removing rhododendron flowers, because some are very sticky and it is difficult to get the goo off your hands. As you pick off the spent flowers, be careful not to damage the new growth, which begins at the same time right below the old bloom.

Weeding Shrubs

Do Not Cultivate Under Rhododendrons

Rhododendrons are surface-rooting plants, so any cultivation under the plants is apt to damage the surface feeder roots. The roots are so dense at the surface that it is difficult for weeds or nuisance grasses to take hold, so the need for cultivation should be minimal anyhow. If weeds appear, just pull them by hand.

Controlling Insect and Disease Problems

Root Weevils—The Rhododendron's Biggest Enemy

This little creature comes from the soil at night, chews along the edge of the leaves, and returns to the soil, doing its damage during the night. When you look for it during the daylight hours, you'll find nothing. I am told that the babies in the soil chew the skins of the roots of the plant and can do potential damage to the roots.

In our garden, I have had the best results controlling this pest by simply making a 3- or 4-inch band of masking tape around the trunk of the plant, about 1 foot above ground level. Cinch it tight so the weevils cannot get under the tape. Then apply a band of a sticky substance, such as Tanglefoot, right onto the masking tape. Then as the weevils crawl up onto the plant, they get stuck. Check every now and then to be certain they have not formed a bridge of dead weevils. Since Tanglefoot is very sticky, be sure to wear gloves when applying it.

Protecting Half-Hardy Shrubs from Cold Weather

This group includes hibiscus, gardenias, citrus, etc. In the Pacific Northwest and other areas where the temperatures dip below freezing, these plants should be treated as indoor houseplants over winter.

Choosing Shrubs

The following categories will be of the most value to you. I have tried to present them in an easy-to-understand format. Once you choose the plants you think will suit your landscape needs, make a list or take this book with you to the nursery and evaluate the plants. Are the leaf color, texture, growing shape, and flower color appealing to you? If so, you've got a winner!

By Size

Low-Growing

Here are a few of the lower-growing plants that are ideal for borders, for rockery plantings, or as edging plants. Many of these low-growing plants may also be used along the edge of containers or window boxes. Here are ten of my favorites that grow less than 2 feet high:

azaleas, various evergreen
cotoneasters, various
Euonymus fortunei, various varieties
grasses, including *Festuca glauca*
heather, *Erica* and *Calluna,* etc.
juniper, *Juniperus horizontalis* 'Tam', 'Wiltoni', etc.
rhododendrons, dwarf species
rock daphne, *Daphne cneorum*
sarcococca, *S. hookerana humilus*
veronica, *Hebe,* various

Medium-Growing

There is an almost unlimited amount of medium-size evergreen and deciduous shrubs. You may want to look at those mentioned here and ask to see others. Here are eighteen of my favorites. These are shrubs that can be kept under 6 feet tall with minimal pruning:

azalea, dozens of varieties
Camellia sasanqua species

Ceanothus 'Victoria' and others
conifers, many varieties
escallonia, several varieties
hydrangea, several varieties
laurustinus, *Viburnum tinus* (dwarf)
Leucothoe fontanesiana
lily-of-the-valley shrub, *Pieris japonica*
Mexican orange, *Choisya ternata*
mollis azaleas, many colors
mugho pine, *Pinus mugo pumilio*
Oregon grape, *Mahonia aquifolium*
osmanthus, several varieties
Potentilla, various
rhododendron, countless varieties
stranvaesia, *S. davidiana*
winter daphne, *Daphne odora,* and others

Tall-Growing

Tall-growing shrubs are often used toward the back of flower and shrub beds, as perimeter shrubs, as screening plants, to help cover large fences, or to cover blank walls on the exterior of the house or outbuildings. In this grouping I list eighteen of my favorites that will grow over 6 feet in height:

American arborvitae, *Thuja occidentalis* 'Pyramidalis', 'Emerald Green', others
aralia, *Fatsia japonica*
Aucuba, several varieties
bamboo, several varieties
butterfly bush, *Buddleia davidii*
camellias, many varieties
cotoneasters, several varieties
English laurel, *Prunus laurocerasus*
firethorn, *Pyracantha coccinea,* several varieties
forsythia, several varieties
juniper, many upright varieties
Leyland cypress, x *Cupressocyparis leylandii*
mock orange, *Philadelphus* x *virginalis*
Photinia serrulata
Portugal laurel, *Prunus lusitanica*
rhododendrons, many varieties
strawberry tree, *Arbutus unedo*
weigela, several varieties

Flowering Shrubs

Evergreen

It's so nice to include shrubs that maintain leaves all twelve months of the year and have flowers as well. Here are eleven of the best for this region:

andromeda, *Pieris japonica* (several)
azaleas, evergreen varieties (most are dwarf)
camellias, both winter and spring types
ceanothus, several
escallonia, several varieties
heathers, wide range of colors
Mexican orange, *Choisya ternata*
mountain laurel, *Kalmia latifolia*
rhododendrons, almost all varieties
veronica, *Hebe,* several varieties
Viburnum (*V. davidii),* laurustinus *(V. tinus),* and others

Deciduous

Some of the prettiest flowering plants lose their leaves over winter. These plants can be nicely combined with evergreens so that the loss of leaves over winter is barely noticeable. The following twelve are among my favorites:

beauty bush, *Kolkwitzia amabilis*
broom, *Cytisus praecox*
flowering quince, several colors
forsythia, several varieties
hydrangeas, many varieties
magnolia, several varieties
mock orange, *Philadelphus* x *virginalis*
potentilla, several varieties
rockrose, *Cistus* sp., several colors
rose of sharon, *Hibiscus syriacus*
snowball, *Viburnum carlcephalum*
weigela, *W. florida*

Fragrant

Here are a dozen wonderfully fragrant shrubs. These are ideal shrubs to plant in spots where their fragrance can be fully appreciated and enjoyed. Ideal planting areas would be near the entry area, by a heavily traveled walkway, near the patio, or in a container on the lanai:

butterfly bush, *Buddeia davidii*
carolina allspice, *Calycanthus floridus*

Chinese witch hazel, *Hamamelis mollis*
daphne, all varieties
lilac, *Syringa* varieties
Mexican orange, *Choisya ternata*
mock orange, *Philadelphus* x *virginalis*
Osmanthus delavayi
pittosporum, *P. tobira*
rhododendron, *R. fragrantissimum*
sarcococca, *S. hookerana humilis, S. ruscifolia*
viburnum, several varieties

Winter-Flowering

There are several really nice shrubs you can use to add interest to the winter garden. Many of the winter-flowering shrubs are fragrant, because fragrance draws the insects to pollinate the flowers. As a bonus, some of the winter-flowering plants can be used as cut flowers in the home. Here are a few top-notch choices:

Chinese witch hazel, *Hamamelis mollis*
Corylopsis glabrescens
heather, many varieties
laurustinus, *Viburnum tinus*
Mahonia, several varieties
rhododendron, *R. mucronulatum*
sarcococca, *S. hookerana humilis, S. ruscifolia*
Viburnum bodnantense
winter camellias, *C. sasanqua*
winter jasmine, *Jasminum nudiflorum*

Spring-Flowering

Here are a dozen of my favorites for spring garden color. These plants can provide a mass of garden color when base planted with the spring-flowering bulbs, perennials, and early-flowering annuals. Mix 'em up for a delightful mass of early garden color:

azaleas, evergreen and deciduous types
camellias, many varieties
ceanothus, several varieties
Choisya ternata
forsythia, several varieties
kerria, *K. japonica*
lilac, *Syringa,* many varieties
mock orange, *Philadelphus* x *virginalis*
mountain laurel, *Kalmia latifolia,* several varieties

rhododendrons, countless varieties
rock daphne, *D. cneorum*
viburnum, several varieties

Summer-Flowering

During the period right after the spring plants are finished flowering, the garden can be kind of drab, so it's good to have a few shrubs that will fill the garden with bright color just before the summer annuals and perennials reach their peak of beauty. Here are a dozen of my favorite summer-flowering shrubs:

abelia, *A. grandiflora* 'Edward Goucher'
broom, *Genista* 'Vancouver Gold'
butterfly bush, *Buddleia davidii*
crape myrtle, *Lagerstroemia* (several)
escallonia, several varieties
fatsia, *Aralia japonica*
heather, many varieties
Hibiscus syriacus
hydrangeas, several varieties
potentilla, *P. fruticosa*
rockrose, *Cistus,* several varieties
veronica, *Hebe,* several varieties

For Specific Sites

In Shade

These are shrubs that will tolerate a shady spot in the garden. Typical shady areas are the north side of the house, under tall trees, and between buildings. These plants will grow in shady areas as long as they get indirect light. Here are some of the best ones for this region:

aucuba, *A. japonica,* several varieties
camellias, many varieties
evergreen azaleas, many varieties
Oregon grape, *Mahonia aquifolium,* and *M. nervosa*
rhododendrons, many varieties
salal, *Gaultheria shallon*
sarcococca, *S. hookerana humilis*
skimmia, *S. japonica*

In Partial Sun and Shade

These shrubs are perfect for areas of your garden where it is sunny part of the day and shady at other times. However, they do need a little protection from the hot midday sun:

camellia, *C. sasanqua* varieties
enkianthus, *E. campanulatus*
evergreen azaleas, many varieties
hydrangeas, several varieties
leucothoe, *L. fontanesiana*
lily-of-the-valley shrub, *Pieris japonica*
mountain laurel, *Kalmia latifolia*
nandina, *N. domestica* varieties
osmanthus, several varieties
rhododendrons, many species
stranvaesia, *S. davidiana*
winter daphne, *D. odora*

In Sun

There is a lot of difference between full sun exposure and full sun plus reflected sunlight, which occurs when shrubs are planted next to the house on the south or west side. The plants mentioned here are quite tolerant of both conditions. If you want to add a bright spot of color or interest to your garden in a sunny spot, here are twelve of my favorites:

abelia, *A. grandiflora* and *A. g.* 'Edward Goucher'
ceanothus, several varieties
cotoneasters, all varieties
escallonia, several varieties
firethorn, *Pyracantha coccinea*
heather, many varieties
junipers, cypress, conifers, all
laurustinus, *Viburnum tinus*
Mexican orange, *Choisya ternata*
mollis azaleas (deciduous)
photinia, all varieties
veronica, *Hebe,* many varieties

For Privacy and Screening

Here are some plants that are ideal to provide screening privacy. Whether it's neighbors, telephone poles, fire hydrants, or areas of the neighborhood that are unsightly, you can provide privacy by using the right types of plants. Here are a few evergreens I recommend:

American arborvitae, *Thuja occidentalis,* several varieties
bamboo, many varieties
camellias, a few tall ones
cotoneasters, several upright varieties
English holly, *Ilex aquifolium*

English laurel, *Prunus laurocerasus*
laurustinus, *Viburnum tinus*
Lawson cypress, *Chamaecyparis lawsoniana*
Leyland cypress, *Cupressocyparis leylandii*
photinia, *P. serrulata* 'Frazeri' and 'Glabra'
Portugal laurel, *Prunus lusitanica*
rhododendron, several fast-growing varieties

For the Seaside

Myrna and I owned a home at the ocean for three years, and we quickly found out which plants will tolerate the strong winds and salty sea breezes. When I visited the nearby nurseries, they were quick to tell me which plants didn't grow at the ocean, but didn't really have advice as to which ones did well. So I solved the problem by visiting old residential areas along the coast, and making note of which plants were doing especially well in their gardens. Here are a few we found that did very well in full exposure to the ocean winds and salty sea breezes:

butterfly bush, *Buddleia davidii,* many varieties
cotoneasters, several varieties
Elaeagnus angustifolia
escallonia, several varieties
heather, several types and varieties
hydrangeas, several varieties
kinnikinnick, *Arctostaphylos uva-ursi*
mugho pine, *Pinus mugo pumilio*
potentilla, several varieties
strawberry tree, *Arbutus unedo*
veronica, *Hebe,* several varieties
wild lilac, *Ceanothus*

In Moist Soil

If you have a low, wet area of your garden, you know how difficult it is to grow plants in that spot. Here are a few plants that do quite well in rather wet areas where drainage tends to be rather poor. Remember, the roots of plants must have oxygen, so these plants cannot sit in water continually:

bog kalmia, *Kalmia polifolia nana*
flowering quince, *Chaenomeles* spp.
privet, *Ligustrum vulgare*
pussy willows, *Salix gracilistyla*
red-osier dogwood, *Cornus stolonifera*
spiraea, *Spiraea* spp.

In Dry Soil

It's not unusual to have at least one spot in the garden where the soil tends to dry out. Often this is a spot where the hose won't reach or where it's tough to get to, such as the top of a rockery or a hillside. These shrubs will adapt to dry soil areas:

broom, *Genista*
kinnikinnick, *Arctostaphylos, uva-ursi*
potentilla, several varieties
rockrose, *Cistus*
sumac, *Rhus,* all species
yucca, *Yucca flaccida*

By Particular Features

Special Interest in Fall

In addition to flowers, there are many plants that have interesting leaf color or showy berries during the autumn. These plants can be effectively base planted with the fall- and winter-flowering pansies, flowering cabbage or kale, fall perennials, and 'Bright Lights' Swiss chard. Here are a few shrubs that merit consideration for fall garden color:

Abelia grandiflora and *A. g.* 'Edward Goucher'
Azalea mollis (autumn leaf color)
burning bush, *Euonymus alata* (autumn leaf color)
camellias, winter types, *C. sasanqua*
cotoneaster, many varieties (berries)
heather, several fall and winter varieties
heavenly bamboo, *Nandina domestica* (leaves)
peegee hydrangea, *H. paniculata*
Pernettya mucronata (berries)
skimmia, *S. japonica* (berries), several varieties
sourwood, *Oxydendrum arboreum*
strawberry tree, *Arbutus unedo* (unusual berries)

With Unusual Shapes

Topiary, espaliered, and bonsai shaped plants have become a popular feature in many gardens. In addition to these shaped shrubs, there are many plants that have special characteristics of their own. Here are just a few to consider:

hinoki cypress, *Chamaecyparis obtusa*
Hollywood juniper, *Juniperus chinensis* 'Torulosa'
laceleaf maples, *Acer palmatum*
weeping blue atlas cedar, *Cedrus atlantica*
weeping blue spruce, *Picea pungens* 'Pendula'
weeping Japanese red pine, *Pinus densiflora* 'Pendula'

To Attract Hummingbirds

One of the most fascinating birds is the hummingbird. Here are six plants that are especially appealing to hummingbirds. Include them in the garden, and you stand a better chance of enticing this beautiful bird into your yard:

beauty bush, *Kolkwitzia amabilis*
butterfly bush, *Buddleia davidii*
flowering currant, *Ribes sanguineum*
flowering quince, *Chaenomeles*
mollis azalea, many varieties
weigela, several varieties

To Attract Butterflies

One of the prettiest garden creatures is the butterfly. It is always fun to include some of the shrubs that encourage them to visit your garden. The following are six of their favorites:

butterfly bush, *Buddleia davidii,* several varieties
escallonia, several varieties
Mexican orange, *Choisya ternata*
potentilla, several varieties
veronica, *Hebe,* several varieties
wild lilac, *Ceanothus,* several varieties

Berries to Attract Birds

Birds are especially attracted to the fall- and winter-berried plants, as this is the time of the year when their food sources are limited. In addition to strawberries, raspberries, and blueberries (see Chapter 6, Berries and Grapes), here are half a dozen of the best-berried shrubs that attract birds:

cotoneasters, several varieties
firethorn, *Pyracantha,* several varieties
holly, *Ilex,* several varieties
huckleberries, *Vaccinium ovatum*
Pernettya mucronata
salal, *Gaultheria shallon*

Native Shrubs That Add Interest

In recent years, native shrubs have gained in popularity because they require minimal maintenance and water, plus many of them make very attractive landscape plants. Here are some of my favorites:

dogwood, *Cornus canadensis*
huckleberry, *Vaccinium ovatum*
kinnikinnick, *Arctostaphylos uva-ursi*

native ferns, maidenhair and others
Oregon grape, *Mahonia aquifolium*
salal, *Gaultheria shallon*

Choosing Rhododendrons

Without question, rhododendrons are some of the most popular plants in this region. Varieties number into the thousands, from some that grow just a few inches high to others that may grow up to 20 feet or more. In the garden, rhododendrons have just about unlimited uses, from the low-growing types ideal in rockeries or as ground covers to the medium-size ones well suited for shrub beds or as foundation plants; to the tall ones that are excellent as background plants.

Most flower in April and May, but some flower as early as January and others flower into June. By carefully choosing varieties, it is possible to have rhododendrons flowering in the garden for about six months of the year. Flower colors practically span the color spectrum, and the blooms come in a variety of sizes, some with pleasant fragrances. I think the biggest mistake made in selecting a rhododendron for the garden is to make the choice simply by flower size and color. Remember, the plant is only in bloom for about three weeks, so isn't it more important that the leaves (which you look at all twelve months) be really nice looking?

By Size

Dwarf and Low-Growing

When we think of rhododendrons, we immediately think of the large, tall-growing varieties, but there are also some magnificent dwarf and low-growing varieties. These lower-growing varieties are ideal to use as rockery plants, border shrubs, or low ground cover–type plants. Here are eight of my favorites (they will grow less than 2 feet in ten years):

'Bric-a-Brac' (white)
'Ramapo' (deep lavender)
R. impeditum (mauve to dark blue)
R. moupinense (white to rose)
R. pemakoense (pinkish purple)
'Rose Elf' (white tinge of pink)
'Sapphire' (light blue)
'Scarlet Wonder' (scarlet red)

Medium-Growing

Here are some of my favorite average-size rhododendrons that will grow less than 4 feet in ten years. Ideal plants for midbed plantings, foundation plantings (next to the house or fence), and to use in small groups in large planting areas:

'Blue Diamond' (violet blue)
'Blue Peter' (lav/blue with dark blotch)
'Bow Bells' (pink)
'Carita' (yellow)
'Christmas Cheer' (pink, fades white)
'Elizabeth' (red)
'Jean Marie de Montague' (red)
'Loder's White' (white)
'Lord Roberts' (dark red)
'Mrs. Furnival' (pink with dark blotch)
'PJM' (fuchsia)
'Purple Splendour' (purple)
'Unique' (pale yellow)
'Vulcan' (bright red)

Taller-Growing

These varieties do not get big overnight, but with time can grow quite large. They are excellent varieties to use for privacy screening, hedging, or background shrubs in shady landscape beds. Here are eight of my favorites:

'Anna Rose Whitney' (deep rose pink)
'Antoon Van Welie' (pink)
'Cynthia' (rosy crimson)
'Fastuosum Flore Pleno' (double, mauve)
'Loder's White' (white)
'Mrs. G. W. Leak' (pink with dark blotch)
'Pink Pearl' (pink)
'Sappho' (white with purple blotch)

For Specific Sites

In Considerable Sun

Most varieties of rhododendrons will not tolerate full sun or a lot of heat, but there are few that will. If you attend to their needs of water, food, mulch, and grooming, these ten should do quite well in the sunny part of the garden:

'Anna Rose Whitney' (bright rose)
'Blue Peter' (lavender/blue with dark blotch)
'Cynthia' (rosy crimson)

R. daphnoides (soft purple)
'Dora Amateis' (white)
'Gomer Waterer' (white, tinge of pink)
'Jean Marie de Montague' (red)
'Lord Roberts' (dark red)
'PJM' (fuchsia)
'Trilby' (deep crimson)

For Cold Weather

Here are six varieties that are known for their ability to withstand cold winter weather. Of course, they must be planted in acid soil in a shady spot, and if the temperature drops below minus 10 degrees Fahrenheit, cover the plants for added protection.

'America' (red)
'Cunningham's White' (white)
'Nova Zembla' (red)
'PJM' (fuchsia)
'Purple Gem' (soft purple)
'Ramapo' (deep lavender)

By Particular Features

Very Early-Flowering (Before April 1)

It's possible to have rhododendrons blooming in your garden for up to four to six months of the year. Simply choose them by the season in which they bloom, starting with these very early ones and combining them with a few of the others that flower during the later seasons. Here are six of my favorite very early-flowering varieties:

'Bric-a-Brac' (white)
'Christmas Cheer' (pink, fades white)
'Else Frye' (pink/white, gold blotch)
R. mucronulatum (rosy purple)
R. praecox (rosy purple)
'Rosamundi' (pale pink)

Early-Flowering (Early April)

This is the next group of rhododendrons to bloom. These are very dependable varieties and the flowers are not as apt to be ruined by frost as are the very early ones. I have had all six of these varieties in my garden and find them nice ones to have for early color:

'Blue Diamond' (violet blue)
'Elizabeth' (red)
'PJM' (fuchsia)
R. pemakoense (pinkish purple)

R. racemosum (soft to bright pink)
'Unknown Warrior' (light red)

Midseason-Flowering (Early May)

This is the peak flowering time for rhododendrons, so the list of varieties is endless. However, here are just a dozen of my favorites:

'Blue Peter' (lavender/blue with dark blotch)
'David' (blood red)
'Dora Amateis' (white)
'Fastuosum Flore Pleno' (double, mauve)
'Jean Marie de Montague' (bright red)
'Lady Primrose' (yellow)
'Loder's White' (white)
'Moonstone' (cream)
'Mrs. Furnival' (pink with dark blotch)
'Pink Pearl' (pink)
'Ramapo' (deep lavender)
'Sappho' (white with purple blotch)

Late- to Midseason-Blooming (Late May)

These rhododendrons that flower just a little later than the peak of bloom are ideal to include in the landscape because they extend the flowering season just a bit longer. Here are eight I know and like:

'Britannia' (red)
'Canary' (yellow)
'Cynthia' (fuchsia)
'Gomer Waterer' (white, tinge of pink)
'Lady Bligh' (strawberry red)
'Madame Mason' (white, yellow blotch)
'Purple Splendour' (purple)
'Trilby' (deep crimson)

Late-Flowering (June)

If you want to extend the flowering time of rhododendrons just a little longer, then these are eight varieties you might want to consider:

'Autumn Gold' (salmon/pink, orange center)
'Cunningham's Blush' (pink/white)
'King of Shrubs' (apricot yellow)
'Lee's Dark Purple' (dark purple)
'Lord Roberts' (dark red)
'Plum Beautiful' (lavender/plum)
'Trilby' (deep crimson)
'Vulcan' (bright red)

With Fragrant Flowers

Rhododendrons are really best known for their beautiful flowers and handsome foliage, but there are a few that have the added advantage of fragrant flowers. Here are six of my favorites:

'Dora Amateis' (white)
'Fragrantissimum' (white, tinged pink)
'Loder's White' (white)
'Naomi' (pink)
R. loderi 'King George' (light pink, white)
'Sapphire' (light blue)

Ed's Favorite Rhododendrons

This is my favorite part of this chapter, because I get to share with you some of the rhodys I like best. However, it should be noted that there are thousands of varieties (many new ones), and you may find many that you like even better. Remember, these are my choices! I select mine by growth habit, foliage appearance, and color:

yellow—'Odee Wright'
orange—'Polynesian Sunset'
red—'Jean Marie de Montague'
pink—'Anna Rose Whitney'
lavender—'PJM' (fuchsia color)
blue—'Blue Diamond'
purple—'Lee's Dark Purple'
white—'Dora Amateis'
bicolor—'Mrs. Furnival'
variegated leaves—'Silver Edge'

With Some Resistance to Weevils

Root weevils are the insects that notch along the edge of the leaves of rhododendrons, azaleas, and other plants. The ten varieties listed below seem to have at least partial resistance to this pest:

'Cilpinense' (pale shell pink)
'Dora Amateis' (white)
'Jock' (dark pink)
'Moonstone' (cream)
'Naomi' (pink)
'Odee Wright' (yellow)
'PJM' (fuchsia)
'Rose Elfe' (rose)
'Sapphire' (lavender blue)
'Virginia Richards' (yellow, dark red blotch)

Choosing Azaleas

There are two basic types of azaleas: evergreen and deciduous (called mollis azaleas). Both require the same care as rhododendrons. However, both will tolerate more sun. The deciduous varieties grow taller, so they should be used in midbed to background plantings in the landscape; the evergreen varieties tend to grow lower and are most often (depending upon variety) used in the foreground or as border plants. In Japan, it is not unusual for the evergreen azaleas to be used for edging, much like we grow and trim boxwood. Both are very attractive used individually, in groups, or massed together in large areas.

Evergreen Azaleas

Most of these average 1 to 4 feet in height and have evergreen leaves and showy spring flowers. Some have very attractive bronze to reddish fall leaf color. If pruning is needed, it is best done immediately after flowering. They will grow in sun, but avoid planting them where they would be exposed to hot reflected sunlight. If they are planted too deep, they will grow but will not flower, so it is essential that they be planted so that the top of the root ball is level with the soil surface. Mulching for winter protection is fine, but the mulch must be pulled away during the spring and summer growing season or it is apt to affect the next year's flowering. Provide good drainage for all evergreen azaleas.

Ed's Favorite Evergreen Azaleas

These evergreen varieties flower for several weeks. Here are twelve of my favorites:

'Coral Bells' (coral pink)
Gable hybrid 'Purple Splendour' (purple)
Gable hybrid 'Rosebud' (pink)
Girard hybrid 'Girard's Roberta' (double pink)
Glenn Dale hybrid 'Everest' (white)
Glenn Dale hybrid 'Glacier' (white)
Gumpo/Macrantha hybrid 'Gumpo' (pink or white)
Gumpo/Macrantha hybrid 'Macrantha' (rose pink)
kurume hybrid 'Hino-crimson' (dark crimson)
kurume hybrid 'Hinodegiri' (bright red)
kurume hybrid 'Sherwood Red' (orange red)
Rhododendron kaempferi 'Holland' (large red)

Deciduous Azaleas

Larger flowers in brilliant shades of orange, yellow, red, and whites, plus combinations of colors, are the outstanding features of the deciduous azaleas. Then as a bonus the leaves turn brilliant autumn leaf colors before dropping. These deciduous azaleas will tolerate more bright sunlight than either rhododendrons or the evergreen varieties of azaleas. They are very effective when used individually or in small groups of three or five plants. Most grow about 4 to 6 feet tall, some lower, a few taller. If needed, prune immediately after flowering. There are several strains; probably the best-known are Mollis and Knap Hill-Exbury hybrids.

> Always plant rhododendrons, azaleas, and camellias right at ground level. The top of the root ball must be level with the soil surface. I find that about 85 percent of the time if these plants are planted or mulched too deeply, they will grow but will not flower. If you have one that is not flowering, check the planting depth and pull away some of the surplus surface soil.

Ed's Favorite Deciduous Azaleas

Many of the varieties are not named, so one should select them when they are in bloom, then you can choose the color and growth habit desired. The University of Minnesota developed a very hardy series named Northern Lights hybrids. These would be an excellent choice east of the Cascades or for gardening at higher elevations. The following are a few named varieties worth considering:

'Golden Flare' (yellow with red center)
'Golden Lights' (golden yellow)
'Homebush' (pink, double flowers)
'Irene Koster' (white/pink)
Knap Hill-Exbury hybrid 'Cannon's Double' (gold with orange center)
Knap Hill-Exbury hybrid 'Klondyke' (tangerine)
'Sunset Pink' (rose-pink, orange center)
'Tutti Frutti' (rose, with red center)

Shrub Encyclopedia

Abelia (*A. grandiflora* and *A. g.* 'Edward Goucher'). These are two prolific summer-flowering shrubs. Flowers first appear in July and continue until late September or early October. *Grandiflora,* 7–8 feet, is the taller of the two. It has white flowers with a tinge of pink. 'Edward Goucher' grows about 2½–3 feet, with dark pink to pinkish-purple flowers. New growth is bronze, maturing green with age. Plants will often develop two or three straggly, long growths that will need to be pruned back. We have the new variegated variety 'Francis Mason', which has green and yellow foliage and grows 2½–3 feet in our garden. All are semi-evergreen, meaning they lose some leaves over winter. All are nice additions to the landscape because of their long flowering period. Plant in full sun for best flowering and foliage color. Provide fertile, well-drained planting soil.

American arborvitae *(Thuja occidentalis).* These are upright pyramidal-type evergreens most often used for privacy screens or hedges. The varieties of 'Pyramidalis' and 'Emerald Green' are the two most popular ones. Either can be sheared and kept at a desired height. Plant them 3 feet apart for a dense privacy screen, closer if an immediate screen is desired. Plant in full sun or partial shade in rich, well-drained garden soil.

'Emerald Green'. Has bright emerald-green foliage and grows a little lower, 12–15 feet.

'Pyramidalis'. 20–25 feet, has dark green foliage and is not quite as dense.

Andromeda *(Pieris japonica).* Also called lily-of-the-valley shrub. Their early spring clusters of hanging flowers are very showy. In my opinion, this plant is a must, not only because of its attractive flowers, but because some varieties have spectacular new growth color. The standard Japanese lily-of-the-valley shrub has white flowers and the new growth in bronze; 8–10 feet. Plant in partial shade, protected from the hot midday sun. Need moist, fertile, well-drained soil. There are many varieties, but here are a few you might want to consider.

'Forest Flame'. 6–7 feet; new growth in shades of pink, red, creamy white, and green.

'Mountain Fire'. 3–6 feet; brilliant new red growth.

'Purity'. 3–4 feet; pure white flowers.

'Valley Rose'. 3–5 feet; has light pink flowers.

'Valley Valentine'. 5–7 feet; deep red flowers and attractive new growth.

'Variegata'. 3–5 feet; with green foliage with white margins and occasional pink tinges in the old growth.

Aralia *(Fatsia japonica).* The large maplelike leaves give this plant an interesting tropical look. Often grown as a houseplant, it will also grow outdoors in a shady spot. In a really severe winter (5 degrees Fahrenheit), ours froze to the ground, but quickly came back. It is not unusual for the plant to have clusters of creamy-white flowers in late summer. Plant in a shady spot, in moist, organic-rich, well-drained soil.

Aucuba *(A. japonica).* The 6- to 8-inch leaves of this colorful broadleaf evergreen provide interest in the shady garden. The common Japanese aucuba, 10–12 feet, has large, shiny, dark green leaves. Plants flower and occasionally produce large red berries if a pollinizing plant is nearby. Plus there are few other varieties of merit. Plant in part to full shade in moist, rich, well-drained garden soil.

'Picturata'. 8–10 feet; has green leaves with yellow centers. I have seen this plant sold locally under the name of 'Gold Center'.

'Variegata'. 10–12 feet; has attractive green leaves splashed with gold.

Azalea. Deciduous azaleas are described in Choosing Azaleas; there are countless varieties. See also evergreen azalea. Deciduous, spring-flowering azaleas come in a wide range of colors. The Knap Hill–Exbury and Mollis hybrids are popular series. For care, see Choosing Azaleas.

Bamboo (various species). See heavenly bamboo; see also Chapter 3, Trees, and Chapter 12, Ground Covers.

Beauty bush *(Kolkwitzia amabilis).* Pink flowers cover the plant in profusion during the early part of June. This deciduous 10-foot shrub has an upright growth habit with arching branches. Use it as a tall border shrub or for summer privacy. Plant in full sun in ordinary garden soil.

Bog kalmia *(Kalmia polifolia nana).* This and *K. microphylla* (western bog laurel) both grow in moist peat soils. These two dwarf varieties are native to the United States. Average height is approximately 2 feet, with a width of 8 to 12 inches. Late spring flowers are rosy-lilac.

Broom (*Cytisus praecox* 'Moonlight'). This is the soft yellow April-flowering plant you often see used along freeways as a cover on hillsides. It has light gray-green spreading branches. Can be pruned after blooming to reduce height. Plants thrive on a certain amount of neglect, as witnessed by where they are growing along the freeways. Plant in full sun in ordinary garden soil.

Broom (*Genista pilosa* 'Vancouver Gold'). See Chapter 12, Ground Covers.

Bunchberry. See dogwood.

Burning bush *(Euonymus alata).* Commonly called the winged euonymus. This shrub, 15–18 feet, is grown for its brilliant red autumn leaf color. There is a garden variety, 'Compacta', which only grows 6–10 feet high, but can be pruned and

Left: The unusual flowers and bold leaves of lacecap hydrangea contrast nicely with other shrubs.

Below: Low-growing andromeda 'Purity' mixes will with variegated hebe and other evergreens.

kept at half the height if desired. This plant is occasionally used in highway plantings because of its easy growth and brilliant scarlet-red fall foliage color. Growth tends to be horizontal and new growth is rough and corky in appearance. Although the plant will grow in part shade, best leaf color is obtained in full sun. Plant in ordinary garden soil.

Butterfly bush *(Buddleia davidii).* There are some great new varieties with long, showy flowers. As the name implies, this is a great plant for bringing butterflies, bees, and hummingbirds to the garden. Very attractive, long, narrow, spikelike clusters of flowers are often 6–12 inches. This deciduous shrub also has long, narrow, 4- to 10-inch leaves with white, feltlike undersides. There are several others that merit use in the garden. Plant them in full or part sun, in rich, well-drained garden soil. Here a few special varieties you should consider.

'Black Knight'. Has deep, dark violet-purple spikes.

'Harlequin'. Has variegated green and creamy-white leaves, with bright reddish-purple flower clusters.

'Petite Snow'. Dwarf white.

'Pink Delight'. Has large clusters of rose-pink.

'White Bouquet'. White.

Camellia *(C. japonica* and *C. sasanqua).* These are terrific autumn-, winter-, and spring-flowering evergreens. Our sasanqua camellias flower mainly in November and December. We have a couple of them in containers, in the entry area. What we like about them is that they flower when there are very few other plants in bloom. I feel the sasanqua type are a little hardier than the spring-blooming japonica type. They will take a bit more sun and wind, and still look great. Flowers are generally smaller, but quite prolific. The late-winter and spring-flowering japonica camellias usually have larger flowers and the plants grow bigger. Both have single, semi-double, and double flowering varieties. There are a few thousand varieties in all shades of pink, rose, crimson, and white. Color descriptions are not always that accurate, so it's best to pick out varieties when they are in bloom. Camellias grow and flower best in a spot where they are protected from the hot midday sun. Plant them in organic-rich, well-drained garden soil.

Carolina allspice *(Calycanthus floridus).* Native to eastern states, this deciduous shrub has dark reddish-brown spring flowers. Dense, glossy green foliage is quite aromatic when crushed. Plants grow 8–10 feet, but can be kept lower with simple pruning. Plant in most any ordinary garden soil.

Ceanothus (several species). Blue is a difficult flower color to find in shrubs, and the ceanothus is one of the best. There are dozens of varieties, but not all are hardy in the Northwest. Many other varieties merit consideration; ask your nurseryperson which ones they recommend for your area. There is a tendency to overwater them late in the season, so start withholding water in August to harden the plants for winter. Plant in organic-rich, well-drained garden soil.

'Victoria'. We have a couple of this variety and they grow and flower prolifically for us. The spikelike clusters of deep-blue flowers stand out above the dark green leaves.

Ceanothus gloriosus 'Point Reyes'. A low-growing, ground cover–type, blue-flowering ceanothus. It only grows 12–18 inches high, but will spread several feet.

Chinese holly. See holly shrubs.

Chinese sacred bamboo. See heavenly bamboo.

Chinese witch hazel *(Hamamelis mollis).* Yellow, spiderlike, fragrant flowers along the branches in midwinter. Provides interest and a little color at a time when not much is in bloom. This deciduous plant has an interesting irregular growth habit. Many new varieties have been introduced in recent years in varying shades of yellow, orange, copper, and light red. Plant them in a spot where you can enjoy both the fragrance and winter flowers. Plant in full or part sun in organic-rich, well-drained soil.

Choisya *(C. ternata).* Commonly called the Mexican orange, probably because the white spring flower clusters have a citruslike fragrance. Glossy foliage is a bright medium green, making an excellent background for the showy, pure white flowers. This evergreen shrub grows 6–8 feet high. Plant in full sun, in rich, well-drained garden soil.

Conifer (many species). This term refers to a wide range of cone-bearing evergreen shrubs. Cypress, juniper, spruce, pine, and fir are some of the plants in this category. Plants range from low-spreading ones to large shrubs. See also Chapter 3, Trees.

Corylopsis *(C. glabrescens).* Commonly called the fragrant winter hazel. In March its branches are covered with pale yellow, hanging, bell-shaped flowers. Coarse-textured leaves are similar to those of hazelnut. This deciduous shrub grows 8–12 feet at maturity. Plant in full or filtered sun, in ordinary, well-drained garden soil.

Cotoneaster (many varieties). Spring flowers, fall and winter berries, attractive evergreen foliage, and varying growth habits combine to make the cotoneasters very useful landscape shrubs. The low-growing varieties are excellent ground cover plants, while the taller-spreading ones are ideal to use in foundations planting and shrub borders. (See Chapter 12, Ground Covers, for suggestions on low-growing varieties.) Plus there are many others that merit consideration for use in the landscape. Plant in full or part sun, in enriched, well-drained garden soil.

Cotoneaster franchetii. Has gray-green leaves, light pink flowers, and orange berries. Large plant to 12 feet, but can be pruned and kept lower.

C. henryana 'Henry'. A large plant to 12 feet. Nice arching growth, with large, 3- to 5-inch-long leaves. White flowers, dark red berries.

C. lacteus 'Parneyi'. Personally, I prefer the evergreen varieties like this, which grow about 8–10 feet high. Graceful arching branches are covered with white spring flowers, followed by colorful red fall and winter berries.

Rock cotoneaster *(C. horizontalis).* This deciduous shrub grows 3–4 feet high and has horizontal spreading branches (4–6 feet), light whitish pink flowers, and red berries. It also comes in a variety with variegated green and white leaves. This one is excellent in rock gardens or to use as a wall plant.

Crape myrtle (*Lagerstroemia* hybrids). Some great new hardier varieties have been hybridized and are being featured more often in garden outlets. Monrovia Nursery has developed a whole strain of 5-foot-high, 4-foot-wide dwarf crape myrtles called 'Petite'. These include varieties with flowers in shades of rose-red, orchid, pink, plum, red, and white. Check with your garden outlet to see which ones they carry and recommend. Their hardiness is a little on the marginal side here, but worth a try because of the prolific flower display. Give protection during severe winter weather. The taller-growing ones are discussed in Chapter 3, Trees. Plant in full sun in organic-rich, well-drained garden soil.

Cypress.

Hinoki cypress *(Chamaecyparis obtusa).* A beautiful, irregular-shaped, slow-growing evergreen shrub. The dwarf varieties are often used as container plants or specimen plants in landscape borders. Plant in full or filter sun, in enriched, well-drained garden soil.

Lawson cypress *(C. lawsoniana).* These are several rather pyramidal shrubs that can be used for hedging, privacy screens, or where an upright evergreen shrub is needed. (The tree varieties are not included here.) Probably the two best-known ones are 'Allumii', which has blue-green foliage, and 'Stewartii', which has a yellow variegation. Both grow about 30 feet high over time. Plant in full or partial sun, in enriched, well-drained garden soil.

Leyland cypress *(x Cupressocyparis leylandii).* See Chapter 3, Trees.

Daphne (*Daphne,* several varieties). If you want to add some fragrance to your garden, these are the plants for you. Other varieties are available, but I think you'll like these the best. Plant in organic-enriched, well-drained garden soil. Here are a few of my favorites.

Daphne retusa. A variety that is occasionally available; only grows 2–3 feet high. The evergreen leaves are quite small. Fragrant flowers are white inside, purplish-red outside.

February daphne *(D. mezereum).* This variety is deciduous, but as the common names implies, it flowers very early, in the month of February. It has a stiff,

Above left: Hydrangea macrophylla is a showy plant in the garden, and its flowers can be dried for use in winter arrangements.

Left: Winter-flowering 'Springwood White' heather in bud. It will flower from January to April.

upright, vase-shape growing habit. Purplish flowers are very fragrant. Berries that follow flowers are red and toxic. Grow in full or part sun.

Rose, rock, or garland daphne *(Daphne cneorum).* A low-growing, spreading, ground cover–type variety. Pink, sweetly scented flowers cover the plant in May. Plant grows 1 foot high and approximately 2½–3 feet wide. 'Ruby Glow' has darker flowers and often flowers again in the late summer. A great rock-garden plant or one to use by a sunny entry where the fragrance can be thoroughly enjoyed.

Winter daphne *(D. odora).* This variety grows 3–4 feet high in a partially shady location. Flowers are rosy purple with a tinge of white. Leaves are variegated green and gold.

Dogwood *(Cornus canadensis).* Common name is bunchberry. This is actually a native perennial ground-cover plant. It is a deciduous plant that only grows 6–10 inches high, with small, typically dogwood-shaped flowers, followed by red berries. Dark green leaves turn yellow in the fall. A wonderful plant to use under rhododendrons or azaleas, or in a naturalized planting. Plant in full or filtered shade in moist, organic-enriched, well-drained garden soil. See also Chapter 3, Trees.

Elaeagnus *(E. angustifolia).* These are mostly large shrubs or small trees, also called Russian olive; can grow up to 20 feet or it can be trained into a large shrub. Narrow foliage, small, fragrant, greenish flowers in early summer, followed by small round fruit.

E. x *ebbingei.* The new hybrids are considerably lower growing; 10–12 feet. Red berries follow small fragrant flowers. The variety 'Gilt Edge' has attractive variegated yellow and green leaves.

English holly *(Ilex aquifolium).* See Chapter 3, Trees.

English laurel *(Prunus laurocerasus).* See Chapter 3, Trees, for this particular species. However, the variety 'Zabeliana' makes a nice landscape shrub. It grows 4–6 feet tall and even wider. Leaves are narrower than English laurel and only about 3–4 inches long. The variety 'Otto Luyken' grows 3–4 feet high and spreads 5–7 feet or wider. Leaves are a little longer and darker green. Plant in full or part sun, in organic-enriched, well-drained garden soil.

Enkianthus *(E. campanulatus).* It has a very interesting tiered growth structure. Attractive deciduous shrub to about 10–12 feet. Bell-shaped hanging flower clusters (May flowering) are yellowish to soft orange. Autumn leaf color is bright red. Myrna and I love this plant, and moved one plant to five different homes because we couldn't part with it. The structure, flowers, and autumn leaf color are really outstanding. Plant in full sun, in fertile, well-drained garden soil.

Escallonia (several varieties). This is a nice evergreen that flowers right after the spring shrubs and before the summer ones. Plants vary from varieties that grow

2½–15 feet high. Flower clusters range in shades of pink, rose, red, crimson, or pinkish white. Most have dark, glossy green, 1- to 4-inch-long leaves. Bees are attracted to this plant. There are several new named varieties, so I suggest you check with your local nursery to see which varieties they feature and recommend. Mine has died back in severe freezes, but comes back quickly. It flowers best in full to part sun. Plant in fertile, well-drained garden soil.

Euonymus *(E. fortunei,* several varieties). Several evergreen bush varieties deserve a place in the landscape. Many have colorful leaf variegations and compact, bushy growth. Here are a few of my favorites. Check to see what other varieties are available locally. Plant in full or part sun, in enriched, well-drained garden soil.

'Emerald Gaiety'. Grows upright 3–5 feet, with dark green leaves with white margins.

'Emerald 'n Gold'. Similar to 'Emerald Gaiety', except leaf margins are golden yellow.

'Ivory Jade'. Grows 3–4 feet with creamy white margins. Plants can be kept lower with simple shearing.

Evergreen azalea. There are thousands of varieties. For care and some notable varieties, see Choosing Azaleas.

Fatsia *(Aralia japonica).* See aralia.

Firethorn (*Pyracantha coccinea* and hybrids). These are very versatile wall plants, freestanding shrubs, hedge plants, or ground covers. The thorns on these evergreens will keep pets and humans away; that's why they are often used in hedging or privacy screens. Plants are covered with clusters of white flowers in springtime, followed by red or orange fall and winter berries. Bees are attracted to the flowers and birds feast on the berries as winter food. This is the plant you will very often see trained up against a fireplace or espaliered against a wall of the house. Plant in full sun for best flowering and berries. Prepare soil by mixing organic humus with the existing garden soil. Provide well-drained soil. Here are a few of my favorite varieties.

'Kasan'. 8–10 feet with bright orange berries.

'Lalandei'. Has orange berries and is considered one of the hardiest.

'Mohave'. 8–10 feet with bright orange-red berries.

'Ruby Mound'. 3–4 feet; is a nice, red-berried variety to use as a spreading 4- to 6-foot plant or high ground cover.

Flowering currant *(Ribes sanguineum).* The red-flowering native currant. This deciduous 5- to 10-foot plant has hanging clusters of red flowers. (There are also varieties with pink or white flowers.) They should not be grown near white pines, because they are hosts to white pine blister rust. A nice plant for a naturalized garden or in a shrub border. Plant in full or part sun, in ordinary, well-drained garden soil.

Forsythia (*F. intermedia,* several varieties). One of the earliest late-winter, early-spring deciduous flowering shrubs. Very showy, prolific-flowering garden shrubs. The branches can be cut and used as cut flowers, and can even be forced into bloom before the flowers open. Plant in full sun for best flowering. Add organic humus, and provide good drainage at planting time. There are many varieties, but here are three I think do very well in this region.

'Beatrix Farrand'. This vigorous-growing 8-foot plant has deep golden yellow flowers.

'Lynwood Gold'. 5–7 feet; early flowers are bright yellow. Popular one for cut flowers.

'Spring Glory'. 6–8 feet; lighter yellow flowers completely cover the branches.

Fragrant winter hazel. See corylopsis.

Grasses. See Chapter 10, Ornamental Grasses.

Heather/heath (several varieties). Care of these plants is discussed in Chapter 12, Ground Covers. Here are just a few varieties I like for seasonal color.

Calluna vulgaris 'County Wicklow' (double pink), 'David Eason' (reddish purple), 'H. E. Beale' (gray foliage, double pink blooms), 'Mrs. Pat' (dwarf purple), and 'Searlei' (variegated golden foliage, white flowers). Summer/fall.

Erica carnea 'Springwood White', Springwood Pink', and 'Vivellii' (carmine red). Winter/early spring.

E. darleyensis 'Furzey' (rose pink), 'Mediterranea Hybrid White' (white), and 'Mediterranea Hybrid Pink'. Winter/early spring.

E. vagans 'Mrs. D. F. Maxwell'. Rose pink. Summer/fall.

Heavenly bamboo *(Nandina domestica).* Sometimes also called Chinese sacred bamboo. It is important to note that this is not a bamboo and does not spread like bamboo. New growth is lacy, giving the effect of bamboo. Leaf color at first is yellow, bronze, and red, turning green during the summer, then turning reddish in the autumn. Plants often have clusters of flowers on stiff stems, followed by red berries. Nandina grows best and colors up the best when planted in full sun. However, plants will also do all right in part shade. Plant in enriched, well-drained garden soil. Many new varieties. Here are a few of my favorites:

'Gulf Stream'. Low 4-foot shrub, red fall color.

'Moon Bay'. 2-foot dwarf compact plants; lime-green leaves turn red in fall.

'Plum Passion'. 4–5 feet; new leaves plum colored, turn green in summer then reddish-purple in autumn.

'Woods Dwarf'. Developed by my late friend Ed Woods of Portland, Oregon. Grows 18 inches high with dense, compact growth. Light green leaves turn crimson, orange, and scarlet in the late autumn.

Hibiscus *(Hibiscus syriacus).* Commonly called rose of sharon. When I first started 50 years ago, these were known as althaea, and were occasionally used as parking-strip trees. The 2- to 3-inch August-September flowers come in single, semi-double, and fully double. We have two in our garden and everyone goes wild over them. (Ours are double purple and single white.) They are sometimes hard to find, and the selection of varieties may be quite limited. They range in shades of rose, red, purple, violet, or white. Some have centers of a darker color. On a single trunk they grow 10–12 feet, or they can be trained into multiple-stemmed shrubs. Plant in full sun, in enriched, well-drained garden soil.

Hinoki cypress. See cypress.

Holly shrubs *(Ilex cornuta* and *Ilex crenata).* These are the shrub types known as Chinese holly and Japanese holly. Both are evergreens and have merit in the home garden. Plus there are many new hybrids that also merit consideration. Plant in full or part sun, in enriched, well-drained garden soil.

Dwarf Burford (*Ilex cornuta* 'Burfordii nana'). Has small, 1½-inch, spineless, hollylike leaves. It only grows about 6 feet, but can be trained to become a lower, bushier plant.

Left: Pure-white flowers, brilliant new foliage growth, and deep-green mature leaf color make andromeda a popular spring-flowering plant.

Rotunda (*Ilex cornuta* 'Rotunda'). Only grows 3–4 feet but it has a few spines.

Dwarf Japanese holly (*Ilex crenata* 'Compacta'). A very compact, 4- to 6-foot variety with small, dark green leaves.

Hollywood juniper. See juniper.

Huckleberry *(Vaccinium ovatum).* This is a native evergreen with radiant leaves, bronze at first, turning green. Plants only grow 3–4 feet in the shade, but up to two or three times higher in the sun. Berries follow the white to pinkish flowers. The black berries are often used to make jams, jellies, and pies. Plant in full sun or shade, in woodsy-type, well-drained soil.

Hydrangea (*H. macrophylla* varieties). This group is the common hydrangea. Then within this are two groups: the large-flowering cluster type and the group called lace cap, with sterile flowers along the edge and darker fertile ones in the center. We have several varieties of both and think they are magnificent summer-flowering deciduous shrubs. Myrna loves to dry the blossoms and we enjoy them as dried flowers all winter. Flower colors, of both types, range in shades of blue, pink, rose, red, white, and bicolor. Plant hydrangeas in a partially shady area of the garden, where they are protected from the hot midday sun. Plant in soil that has been enriched with organic matter and is moist but well-drained. Here are half a dozen varieties you might want to check out.

'Bluebird'. This is the lace-cap type; 'Tricolor' (white to bluish pink) and 'Lanarth White'. These plants range from 1½–8 feet tall.

'Pink Elf'. One of my favorites is this new dwarf, which only grows 18 inches tall and is loaded with bright pink blossoms. Full-cluster varieties include 'Nikko Blue', 'Red and Pretty', and 'Unique' (double white).

Peegee hydrangea (*H. paniculata* 'Grandiflora'). This one has a totally different type of blossom and growth habit. It can grow 10–25 feet high, but is best kept as a shrub 10–12 feet high. The blossoms are conical and 12–15 inches long. The upright flower clusters are creamy white, eventually fading pink. Fall foliage color is yellow. Plant in full or partial sun in enriched, well-drained garden soil.

Japanese aucuba. See aucuba.

Japanese holly. See holly shrubs.

Junipers (various varieties). This is a huge plant family of evergreen plants with various growing heights, shapes, and colors. The low-growing ones are most often used as ground cover plants (see Chapter 12, Ground Covers), while the mid-sized ones are most often used for screening and the tall ones for specimen plants, as trees, or for privacy. *Juniperus horizontalis* 'Tam' and *J. h.* 'Wiltonii' are a couple to consider. I suggest you visit your local nursery to see which ones they feature and how they might fit into your landscape. Plant them in full or part sun, in most any ordinary, well-drained garden soil. They will not tolerate wet feet.

Hollywood juniper (*J. chinensis* 'Torulosa'). This is one of our favorite upright junipers. We have ours planted as the focal point when you enter our garden. Darkest green foliage and a rather twisted, irregular growth habit can really make it stand out as a specimen plant. It can eventually grow up to 12–15 feet, but with a little training, we will keep ours lower. Plant in full or part sun, in enriched, well-drained garden soil.

Kerria *(K. japonica)*. This deciduous shrub has interesting double yellow 1- to 2-inch flowers along the stem. After bloom, prune out flowering stems and keep the new ones. Spring flowers appear on greenish yellow branches (8–10 feet) that hold their color throughout the year. Plant in full sun or part sun in shade, because if it's too sunny the flowers will discolor and fade quicker. Prepare the planting soil by adding enriched organic matter and provide good drainage.

Kinnikinnick *(Arctostaphylos uva-ursi)*. See Chapter 12, Ground Covers.

Laceleaf maple *(Acer palmatum)*. Has green leaves, which turn beautiful autumn leaf colors. The low-spreading habit of growth makes it ideal as a rock garden or specimen plant. Some varieties are red-leafed, other have green leaves. All have very lacy, deeply cut leaves, hence the name "lacy leaf." It's best to choose them for leaf color and texture. Plant them in full sun or filtered sun, protected from the hot midday sun and cold winds. Prepare the planting hole with enriched garden soil. These laceleaf maples must have good drainage.

'Crimson Queen' (8–10 feet), 'Dissectum Viridis' (6–8 feet), 'Ever Red' (10–12 feet), and many others.

Laurustinus *(Viburnum tinus)*. I think this is one of the best fall- and winter-flowering evergreen shrubs. In our garden they start flowering in October or November and continue to flower a little all winter, coming into full bloom in March or early April. Cut branches are great for winter arrangements. Plants vary from 3 to 12 feet high, depending upon variety. Leathery, dark green leaves, with flower clusters that are pink in bud then open white. The dwarf variety only grows 3–5 feet. Hold back on watering late in the summer and early fall to give these plants a chance to harden before winter sets in. Plant in full sun or light shade, in organic-enriched, well-drained garden soil.

Roundleaf laurustinus ('Robustum'). Grows up to 6–12 feet high.

'Spring Bouquet'. A nice in-between variety that grows 5–7 feet high.

'Variegatum'. Has attractive green, white, and pale yellow leaves. In our garden, it is really slow-growing in comparison to the others.

Lawson cypress. See cypress.

Leyland cypress. See cypress.

Leucothoe *(L. fontanesiana).* Commonly called the drooping leucothoe. 'Rainbow' (4–6 feet), with its green, marked cream-and-pink leaves, is really colorful in the garden. Myrna loves to use the cut foliage as filler in arrangements, and the more she cuts it, the bushier and more beautiful the plant becomes. The green-leaf varieties (2–6 feet) are also attractive. Both have clusters of creamy-white spring flowers. The green-leaf varieties will take full sun, but the variegated needs protection from the hot midday sun. Plant in rich, well-drained garden soil.

Lilac (*Syringa,* many varieties). Grow these as small trees or large shrubs. One of the most outstanding large flowering shrubs. Gorgeous spring conical flower clusters stand upright at the tips of the branches. There are hundreds of varieties with either single or double flowers. Many varieties have fragrant flowers. The average size of this shrub or small tree is about 18–20 feet. Flower colors range in shades of pink, lavender, reddish-purple, purple, white, or yellow. The French lilacs are a little later-flowering than the common lilacs. Plants may need lime in the typically acid soils of the Northwest. Plant in full sun for best flowering, in fertile, well-drained soil.

Lily-of-the-valley shrub *(Pieris japonica).* See andromeda.

Magnolia (various varieties). Many species can be grown as large shrubs or small trees. See Chapter 3, Trees, for information on growing as trees. The most popular shrub species are listed below. Plant in enriched, well-drained garden soil.

> **Lily magnolia** *(M. liliiflora).* 12–15 feet; long pointed buds, comes in a combination of white and purple flowers. Often blooms twice in the Northwest.
>
> **Saucer magnolia** *(M.* x *soulangiana).* 18–25 feet; large cupped flowers; that's why it is often mistakenly called the tulip tree. Flowers range in shades of pink, purple, or white.
>
> **Star magnolia** *(M. stellata).* 10–15 feet; attractive multiple flower petals in pink and white varieties.

Mahonia (several species). Several other species are grown here, but these are the two most popular and most readily available. More on this plant family in Chapter 12, Ground Covers. Plant in filtered sun to partial shade, in enriched, well-drained soil.

> **Longleaf mahonia** *(M. nervosa).* A native that only grows 2 feet high, taller if crowded.
>
> **Oregon grape** *(M. aquifolium).* 2–6 feet. Probably the most popular variety. Hollylike leaflets 9–12 inches long. Late-winter, early-spring clusters of flowers are bright yellow. Dwarf variety only grows 2–2½ feet high. New foliage is greenish bronze, then turns green, then takes on a purplish cast in the autumn.

Above left: The large berries of *Pernettya mucronata* provide quite a show in the fall and early winter garden.

Left: My favorite blue-flowering shrub is ceanothus. Its June-through-July blooms come at a time when not much else is in flower.

Mexican orange *(Choisya ternata)*. See choisya.

Mock orange *(Philadelphus* x *virginalis)*. The fragrant double and semi-double pure-white flowers in late spring cover the 6- to 8-foot-high deciduous shrub, which has a nice, spreading form. There is also a dwarf variety, 'Dwarf Minnesota Snowflake', with double flowers, which grows 3–4 feet, about half as high. Plant them in full or part sun, in rich, well-drained soil.

Mollis azalea. See azalea.

Mountain laurel *(Kalmia latifolia)*. Some really outstanding varieties have been introduced in recent years. This slow-growing, 6- to 8-foot evergreen shrub has dark, glossy green leaves and 4- to 5-inch clusters of small cup-shaped flowers. Here are a few of my favorite varieties. Plus there are several dwarf varieties that grow 3–3½ feet, half as high. Grow them in partial shade, in rich, well-drained soil.

'Carousel'. A combination of pink, white, and purplish red.

'Olympic Fire'. Buds are red, opening pink.

'Ostbo Red'. Pink, opening red.

'Peppermint'. White and red.

Mugho pine *(Pinus mugo pumilio)*. This dwarf pine is slow-growing to about 4 feet high and up to twice as wide. Needles are short and dark green. This is a confusing group of dwarf pines, because some are sold as dwarf Mugho pines, but my experience has been that the longer the needles, the quicker and taller the plants grow. So if you want a truly dwarf plant, look for plants with short needles. Pines grow best in full sun (but will take part sun) in ordinary, well-drained garden soil. See also Chapter 3, Trees.

Nandina *(N. domestica)*. See heavenly bamboo.

Native ferns (maidenhair and other varieties). Probably the two most popular natives are the maidenhair and sword ferns. That's too bad because there are some really nice ones, plus many species that certainly merit a place in the shade garden. If you have a shady spot in the garden that calls for ferns, I hope you'll take the time to explore this fascinating group of plants. Plant them in the shady garden, in moist, organic-enriched garden soil.

Western maidenhair *(Adiantum aleuticum)*. Grows 18–30 inches high. The black stems are topped with delicate, small, lacy leaves.

Western sword fern *(Polystichum munitum)*. Best known for its large, leathery, deep-green fronds.

Oregon grape *(Mahonia aquifolium)*. See mahonia.

Osmanthus *(O. delavayi)*. This is one of my favorite "most-overlooked" evergreen shrubs. Small dark green leaves, very fragrant white flowers, versatility, and a nice growth habit combine to make this a super garden plant, in my opinion. It is truly overlooked by many professionals and the home gardener. (On a scale of 1 to 10, I give this an 8 for fragrance alone.) Will grow 4–6 feet high and up to 6–8 feet wide, but can easily be sheared and kept lower. They can be used individually, in low hedges, or in borders. Quite tolerant of soils, as long as good drainage is provided. Plant in full or part sun.

Pernettya *(P. mucronata).* This is a top-notch berried plant. Plants grow 2–3 feet high with late-spring small white flowers followed by large berries. Berries are pink, rose, red, purple, or white. Clumps spread by underground runners to 3–4 feet. You need to plant more than one plant for proper cross-pollination. You can control the width of the plant by cutting the side shoots with a spade or by separating them to make more plants. Plant in full or part sun, in organic-enriched well-drained garden soil.

Philadelphus. See mock orange.

Photinia (*P. serrulata* 'Frazeri' and 'Glabra'). Two popular varieties of special interest because of their new red foliage growth. 'Frazeri' (12–15 feet) is probably the most popular, with new growth that is bright red. 'Glabra' (6–8 feet) is not as high, and its new leaves are a coppery red. Spring flower clusters are white. They are often used as privacy screens or trimmed as hedges. They are susceptible to a leaf spot disease (like blackspot on roses) that can spoil the appearance of the new red leaves. Place in full sun for best leaf color. Plant in enriched, well-drained garden soil.

Pittosporum *(P. tobira).* This is an interesting plant with whorls of dark-green leaves and clusters of cream-colored, fragrant flowers. The clusters of flowers appear surrounded by the green leaves. Plants may grow up to 8–10 feet, and I have seen a few in old gardens even taller, especially when crowded by surrounding plants. There is also a variegated variety with white margins along the green leaves. There are several dwarf varieties. I think this is another of the overlooked evergreens. Grows best in filtered sunlight, but will take even more shade. Plant in organic-enriched, well-drained garden soil.

Portugal laurel *(Prunus lusitanica).* This can be grown as a small tree or as a large shrub. Very dark-green leaves 3–5 inches long. Plants grow slowly up to 25 feet, usually less. Often used for privacy screening or as a hedge plant. Clusters of tiny black berries follow clusters of tiny white flowers. Plant in full or partial sun, in enriched, well-drained garden soil.

Potentilla *(P. fruticosa).* These deciduous shrubs flower all summer, from June to frost. Most varieties grow 2–4 feet. Flowers (1–2 inches) are somewhat shaped like those of strawberries. Single or double flowers come in shades of creamy yellow, yellow, orange, pink, red, or white. A few of my favorite varieties are 'Goldfinger' (golden yellow), 'Katherine Dykes' (soft yellow), 'Mount Everest' (white), 'Red Ace' (red and yellow), and 'Tangerine' (orange with tinge of yellow). Full to part sun is the best location to plant them. The deeper colors need a bit more shade or the flowers will fade quicker. Plant in rich, well-drained garden soil.

Privet *(Ligustrum vulgare).* This plant is most often used for hedging. Left unpruned, the plants will grow up to 10–12 feet and almost as wide. Small black fruit follows white summer flower clusters. Individual plants can be used as background plants in borders or for privacy. Plant in full or partial shade, in ordinary, well-drained garden soil.

Pussy willows *(Salix gracilistyla).* This is the bush species (6–8 feet) with large 1- to 1½-inch catkins. Very popular variety to use for cutting. Benefits from severe pruning every few years. Plant in full sun, in ordinary, well-drained soil.

Pyramidalis *(Thuja occidentalis).* See American arborvitae.

Flowering quince *(Chaenomeles).* These are the beautiful flowering varieties of quince, some of which also produce fruit. Varieties range 2–6 feet high or taller. Flowers 1–2 inches are single, semi-double, or fully double and range in shades of pink, apricot, salmon, red, orange, or white. Nurseries may sell them by color or by named varieties. Plant in full to part sun, in ordinary, well-drained garden soil.

Red-osier dogwood *(Cornus stolonifera).* This shrubby dogwood is also known as the redtwig dogwood. Multiple-stemmed plants grow about 6–8 feet high and 3–4 feet wide. Stems and branches are red and attractive year-round. Autumn leaf color is also bright red. Plant spreads by underground stems, which may need to be cut to confine growth. Deep green leaves are 2–2½ inches long. Although it has clusters of small white summer flowers, it is really grown for its red twigs and autumn leaf color. Plant in sun, part sun, or shade, in moist, enriched garden soil. See also Chapter 3, Trees.

Rhododendron (many varieties). For care, see Choosing Rhododendrons. Some species rhododendrons include *R. daphnoides* (soft purple); *R. impeditum* (mauve to dark blue); *R. loderi* 'King George' (light pink, white); *R. moupinense* (white to rose); *R. mucronulatum; R. pemakoense* (pinkish purple); *R. praecox* (rosy purple); and *R. racemosum* (soft to bright pink).

Favorite varieties include 'America' (red); 'Anna Rose Whitney' (deep rose pink); 'Antoon Van Welie' (pink); 'Autumn Gold' (salmon/pink, orange center); 'Blue Diamond' (violet blue); 'Blue Peter' (lavender/blue with dark blotch); 'Bow Bells' (pink); 'Bric-a-Brac' (white); 'Britannia' (red); 'Canary' (yellow); 'Carita' (yellow); 'Christmas Cheer' (pink, fades white); 'Cilpinense' (pale shell pink); 'Cunningham's Blush' (pink/white); 'Cunningham's White' (white); 'Cynthia' (rosy crimson); 'David' (blood red); 'Dora Amateis' (white); 'Elizabeth' (red); 'Else Frye' (pink/white, gold blotch); 'Fastuosum Flore Pleno' (double, mauve); 'Fragrantissimum' (white-touched pink); 'Gomer Waterer' (white, tinge of pink); 'Jean Marie de Montague' (red); 'Jock' (dark pink); 'King of Shrubs' (apricot yellow); 'Lady Bligh' (strawberry red); 'Lady Primrose' (yellow); 'Lee's Dark Purple' (dark purple); 'Loder's White' (white); 'Lord Roberts' (dark red); 'Madame Mason' (white, yellow blotch); 'Moonstone' (cream); 'Mrs. Furnival' (pink with dark blotch); 'Mrs. G. W. Leak' (pink with dark blotch); 'Naomi' (pink); 'Nova Zembla' (red); 'Odee Wright'; 'Pink Pearl' (pink); 'PJM' (fuchsia); 'Plum Beautiful' (lavender/plum); 'Polynesian Sunset' (orange); 'Purple Gem' (soft purple); 'Purple Splendour' (purple); 'Ramapo' (deep lavender); 'Rosamundi' (pale pink); 'Rose Elf' (white tinge of pink); 'Sapphire' (light blue); 'Sappho' (white with purple blotch); 'Scarlet Wonder' (scarlet red); 'Silver Edge' (variegated leaves, green with white edge; lavender flowers); 'Trilby' (deep crimson); 'Unique' (pale yellow); 'Unknown Warrior' (light red); 'Virginia Richards' (yellow, dark red blotch); and 'Vulcan' (bright red).

Rock daphne *(Daphne cneorum).* See daphne.

Rockrose (*Cistus* species). These plants love a bright, hot, sunny spot in the garden and thrive on a certain amount of neglect. They get their name from the single flowers, like the old-fashioned single rose. Many species, ranging in height from 2 to 8 feet. Flowers cover the plants for about a month in June and early July. Flowers (1½–2 inches) come in shades of pink, rose, orchid, purplish tints, or white. New growth can be pinched to encourage bushiness. Plant in full sun, in ordinary, well-drained garden soil.

Rose of sharon *(Hibiscus syriacus).* See hibiscus.

Russian olive. See elaeagnus.

Salal *(Gaultheria shallon).* See Chapter 12, Ground Covers.

Sarcococca *(S. hookerana humilis* and *S. ruscifolia).* Nice fragrant plants for the shady garden. *S. h. humilis* is a low-growing, 12- to 18-inch ground cover–type evergreen (see Chapter 12, Ground Covers). *S. ruscifolia* is a tall, 3- to 6-foot evergreen with very fragrant white flowers in January and February. The flowers appear close to the stems and are not too noticeable. Dark-green, 2-inch leaves. Plant in the shady garden, in organic-enriched, moist, but well-drained soil.

Skimmia *(S. japonica).* Showy red winter berries provide a nice spot of color in the fall and winter shady garden. Skimmia has a nice bushy growth habit when young, but may stretch out a little with age. Plants grow 5–6 feet high, with a dwarf variety that only grows 18–24 inches tall. Spring flower buds are pink, opening white. Fall and winter berries are bright red and stand out above the dark, glossy, 3- to 4-inch green leaves. This plant is sometime susceptible to mites in this region, which will give the leaves a mottled white appearance. Refined garden oil spray can often be used to help control them. Ask the certified nurseryperson at your garden outlet which product you should use. Plant skimmia in a shady spot where the showy berries can be enjoyed to the fullest. Add organic humus to the planting soil and provide good drainage.

Snowball *(Viburnum* x *carlcephalum).* Sometimes called the fragrant snowball viburnum. The large, 4- to 5-inch, ball-shaped spring clusters of cream-white, lightly fragrant flowers are very attractive. Attractive, 2- to 3-inch leaves are dull green. This deciduous shrub does very well in full or part sun, in organic-rich, well-drained garden soil.

Sourwood *(Oxydendrum arboreum).* See Chapter 3, Trees.

Spiraea (*S. japonica* and other species). There are several species. The *S. japonica* varieties have flowers on the ends of the stems and flower mostly during the summer and fall. One of my favorites is 'Magic Carpet', which only grows 24–30 inches and has bright bronze-red new growth that matures bronze-green, then reddish in autumn. The flowers are pink. 'Anthony Waterer', one of the best known, grows 3–5 feet with rose-pink flower clusters. Check with your garden outlets to see which varieties they feature. Plant spiraea in full or part sun, in ordinary, well-drained garden soil.

> **Bridal wreath spiraea.** *S. prunifolia* 'Plena'. Starts flowering in early spring; single variety. Probably the best known are these white-flowering spiraeas. They are the ones you undoubtedly saw in your grandparents' garden. The arching branches are covered with small single flowers.
>
> *S. cantoniensis* 'Flore-Pleno'. Begins blooming in late spring; double-flowering variety.

Stranvaesia *(S. davidiana).* This is a large shrub or small tree. Can grow up to 20 feet high, but if pruned can be kept lower. Upright broad-leaved evergreen with spring clusters of flowers, followed by red berries in the fall. The variety *S. d. undulata* is much lower-growing (4½–5 feet) and has wavy leaves. New growth on both is bronze, maturing green. Flowers attract bees, and berries attract birds. This plant will take full sun, even a southern exposure with reflected sun. Plant in enriched, well-drained garden soil.

Strawberry tree *(Arbutus unedo).* Here's an interesting large shrub or small tree that has fall berries that look like strawberries, hence the name. The plant generally has an open, upright growth habit (15–20 feet), with red bark and white flower clusters. Flowers appear at the same time as the fruit. There are dwarf forms that grow about half as tall. Plant in full or partial sun, in enriched, well-drained garden soil.

Sumac (*Rhus* species). All are grown for their brilliant autumn leaf colors. These plants have a tendency to develop suckers, which may need to be removed. Plant sumac in full sun, in ordinary, well-drained garden soil.

Above left: Fall, winter, and early spring flowers of laurustinus *(Viburnum tinus)* provide color from months and are lovely in cut flower arrangements.

Left: You can create a wonderful spring floral display with azaleas and rhododendrons.

Cut-leaf sumac (*R. typhina* 'Laciniata') is the same as staghorn sumac except the leaves are more finely cut.

Smooth sumac *(R. glabra).* Grows 10–12 feet; has leaves that are divided into several rather narrow, 3- to 5-inch-long leaflets. Autumn leaf color is scarlet red, with scarlet fruit (fall and early winter) on the ends of the branches.

Staghorn sumac *(R. typhina).* Very similar to *S. glabra* except it has fuzzy, short brownish hairs on the branches, much like the velvet of a deer's antlers. Autumn leaf color is in shades of yellow through red, with 4- to 8-inch dark-red velvet fruit.

Veronica (*Hebe* varieties). These are the shrub varieties, not to be confused with the perennial varieties of veronica. These are marginally hardy in our gardens, but it's worth trying to grow them. The varieties below have done really well in our garden for the past three years. Growers tell me the smaller-leaf varieties are the hardiest. Plants are covered with clusters of small spikelike flower clusters. Most start flowering in June and will continue for months if the spent flowers are kept picked. Flowers appear on new growth, so just pick the spent flowers, not the tip growth. Plant them in full or part sun, in enriched, well-drained garden soil.

'Autumn Glory'. 2–3 feet; lavender blue flowers.

H. buxifolia. 2–3 feet; small leaves and white flowers.

'Tricolor'. 3–4 feet; variegated green and cream leaves and purple flowers.

'Wiri-Charm'. 12–18 inches; fuchsia flowers.

Viburnum *(V. bodnantense).* A nice deciduous, 6- to 8-foot shrub with fragrant winter flowers. Rich, deep-green leaves on an erect, upright-growing shrub. Pink winter flowers are very fragrant. If possible this plant should be used in heavily traveled areas where the winter fragrance can be enjoyed to its fullest. Plant in full sun, in rich, well-drained garden soil.

Viburnum davidii *(V. davidii).* Large, bold, dark-green leaves 6 inches long provide a nice texture in the landscape. This evergreen shrub usually grows 3 feet high and 4 feet wide. I have seen them grow wider, but they usually will stay low unless crowded by nearby shrubs. In spring, 3-inch white flower clusters are sometimes followed by tiny metallic blue berries. Plant in partial shade in organic-enriched, well-drained garden soil.

Weeping blue atlas cedar (*Cedrus atlantica* 'Glauca Pendula'). This is really a tree instead of a shrub, but it is an excellent specimen tree to use in shrub plantings. They can be trained upright, then allowed to extend vertically for yards over a planting area. In one of our gardens, we had one 6 feet high and probably 9 feet or more in vertical length, and it was only ten years old. Bright bluish needles were only about 1 inch long. Plant in full sun, in enriched, well-drained garden soil.

Weeping blue spruce (*Picea pungens* 'Pendula'). It can be staked upright, then trained to grow vertical across a landscape planting, or allowed to grow on the ground as a ground cover. The silvery blue-green needles provide a bright spot of color in the garden. Often used as a specimen plant in a rock-garden outcropping. It is a magnificent (expensive) specimen plant for use in large containers. Plant in full sun or part shade, in organic-rich, well-drained soil. See also spruce, Chapter 3, Trees.

Weeping Japanese red pine (*Pinus densiflora* 'Pendula'). A low-growing weeping variety with bright green, 2½- to 4½-inch needles. Ideal to use in containers or a rock garden. Plant in full or part sun, protected from strong wind exposure. Grows in ordinary, well-drained garden soil. See also pine, Chapter 3, Trees.

Weigela (*W. florida* and hybrids). Late-spring tubular flowers are quite showy in shades of ruby red, pink, or white. Most varieties have dark-green leaves; however, there are a couple of variegated leaf forms. Most of the new introductions grow 3–7 feet high. I find most nurseries do not carry more than one or two varieties, so check to see which ones they feature. Plant in full or partial sun in organic-enriched, well-drained garden soil.

Wild lilac *(Ceanothus)*. See ceanothus.

Winged euonymus. See burning bush.

Winter daphne *(D. odora)*. See daphne.

Winter jasmine *(J. nudiflorum)*. See Chapter 7, Vines.

Yucca *(Y. flaccida)*. We have a couple of the variegated leaf forms; we really enjoy the foliage and then the large, 3- to 6-inch, creamy-white clusters of July and August flowers. Ours is a variety called 'Bright Edge', which has leaves that are green with yellow margins. We have them set back into the borders, so the sharp-pointed, 1½- to 2-foot leaves do not cut anyone. Easy to grow; provide well-drained, ordinary garden soil.

5 • Roses

Over the years, I doubt that there has been a more popular garden flower than the rose! Of the thousands of varieties introduced, most grow and flower prolifically in this region. The showy flowers come in practically every color of the rainbow. Flowers come in various sizes from miniature to large, from single to fully double. Although roses require a little more care than most plants, they're worth it because of the profusion of gorgeous flowers they produce throughout the summer.

Facing page: Large-flowering hybrid teas are colorful in the garden and showy as cut flowers.

Below: An attractive blend of yellow-and-pink flowers, dark-green foliage, and sturdy growth habit make 'Peace' one of the most popular garden roses.

Roses are one of the most popular garden plants simply because they flower prolifically, often have fragrance, and are such versatile plants because of their many growing forms. If you have a bright, sunny spot in your garden, there is a variety of bush, climbing, or tree rose that will provide a wealth of summer color. Their value in the garden and as cut flowers is unsurpassed by just about any other garden plant. Practically every garden has at least one rosebush, so here are a few of my suggestions on how to care for them in your garden.

Choosing a Location

I've planted a few rosebushes in areas of my garden where they only got about four hours of sunshine and others where they were exposed to six to eight hours of sunshine. Without question, the ones exposed to more bright sunlight did the best. Rose specialists recommend full sun. It should also be noted that most of the rose display gardens in this region are exposed to full sun most of the day. So go with the experts and plant your roses in a bright, sunny spot. Be certain the soil is well drained or mound the beds to provide additional drainage for the roots.

My Favorite Spot to Plant Roses

When I was growing up, Mom had all of her rosebushes planted in one area, the rose garden. Her perennials and annuals were in yet another area. The roses were beautiful when in bloom, but during the winter that area looked terrible; bare rose canes and nothing else. Today, for three reasons, I recommend that you mix the rosebushes in with other shrubs, perennials, and annual flowers:

- During the winter, the other plants tend to hide the ugly, bare canes of the roses.
- Separating the bushes tends to isolate and lessen insect and disease problems. When rosebushes are planted close together, mildew, blackspot, rose aphids, and other rose problems can be intensified.
- The bushes show off individually and provide quite a show in the garden. From experience, I can tell you the rosebushes do not suffer from competition with the other plants. In fact, they complement one another and this seems to offer the roses some additional winter protection.

In Containers

For summer color, it's hard to beat the beauty of a rose. In recent years they have become very popular bushes to grow in pots or containers. In some yards the only sunny spot is on the deck or lanai, so the only way to enjoy roses is to have them in pots in those areas.

When asked how to prune roses, an English rose authority once said, "Prune your roses. Go in and have a cup of tea. Then go back out and prune them some more." For hybrid tea roses, that probably isn't a bad idea! Severe pruning generally results in long stems and large flowers, and bushier rosebushes.

Indoors

Miniature roses are often sold as houseplants, but I don't think it's a good idea to grow them indoors. They are too susceptible to mildew because of stagnant air and lack of humidity. However, they are all right for a while in a greenhouse window or on a sun porch. At the first sign of any problems, plant them in a sunny spot outdoors. The rose will be happier and so will you.

Tree Roses

Some of the most popular bush varieties of roses are also offered as tree roses. These majestic plants are extremely popular in containers, as the focal point within a bed of roses, or as a stand-alone specimen plant. A cane of a climbing rose is grafted onto a rose rootstock then, 3 to 5 feet up that cane, the desired variety is grafted, thus producing a gorgeous tree rose. Care is the same as for all other types of roses, except they need special winter protection and may need staking to protect them from wind whipping during strong windstorms.

Buying a Rosebush

Choose rosebushes that have three to five healthy canes. Examine the canes to be certain they are not damaged (bruised). If you can see the roots, make sure that none are broken and that the canes and roots are healthy (not shriveled). Check the buds along the rose canes to be certain that they are not dried up, shriveled, or dead. I doubt you're going to find such rosebushes at reputable garden outlets or from specialty rose catalog firms, but who wants to waste their time and money planting inferior rosebushes?

Roses

Planting Roses

Bare-Root or Packaged Rosebushes

Remember to select a spot where the rosebush will get at least six to eight hours (or more) of bright sunlight. Roses that you purchase during the winter or in earliest spring usually do not have soil around the roots, hence the term *bare root.* Others will be in packages, usually in cardboard or polyethylene. I suggest you plant them just like a bare-root rose, unless they are in full growth and blooming.

Dig the Planting Hole

Dig a planting hole about 18 to 24 inches in width and depth.

Prepare the Soil for Planting

Into the existing soil mix generous amounts of organic humus in the form of compost, processed manure (the bagged steer manure), and peat moss. Mix thoroughly together and make a cone in the center of the planting hole.

Set the Bush at the Right Depth

In cold regions, set the bush in the soil so the graft (bud) is 2 inches below soil level. In moderate climates, like west of the Cascade Mountains, the graft can be placed right at ground level. And in warm southern climates, the graft is often set an inch or two above soil level.

Next, spread the roots of the rose over the cone, fill soil over the top of the roots, and firm the soil around the plant. Leave a concave soil area (well) at the base to make it easier to water each bush.

Container-Grown Roses

Today, with the advent of container-grown roses, many bushes are purchased already growing in pots. These are sometimes purchased when the rose is in full bloom. Ask the dealer how long the rosebushes have been in the container. If they have been in the pots for less than sixty to ninety days, I recommend that the rosebushes be planted container and all, then taken out of the pot and replanted in the fall. Otherwise you take a chance of the roots not being fully developed and the soil falling away from the rose roots. Consequently, transplanting could measurably affect the heath and vigor of, or even result in loss of, the bush. It's not worth the risk!

Wondering which variety of rose to plant, even after you've reviewed the varieties listed in this book? Visit one of the regional rose gardens. Practically every major Northwest city has a rose garden. See the roses firsthand, and you can judge them for their beauty, fragrance, growth habit, and disease resistance.

In Containers

Roses will do very well in pots, as long as the pot/container is large enough, has good drainage, and is given sufficient water, food, and extra winter protection. The container should be at least 24 inches by 24 inches by 24 inches. That's large enough for a bush or climber and still gives a little space at the base for a few summer-flowering annuals. If the container is too small, the plant will become top-heavy and is apt to blow over in a strong windstorm. Plus the bush needs a large enough root space to grow and flower at its best.

When to Transplant Established Roses

Have a rosebush in your garden that needs to be moved? The best time to move it is during the winter dormant season, after the leaves have fallen. Even if the leaves have not fallen, the months of November to February are the best for moving any kind of rosebush.

What do you do if you are moving or are adding an addition to your home, and you must move the rosebush in the late spring or summer when it is flowering and in full growth? If you are moving, you can probably get by with tagging the plant and making arrangements with the new owner to dig the plant in the fall. (This is a commonly accepted practice.) But if you are moving out of town or are doing some remodeling, you can try to save the rosebush by spraying an anti-transpirant such as Wilt-Pruf or Cloud Cover onto the foliage. This type of product helps retain moisture within the leaves and often reduces the trauma of replanting during the growing season. Don't do it unless you absolutely have to, but if you must, it's worth a try.

Heel in Roses Until Ready to Plant

What happens if you get a rose and do not have a place ready to plant it? Simply *heel it in*. What does that mean? Dig a hole anywhere and temporarily set the bush in the ground. Or place the roots on the soil surface and mound some bark, sawdust, or soil up over the root system. That's heeling it in! It's just a temporary place to keep the plant until the new planting soil is ready.

Feeding Roses

When to Feed Roses

Roses are prolific-flowering, robust-growing garden plants and will benefit from regular feeding during the growing season. I recommend feeding them in mid-February to encourage good root growth, then again monthly from May through August.

What to Feed Roses

Plants that lose their leaves over winter are called *deciduous*. A rose or all-purpose garden fertilizer (vegetable fertilizer too) can be used to feed deciduous plants; for example, roses. Select a quality fertilizer that contains micronutrients, such as iron, zinc, magnesium, boron, etc. Water in the fertilizer after application. The amount of fertilizer you apply depends upon the label recommendations of the fertilizer you use.

Left: Beautiful new floribunda roses like 'Betty Boop' are excellent as border or foreground plants in the landscape.

Pruning Roses

This is a major factor in having really attractive roses. These bushes need special pruning attention.

When to Prune

Dormant Pruning

Dormant pruning is done in late February to mid-March west of the Cascade Mountains, and in mid- to late April (weather permitting) at high elevations and east of the Cascades.

Summer Pruning

When cutting a flower or removing an old spent flower, cut the flower stem back to the first five-leaflet stem. This form of pruning encourages at least one new flowering stem and often two, so it not only helps maintain the size of the bush, but improves the appearance and at the same time encourages additional flowering on the repeat-blooming varieties.

Fall Pruning

We prune our bush roses back to waist high in late October or November. It certainly improves the appearance of the bushes, and at the same time keeps them from wind whipping during strong winter windstorms. If the wind whips the canes, it is apt to loosen them at the base, expose the roots to air, and make them more susceptible to freeze damage, which could cause possible loss of the entire rosebush.

How to Prune

All rose pruning starts with the removal of dead, decayed, or broken canes. Remove some of the center growth to open up the bush for good air circulation and sunlight exposure. Always make your pruning cut above an outside bud, to encourage new outward growth. Sucker growth that appears from below the graft should be removed immediately.

Each of the various types of roses have varying pruning requirements, so here are a few hints on how to prune each of them.

Hybrid Tea and Grandiflora Roses

These are unquestionably the most popular of all types of roses. Years ago, an English rose hobbyist shared with me his favorite method of pruning the large-flowering hybrid teas and grandifloras, and it sure has worked wonders for Myrna and me. He recommended that each bush be limited to three to five of the strongest canes. Prune those three to five canes in this manner:

- Canes the diameter of a pencil or pen: Prune to 6 inches.
- Canes the size of your little finger: Prune to 12 inches.
- Canes the size of your forefinger: Prune to 18 inches.
- Canes the size of your thumb or larger: Prune to 24 inches or less.

In cold climates, these two rose types may need to be pruned more severely during late spring. As the seasons pass, try to eliminate some of the old canes, replacing them with new ones as they develop.

A radio listener called in the other day and said she was reading an English book on gardening. In it, the author recommended that you prune your roses, then go have a cup of tea and come out and prune them some more. That's probably the best advice I have ever heard! In my opinion, home gardeners seldom prune their roses enough. They prune them too high, and as a consequence one looks at ugly, tall rose canes instead of a nice bush with beautiful flowers and attractive leaves from the ground up.

Floribunda and Polyanthus Roses

These bushes have many canes, and it is a good practice to encourage new canes from the base by removing a few old canes. Little if any pruning of the new canes is required, but the old canes should be pruned about halfway back at the same time as you prune all your other roses.

Climbing Roses

The key to growing really nice climbing roses is not so much pruning as it is training. The natural growth of most climbing roses is rather vase-shaped, and when they are allowed to grow in this manner, most of the rose flowers appear near the top of the canes. On the other hand, if you spread the canes outward so they grow horizontally, additional secondary growth will develop and bloom like crazy. In some rose gardens, the climbing roses are actually grown in an espaliered crisscrossing manner. Next time you're in a rose garden, take a close look at how the climbers are trained.

It's easy to do the little pruning required on climbing roses. The secondary growth—the side growth from a main cane—should be shortened back to the second growth bud from the main cane. As a new cane grows from above the bud, let it grow and prune out one of the old canes to replace it. That way, you are continually renewing the old plant.

Having an insect or disease problem with your roses? Before blasting them with everything on the garden shelf, take a few leaves in to your local garden outlet and have the certified nurseryperson make an on-the-spot diagnosis. They may be able to recommend a very simple, environmentally friendly means of insect or disease control.

Miniature Roses

These plants require very little pruning. I cut mine back about one-third to one-half every year. Prune out any dead tips and thin out a few stems if they are too crowded.

Ground Cover Roses

I have only two ground cover roses in my garden, but I find they will sometimes send a cane straight up, completely out of shape with the rest of the plant. So these canes I prune at any time. The only other pruning I do is to shape the plants for appearance's sake only. However, if they tend to grow a little spindly, prune back the tips to encourage side-branching and a better-looking, bushier plant.

Shrub/Landscape Roses

Limited pruning of these may be needed. Primarily prune to shape. If the bushes get too big, give them a haircut. I sometimes cut mine back as much as 50 percent.

David Austin Roses

We do not have any Austin roses in our garden, so I have to take the word of friends who say they prune their bushes about 50 percent each year. It may be necessary to thin them a little for good air circulation and sun exposure.

Old Garden Roses

How do I recommend to prune these? I've seen some around abandoned farmhouses and in old cemeteries that I am sure have not been pruned for the last decade, and they are truly beautiful. I would say prune them to fit your garden, and prune back any growth that ruins the shape of the bush.

Tree Roses

Since tree roses can be created from hybrid teas, floribundas, and even miniature roses, each should be pruned by type. Use the same general rules above, except do not prune quite as severely. Why? Severe pruning stimulates strong new growth, which is apt to be too vigorous for the stem to support. Make certain all canes are pruned at an equal distance from the trunk.

Protecting Roses from Cold Weather

Mound mulch up over the base of rose canes to a depth of 8 to 12 inches. Bark, sawdust, and straw are among the best materials to use for this job.

Pull the mulch material away in early spring. A frame of rabbit or chicken wire can be made around tree roses, then filled with straw to completely protect the stem and upper parts of the tree rose. Most climbing roses are very hardy and seldom need this type of protection.

Controlling Weeds Around Roses

Weeds and grasses are hosts to many insects and diseases, so it is important to keep them pulled. Note I said to keep them pulled, because it's best to avoid cultivating near the bushes, which is apt to damage the surface-feeder rose roots. Another way to help control weeds is with some types of preemergent weed killers.

Mulching or Underplanting Roses

Can you use bark, sawdust, or other mulching material around rosebushes to cut down on weed growth? Of course! Be certain you leave a small well around the base of the rose canes to collect and hold water. As bark and sawdust decay, they will use up nitrogen, so you may need to give the rosebushes a little additional feeding.

You can also plant low-growing ground covers at the base of roses to help deter weed and nuisance grass growth. One of the most attractive

Left: 'English Garden' is one of the most attractive old English roses, providing an abundance of summer color.

rose gardens Myrna and I ever had was base planted with blue-flowering lithodora (see Chapter 9, Perennials). My friend Eric Dupee in England uses the perennial aubrieta at the base of his roses. It's a beautiful combination, because the aubrieta flowers just before the roses; he then trims it back and it flowers again in midsummer. It doesn't seem to hurt the perennial plants to step on them when pruning the roses, cutting flowers, etc.

Controlling Insect and Disease Problems

The following are a few of the most common ailments that roses may suffer in Northwest home gardens.

Insects on Roses

Aphids, spider mites, caterpillars, and budworms are just a few of the pests that sometimes find their way onto rosebushes. Rose sprays or dusts can be used to help keep these pests under control. Sprays containing the natural insecticide neem oil are also being used to help control insects on rosebushes. Always apply these products according to label instructions.

Mildew and Blackspot

Mildew is noted by a whitish to grayish film that forms on the rose leaves. Blackspot, as the name implies, are black spots that develop on the leaves. Sometimes the condition will get so bad that the leaves will turn yellow (with the black spots on them), then drop from the bushes. Rose fungicides are often used to help control both of these problems.

One research project recommends using 3 teaspoonfuls of baking soda and 1 teaspoonful of refined spray oil, mixed into 1 gallon of water. Spray the mixture on the leaves of the affected bushes once every ten to fourteen days throughout the growing season, or until the mildew and blackspot are under control. Several rose hobbyists I have talked to lately claim that natural products containing neem oil are also quite effective in controlling both mildew and blackspot. Read and follow label instructions.

Rose Suckers

Long, fast growth from below the graft on a rose cane is called sucker growth. It is from the rootstock and is of no value. In fact, it should be removed as soon as it appears, because it robs the bush of needed energy and distracts from the neat appearance of your rose plant. You may have to dig into the soil an inch or two to find the point at which it originates, which is where it should be cut off.

Blindness in Rose Bushes

This is a condition in which the rose grows but never flowers. The tip growth that should produce the rosebuds and flowers never does. This seldom happens, but when it does, one is at a loss as to what to do. It's easy; prune the stems back to just above a five-leaflet stem, as you would if you were cutting a flower. If it continues to grow but not flower, the best solution is to replace the plant with another variety.

Rose Gall

This condition is noted by the development of a swelling around the base of the rose canes. It can be fatal, or it may exist for several years before affecting the health of the rosebush. To date, there is nothing one can do to control this disease. The best solution is to dig the bush and send it away with the garbage carrier. Do not replant a rose in the same spot unless the soil has been completely replaced with new soil.

Rust on Roses

Rust simply looks like rust on the leaves. It is most noticeable on the undersides of the leaves. Because it is a disease, simply use a rose fungicide to help control rust. Read the label of the fungicide you are using to be certain that it will control rust on roses, and apply as directed.

Choosing Roses

By Size

Ground Cover Roses

These are fast-growing, sprawling plants (seldom over 2 feet tall) for use in large areas to provide abundant color, help cover the soil, and cut down on maintenance. They are particularly useful on a hillside, as a means to restrict animal traffic, or to serve as a low screen or fence. Here are five super varieties for use in regional gardens:

'Cape Cod' (light pink)
'Kent' (white)
'Martha's Vineyard' (bright pink)
'Napa Valley' (red)
'Newport' (light pink)

Miniature Roses

These are rapidly growing in popularity. Easy to grow, these miniatures are ideal in containers, for low edging or borders, in rockeries, or individually in a sunny part of the garden. Most grow only 8 to 15 inches or less and bloom all summer. The cut flowers are great for small arrangements and as boutonnières. Contrary to popular belief, they are quite hardy. They often are sold as indoor flowering plants, but are much more satisfactory and much easier to grow outdoors. Here are six of the best ones to grow in your garden:

'Black Jade' (midnight red)
'Hot Tamale' (orange/yellow reverse)
'Incognito' (mauve/yellow reverse)
'Irresistible' (white)
'Jean Kenneally' (blend)
'Minnie Pearl' (blend)

Floribunda Roses

Probably the showiest of all roses, their flower clusters, with several flowers per cluster, provide a splash of color most of the summer. The flowers open one at a time, so each cluster provides color for several weeks. The flowers are smaller and the stems shorter than hybrid tea roses, but what they lack in size, they gain in profusion of color. These are ideal to use as a border bush when planted in the foreground of the taller types of roses. Use them in groups or individually for a splash of color anywhere in the sunny garden. They are also very attractive when grown in pots, tubs, or planter boxes. Here are eight top-notch varieties to consider growing in your garden:

'Amber Queen' (golden amber)
'Betty Boop' (white to yellow, edged with red)
'Blueberry Hill' (vivid lilac)
'Easy Going' (yellow)
'Iceberg' (crystal white)
'Lavaglut' (red)
'Livin' Easy' (apricot and orange)
'Playboy' (scarlet with yellow center)

Polyanthus Roses

This is another class of attractive, cluster-type, small-flowering roses that are low growing and prolific blooming. They are often grown as a low border or edging. These combine well with the other classes of roses. Cut flowers are fine for small arrangements, or individual flowers are often used as boutonnières. Here are four of the best for this region:

'Ballerina' (pale/white center)

'China Doll' (pink)
'The Fairy' (pale pink)
'Mother's Day' (dark red)

Shrub/Landscape Roses

This is a relatively new group of roses that are ideal for edging, hedging, and individual planting. Much emphasis is being placed on developing hardy varieties that have considerable resistance to disease. Here are eight varieties that certainly merit a place in the garden:

'Baby Love' (medium yellow)
'Bonica' (warm pink)
'Carefree Delight' (light pink)
'Knock Out' (cherry red)
'Sally Holmes' (creamy white)
'Scarlet Meidiland' (scarlet)
'Sea Foam' (creamy white)
'White Meidiland' (white)

Hybrid Tea/Grandiflora Roses

These are the granddaddy of all roses. I dare say, when most people think of roses, these are the ones they know best. They are the cutting rose that florists feature. Long stems and medium to large flowers are their greatest attributes. Flowers on the hybrid teas are generally borne one per stem, whereas the robust grandiflora roses may have one or more flowers per stem. Here are more than two dozen favorites:

'Barbra Streisand' (intense lavender)
'Double Delight' (hybrid tea; creamy white/rose)
'Elina' (light yellow)

Left: Fragrance, color, and dependability combine to make 'Double Delight' a popular hybrid tea rose.

'Fame' (pink blend)
'Full Sail' (white)
'Gemini' (pink)
'Gold Medal' (deep gold)
'Ingrid Bergman' (deep velvety red)
'Karen Blixen' (pure white)
'Liverpool Remembers' (orange red)
'Melody Parfumee' (purple)
'Mr. Lincoln' (hybrid tea; fragrant; deep red)
'Moonstone' (white/light pink edge)
'New Zealand' (creamy light pink)
'Octoberfest' (orange/yellow reverse)
'Olympiad' (hybrid tea; scarlet)
'Opening Night' (red)
'Peace' (hybrid tea; yellow and pink)
'Peter Frankenfeld' (deep pink)
'Pristine' (white/brushed pink)
'Queen Elizabeth' (grandiflora; coral/shaded pink)
'Reba McEntire' (orange red)
'Rina Hugo' (deep pink)
'Secret' (hybrid tea; white/pink edge)
'Sunset Celebration' (apricot)
'Veteran's Honor' (red)

Climbing Roses

Need a little height in your garden? Climbing roses may be the perfect solution on a fence, post, trellis, or arbor. Climbing roses need support in order to encourage them to climb. Many varieties are repeat bloomers, and some provide excellent cut flowers. Here are half a dozen choice varieties:

Cl. 'Altissimo' (deep crimson)
Cl. 'Autumn Sunset' (apricot gold)
Cl. 'Berries and Cream' (rose/white markings)
Cl. 'Cécile Brunner' (polyantha; shell pink)
Cl. 'Dublin Bay' (red)
Cl. 'Royal Sunset' (apricot)

By Particular Features

David Austin Roses

The David Austin roses are a selection of English roses. Austin bred old-fashioned roses with modern varieties for fragrance, durability, and repeat bloom. It is said that some are also bred for their resistance to disease. Rose friends recommend these varieties:

'Belle Story' (delicate pink)
'English Garden' (white, yellow center)

'Golden Celebration' (golden yellow)
'Graham Thomas' (apricot/yellow)
'Heritage' (clear shell pink)
'Lord D. Braithwaite' (red)
'Mary Rose' (rose pink)

Old Garden Roses

Many of the old rose varieties date back well over 100 years and some are among the hardiest garden roses of today. Much to my surprise, many of these old roses have been discovered growing in cemeteries around the world, which means they truly have survived harsh winters. Some flower only once a year, while others are repeat bloomers. I am not really familiar with many old roses, so I relied on rose specialists for their recommendations, and here are nine of their favorites:

Cl. 'Frau Dagmar Hastrup' (pink)
Cl. 'Sombreuil' (creamy white)
'Lyda Rose' (white, edged lavender pink)
'Reine des Violettes' (violet purple)
Rosa alba (white)
R. damascena 'Mme. Hardy' (white)
R. gallica 'Rosa Mundi' (rose/splashed white)
'Rose de Rescht' (white/strawberry markings)
'Zéphrine Drouhin' (deep rose pink)

Roses with Pleasant Fragrances

Without question, flower form and fragrance are the two features to look for when selecting rosebushes for the garden. Although most people think the old varieties were more fragrant, you'll notice the newer ones (listed here) are the ones with the most fragrance. In order to keep these comments in perspective, I must add that most David Austin and old garden roses are also noted for their fragrance. Here are eleven of today's most fragrant roses:

'Barbra Streisand' (hybrid tea/grandiflora; intense lavender)
'Big Purple' (grape juice purple)
'Blueberry Hill' (floribunda; vivid lilac)
'Cologne' (light lavender)
'Double Delight' (hybrid tea; white, strawberry markings)
'Fragrant Cloud' (hybrid tea; deep orange red)
'Full Sail' (hybrid tea/grandiflora; white)
'Mr. Lincoln' (hybrid tea; dark red)
'New Zealand' (hybrid tea/grandiflora; creamy light pink)
'The Oregonian' (pink)
'Secret' (hybrid tea; creamy white/pink edge)

6 Berries & Grapes

One of the really enjoyable parts of gardening is to be able to go out into the garden and pick fresh, luscious, nutritious berries and small fruits such as grapes right off the plants and vines. If you have a surplus, they can be used in pies, cobblers, jams, jellies, muffins, and breads, or be canned or frozen for later use.

Choosing the Location

Relatively easy to grow, berries and grapes can often be incorporated into landscape plantings. For example, strawberries can be used as ground covers, blueberries for their bright autumn foliage color, raspberries in the background for seasonal privacy, and blackberry vines as a thorny natural fence. The vines of small fruits like kiwis and grapes can be used effectively for privacy or to help screen parts of the garden. If you have a limited garden area, you can probably still find at least one or two spots that are just right for berries or grapes.

- Berries grow best in a bright sunny spot. Choose a spot where they will get at least half a day (more if possible) of bright sunlight.
- Well-drained soil is a must, except for blueberries and elderberries. All berries do best when grown on raised soil, where the best possible drainage and warmer soil are assured.
- Avoid planting smaller-growing berry plants where roots of nearby trees would be in competition with the berries.

Facing page: Currants are easy to grow, and the berries are tasty in jams and jellies.

Left: It's hard to beat the flavor of strawberries picked fresh from your own garden.

Planting Berries and Small Fruit Vines

When to Plant

As for all deciduous plants (plants that lose their leaves over winter), the ideal time to plant or transplant berries and vines is during the dormant season. Berries can be planted bare-root if they are planted/transplanted during the dormant season. Late November through mid-March is the ideal time.

New Plants

You will get the best selection of varieties and plants if you wait until late winter/early spring when the nurseries get in their new stock.

Transplants and Divisions

I prefer fall transplanting so the plants have the fall and winter months to reestablish a new root system.

A young strawberry plant that is set out by April 15 will produce a small crop of berries the first year. If you prune off the runners that develop the first year, they will produce larger berries.

Prepare the Soil for Planting

Whether you are planting for the first time or transplanting established plants from your garden (or a neighbor's), take time to prepare the soil properly. Remember, the only time you have a chance to get the nutrients and soil amendments into the root zone is at planting time. So please do it right; you'll be rewarded with healthier plants, better yields, and easier-to-maintain berries, vines, and small fruits.

First raise the soil 6 to 8 inches above ground level. Then add about one-third to one-half part organic matter to your existing soil. Peat moss, well-rotted manure, processed manure (the bagged stuff), and compost are all good forms of organic humus. I like to use a little peat moss and processed manure when I plant, or I'll use compost instead of the peat moss if I have some. Also add a nonburning transplanting fertilizer, mixing it thoroughly with the planting soil. Now you're ready to plant! See the Tips on Planting and Transplanting sidebar on pages 16–17.

Feeding Berries

Over the years, I have found the best time to fertilize berries is in late winter or earliest spring. The months of mid-February to mid-April are the best. Use a vegetable or rose food to feed the berries. (If you use a rose food, be certain it does not contain a systemic insecticide.) See Chapter 16, Composting and Fertilizing, for more information on when to feed all types of plants.

Protecting Cane Berries from Cold Weather

Berries such as raspberries seldom need winter protection. However, if you live in a very cold spot, you can mound 10 to 12 inches of mulch around the base of the canes. Straw is excellent for this. Then, in springtime, use the straw as mulch between the rows.

Controlling Insects and Disease Problems

Dormant Spraying

Winter dormant sprays can be used on the deciduous cane and vine-type berries to help control overwintering insects and diseases. The months of November (first spray), December (second spray), and early February (third spray) are the best times for winter spraying.

Summer Spraying

If insects become a problem during the growing season, you can use a product such as Fruit & Berry Insect Control (that's the actual name of the product), following directions on the label. Or for insect and disease problems you could use a combination vegetable garden-type dust or spray.

Controlling Birds That Love Fruit

There are several quite effective ways of keeping birds from devouring your berries. They include covering or surrounding your trees or plants with netting, using loud noises, or hanging strips of the mylar or nylon tapes currently on the market. See Chapter 17, Protecting Plants from Creatures, for details and more ideas.

Blackberries

There's nothing like a fresh blackberry pie or cobbler! How many ways can one use blackberries? Pies, cobblers, jams, jellies, sauces, wine, in muffins, eating fresh, etc. Domesticated blackberries should not be confused with the wild ones, as they have a delicious difference in flavor, are easier to control, and several that I mention are thornless.

Choosing a Location

Easy to grow, blackberries thrive in full sun or part sun and shade. The thornless vines make a nice barrier or seasonal fence. It's best to train blackberries on a trellis or support so the fruit does not touch the ground. Blackberries are quite tolerant of soils and will adapt to moist (not continually wet) soil conditions.

Pruning Blackberries

They bear on the previous season's growth, so prune out the old canes as soon as they are through bearing fruit.

Varieties

'Arapaho'—a new (early) thornless variety
'Cascade'—thorns
'Loch Ness'—thornless (late)
'Marionberry'—thorns
'Tayberry'—thorns
'Triple Crown'—thornless

Blueberries

Attractive bushes with colorful autumn foliage color make blueberries an ideal bush berry for the landscape. This one's so easy to grow, it's a winner for the first-time gardener or the old-dirt gardener. Eat the berries fresh from the bush; use them in pies, muffins, breads, and jams; or mix them up in a fruit compote. We have two bushes in our garden, and not one blueberry ever makes it to the kitchen; they are all eaten fresh right off the bushes.

The average bush, with care, will produce fifty years or more. It is sometime said that blueberries need pollinating from a second bush of a different variety. This does not seem to be true; they bear just fine alone. However, it is sure nice to have two plants, one early bearing and the second one fruiting a little later.

Planting Blueberries

Most plants are spaced 6 to 7 feet apart. Dwarf varieties can be planted 3 to 4 feet apart. Blueberries should always be planted or transplanted with a root ball (soil with the roots), except young starts. Mix generous amounts of peat moss into the planting soil; they like an acid soil.

Blueberry Care

They like more moisture than most berries. However, they should not sit in waterlogged soil. Use a rhododendron-type fertilizer to feed them. Organic gardeners can use cottonseed meal to feed blueberries.

Pruning Blueberries

As the plants mature, it is a good practice to thin tangled growth. Also, remove one-third of the oldest growth yearly to encourage regrowth of new shoots. If flowering is heavy, remove some of the flowers so the bush can yield a moderate crop of good-size berries. Remove suckers as they appear. Best time to prune is during the late winter.

Varieties

Early

'Northcountry'
'Patriot'
'Spartan'

Midseason

'Bluecrop'
'Northblue'
'Olympia'

Late

'Darrow'
'Jersey'
'Legacy'
'Sunshine Blue'

Dwarf

'Chippewa'
'Northsky'

Blueberries are one of the most versatile of all berry plants. They make very attractive landscape plants, grow nicely in containers, or you can grow them as a summer hedge. Their bright red and yellow fall color is a bonus.

CURRANTS

Currants are not as well known to home gardeners, so they are not as popular as blueberries, raspberries, and strawberries. The red currants are often used in jams and jellies, while the black currants are popular in jellies, juices, and syrups. The red varieties have very attractive, bright-red fruit and in Europe are often grown in the garden as a deciduous hedge. The sweet-flavored white currants are quite rare and are used in the same way as the red and black ones. Currants usually ripen in late June to early July.

Planting Currants

Leave approximately 4 feet between plants, a little closer if they are to be grown as a hedge.

Pruning Currants

This is best done during the winter when they are dormant. Prune out old shoots, but leave the current year's growth, because it will produce the crop for the next season. (Shoots grow one year, produce the second.)

Varieties

Here are a few varieties of currants that are recommended for growing in the home garden:

Red

'Cascade'
'Red Lake'

Black

'Hilltop Baldwin'

White

'White Imperial'

Gooseberries

Here's a berry that's not really too well known to most homeowners. Early varieties were quite tart and disappointing to many, but the introduction of sweeter-tasting varieties has helped them gain in popularity. Gooseberries are easy to grow; they are often used in jams, jelly, and sauces, or eaten fresh. Plants are self-fertile.

Choosing a Location

Gooseberries will grow and produce in full sun or part sun and shade. In hot climates, give them a part sun and shade exposure.

Pruning Gooseberries

Like currants, the idea is to prune out old growth to encourage the development of new growth. Removing the old inner growth opens up the plants to more air circulation and better light exposure. Leave six or seven canes. Do this pruning during the winter dormant season.

Varieties

'Hinnomaki Yellow'

'Invicta'
'Poorman'

Strawberries

Planting Strawberries

Remember, this is one berry plant that can very effectively be used in the landscape as a ground cover. Many have runners so the plants will fill in quite quickly. In the vegetable garden, space the new starts about 12 to 15 inches apart, a little closer in the landscape. *Important Note:* If strawberries are used in the landscape, be certain no harsh pesticides or herbicides are used in the areas where they are planted.

Feeding Strawberries

The June-bearing varieties set flower buds in the fall for the following spring, so feed the strawberries with 0-10-10 fertilizer in August or September (see Chapter 16, Composting and Fertilizing). A light feeding in late winter (February 15) is beneficial in getting the plants off to a good start in early spring. Use a vegetable garden–type fertilizer for this feeding.

Everbearing strawberries produce throughout the summer, so feed them monthly during the summer, using a vegetable-type plant food.

Left: Tasty, heavy-bearing blueberries make attractive landscape plants. Plant early-, mid-, and late-season varieties for extended harvest.

Watering Strawberries

Water by irrigating the plants. Do not water overhead during their bearing season. They should not lack for moisture during the harvest season. Lack of moisture and/or fertilizer can reduce yield or result in smaller berries.

Fall Care of Strawberries

Dead leaves should be removed. Mulching with a light layer of straw, sawdust, or bark will provide extra protection to the plants over winter. The mulch will also help control overwintering weed growth.

Varieties

June-Bearing

'Benton'
'Puget Summer'
'Rainier'
'Shuksan'

Everbearing

'Quinault'
'Tristar'

Raspberries

We are extremely lucky in that our generous, sharing next-door neighbor has a huge patch of raspberries, so we enjoy the benefits of this fabulous fruit without giving up any garden space for it. Raspberries are delicious picked and eaten fresh, sprinkled over some ice cream, used in pies, jams, and jellies, or frozen for later use. Along with strawberries, this is another berry that kids seem to thrive on.

Easy to grow, raspberries can be used in the landscape as a seasonal screen or they can be grown in small clusters (supported by wire rings), instead of on wire supports in rows as grandma and grandpa used to grow them. There are two types: the single crop and everbearing varieties. Try them, you'll like 'em! Average height is 5 to 6 feet.

Planting Raspberries

Leave about 18 to 21 inches between plants at planting time. Space rows about 4 to 5 feet apart. Or in small gardens, plant raspberries in clusters, placing plants in a circle 15 inches apart.

Raspberry Care

Plants that are well tended in the garden will remain productive for up to eighteen to twenty years. Watering and feeding requirements are the same as for other berries. (See earlier in this chapter.)

Pruning Raspberries

On the single-crop varieties, cut off the old canes to the ground as soon as they are through bearing fruit. Do not cut the new canes, because they are the ones that bear next year's crop. (However, those new canes can be topped at 4 to 5 feet in the fall, so they do not wind-whip during winter windstorms.)

On the everbearing varieties, cut the canes to the ground after they are through bearing in the autumn.

Varieties

Single-Crop

'Chilliwack'
'Meeker'
'Tulameen'
'Willamette'

Everbearing

'Autumn Bliss'
'Dinkum'
'Heritage'
'Summit'

Other Berries

Elderberries, cranberries, huckleberries, and lingonberries are other berries that merit a spot in the home garden. All are easy to grow, and the lingonberries and cranberries both make excellent ground-cover plants in the landscape (see Chapter 12, Ground Covers). If you have a shady garden and are unable to grow many types of fruit or berries, the evergreen huckleberries are the ideal berry plants for you (see Chapter 4, Shrubs). Jostaberry is a cross between the gooseberry and black currant. It turns almost black when ripe. High in vitamin C, the berries can be used to make jam or jelly or can be eaten fresh. Pruning and care in general are the same as for currants.

Note: Due to space limitations, I cannot cover every type of berry or each of the hundreds of varieties available, so I have listed just a few of the best and most productive ones. New varieties are being introduced and old ones being rediscovered yearly, so please ask an experienced certified nurseryperson, Master Gardener, or fruit and berry specialist for additional suggestions.

Grapes

Here's a vine that has value for it beauty in the landscape and, as a bonus, produces tasty table or wine grapes. Grapes are a great fruit for eating fresh; they are good for making juice, jams, and raisins; and some varieties are ideal for making wines. Grapes are self-fertile, so only one vine is needed to produce fruit. Vines usually produce grapes about two to four years after planting.

Choosing a Location

If you need a vine for a bright, sunny spot in the garden, a grapevine may the perfect solution. In recent years, home gardeners and fruit specialists have discovered many grape varieties that thrive in cool, short-season climates. Their big, bold foliage and robust growth make them great vines for providing shade, privacy, and delicious fruit. I have mentioned the importance of planting them in a sunny spot. That is not to say that grapes will not grow in part sun and shade, but the fruit usually will not ripen. They need well-drained soil in which to grow.

Planting Grapes

At planting time, mix in some organic humus in the form of peat moss, compost, or well-rotted manure. Peat moss is an excellent additive because grapes like a slightly acid soil. Add a little organic, nonburning, acidic rhododendron fertilizer into the planting hole to aid in the development of their deep root growth. If you are growing several vines, space them about 8 to 10 feet apart.

Watering Grapes

I have asked several vineyard owners about watering grapes, and the answers vary just a little. Most say to water to get the vines established the first year, then go light on watering afterward. In the Napa Valley of California, one owner said, "On average we water the vines twice a year." That's not very much for that region. Over the years I have found that overwatering and overfeeding stimulate too much vegetative growth and reduce the yield, so go light on watering. (Make certain the vines are not situated in a spot where they get sprinkler water every time you water the lawn.)

Feeding Grapes

Go light on feeding, which tends to produce too much vegetative growth instead of fruit. Look for signs of yellowing leaves; if they occur, then feed the vines. Use an organic, acidic rhododendron-type plant food. If feeding is needed, late winter to late spring is the best time to do it.

Pruning Grapes

I prune our grapevine hard every February, and it's loaded with grapes every year. Here's how to start: The first year, select one stem and cut it back to three or four buds. (That's quite severe, sometimes only 3 to 5 feet high.) The second year, train four canes from that main stem, two on each side, growing in opposite directions. Train them on supports of wire or a trellis support. Then in subsequent years prune out some of the three-year-old growth. My vines get so long, sometimes up to 15 or 20 feet, during the summer, that I cut about one-third to one-half of the tip growth during the growing season. Otherwise it takes too much space, and too much of the vines' energies are wasted on vegetative growth instead of fruit.

Varieties

Seedless Table Grapes

'Einset' (red/pink)
'Venus' (blue)
Vitis labrusca 'Canadice' (red/pink)
V. l. 'Himrod' (green)
V. l. 'Interlaken' (green)

Wine Grapes

The best advice I can give is to ask a winery near you. So much depends upon the microclimate in your garden, and your results are apt to vary from one year to another depending upon weather. Nevertheless, here are a couple of maybes:

Vitis vinifera 'Madeleine Angevine' (Riesling)
V. v. 'Pinot Noir' (Burgundy)

Other Fruiting Vines

Kiwi, passion vine, and akebia are other vines that merit a spot in the garden because of their appearance and tasty fruit. (See Chapter 7, Vines.)

Berries and Grapes Encyclopedia

Akebia *(Akebia quinata)*. See Chapter 7, Vines.

Blackberry.

'Arapaho'. A new, very hardy variety developed by the University of Arkansas. This is a popular *freestanding* (does not need trellis support), thornless variety. Large round berries. First year, let canes grow to 4 feet, then tip-prune and fruiting laterals will develop. Following spring, head back laterals to 2-foot lengths and mid-June berries develop. After fruiting, cut out old canes and prune new ones as you did the previous year. Ripens June/July.

'Cascade'. Years ago this was a favorite in our garden. Some think it is a cross between the native trailing Cascade blackberry and the 'Loganberry'. Much larger in size than the native, but with similar flavor. Ripens July.

'Loch Ness'. Thornless, semi-upright Scottish variety. Tart flavor; large, shiny, black berries. Can be trained upright on supports, like raspberries. Very productive. Ripens August/September.

'Loganberry'. This blackberry is actually red. Some think this red berry is a wild cross between a blackberry and red raspberry. Excellent flavor. It has lost some of its popularity because it does not bear as heavily as some of the other blackberries. Nevertheless a good garden variety. Trailing vines.

'Marionberry'. One of the sweetest and most popular eating berries. It is also excellent in making pies, cobblers, jellies, and juices. Good heavy producer of high-quality berries. Ripens July. The trailing vines are not hardy in the coldest areas.

'Tayberry'. Developed in Scotland, this is a cross of 'Loganberry' and the black raspberry. Large, long, narrow, reddish-black berries are flavorful. Vigorous canes can be grown in a sprawling clump, like black raspberries.

"Triple Crown'. Very sweet, large, shiny blackberries. They ripen in early August, a little later than most varieties, and so tend to extend the berry season. Vigorous vines may produce up to 30 pounds of berries per plant. Ideal for eating fresh, jellies, toppings, or juice.

Blueberry.

'Bluecrop.' Extremely heavy-bearing, very large, light blue berries. This flavorful variety has an upright growth habit. Ripens from mid-July to mid-August. Excellent red fall leaf color.

Left: Large bold leaves, attractive vines, and tasty fruit make grapes a great garden vine.

'Chippewa'. A new dwarf, hardy variety from the University of Minnesota. Large, light-blue berries with excellent flavor. Plants grow 3–4 feet tall and produce 4–7 pounds at maturity. Fiery red fall foliage.

'Darrow'. Fruit up to a quarter in size. The largest blueberry of all. Vigorous, upright growth habits. Heavy producer of firm, tart, flavorful berries. A good variety for Northwest home gardens. August-bearing.

'Jersey'. An old-time favorite. A heavy producer of spicy-flavored berries. Vigorous, upright growth habit with bright yellow autumn leaf color. Fruit ripens mid-August to frost. This is one of the varieties we have in our garden and we thoroughly enjoy the long harvest season.

'Legacy'. This is heavy producer of tasty berries, which ripen in August. Introduced by the USDA, this variety extends the season by almost a month. Colorful autumn leaf color makes this an attractive landscape plant.

'Northblue'. One of the new lower-growing varieties, 3 to 4 feet tall. Great for small gardens. It produces large, sweet, dark-blue berries.

'Northcountry'. New dwarf-type blueberry that grows to only 3 feet high. A wonderful landscape plant. Delicious berries are light blue. Nice autumn leaf color.

'Northsky'. Here's a real dwarf that only grows 18 inches high and spreads to 3 feet. It only produces about 1–2 pounds (per year) of medium-sized light-blue berries, but they have the delicious wild blueberry flavor. Autumn leaf color is bright red. Great as a ground cover or for use in containers. Bears in mid-July.

'Olympia'. The folks at Raintree Nursery describe this one as one of the West's best-kept secrets—this berry does well where others are less successful. The fruit is large with a superb flavor. Highly productive, the plants have a vigorous, spreading growth habit. Autumn leaf color is red. Ripens in late July.

'Patriot'. Large, dark-blue berries are highly flavored. Hardy, consistent-bearing variety. Low-growing, bushy growth, spreading to 4 feet. Will grow even in wet soils. A selection from the University of Maine. Autumn leaf color is bright orange.

'Spartan'. Very large berry of excellent flavor. New mummy berry–resistant variety. One of the best heavy-bearing, early varieties. Plant in well-drained soil. Ripens in July.

'Sunshine Blue'. This evergreen variety has colorful, bright pink spring flowers and light-blue, medium-sized berries. Plants grow 4 feet high and yield up to 10 pounds of delicious berries. Berries ripen from early August through early September. Very hardy to 0 degrees Fahrenheit.

Cranberry. See Chapter 12, Ground Covers.

Currant.

'Cascade' (red). A proven Northwest variety. Large, sweet berries are produced in abundance. Provide support for this easy-to-grow variety. Winter hardy.

'Hilltop Baldwin' (black). This English variety has been rated highest in vitamin C. Heavy producer of sweet, black berries. One of the best (if not the best) for jellies.

'Red Lake'. Bright-red berries in grapelike clusters cover the plant in late July. Showy spring flowers. Ideal for pies and preserves.

'White Imperial'. This is one of the old-time favorites. Introduced more than 100 years ago, the white, pink-blushed fruit has a rich, sweet flavor. Very productive in Northwest gardens.

Gooseberry.

'Hinnomaki Yellow.' This Finnish variety is winter hardy and has sweet, yellow-green berries. The medium-sized berries have an aromatic aftertaste reminiscent of apricot. Low-spreading growth habit. Ripens in mid-July.

'Invicta'. An excellent, mildew-resistant selection from England. Good producer of flavorful, large green berries that hang in clusters along the branches. Berries are ideal for jams, pies, or freezing.

'Poorman'. A very popular American variety with some mildew resistance. The berries are so sweet they can be eaten fresh off the bush. Sweet, highly flavorful. Green berries turn red when ripe.

Grape. *Vitis labrusca.*

V. l. 'Canadice'. A hardy, productive, pink seedless grape. It has a delicious, spicy flavor. Ripens in the Northwest in early October.

V. l. 'Einset'. This seedless pink grape has medium-sized fruit and fine flavor that has a hint of strawberries. Early ripening (about a week before Canadice), it is an introduction from New York. Grapes store well, and it is resistant to *botrytis* (gray mold).

V. l. 'Himrod'. This early-bearing variety is vigorous growing. Similar to 'Interlaken', the golden, oval seedless berries develop in long, loose clusters. Ideal to plant on a trellis or arbor.

V. l. 'Interlaken'. This is considered the most reliable seedless grape for west of the Cascades. Small fruit ripens in mid-September. Green to golden berries are excellent in fruit salads, and they make great raisins. Excellent flavor for eating fresh. Very hardy variety.

V. vinifera 'Madeleine Angevine' (Riesling). This is a heavy-producing, golden-yellow variety that makes an excellent white Riesling-type wine. This variety consistently ripens in the Pacific Northwest; early October.

V. v. 'Pinot Noir' (Burgundy). This is the variety used to produce the award-winning dry red wine of Burgundy. Grown in California, western Oregon, and the warmer areas of western Washington. This variety produces moderate yields of small, dark-blue grapes. *Note:* There are different types, so be certain to pick an appropriate one for your area.

'Venus'. Here's a seedless blue grape with excellent flavor. An introduction from the University of Arkansas. Considered a real winner in Northwest gardens. Very large, productive, early, attractive blue grape. Fruit may have soft seed vestiges. (Patented.)

Huckleberry. See Chapter 4, Shrubs.

Kiwi *(Actinidia arguta).* A hardy, fruit-bearing kiwi. See Chapter 7, Vines.

Lingonberry. See Chapter 12, Ground Covers.

Passion vine *(Passiflora caerulea).* See Chapter 7, Vines.

Raspberry.

'Autumn Bliss'. A nice, early fall-fruiting, home garden, everbearing variety. Sturdy canes require little support, except in windy areas. Large, firm berries have excellent flavor.

'Chilliwack'. Wonderful flavor, large berries, high productivity, and good berry color combine to make this a popular home garden variety. It has better root-rot resistance than many varieties.

'Dinkum.' This new everbearing variety comes from Australia, has excellent flavor, and is easy to pick. It produces lots of berries from August to frost. Excellent variety for the backyard garden.

'Heritage'. Dark-red berries with good mild flavor. Produces a bit later then most raspberries, extending the season. Provide support for the vigorous canes.

'Meeker'. One of this area's favorite varieties. Very productive, with excellent flavor. Ripens in July. Berries are excellent for eating fresh and in jams, jellies, and cobbler.

'Summit'. This is considered one of the best everbearing varieties for this area. Heavy late-summer and fall producer of delicious, medium-sized berries. Resistant to root rot and does better than most varieties in wetter soils. A wonderful home garden variety. 'Golden Summit', which has beautiful golden berries of similar qualities, is a mutation of this variety.

'Tulameen'. Here's a great new single-crop raspberry for the home garden. Berries are up to 25 percent larger than others. Light red fruit has fine flavor. An introduction from British Columbia, it produces for up to 50 days during

July and August. This variety is susceptible to root rot, so it must be planted in well-drained soil.

'Willamette'. Dark red with sharp raspberry flavor. A popular, commercially grown variety. Vigorous growing plants must have good drainage.

Strawberry.

'Benton'. This late-June variety has very tasty, large berries. It will tolerate a wide range of soils. An easy-to-grow variety that has a great flavor. Ideal for eating fresh or to freeze for later use.

'Puget Summer'. One of the best new varieties for the backyard gardener. Large, firm berries with rich color and good yields. Very sweet, with full strawberry flavor. Late June-bearing. A selection from Washington State University.

'Quinault'. This has been one of the most popular everbearing varieties. Semi-large berries of good quality. Easy to grow in Northwest home gardens but not as productive as the *day-neutral* varieties. (Day-neutral strawberries do not depend upon day length to initiate bloom, like the single-crop, June-bearing varieties. Instead they bear lightly in June and then continue to bear heavier from July until frost.)

'Rainier'. In recent years, there have been many new strawberry variety introductions, but this is one that continues to be popular because of its flavor and large berries. Ripens in late June.

'Shuksan'. Medium-sized to large berries have dark red color and excellent flavor. One of the best for freezing or eating fresh. Productive and well suited to the Northwest home garden. It's one of the hardier varieties. Ripens in late June.

'Tristar'. This is a very popular day-neutral strawberry that produces from June until frost. One of the favorites of researchers and growers throughout the Northwest and many areas of the United States. It's a highly productive variety with large, flavorful berries. A favorite for eating fresh or freezing. Give this one five stars!

7 · Vines

Some vines are evergreen, others are deciduous, and still others are seasonal (annual) vines that provide an abundance of summer color. Many vines are self-clinging, with tendrils, aerial roots, or intertwining vines; others need support. All vines need support until they are established. In our garden, in the spring we plant summer annual flowers at the base of our vines, which makes for a very attractive flower display during the months we are using the patio the most.

Choosing a Location

Facing page: Clematis 'Nelly Moser' adds a bright spot to the summer garden.

Above: Honeysuckle vines provide showy flowers and great fragrance. Use them on a trellis, post, or fence.

Practically every garden has at least one spot where a vine can be used very effectively. Some typical spots for vines include using them on trellises, arbors, pergolas, pillars, downspouts, posts, old tree stumps, or old retaining walls. Today vines are often used in the landscape to provide privacy or to screen out an unpleasant neighborhood eyesore. Vines are excellent for adding height to the garden and providing a bit more interest and seasonal color to the garden. There are even a few vines that can be effectively used like ground covers, especially on hard-to-maintain hillsides, or to hang over low banks.

In Containers

Can vines be grown in containers? Certainly; sometimes because of paved surroundings, it is impossible to plant vines in the open ground, so if a vine is desired in such an area the only solution is to plant it in a container.

Of course, the size of container will determine which vines can be planted. For example, we have four vines on our deck: clematis, honeysuckle, akebia, and evergreen clematis. They are all planted in containers 24 inches by 24 inches and about 18 inches deep; all are doing very well. However, these containers would be too small for fast-growing vines such as wisteria, grapes, or kiwis. The faster- and larger-growing vines need containers about the size of a half-whiskey barrel in order to survive.

Planting Vines

When to Plant or Transplant

If you want to add a new vine to the garden, it can be done at practically any time of the year, providing the ground is not frozen. Because all vines you buy are grown in containers, they can easily be planted almost year-round. If you want to transplant an established vine in your garden, the best time to do this is during the winter dormant-season months of November, December, January, or February.

Prepare the Soil for Planting

Mix organic humus with your existing soil at planting time. It's a good practice to add one-third part compost, peat moss, or processed manure, plus one-third part planting mix, to one-third part your existing soil. This will give the new plant roots a better chance of becoming established in the early stages of growth.

Dig the Planting Hole

Make the planting hole about twice as deep and twice as wide as the actual size of the root ball of the plant you are setting out.

Set the Plant at the Proper Depth

Be certain to set the plant in the new planting hole so that the surface roots are right at ground level. Some vines, such as clematis, can actually be planted deeper, but that's the exception, not the rule.

Looking for a vine that has evergreen foliage all twelve months of the year? Take a look at *Clematis armandii.* The rich, dark-green, bold foliage and white clusters of fragrant flowers in late winter and early spring make this a wonderful vine for Northwest gardens.

Pruning Vines

Vines that flower during the spring months produce their flowers on the previous season's growth (old wood), so they are pruned or shaped immediately after they finish flowering. On the other hand, vines that flower during the summer and into the fall flower on the current season's growth (new growth), so they can be pruned anytime during the fall or winter. The reason this is so important is that if you prune or shape at the wrong time, you'll be inadvertently cutting off the next season's flowers.

Vines can easily become overgrown or misshapen, and a little corrective shearing can keep them within bounds. Some vines are so robust that it is not unusual for the lower vines to become barren, with flowers and foliage occurring much higher on the vines. Pruning will help correct this condition, but sometimes the better solution is to plant a second slower-(lower-) growing vine to cover the bare stems.

Feeding Vines

When to Feed

If needed, the best time to fertilize vines is in early spring, and the second application, if needed, can be made in late spring. How do you know whether a vine needs feeding? If it is growing prolifically and flowering abundantly, and has nice, green, healthy leaves, there is no need to feed it. In fact, this is true of any garden plant; overfeeding is apt to push a plant too much, encouraging unwanted growth and often limiting flowers, because the prolific new growth bypasses the flower buds.

What and How to Feed

Use a rhododendron- or evergreen-type fertilizer to feed evergreen vines, and a rose-type food to feed the deciduous and annual vines. Apply the fertilizer on the soil surface at least 1 foot away from the main stem, and water in thoroughly after application.

I think one of the most overlooked vines is the spring-flowering *Akebia quinata*. The unusual fragrant purple spring flowers provide quite a show in the garden. If the roots are shaded, this vine can grow in partial shade or full sun.

Controlling Insect and Disease Problems

This is a tough one to cover, because pest problems vary by plant species. Most of the vines we grow in our gardens are not often bothered by pests.

Aphids

Some vines, however, including clematis and honeysuckle, can be visited occasionally by aphids. These plants attract beneficial insects too, so be sure to use an organic or natural spray to control the aphids. Best time to spray is in the early evening.

Mildew

Mildew can be a problem on a few vines, especially if they are planted in a spot with poor air circulation or not enough sun exposure. Climbing roses, clematis, and honeysuckle are the most likely victims. Neem oil and several other natural fungicides are now available, so check with your local certified nurseryperson or Master Gardener for the very latest environmentally friendly recommendation.

Choosing Vines

Is it important that your vine be evergreen? Is it important that it have flowers? Is it going to grow in the sun or shade? Do you want a vine that produces fruit? If it's being used to provide shade, the leaves should be large or at least dense enough to accomplish the job. Study the site, then select the vine that will fulfill all your needs.

Needless to say, below are only a few of the choice vines that can be effectively used in the home garden. Take time to observe vines growing in your neighborhood, at local parks, or in area display gardens so you can see these vines as they reach maturity. Likewise, large retail nurseries often feature these vines, along with others you might even like better.

By Particular Features

Annual Summer-Flowering

These are vines that you start from seed in springtime; they flower during the summer, then die with the first frost in fall. Most annual vines flower prolifically, some provide excellent cut flowers, and a couple even produce edible beans:

black-eyed susan vine, *Thunbergia alata*
canary vine, *Tropaeolum peregrinum*
climbing nasturtiums, *Tropaeolum majus*
cup-and-saucer vine, *Cobaea scandens*
hops, *Humulus japonicus*
hyacinth bean, *Dolichos lablab*
moonflower, *Ipomoea alba*
morning glory, *Ipomoea nil*
scarlet runner bean, *Phaseolus coccineus*
sweet pea, *Lathyrus odoratus*

Deciduous

These vines will lose their leaves over winter. Winter leaf loss may be a drawback, but in summer their profusion of flowers or fruit more than makes up for it. Actually, the bare stems of many of these vines create an interesting structure during the winter months, and summer privacy or shading is not a factor during the winter, so the loss of leaves is not all that important. Here are a few of the best ones:

akebia, *Akebia quinata*
blueberry climber, *Ampelopsis brevipedunculata*
Boston ivy, *Parthenocissus tricuspidata*
climbing hydrangea, *Hydrangea anomala petiolaris*
climbing rose, *Rosa* spp.
clematis, *Clematis* spp.
gourds, many varieties
grape, *Vitis vinifera* 'Purpurea'
honeysuckle, *Lonicera* spp.
kiwi, *Actinidia arguta* and *A. kolomikta*
passion vine, *Passiflora alatocaerulea*
silver lace vine, *Polygonum aubertii*
trumpet vine, *Campsis radicans*
Virginia creeper, *Parthenocissus quinquefolia*
wisteria, *Wisteria* spp.

Below: A climbing hydrangea creates a wonderful spot of color in partial shade at the VanDusen Botanical Gardens in Vancouver, B.C.

Evergreen

Here are some vines that will provide year-round interest because they maintain their leaves all twelve months of the year. These vines are ideal for providing privacy screening and can be used to soften structures or help hide visual eyesores such as telephone poles, mailboxes, utility boxes, etc.:

clematis, *Clematis armandii*
fatshedera, *Fatshedera lizei*
firethorn, *Pyracantha* spp.
English ivy, *Hedera helix*
jasmine, *Jasminum officinale* (semi-evergreen)
winter creeper, *Euonymus fortunei radicans*

With Pleasant Fragrance

It's a great bonus anytime you can find a vine that flowers and has a pleasant fragrance. These are the vines you want to use near the entry area, patio, deck, or any part of the garden where the fragrance of the flowers can be fully enjoyed and appreciated. Here are a few of the best ones for this region:

akebia, *Akebia quinata*
climbing hydrangea, *Hydrangea anomala petiolaris*
climbing rose, *Rosa* (some spp.)
clematis, *Clematis armandii*
honeysuckle, *Lonicera* spp.
hyacinth bean, *Dolichos lablab*
Japanese wisteria, *Wisteria floribunda*
jasmine, *Jasminum officinale*
passion vine, *Passiflora alatocaerulea*
sweet pea, *Lathyrus odoratus*

With Colorful Foliage

Vines with bright foliage color can add a whole new dimension to any garden. Sometimes instead of using flower color to provide seasonal color, a vine with attractive bright leaves will create the same effect, but for a much longer period of time. Here are six of my favorites:

fatshedera, *Fatshedera lizei* 'Variegata'
grape, *Vitis vinifera* 'Purpurea'
honeysuckle, *Lonicera japonica* 'Purpurea'
hops, *Humulus japonicus* 'Variegatus'
ivy, *Hedera canariensis* 'Variegata'
kiwi, *Actinidia kolomikta*

For Specific Sites

In Mostly Shady Spots

Every garden has at least one shady spot, and sometimes a vine is needed in those areas to create interest or provide privacy. Shade-loving vines may require a little more training than those grown in more exposed areas of the garden. Here are four of the ones most commonly used in home gardens:

blueberry climber, *Ampelopsis brevipedunculata*
clematis, *Clematis armandii*
English ivy, *Hedera helix* (and other species)
fatshedera, *Fatshedera lizei*

In Part Sun and Shade

If you are looking for a vine to grow on the east side of the house or in any spot where it will only receive sun for part of the day, these will do the job. Needless to say, there are many others. In fact, almost all of the ones that grow in full sun will also do quite well in partial sun. Here are six popular vines that love a semi-sunny spot in the garden:

akebia, *Akebia quinata*
climbing hydrangea, *Hydrangea anomala petiolaris*
honeysuckle, *Lonicera* spp.
jasmine, *Jasminum officinale*
passion vine, *Passiflora alatocaerulea*
silver lace vine, *Polygonum aubertii*

In Full Sun

Vines are often situated in a bright, sunny part of the garden as a mean of providing shade on a patio, deck, or entry area. Likewise, vines are used in these same areas as a way of providing privacy or as a means of screening out unpleasant views. The amount of direct sun and reflected sunlight will greatly affect which vines you can use. Here are eight that will tolerate full sun exposure:

Boston ivy, *Parthenocissus tricuspidata*
climbing rose, *Rosa* spp.
clematis, *Clematis* spp.
grape, *Vitis* spp.
kiwi, *Actinidia arguta*
trumpet vine, *Campsis radicans*
Virginia creeper, *Parthenocissus quinquefolia*
wisteria, *Wisteria* spp.

In Soil That Is Sometimes Dry

If you have an area away from the house, at the top of a hillside, or anywhere that is difficult to reach with a garden hose, the soil is apt to be dry at times. Here are four common vines that will tolerate a certain amount of dryness:

English ivy, *Hedera helix* (keep this one confined or it can become unruly)
honeysuckle, *Lonicera* spp.
silver lace vine, *Polygonum aubertii*
wisteria, *Wisteria* spp.

In Occasionally Moist/Wet Soils

Soils that are not continually wet but, rather, moist at times throughout the year are trouble spots that can be a challenge to any home gardener. By selecting the right plant for the right location, your chances of success are greatly increased. Here are what I consider the best vines for occasionally moist soils:

English ivy, *Hedera helix* (keep this one confined or it can become unruly)
honeysuckle, *Lonicera* spp.
hops, *Humulus japonicus*
silver lace vine, *Polygonum aubertii*

Vines Encyclopedia

Akebia *(A. quinata)*. Primarily grown as a decorative vine in the flower garden. Beautiful, fast-growing vine with fragrant white, pink, or purple (depending upon variety) mid-spring flowers. Occasionally produces unusual, small (4–5 inches), sausage-shaped pinkish fruit. Use pulp in tropical-type drinks or as jelly. It is an inconsistent bearer. Plant two different varieties for pollination. Evergreen in our garden, but can be deciduous in cold climates. Plant in part shade, although it is all right to have roots and base of plant in shade and top flowering part in sun. Must have good drainage. Plant in fertile soil.

Black-eyed susan vine *(Thunbergia alata)*. Showy yellow flowers with a black center. This annual vine grows up to 6 feet high and blooms all summer. Use on trellis or in hanging baskets. Requires a sunny location and moist, rich, well-drained soil. Easy to grow from seed.

Blueberry climber *(Ampelopsis brevipedunculata)*. This is also known by the common name porcelain berry. This sturdy deciduous vine is fine for tough surfaces. Clusters of fall and winter berries are metallic blue. Rampant grower to 25–30 feet or more. Give it strong, sturdy support. Will grow well on concrete or brick surfaces. Berries attract birds. Prune in the spring. Plant in sun or part shade, in well-drained, ordinary garden soil.

Boston ivy *(Parthenocissus tricuspidata)*. Brilliant orange to red autumn leaf color. This vine is semi-evergreen, but will lose all of its leaves in a cold winter. A rampant grower with suction-cup disks that hold it to brick or concrete surfaces. Prune to fit the location, or vine will grow 50 feet or more. Leaves are divided and cover the vines. Do not let the vines get under roof shingles, siding, or any wood surfaces, or they are apt to lift them off. Plant in sun or partial shade in fertile, well-drained soil.

Canary vine *(Tropaeolum peregrinum)*. Also called canary bird vine, because the small yellow flowers are said to look like miniature canaries. This interesting vine is a member of the nasturtium family. The unusual 1- to 1½-inch flowers cover the 8- to 12-foot vines in summer. It grows best in full sun in areas with cool summers. Give it part sun and shade in warm climates. Plant in well-drained, average soil.

Climbing hydrangea *(H. anomala petiolaris)*. Beautiful white lace-cap-like flowers. The prettiest one I have ever seen is at VanDusen Botanical Gardens in Vancouver, B.C. It is planted on the north side of the entrance building and is stunning when in bloom. Vines are self-clinging, and can grow up to 50 feet or more. Light pruning after bloom helps confine growth and encourage additional flowering the next season. More severe pruning can be done anytime during the dormant season. Grows well in organic-rich, well-drained soil.

Climbing nasturtiums *(Tropaeolum majus).* One of the most popular old-time annual vines. The climbing/trailing type grows 3–6 feet and is a great summer-blooming annual vine. Showy flowers come in either single or doubles, in shades of yellow, orange, creamy white, red, and reddish brown. Cut flowers are excellent for small bouquets. Flowers (2–2 ½ inches) stand out above the bright green leaves. They are easy, quick-growing vines. Thrive on considerable neglect. Plant in full or part sun, in ordinary garden soil.

Climbing rose (*Rosa,* many varieties). See Chapter 5, Roses, for full details on climbing roses, recommended varieties, and pruning hints.

Clematis (*Clematis* species). This group includes both the deciduous and evergreen types. Deciduous varieties predominate. They are considered one of the most attractive spring-, summer- or fall-flowering vines. The large summer-flowering ones are the favorites, but don't overlook those that bloom at other times. Flower colors practically span the color spectrum, with some that have stripes of contrasting colors. Pink, red, blue, and purple are the most common colors in the large-flowering category. Most are single, but there a few that have double flowers. Prune the spring-flowering varieties right after they finish blooming. The summer and fall ones are pruned in the fall or late winter. If you prune back about half the growth, they will respond with bushier growth and usually more flowers. This is one plant that can be planted deeper in the soil. In other words, to cover the roots with 3–6 inches of soil is all right. Shade the root-growing area with some type of plants, as they like a cool growing spot but enjoy full sun on the upper parts of the vines. Vines will also do quite well in filtered sun. One of the large Canadian growers of clematis has several varieties growing right up into the trees in his yard. They need a lime (sweet) soil in which to grow. Apply the lime in late winter or earliest spring. Feed with a rose-type fertilizer in mid-February and again in mid-May, if needed.

Clematis armandii. This one is the evergreen variety of clematis. Long, 5- to 6-inch, dark glossy green leaves are excellent background for 2-inch white, early-spring flowers. We have several vines in our garden, two in the entry area, and the early spring fragrance is delightful to say the least. Our vines are fast growing and easily cover 20 feet or more in the three seasons we have had them. Our vines need to be trained, if support is not provided. There is a pink-flowering variety, 'Hendersoni Rubra', but in my opinion it is a washed-out pink and not nearly as attractive as the white-flowering ones. Light shearing after bloom encourages bushiness and helps confine rampant growth on established vines. Although it grows in full sun, our vines do better where they are protected from the hot midday sun. Plant in organic-rich, well-drained soil.

Above left: Pretty scarlet-red flowers followed by edible beans make the scarlet runner bean a popular annual vine.

Left: Grapes, edible or simply ornamental, are excellent vines for the garden.

Cup-and-saucer vine *(Cobaea scandens).* This is a showy annual vine with "cup and saucer"-like 2-inch flowers. This fast-growing vine can grow up to 15 feet or more in one season. Start seeds indoors in pots to get a jump on the growing season. Then transplant outside in warm weather. Feed twice during the summer with liquid fertilizer. Plant in full sun, in rich, fertile, well-drained soil.

English ivy (*Hedera helix* and other species). This evergreen vine can be used as a climbing vine or ground cover, but it will run rampant if not kept under control. (The State of Oregon has already classified English ivy as a nuisance—actually, the wording is more severe than my comments—and a few other states may not be far behind in limiting its use.) See Chapter 12, Ground Covers.

Fatshedera *(F. lizei).* Large 6- to 10-inch leaves look somewhat like tropical, glossy green maple foliage. The stems and leaves are heavy so it will need a strong support. The vine does not have tendrils, so it needs to be trained and tied in place. *F. l.* 'Variegata' has green leaves with an attractive white margin. Over time this vine can grow a considerable height. Plant in full to part shade in enriched, well-drained garden soil.

Firethorn (*Pyracantha* species). This evergreen to semi-evergreen shrub is often grown in place of a vine. It is easy to train against concrete, brick, or a wooden surface. Plants can also be trained on a trellis. Evergreen leaves 2–4 inches long make a nice background for spring clusters of flowers that are followed in the fall

Below: Gorgeous clusters of flowers on vigorous vines make wisteria a favorite for large areas.

and winter by colorful orange, red, or white berries. Berries attract birds. Many varieties range from 8 to 12 feet high. Plant in full or part sun, in organic-rich, well-drained soil.

Gourd (many varieties). A great fast-growing annual vine: up to 15 feet in a single season. Grow on a trellis to show off the colorful and unusual-shaped gourds. Dry and use them as table decorations. This is one vine kids really enjoy growing because the decorative fruit is a real conversation piece. Plant in a sunny spot, with well-drained, fertile soil.

Grape (*Vitis vinifera,* several varieties). The standard varieties of garden grapes are excellent vines to use in the landscape; the advantage of using them is that one can enjoy the beauty of the vines and have tasty edible grapes at the same time. In addition to the edible types, there are several ornamental varieties. One of my favorites of the ornamentals is the variety *V. vinifera* 'Purpurea', which has leaves that open green, turn purplish, then even deeper in color during the autumn. Most grapevines will grow 20–30 feet or more, but can be kept shorter by yearly pruning. Plant in full or partial sun, in organic-rich, well-drained garden soil.

Honeysuckle (*Lonicera,* several species). Some varieties have a very pleasant fragrance. Flowers on many varieties are tubular and attract hummingbirds. The Japanese honeysuckle *(L. japonica)* is one of the most popular, but one that has rampant growth habits and tends to reseed itself. The variety *L. japonica* 'Purpurea' has attractive greenish purple leaves, with purple and white flowers. Vines will grow 10–30 feet depending upon varieties. They grow well in full or part sun, in ordinary, well-drained garden soil.

Hops (*Humulus japonicus* and *H. j.* 'Variegatus'). This is the Japanese hop, and is often used as an ornamental vine in the home garden. Lobed leaves are green and cover the 20- to 25-foot vines. The variety 'Variegatus' has green leaves with white edges. This deciduous vine is cut to the ground after the first heavy fall frost. Chartreuse flower spikes are oblong and quite noticeable close up. Easy to grow, the vines grow best in full sun, in enriched, well-drained soil.

Hyacinth bean *(Dolichos lablab).* A nice, fast-growing ornamental vine that needs warm weather to do well. Actually this is neither a hyacinth nor a true bean. Its fragrant, 1½-inch, sweet, pink-and-white flowers stand out above its dark-veined green leaves. Flowers give way to decorative, magenta, 3- to 4-inch pods. Do not plant outdoors too early, as this is a tropical vine and will not tolerate cold weather or cold soil. Plant in fertile, well-drained soil, in full sun.

Ivy *Hedera canariensis* 'Variegata'). The large, variegated cream-and-green leaves of this shrubby variety are quite showy. It can be trained into a vining type plant. As such, it is quite effective when used in the darker areas of the garden. Flowers and berries are rather insignificant. Grows most anywhere, but this variegated form does best when planted in a spot where it is protected from the hot midday sun. Cut greens are often used as filler in flower arrangements. Use on trellises, fences, and walls. It is a robust-growing vine. Plant in average, well-drained garden soil.

Jasmine *(Jasminum officinale)*. The hardiness of this vine is marginal in some of the cooler areas west of the Cascade Mountains. In summer and early fall, 1-inch white flowers have a very pleasant fragrance. Small, dark green leaves are excellent background for the flowers. Many home gardeners will grow this one in a container and bring the plant indoors or into a greenhouse over winter. One of my horticulturist friends suggests the vine be left outdoors. But he says to cut it back to a couple of inches from the ground after a light frost, then mulch with a few inches of straw for added winter protection. When treated in this manner, the plant flowers heavily and usually only grows 6–12 feet per year. If this vine is grown as an indoor plant, it can grow up to 25–30 feet unless pruned. When grown outdoors, plant in rich, well-drained garden soil. Plant in full sun or in partial shade.

Kiwi *(Actinidia arguta* and *A. kolomikta)*. One is the hardy fruiting kiwi, the other an ornamental vine; both are nice garden vines. Vines of this species grow about 12–15 feet. Provide support and train vines. Both are robust growers. Grow them in full sun or partial shade. Plant in fertile, well-drained soil.

A. arguta. The fruit-producing kiwi. The bold leaves of this type provide dense shade and it is often used on a trellis as a vine to cover a patio.

A. kolomikta. Ornamental vine. The leaves of this one are gorgeous—some leaves have a combination of green, cream, and pink; others are just green and cream; and others might be just green, all on the same vine. The male plants of this species tend to have the best leaf color. The leaves are somewhat heart shaped and make a nice cover.

Moonflower *(Ipomoea alba)*. This is an evening-blooming variety with white fragrant flowers. Grow as an annual in containers in the Northwest. Flowers are up to 6 inches across and open only at night or on cloudy days. Plant by entry area or patio where evening fragrance can best be enjoyed. Vines will grow up to 10–25 feet in a single season. This one must be planted in a warm, sunny spot, in ordinary garden soil.

Morning glory *(Ipomoea nil* and *I. tricolor)*. These are both annual morning glories, one-season plants that you have to start from seed each year, not to be confused with the pesky perennial bindweed that is such a nuisance. Flowers up to 6 inches across come in shades of blue, scarlet, and mixed colors. (For the dwarf variety, which does not vine, see convolvulus in Chapter 13, Annuals.) Vine growth varies by variety, 6–15 feet in a single season. Very showy, fast-growing vines that thrive on a certain amount of neglect. These grow and flower best in full sun, in fertile, well-drained soil.

Above left: Honeysuckle, with its fragrant, unusual-looking flowers, is a popular garden vine.

Left: Blooming in late winter or early spring, *Clematis armandii* brings welcome color and fragrance to the garden.

Passion vine *(Passiflora alatocaerulea* and *P. caerulea).* When in bloom, this vine gets more comments than any of the others in our garden. The unusual, multicolored flowers are unlike any other. *P. alatocaerulea* has fragrant, 3- to 4-inch summer flowers with white, pink, lavender, and deepest blue colors in each flower. The name has a religious context in that the crown of the flower is thought to represent a halo, the five stamens the five wounds to Christ's body, and the ten outer flower petals the ten apostles. The attractive, medium-green leaves are three-lobed, making a nice background for the unusual flowers. Ours is planted on a north/south fence, so most of the flowers face west, toward the sun. In a cold winter the leaves fall, making the vine almost deciduous. However, in a mild winter the leaves remain evergreen. Our vine grows about 6–10 feet a year, now that it is established. Plant in full sun or partial shade, in enriched garden soil. *P. caerulea* produces a small, orange, edible fruit.

Porcelain berry. See blueberry climber.

Scarlet runner bean *(Phaseolus coccineus).* A very popular, fast-growing, scarlet-flowering annual vine. This ornamental vine has clusters of bright red flowers, which produce snap beans when young or shell (lima type) beans when more mature. A great vine for summer privacy, for trellising, or for covering a fence, post, or stump. Height 8–12 feet. Plant in a sunny location, with loamy, warm soil.

Silver lace vine *(Polygonum aubertii).* Actually the new botanical name is *Fallopia baldschuanica;* it is the same plant, just a new name. (This is happening a lot now, and is really confusing to some of us old-time gardeners.) The vine is covered with creamy-white, lacy flower clusters from spring to fall. Leaves 1½–2 inches long are somewhat heart-shaped. Vines are quite robust and may cover 30–40 feet over time. Don't be afraid to prune and keep them in bounds, as the vine takes very well to pruning. Plant in full sun for best flower display. Plant in ordinary, well-drained garden soil.

Sweet pea *(Lathyrus odoratus).* A great annual vine that produces showy, fragrant flowers. Cut flowers are ideal to use in early summer arrangements. Seeds should be sown in about mid-February in most areas. You will find sweet peas in individual flower colors or mixed collections. Fragrance varies between varieties, so if it's fragrance you want, you may like the 'Old Spice' collection. Provide support for the 6- to 8-foot climbing-type sweet peas. I suggest you grow the vines in a north-south direction, for best air circulation and sun exposure. This annual vine likes it cool, so plant them in a sunny spot but do it early. Plant in fertile, well-drained soil.

Trumpet vine *(Campsis radicans).* Attractive, orange to red, 3-inch summer flowers are trumpet shaped. This deciduous vine is a vigorous grower to 30–40 feet or more. Winter-prune to shape and confine growth. Leaves consist of several leaflets, providing a nice background for the attractive flowers. Ideal to use on trellises, on walls, or for screening. Vine clings on its own. Plant in full sun or part shade, in rich, well-drained soil.

Virginia creeper *(Parthenocissus quinquefolia).* This vine is often used to cover concrete or brick surfaces. It can also be used on trellises, on arbors, or as a hillside ground cover. Very hardy deciduous vine with outstanding crimson autumn leaf color. Each leaf consists of five leaflets. May cover 50 feet or more unless pruned and trained. Plant in full sun or part shade, in ordinary, well-drained garden soil.

Winter creeper *(Euonymus fortunei radicans).* Common winter creeper has green leaves. There are also some named varieties with very attractive variegations. Over time it can spread up to 20 feet. Often used to cover hillsides, walls, trellises, etc. Evergreen, 1-inch leaves are dark green. Plant in full sun or shade in organic-rich, well-drained soil.

Wisteria (several species). New varieties of both Japanese and Chinese wisterias are now available. The leaves of both types are divided into ten or more leaflets. Both take the same cultural care. Vines grow very robust, so require ample space and yearly pruning to keep them within bounds. Prune and shape during the winter dormant season. You can even shorten the vines in the summer if they need it. We have several in our garden and they do require summer pruning, because the vines just grow too fast. Look for some new named varieties; you might like them better than the old standards. This vine thrives on a certain amount of neglect, so go light on feeding and watering. Plant in full sun for best bloom, but vines will also grow in shade. Vines grow in most ordinary garden soils.

Chinese wisteria *(W. sinensis).* The smaller 12-inch blossoms of the Chinese wisteria (less fragrant) are predominately lavender-blue or white, but they flower before the leaves open, so they put on a better show of color.

Japanese wisteria *(W. floribunda).* The fragrant flowers of the Japanese wisteria are larger but flower a little later than those of the Chinese varieties, so they are a bit hidden by the leaves. The Japanese wisteria has large, 18-inch hanging flower clusters in blue, lavender, purple, pink, or white.

8 · LAWNS

The lawn is the framework for the entire landscape, so it is important to keep it looking nice. Lawn maintenance becomes easy and very rewarding when you adopt a simple maintenance plan. I think the major factors in creating a really nice-looking lawn are a low cutting height, feeding four times a year, providing an inch of water a week in summer, and overseeding with new grass seed each year.

Facing page: I recommend that you fertilize your lawn four times a year: spring, summer, fall, and late fall.

CHOOSING THE LOCATION

The space to be devoted to lawn should be based on your family's needs. For example, allot sufficient space for the children to play, for pets to roam, and to provide access to the various parts of the yard and garden. If possible, I suggest that you avoid planting a lawn on a hillside, under trees (in most cases), in cramped narrow areas, and in places where there is dense shade.

Under Trees

Many beautiful evergreen and deciduous trees grow in this region, but how do you grow grass under them? The fertilizer you put down on the lawn is quickly taken by the more dominant roots of the trees, so the grass suffers from both lack of nutrients and an abundance of shade provided by the tree above. However, here are several things you can do to help create a better lawn under trees:

- Fertilize the lawn under the tree with a liquid fertilizer. This way, only the grass blades absorb the liquid food.
- Water the area under the tree more frequently. (A large tree can absorb up to 100 gallons of water per day!)
- Introduce more shade-tolerant grass, such as a type of fescue.
- If it doesn't ruin the shape of the tree, trim some of the lower branches to allow more light to reach the lawn underneath.

Below: Dandelions may be the first sign of spring, but they are probably the home gardener's most troublesome weed.

Planting a Lawn

Early in my career I put in many a new lawn, so I speak from experience on this subject, and I can assure you that thorough preparation of the soil for seeding or sodding a new lawn will greatly cut down on maintenance in the future. Here are the basic steps I suggest for soil preparation.

Seeding, Resodding, or Hydra-Seeding

Use these steps for seeding; sodding, or hydra-seeding lawns.

Clean the Area

Remove weeds, large stones, and debris. If the area is very weedy and consists of wild grasses, you may need to apply a weed-and-grass-type herbicide to eliminate them.

Rototill

Till or spade the area, adding fertilizer or topsoil if needed.

Rake

Rough rake, removing large stones and surface debris.

Roll

Begin to establish a level surface by rolling the entire area with a water-filled roller.

Level

Establish a finished grade by using a weighted ladder or frame made of 4-by-4s. This establishes contours and drainage patterns.

Rake Again

Hold the rake handle upright, so the rake skims the surface. This is called finish raking, and it will fill in the low spots and remove the small to medium-sized stones.

Yellow streaks in the lawn after fertilizing usually indicate that your spreader is out of adjustment or faulty. However, yellow (or off-color) streaks in the lawn will also appear if you have not carefully overlapped on each pass with the spreader.

Fertilize

Spread the correct amount of a new lawn–type fertilizer onto the soil surface. This will provide nutrients to help the new seed germinate.

Seed, Put Down Sod, or Hydra-Seed

If you are seeding, broadcast half of the seed in one direction, then spread the other half in the opposite direction, overlapping. If you are putting down sod, everything is ready to go. Likewise, the seedbed is ready for hydra-seeding.

Cover the Seed

Use only about $\frac{1}{16}$ inch of peat moss to cover the seed.

Water

Seed, sod, or hydra-seed will all need to be watered in thoroughly. If seeding, keep the seed moist until it has germinated. Some varieties will take up to three week to germinate. Put up temporary fencing around the area to keep dogs, cats, and children off the newly planted lawn for about one month, or until the grass is established.

Reseeding

This is one of the most important steps in maintaining a nice lawn. Overseeding an established lawn with new grass seed helps fill in bare spots, introduces new young succulent grass plants, makes the lawn thicker, crowds out weeds and moss, and improves the overall appearance of the lawn.

When to Reseed

The best time to sow the seed is between mid-March and mid-October.

How to Reseed

You will need somewhere between 1 to 3 pounds of seed per 1,000 square feet of lawn area. Use 1 pound of seed if the lawn is in reasonably good shape, and up to 3 pounds if the lawn looks sparse. You can either sow the seed by hand or apply it with a fertilizer spreader. It is always a good practice to fertilize the lawn before reseeding, so the nutrients are present to aid in the germination of the new seed. Water thoroughly after applying the fertilizer and again after sowing the seed.

Type of Seed to Use

If possible, match the type of seed already used in your lawn. Sometimes this is not possible, because you are not the one who seeded it or put down the sod. In this case, it is best to use a grass-seed mix suitable for your area. West of the Cascades, turf-type rye grasses and fescues are among the best. East of the Cascades, bluegrass and turf-type rye grasses are favorites. If in doubt as to which will best fit your needs, ask your certified nurseryperson at your local garden store. They will know which is the best blend for the soils in your immediate area. There are four basic types of lawn seed:

- the ultimate "show" lawn
- the all-purpose "family" lawn
- the very durable "play" lawn
- the blend for shady areas

Feeding the Lawn

This is probably the least understood aspect of lawn maintenance. As a rule, lawn fertilizer should not be applied to a wet lawn, because it is likely to burn the lawn. However, most brands should be watered in immediately after application, so the dry fertilizer does not burn either.

When to Feed

Most turf specialists recommend four feedings per year: once in spring, in summer, in early fall, and the last in late fall around Thanksgiving. In my opinion, the lawn should only be fertilized as needed. In some cases, depending upon soil preparation and general care, this may be only once a year. So don't waste your time and money feeding the lawn if it doesn't need it.

What to Feed

A ratio of 3-1-2 is best for fertilizing turf in this region. This translates to a formula of 9-3-6, 12-4-8, 15-5-10, or similar analysis (see Chapter 16, Composting and Fertilizing). If moss is present in the lawn when it's time for a spring or fall application of fertilizer, you can use a combination fertilizer and moss control product. Weed-and-feed products that contain lawn fertilizer and weed control agents should be applied only in late spring or under specific temperature and weather conditions. (See the Weeds section in Diagnosing Lawn Problems.)

Today there is a wide selection of both organic and chemical lawn fertilizers. The organic fertilizers are considered more environmentally friendly but slower acting, so you will not see immediate results, but organics are generally longer-lasting and they ensure grass clippings that can be composted (as well as not contaminating waterways via runoff). The chemical types of fertilizer generally green up the lawn faster, but don't always last as long.

My Lawn-Feeding Hint

If you want the best-looking lawn in the whole neighborhood, here's my suggestion to you. When you apply your lawn fertilizer, apply only half the recommended amount, then apply the other half three to five weeks later. This way you get a longer greening period, not the big spurt of growth, and the lawn generally requires less mowing. This will not work if you are applying a lawn fertilizer that contains a moss- or weed-control product, which must be applied according to label instructions.

Fertilizer Spreaders

The push-type drop-spreaders and broadcast spreaders are the two most popular. Never use the broadcast types for spreading weed-and-feed or moss-control type combination products. Because they cover such a wide area, the weed or moss products will likely land on desirable plants or walkways and burn or stain them. Check the spreader occasionally so there is no chance for fertilizer particles to get tied up in the hopper blades and cause an uneven distribution of fertilizer. This is what often causes yellow streaking in the lawn. Try to keep track of each pass, so that you avoid overlapping and burning the lawn. Also avoid leaving spaces between runs and ending up with yellow and green streaks in the lawn.

Application of Lime

Because the soil in this region tends to be acidic, the application of lime will often make it easier to control moss and mushrooms. A soil test is a valuable aid in determining the need for lime. Dolomite, agricultural lime, and limestone are among the most popular types of lime to apply to the lawn. I use dolomite lime on my lawn at a ratio of 40 pounds per 1,000 square feet. The lime can be applied in either the spring or the fall, or both if needed.

Left: It's easy to repair or seed new lawn areas. Just follow my simple steps in Planting a Lawn.

Mowing Lawns

This is another extremely important step in establishing a nice-looking, easy-to-maintain lawn. I think most Northwest homeowners cut their grass too tall. This may be because they hear and read about cutting heights from other parts of the country. Here in the Pacific Northwest, our marine climate and typically acid soils provides us with a little different environment for the lawn. If we cut the grass too tall, it tends to lie down and grow sideways instead of growing upright. Consequently, the grass mats down and this creates the buildup of thatch, a higher percentage of disease, and increased weed growth.

On the other hand, if we cut the grass shorter, the grass continues its upright growth, looks nice, and is easier to maintain. My recommendation is to cut the grass at 1 to 1½ inches in height if you live west of the Cascades, 1½ to 2 inches in height if you live east of the Cascades. I also suggest that you cut the grass once a week during the growing season. It's a good practice to cut the grass in different directions each time you mow. Otherwise, the grass begins to lie down instead of standing upright as it should.

If you have been cutting your grass too tall, here's what you can do to correct the situation. Lower the cutting height of your mower for the first mowing in the spring. Set the mower one notch lower than your planned cutting height, then raise it to your desired height immediately after the first cutting and leave it there.

Choosing a Mower

Should you use a reel-type, rotary-type, push, power, or riding mower? Of course, that's up to you, but I have a mulching mower and love it! When the grass is dry, it cuts the grass so fine that the clippings disappear into the turf. The lawn looks great, and I have also recycled the clippings as well as a certain amount of moisture and nutrients. However, it's not the best when the lawn is wet, because it tends to plug up with the wet grass. Using a reel-type mower will probably give you the neatest-appearing lawn. The rotary-type mowers are much improved in recent years, and if the cutting blades are sharp, they will also give a neat cut. The push-type mowers are great for the environment, for small areas, and for getting some exercise!

Cutting Wet Grass

Above I suggested that you cut the grass once a week, but what should you do if the grass blades are wet because of recent rains? Easy! Find a rope or garden hose. Take one end and have a second person take the other end. Drag the rope or hose across the lawn, and it will knock the moisture off the blades of the grass. Wait about fifteen minutes, and the grass should be dry enough to mow. If you can't find anyone to pull one end of the rope/hose, simply tie that end to a stake or the faucet and circle around it. It does the job!

Cutting Newly Planted Lawns

Mow for the first time when the new grass is about 1½ to 2 inches tall.

WATERING LAWNS

It's estimated that during average summer weather, the lawn should be watered with 1 inch of water each week. That means if it rains ½ inch, only ½ inch of additional water need be applied that week.

When you set a sprinkler or turn on a sprinkling system, check to see that the lawn is absorbing the water. If some of the water is running off the lawn and down the street, turn off the water and wait a few hours before you finish watering. Don't waste water or your time and money.

A word to the wise: Watering for short periods of time is not advised, because the water penetrates to a very shallow depth and the lawn dries out very rapidly. On the other hand, if you apply the 1 inch of water all at one time, it penetrates deeply into the soil, gets down to where the roots are, and lasts much longer. The best time to water is during the early morning hours when there will be less evaporation and good absorption. It's best to do your sprinkling all at once on the same day.

Overseeding the lawn yearly is unquestionably one of the most important steps you can take to maintain a nice-looking lawn.

DIAGNOSING LAWN PROBLEMS

To quickly assess the current condition of your lawn, use a knife or straight-edged shovel and cut out a 6- to 8-inch square plug of turf 3 to 4 inches deep. Take it from an area of the lawn that doesn't look very good. Lift it out of the turf and examine it. You will be amazed by how much you can see: moss, thatch (if there is any), *red thread* (a plant disease), torn grass blades, black mold, weeds, insects, or other disease. This simple on-the-spot diagnosis will let you know what needs to be done. If you don't feel confident in your own diagnosis, take the sample to a local certified nurseryperson at a nearby garden center and have a diagnosis made for you. When you've finished analyzing the sample, simply place the plug back into the lawn.

Your first impulse after diagnosing the condition of your lawn may be to start all over again, but it is usually possible to get the lawn back in shape without massive reseeding or extensive renovation. The key is to take the necessary steps in the correct order. Don't waste your time and money on things that don't need to be done. That's why the on-the-spot diagnosis is so important. Here are a few suggestions on how to go about maintaining or renovating the lawn.

Uneven Ground

After mowing, you may notice your lawn is scalped in some areas and the grass is too tall in others. This is a good indication that the ground is uneven. Often this is caused by soil settling after the area is seeded or sod is put down.

One of the easiest ways to solve this problem is to cut an x across the high areas, peel back the sod, take out the excess soil, and roll the sod back in place. Start with the same x cut in the low areas, peel back, then add soil to bring up to level, and again roll the sod back in place.

If the lawn is only slightly high and low in places, you can roll the lawn using a water-filled lawn roller. Do this in late winter or early spring when the turf is still somewhat moist. Lawn rollers are available at rental agencies and some garden outlets.

If that doesn't do the job, you may have to top-dress the lawn with new soil, then level with a rake and roll again. When top-dressing, use only an inch or less of soil at any one time. A good-quality sandy-loam-type soil is best for top-dressing.

Unwanted Wide-Blade Grasses

Coarse, wide-blade grasses sometimes make their way into a beautiful lawn and ruin its appearance. If the wide-blade grass is in clumps, you can either pull it out by hand or spot-treat it with a grass-control product such as Round-Up, Finale, or Kleen Up. These grass control products will kill all grasses, so be careful to apply them only to the undesirable grasses. Always read and follow application directions on the label. Approximately six weeks after applying any of these grass killers, the grass will turn white to yellow, and then you may feed and reseed the area. If the entire lawn is full of weedy grasses and weeds, you can spray the whole lawn, wait six weeks, then fertilize and reseed. This drastic procedure is rarely necessary, and is best done during the growing season months of March through October.

Thatch

Thatch is dead grass that accumulates between the roots and the lower blades of the grass. It builds up and creates a layer that sheds water (much like a thatch roof) and ties up fertilizer so that it doesn't reach the soil or roots below. Don't waste your time thatching unless an on-the-spot lawn-plug diagnosis reveals that thatch is a problem. If the thatch is more than ½ inch deep, the lawn should be thatched or aerated.

You can remove the thatch by using a hand-thatching tool, but this is very tedious and generally not recommended. Power thatching machines are available at most rental agencies and some garden centers. You can also buy a blade made to fit most rotary mowers that can be used for thatch removal. These blades can be tough on the mower, so you may want to limit their use. Early spring is the best time for thatching. After thatching, expect the lawn to look like the Mojave desert for about six weeks. The lawn will recover more quickly if you fertilize and reseed the entire area.

Poor Absorption of Water

When water runs off the lawn without being absorbed or sits on the surface, this indicates the need for aeration. Aerating or perforating the lawn is a good way to get fertilizer and water down to the roots of the grass. There are several tools that can be used for this job. Two of the best tools are the manual or power-type aerators that actually pull a plug of soil. The plug is about the size of your forefinger. Manure forks, pitchforks, or root feeders can also be used for aerating the lawn. Another type of power tool used for aerating is made up of a series of blades that cut into the turf and soil below. Aeration or perforation should be done in the spring or fall. Lawns in which clay or compacted soils are a problem may benefit from yearly aeration.

Weeds

If there are only a few weeds in your lawn, pull them by hand or spot-treat with a ready-to-use lawn-weed killer. However, if there are a lot of weeds, it may be easier to control them by broadly applying an all-purpose lawn-weed killer. Check with your local garden outlet, because there are now several types of environmentally friendly herbicides in addition to the chemical types. Weed-and-feed products can also be used to control easy-to-kill weeds and feed the lawn at the same time. All weed-control products must be applied with the utmost care to avoid damaging desirable plants or endangering pets and children. Read and follow all instructions. Apply weed-control products when the wind is not blowing, when the temperature is between 45 and 70 degrees Fahrenheit, and when there is no chance of rain for twenty-four hours. The best time to control weeds is during their growing season of April through early October.

In Newly Planted Lawns

Do not apply any kind of weed killers to a new lawn until it has been mowed at least five times. Many new weeds are annual weeds and will die after being mowed two or three times.

Moss

Eliminating moss sounds great, but how do you do it? Moss grows for a few reasons:

- too much shade
- soil too wet
- clay or compacted soil
- acidic soil
- improper feeding

Correct these conditions, and the moss should go away. The trouble is that often three or four of these conditions exist, and it is impossible to correct the situation. However, here are a few suggestions for things you can do to improve your odds of success (of course, only do the steps that will correct the problems that exist in your lawn):

- After eliminating the moss, aerate the soil in moss-infested areas.
- Top-dress with sand or a sandy-loam-type soil.
- Apply dolomite lime to help correct acidity.
- Feed the lawn on a regular basis.
- Overseed yearly.
- Find ways to provide better drainage.

Moss-control products and fertilizers containing moss control are available to help kill moss, but they are only a very temporary means of control because the conditions causing the moss to flourish in the first place must be corrected. Iron sulfate is used in most moss-control products and can be applied in spring or fall when the temperatures range between 45 and 65 degrees Fahrenheit. After applying the iron sulfate, the moss will turn black. Read and follow label instructions, because some brands recommend that you water the lawn first; others recommend that you apply the product, then water it in. Be especially careful not to get any of the iron sulfate on pavement or walkways, because it will stain them. Never use a lawn-type moss killer for moss growing on the roof, because it will corrode the downspouts. (A separate specialty type of product is used for that job.)

Mushrooms

These may be a good sign that your soil is rich in organic matter, because mushrooms originate from wood or bark chips, or from some type of organic matter in the soil. If they are in clusters, you can simply dig down, find their source, and remove it.

Otherwise there's not much you can do to eliminate mushrooms. As one research specialist told me, "Take out your frustrations on them—and just give them a good swift kick." Others use the standing mushrooms for practicing their golf swing. Or, you can hand-pick the mushrooms and discard them in the garbage can. In addition, liming, aerating, and fertilizing on a regular basis should aid in the elimination of mushrooms.

Below: A really nice-looking lawn is the result of regular feeding, watering, and mowing at the correct height.

Fairy Rings

As the name implies, this fungus appears in a ring and with time the ring keeps getting larger. It is difficult to control, because most fungicides do not work on it. The best method of control is to perforate the area within the ring and 1 foot beyond. Then keep the area wet for thirty days—not moist, but wet. With luck, this deep watering will drown the fungus and it will disappear. Feed the area with a high-nitrogen fertilizer, such as 21-4-4 or similar (see Chapter 16, Composting and Fertilizing).

Torn Grass Blades

This is usually a sign that the blade on your mower is somewhat dull and needs to be sharpened or replaced. It's surprising what a difference this can make in the appearance of the lawn. Make a habit of checking your mower blades several times during the mowing season.

Mini-Mounds in the Lawn

These look like miniature molehills, and you may first notice them because the turf is uneven under your feet. Then, upon closer observation, you will notice small mounds. They are generally caused by night crawlers (a very large worm that surfaces as a result of too much moisture in the soil). This can be annoying because it looks ugly and makes the lawn bumpy as you walk on it. The simple solution is to rake the lawn area with a bamboo or plastic leaf rake. This step alone will usually level out the turf, and the problem is solved. However, if that doesn't do the job, you may have to rake and then roll the lawn with a water-filled lawn roller.

Insects and Diseases

Let me set the record straight from the beginning regarding my credentials in this area: I am not an entomologist (insect specialist) or pathologist (disease specialist), and it is often necessary to consult a specialist for the answers to lawn insect or disease questions. However, here are a few common problems and my advice on the subject of treatment.

Cranefly/Leatherjacket

This pest really wreaks havoc on many Northwestern lawns. Cranefly in the larval stage is grayish brown in color and wormlike in appearance, with a tough outer skin that inspired the common name leatherjacket. They range from ½ to 1½ inches in size. This insect is most active and easiest to control between mid-March and mid-May and also in the late autumn if the insects become active then. They are usually found in areas where there is poor drainage or moderate to heavy buildup of thatch in the lawn. This insect stays underground most of the time, but it will surface to feed aboveground on plant parts during humid nights. In areas of heavy infestations, the lawn will become quite bare. In the fall, the adult returns, looking much like a giant mosquito, hence the other common name, cranefly.

In the past, insecticides such as Diazinon (now banned) have been recommended to control cranefly. As I write this book, environmentally friendly control products are being introduced. Check with your local certified nurseryperson or Master Gardener for their latest product recommendations, and go after this insect during the first eight weeks of spring or late fall if necessary.

Sod Webworm

Small, spiderlike webs a few inches in diameter that appear in the lawn in the early-morning dew reveal the presence of this insect. Referred to as grubworms, sod webworms, caterpillars, grayworms, or larvae, these insects feed on the grass stems and blades right at soil level. This insect is most active from mid-April through the summer. The damage caused by these worms is generally noted by small brown patches about the size of a silver dollar. Check with your local certified nurseryperson or Master Gardener for the latest means of control. If just a few spots exist, it's probably not necessary to eliminate them. Or you may want to spot-treat the small weblike areas individually rather than treat the whole lawn.

Red Thread

This disease is noted by the red, threadlike growth on the blades of grass. You may need a magnifying glass to see them individually. However, in a diseased lawn there will be an obvious reddening of the grass. Applying a lawn fungicide often controls this disease. Also, it can sometimes be controlled by simply applying a high-nitrogen fertilizer, such as ammonium sulphate 21-0-0 (see Chapter 16, Composting and Fertilizing). More than one application per year may be necessary to control this disease. The best time to apply nitrogen is during the summer growing season when the disease is first observed.

9 • Perennials

It's so nice to have plants that provide a colorful flower display, then winter over and come back again to flower year after year, and that's exactly what a perennial plant does. In addition, there are many species that flower at the various seasons of the year, so by selection of varieties you can have perennials blooming during the spring, summer, fall, and even winter. In addition to their beauty in the garden, many perennials provide showy flowers for cutting or to use as dried flowers.

Facing page: Tall, stately delphiniums are beautiful both in the garden and in cut flower arrangements.

Below: The attractive variegated foliage of Jacob's ladder brightens up the perennial garden.

Choosing a Location

There is a perennial flowering plant for just about any spot in the garden, from the low-growing ground cover or rockery types to the medium- or tall-growing kind. Although perennials are often planted in a designated area sometimes referred to as a perennial garden, in my opinion this is not the best way in which to use them. Many perennials die back during the winter or disappear completely, leaving the garden looking rather sparse or untended. On the other hand, if perennials are interplanted with evergreens, it helps conceal their appearance in winter. Plus the taller-growing shrubs often provide an attractive background for the perennials when they are in bloom. These are ideal plants to use in mixed plantings along with the summer-flowering annuals and/or evergreen and deciduous trees and shrubs in landscape beds.

Planting Perennials

Perennial seeds can be seeded directly into the garden during the spring, summer, or autumn gardening seasons, or started indoors during the winter. If you have collected your own seeds, place them in an envelope until you are ready to sow the seeds. Purchased seeds should be left in the packets. You can store the packets and envelopes in the refrigerator. Then about two or three days before you are ready to sow the seeds, put the envelope(s) and seed packet(s) in the freezer. This conditions the seeds (duplicates winter) and helps break hard-shelled seeds, so they will germinate quicker.

I think the gray leaves of dusty miller add light and life to the winter garden, as well as providing fresh gray color for the summer garden. The key to having nice-looking plants is to keep the yellow flowers picked. Cut the flower buds as they develop and shear or pinch back the plant occasionally to enjoy the new gray leaves.

Sow Seeds Outdoors

If you are sowing directly into the garden, during the growing season (March to October), add some organic matter such as compost or peat moss as you cultivate the soil. Then simply scatter the seed. The seed packets will recommend how much soil should be used to cover the seed. (Please keep in mind, when perennials self-seed, the seed is right on the surface of the soil, so Mother Nature is telling us to barely cover the seed.) If it is necessary to cover the seeds, use peat moss or vermiculite to lightly cover them.

Start Seeds Indoors

You can start perennials from seed indoors to get a jump on the gardening season, then set out the seedling starter plants as the weather warms up. Start the seeds in late February or early March indoors.

Choosing a Location for Starting Seeds Indoors

A sunny windowsill, greenhouse window, sun porch, or greenhouse is the best place to start your seeds. However, they can be started in any bright-light part of the home or garage. If possible, place them in a spot where there is warmth from below, such as over a heating duct. Bottom heat or a heating cable really helps the seeds in the germination process. (Heating cables are available at most garden outlets.)

Most seeds germinate best in a warm location, so select a spot where the temperatures will range between 65 and 72 degrees Fahrenheit, unless the seed packet recommends otherwise.

Containers

You can use flats, pots, trays, egg cartons, eggshells, paper cups, or peat pots as containers. Just be sure they have a drainage hole in the bottom, so the new young seedling plants do not sit in water.

Soil Mix

Storebought seedling mixes are the best to use. However, a regular potting soil, vermiculite, perlite, sponge rock, or a combination of sand and peat moss are all suitable mixes for starting seeds. In fact, they can be started in soil from the garden if it is sterilized and porous. One way to sterilize your outdoor soil is to bake it in the oven (in a baking tray) for approximately two hours at 170 to 180 degrees Fahrenheit.

Sowing the Seeds

Read and follow sowing (planting) directions on the back of the seed packet. This is a very important step because some need to be covered with soil; others need to be uncovered and exposed to light in order to germinate. There is a tendency to cover the seeds with too much soil or peat, so be certain to barely cover the seed. Next, water in thoroughly. Use a fine spray (atomizer type) to water the seeds until the plants are at least 1 inch tall. Otherwise, the water tends to wash all the seeds to the edges of the pots or trays.

Preparing Starts for Transplanting

Once the new young seedlings have developed one set of true leaves, or are about 1 to 1½ inches high, they can be individually potted or spaced in a flat or tray. It's best to transplant them in individual containers, so when the time comes they can be easily transplanted with a minimum of shock to their permanent spot in the garden. Of course, do not plant them outdoors until the proper planting time. (See below.)

How to Plant/Transplant

Using a trowel, dig a planting hole about twice as large as the root ball of the plant you are planting. Then enrich the soil by mixing compost, processed manure, or potting soil with your existing soil.

Place the seedling or plant into enriched soil, being careful to set the plant at the same depth as it was previously planted. For transplants, there will often be a soil mark from the prior planting, which indicates the correct soil depth. Be certain to set the crown of the plant right at the same level as it was previously growing.

When to Plant/Transplant

With the advent of container growing, perennials can be planted anytime, except when the ground is frozen. If you are unfamiliar with a type or variety, it may be best to choose the plant when it is in bloom, then plant it into the garden at that time. The label in most containers will also provide the basic information about the plant and proper planting instructions. Many perennials grow one year and then begin flowering the next, so do not expect much other than new growth from the seedling plants the very first year.

Dividing Established Perennials

When plants become overcrowded or begin to diminish in size or flowering, it is often an indication that the clumps are in need of dividing. There is no set rule as to how often perennials should be divided. Some will do just fine for three to five years; others will go much longer without the need of dividing, so you need to evaluate the frequency of dividing by simply observing the health, vigor, and consistency of flowering. Dividing also provides the opportunity to increase the number of plants and/or share new divisions with others.

When to Divide

Dividing is best done in the autumn or earliest spring. As a rule, I suggest you divide summer- and fall-flowering perennials in earliest spring, before the new growth begins. The spring-flowering perennials can be divided immediately after flowering (preferred time) or in the autumn as the plants begin to go into their winter dormant season. Winter-flowering perennials are divided after they flower. Dividing will limit the next year's flowering, but in subsequent years they should be more beautiful than ever.

How to Divide

To divide perennials, simply dig the clump, lifting the plant with a pitchfork or spade, then pull or cut apart the root divisions. For some species you can pull the divisions apart by hand, others you may have to cut with a knife. Some you can divide with soil attached, others you may have to wash the soil away with water, then divide bare-root. Once the divisions are separated, be sure to get them back into the soil as soon as possible, so the air does not dry out the tender roots.

After planting, if cold weather occurs, the new divisions may be heaved out of the soil when it freezes. If this happens, simply reset the divisions right away. Otherwise, air gets to the roots and could cause them to dry out or freeze and die. For newly planted divisions made in the autumn, a light layer of straw mulch placed around (not over) the plants will provide some protection from cold weather.

Feeding Perennials

Many perennials will go an entire lifetime without the need of feeding, especially if the soil was properly prepared prior to planting. On the other hand, stunted growth, off-color leaves, or poor flowering are signs that perennials do need feeding. Use a rose-, all-purpose-, or vegetable-type fertilizer to feed them.

When to Feed

The best time to feed perennials is from late winter to early spring. This early feeding encourages good root development and eventual top growth. The second best time (if needed) is from mid-May to late June. Avoid feeding perennials in late summer as it is apt to cause late growth, which could be damaged by early fall frosts.

What to Feed

Plants that lose their leaves over winter are called *deciduous*. A rose or all-purpose garden fertilizer (vegetable fertilizer too) can be used to feed deciduous plants; for example, perennials.

Protecting Perennials from Cold Weather

Generally perennials will not need any special protection or care during the winter months. However, tender perennials or newly planted ones

Below: The late-summer flowering of black-eyed susan makes a wonderfully bright and cheerful addition to the garden.

may need to be covered during an especially cold spell. Plants such as chrysanthemums, hardy fuchsias, penstemons, and other tender plants can be covered with about 1 inch of straw during a cold winter. (In a mild winter, this is usually not necessary.) Burlap or some type of cloth can be used to cover the plants. Once the weather has moderated (usually this occurs within three to five days), the covering should be removed.

Wintering Geraniums

Though geraniums are perennials, throughout the Northwest, temperatures are too cold during the winter for geraniums to survive outdoors, so you have the choice of replacing them each year (treating them like annuals) or of finding a method of keeping them in a protected spot over the winter. Enjoy the last of the flowers indoors before you begin the wintering process. If you don't have a greenhouse, below are a few methods that work.

Whatever method you use, the plants should be potted and restarted in about mid-February. At that time, bring them into a warmer room and begin a regular watering and twice-monthly feeding schedule, so the plants will begin their growth and be ready to once again plant outdoors in late spring. Do not set the plants outside until all danger of frost has passed.

Indoors as Houseplants

Bring them indoors before the first autumn frost and treat them as houseplants by keeping them in a cool basement, family room, or utility room. Actually the plants can even be kept in the garage if it is semi-heated.

Indoors as Bare-root Plants

Shake the soil loose from around the roots, bare-rooting the plants. Next, cut back the stems to about 6 to 8 inches and remove any remaining foliage. Then simply hang the plants upside down in a cool but semi-heated basement or garage.

Indoors as Dormants

Place the dug plants in pots or trays with soil attached in the crawl space under the house. Check them monthly for insect infestations.

From Cuttings

Take cutting from the tip growth of the established plants, then discard the old plants, replacing them with the younger new starts. Each cutting should be about 3 to 4 inches long. Start the cuttings in a warm room, using a starting mix of 50 percent sand and 50 percent peat moss.

Outdoors

In a mild winter, geraniums are apt to survive outdoors if they are planted close to the foundation of the house, then mulched with straw.

Wintering Fuchsias

Fuchsias, like geraniums, are perennials that can either be overwintered or treated like annuals. Although it's best to bring fuchsias in before frost occurs, most varieties can take temperatures down to about 28 degrees Fahrenheit. It should be noted that there are more than 100 varieties that are considered winter hardy west of the Cascade Mountains. The tender fuchsias can be wintered in the same ways as the geraniums. (See above.)

Here's another idea the hobbyists occasionally use. Dig a trench about 2 to 3 feet deep. Place a few inches of gravel or sawdust in the bottom for drainage. Cut the fuchsia stems back to 6 to 8 inches from the soil. Then lay the fuchsia plants on their sides and carefully fill sawdust, bark, or straw over the top of them. If you have the space, this is an easy way to winter fuchsia baskets too, because you simply lay the baskets on their sides and cover them. Leave them in place until mid- to late February, dig up the plants, and start them all over again. Pot them in new soil, begin a watering schedule, and feed them twice monthly. Do not set them outdoors until you are certain there is no chance of frost occurring.

Choosing Perennials

By Particular Features

Easiest to Grow

Of all the perennials that we can grow in the garden, here are a dozen and a half that I think are the easiest to grow. They are the ones I would suggest that the first-time gardener start with:

astilbe, *Astilbe* x *arendsii*
bee balm, *Monarda didyma*
bellflower, *Campanula* spp.
black-eyed susan, *Rudbeckia* spp.
bleeding heart, *Dicentra* spp.
carnation/double pink, *Dianthus caryophyllus*
columbine, *Aquilegia* hybrids
cranesbill, *Geranium* spp. (perennial)
daylily, *Hemerocalis* hybrids

The late-summer and early-fall flowering Japanese anemones reseed themselves like crazy in our garden, almost becoming a nuisance, but what a beautiful nuisance! There are many single and semi-double flowering varieties that merit a place in the sunny garden.

flowering sage, *Salvia nemorosa*
phlox, *Phlox* spp.
lavender, *Lavandula*
Michaelmas daisy, *Aster novae-belgii*
garden mums, *Chrysanthemum* spp.
obedience plant, *Physostegia virginiana*
pincushion flower, *Scabiosa* spp.
plantain lily, *Hosta* hybrids
Shasta daisy, *Leucanthemum maximum*

With Winter Interest

It's hard to find many perennials that flower during the winter, at a time when garden color is desired. Here are six plants that provide winter color in the garden:

dusty miller, *Senecio cineraria*
flowering kale and cabbage
hellebore, *Helleborus,* many varieties
Swiss chard 'Bright Lights'
winter pansy, *Viola hiemalis* mix
wormwood, *Artemisia stellerana*

With Fragrance

Be sure to place the fragrant perennials in a spot where you can enjoy both their fragrance and beauty. Near the entry area, on the patio, or near heavily traveled walkways are ideal spots to plant the fragrant perennials. Here are eight that have fragrant flowers or leaves:

bee balm, *Monarda didyma*
carnation/double pink, *Dianthus caryophyllus*
daylily, *Hemerocalis* (selected varieties)
garden phlox, *Phlox paniculata*
Lavender cotton, *Santolina* (foliage)
plantain lily, *Hosta* (some hybrids)
primrose, *Primula* (selected varieties)
thyme, *Thymus* spp. (foliage)

For Specific Sites

In Rock Gardens

Are you looking for perennials to plant in a rockery, to cascade down over the rocks and provide bright garden color? Here are a dozen top-notch plants to use:

aubrieta, *A. deltoidea*
basket of gold, *Aurinia saxatilis*

bellflower, *Campanula* (dwarf)
candytuft, *Iberis sempervirens*
creeping thyme, *Thymus* (several)
cushion spurge, *Euphorbia polychroma* (dwarf)
Irish and Scotch moss, *Sagina moss*
lithodora, *Lithospermum diffusum*
pinks
rockcress, *Arabis caucasica*
sedums and succulents
sea thrift, *Armeria maritima*

In Shade

Practically every garden has at least one shady spot, and it is often difficult to choose plants that will do well. So here's my recommendation of ten plants that will grow and flower in the shade:

bleeding heart, *Dicentra* spp.
columbine, *Aguilegia* hybrids
false spirea, *Astilbe* x *arendsii*
forget-me-not, *Myosotis*
hellebore, *Helleborus* varieties
leopard's bane, *Doronicum cordatum*
lungwort, *Pulmonaria saccharata*
plantain lily, *Hosta* hybrids
primrose, *Primula* spp.
pansy, *Viola* spp.

In Moist Soil

Areas with poor drainage or occasional standing water have a special environment where only water-tolerant plants will survive. Here are eight plants that will survive in a spot where the soil is moist:

bee balm, *Monarda didyma*
cardinal flower, *Lobelia cardinalis*
false spirea, *Astilbe* x *arendsii*
globeflower, *Trollius*
heart-leaf bergenia, *Bergenia cordifolia*
Japanese iris, *Iris kaempferi*
marsh marigold, *Caltha palustris*
primrose, *Primula* (selected varieties)

In Dry Soil

Do you have a spot in the garden that is hard to reach with a garden hose, or where it's simply too dry for most plants? Here are ten plants to consider for such spots, but remember that they will need a little watering attention when hot weather persists:

blanket flower, *Gaillardia grandiflora*
cranesbill, *Geranium* varieties (perennial)
flowering sage, *Salvia nemorosa*
gayfeather, *Liatris spicata*
globe thistle, *Echinops exaltatus*
carnation/double pink, *Dianthus caryophyllus*
stonecrop, *Sedum* spp.
tickseed, *Coreopsis grandiflora*
wormwood, *Artemisia stellerana*
yarrow, *Achillea millefolium*

Flowering Perennials

Spring-Flowering

The spring-flowering bulbs provide an abundance of color in the spring garden, but when they're through, you can count on these perennials to brighten the garden and continue to provide some cut flowers for your home. Here are eight of my favorites:

columbine, *Aquilegia* hybrids
delphinium, *Delphinium elatum*
globeflower, *Trollius*
heart-leaf bergenia, *Bergenia cordifolia*
leopard's bane, *Doronicum cordatum*
oriental poppy, *Papaver orientale*
pasque flower, *Anemone pulsatilla*
peony, *Paeonia lactiflora*

Summer-Flowering

So many perennials flower during the summer that I have simply listed what I think are the eighteen easiest to grow. These are ideal to use for garden color, and most make excellent cut flowers:

bee balm/bergamot, *Monarda didyma*
bellflower, *Campanula* spp.
black-eyed susan, *Rudbeckia* spp.
blanket flower, *Gaillardia grandiflora*
carnation/double pink, *Dianthus caryophyllus*
coneflower, *Echinacea purpurea*

cranesbill, *Geranium* varieties (perennial)
daylily, *Hemerocallis* hybrids
garden phlox, *Phlox paniculata*
gaura, *Gaura lindheimeri*
Iceland poppy, *Papaver nudicaule*
pincushion flower, *Scabiosa* spp.
plantain lily, *Hosta* hybrids
Shasta daisy, *Leucanthemum maximum*
Stokes aster, *Stokesia laevis*
sunrose, *Helianthemum nummularium*
tickseed, *Coreopsis grandiflora*
yarrow, *Achillea millefolium*

Autumn-Flowering

As the autumn leaves start to turn color and the garden begins to fade, there are some interesting flowering perennials that just begin to reach their peak of beauty. Here are a dozen plants that merit consideration for autumn interest:

anemone, *Anemone hupehensis japonica*
autumn joy, *Sedum telephium* 'Autumn Joy' (tall varieties)
beard tongue, *Penstemon* x *gloxinoides*
flowering sage, *Salvia* species
fuchsia, hardy varieties
garden mum, *Chrysanthemum* varieties
grasses, ornamental varieties

Left: With its fragrant foliage and showy flowers, lavender makes an excellent perennial ground cover. This bushy plant grows best in full sun.

Michaelmas daisy, *Aster novae-belgii*
pincushion flower, *Scabiosa* spp.
Russian sage, *Perovskia atriplicifolia*
tickseed, *Coreopsis grandiflora*
veronica, *Veronica* species

Yellow

Bright yellow flowers will perk up any garden. They are ideal to use in a dark spot or in front of an evergreen background. Combine them with whites, lavenders, purples, blues, and reds for show in the garden. Here are ten choice perennials with attractive yellow flowers:

basket-of-gold, *Aurinia saxatilis*
black-eyed susan, *Rudbeckia* spp.
cinquefoil, *Potentilla* spp.
cushion spurge, *Euphorbia polychroma*
daylily, *Hemerocallis* hybrids
garden mum, *Chrysanthemum* spp.
globeflower, *Trollius*
leopard's bane, *Doronicum cordatum*
tickseed, *Coreopsis grandiflora*
yarrow, *Achillea millefolium*

Orange/Bronze

There are not a lot of perennials with flowers in these two shades, so they really provide a showy contrast with other flowering plants. In fact, I call plants with flowers of these colors conversation pieces because they draw people to their bright, showy flowers. Here are eight orange or bronze flowering perennials to consider:

avens, *Geum* 'Borisii'
blanket flower, *Gaillardia grandiflora*
champion, *Lychnis arkwrightii*
crocosmia, *Crocosmia*
daylily, *Hemerocallis* hybrids
garden mum, *Chrysanthemum* spp.
garden phlox, *Phlox* 'Orange Perfection'
sunrose, *Helianthemum nummularium*

Red

You can count on red flowering perennials to add a bright spot of color to your garden. They will really stand out in the garden when planted near white and yellow flowering perennials. Here are ten of the best for the garden and flower arranging:

bee balm, *Monarda didyma*
cardinal flower, *Lobelia cardinalis* 'Queen Victoria'
carnation/double pink, *Dianthus caryophyllus*
columbine, *Aquilegia vulgaris plena*
daylily, *Hemerocallis* hybrids
false spirea, *Astilbe* x *arendsii*
garden penstemon, *Penstemon* x *gloxinioides*
garden phlox, *Phlox paniculata* 'Starfire'
oriental poppy, *Papaver orientale*
yarrow, *Achillea millefolium*

Pink/Rose

Flowers in shades of pink and rose add a cheerful presence to any garden. These are two colors that blend well with flowers of any shade. Here are sixteen favorites:

bleeding heart, *Dicentra* spp.
carnation/double pink, *Dianthus caryophyllus*
coneflower, *Echinacea purpurea*
cranesbill, *Geranium* species (perennial)
daylily, *Hemerocallis* hybrids
false spirea, *Astilbe* x *arendsii*
garden mum, *Chrysanthemum* spp.
garden phlox, *Phlox* spp.
mallow, *Malva* spp.
Michaelmas daisy, *Aster novae-belgii*
obedience plant, *Physostegia virginiana*
pincushion flower, *Scabiosa* spp.
spike gayfeather, *Liatris spicata*
spike speedwell, *Veronica* spp.
Stokes aster, *Stokesia laevis*
yarrow, *Achillea millefolium*

Lavender/Purple/Blue

These three colors are difficult to find in plants, and are excellent companion colors with yellows and whites. These colors should be used in the brighter, sunnier parts of the garden. Their beauty is sometimes lost if placed against a dark evergreen background. Here are fourteen of my favorites:

balloon flower, *Platycodon grandiflorus*
bellflower, *Campanula* spp. (many)
cranesbill, *Geranium* spp. (perennial)
delphinium, *Delphinium elatum*

garden phlox, *Phlox* spp.
flowering sage, *Salvia nemorosa*
Jacob's ladder, *Polemonium caeruleum*
lavender, *Lavandula* spp.
Michaelmas daisy, *Aster novae-belgii*
New England aster, *Aster novae-angliae*
pincushion flower, *Scabiosa* spp.
primrose, *Primula* spp.
Russian sage, *Perovskia atriplicifolia*
speedwell, *Veronica* spp.

White

White flowers are especially useful in the garden because they tend to make other colors stand out. When possible, use white flowering plants in dark or shady areas of the garden, because they brighten the area. Likewise, white flowers are often used in the night or "moon" garden. Using them by the entry or on the patio is worthwhile and attractive. The following ten are just a few of the best for Northwest gardens:

anemone, *Anemone hupehensis japonica*
astilbe, *Astilbe* x *arendsii*
bleeding heart, *Dicentra* spp.
candytuft, *Iberis sempervirens*
creeping thyme, *Thymus* (several)
delphinium, *Delphinium elatum*
garden phlox, *Phlox* spp.
Michaelmas daisy, *Aster novae-belgii*
Shasta daisy, *Leucanthemum maximum* varieties
speedwell, *Veronica* spp.

For Cut Flowers

It's so nice to have beautiful flowers in the garden, but doubly nice when they can also be used as cut flowers in the home. Here are eighteen of Myrna's favorite perennials for cutting:

baby's breath, *Gypsophila paniculata*
bee balm, *Monarda didyma*
black-eyed susan, *Rudbeckia* spp.
blanket flower, *Gaillardia grandiflora*
carnation/double pink, *Dianthus caryophyllus*
coneflower, *Echinacea purpurea*
delphinium, *Delphinium elatum*
false spirea, *Astilbe* x *arendsii*
garden mum, *Chrysanthemum* spp.

garden phlox, *Phlox* spp.
globe thistle, *Echinops exaltatus*
lavender, *Lavandula* spp.
Michaelmas daisy, *Aster novae-belgii* varieties
pincushion flower, *Scabiosa* spp.
Shasta daisy, *Leucanthemum maximum*
speedwell, *Veronica* spp.
tickseed, *Coreopsis grandiflora*
yarrow, *Achillea millefolium*

For Dried Flowers

Here are a few beautiful flowering perennials that can be preserved (dried) and used in arrangements year-round. Enjoy their beauty in the garden and as dried cut flowers. Here are twelve of Myrna's favorites:

baby's breath, *Gypsophila paniculata*
carnation/double pink, *Dianthus caryophyllus*
cornflower, *Centaurea montana*
delphinium, *Delphinium elatum*
false spirea, *Astilbe* x *arendsii*
garden mum, *Chrysanthemum* spp.
globe thistle, *Echinops exaltatum*
hellebore, *Helleborus* varieties
lavender, *Lavandula* spp.
spike gayfeather, *Liatris spicata*
sweet william, *Dianthus barbatus*
yarrow, *Achillea millefolium*

By Size

For Borders

Low-growing perennials are ideal plants to use along a border, in rockeries, or as low foreground plants. These are the ones that are most often used at the front edge of flowerbeds. Although they are not generally considered a source for cut flowers, some will provide short-stemmed flowers that are ideal for small floral arrangements. Here are some of my favorites:

candytuft, *Iberis sempervirens*
carnation/double pink, *Dianthus caryophyllus*
cinquefoil, *Potentilla* spp.
columbine, *Aquilegia* hybrids (dwarf varieties)
coral bells, *Heuchera americana*
cranesbill, *Geranium* spp. (dwarf varieties)
creeping phlox, *Phlox subulata*

English daisies, *Bellis perennis*
moss saxifrage, *Saxifraga rosacea*
pasque flower, *Anemone pulsatilla*
plantain lily, *Hosta* hybrids (dwarf)
primrose, *Primula* spp. (many)
rockcress, *Aubrieta caucasica*
sea thrift, *Armeria maritima*
sedums and succulents
silver brocade, *Artemisia stellerana* 'Silver Brocade'
sunrose, *Helianthemum nummularium*
thyme, *Thymus* spp.

For the Midbed

Medium-sized perennials are by far the most popular because they provide the best range of growing height and still provide excellent cut flowers. These are the plants that are placed in a spot behind the low-growing perennials, but in front of the background ones. Here is a list of thirty-five of the most popular midbed perennials:

avens, *Geum chiloense*
balloon flower, *Platycodon grandiflorus*
bellflower, *Campanula* species
black-eyed susan, *Rudbeckia* spp.
bleeding heart, *Dicentra* spp.
cardinal flower, *Lobelia cardinalis*
catnip, *Nepeta*
columbine, *Aquilegia* hybrids
cornflower, *Centaurea montana*
cushion spurge, *Euphorbia polychroma*
daylily, *Hemerocallis* hybrids
false spirea, *Astilbe* x *arendsii*
fleabane, *Erigeron glaucus*
flowering sage, *Salvia nemorosa*
gaura, *Gaura lindheimeri*
heart-leaf bergenia, *Bergenia cordifolia* varieties
Iceland poppy, *Papaver nudicaule*
lamb's ear, *Stachys byzantine*
lavender, *Lavandula* spp.
lavender mist, *Thalictrum* sp.
leopard's bane, *Doronicum cordatum*
obedience plant, *Physostegia virginiana*
ornamental grasses, many varieties
painted daisy, *Tanacetum coccineum*

penstemon, *Penstemon* x *gloxinioides*
pincushion flower, *Scabiosa* spp.
plantain lily, *Hosta* hybrids
Shasta daisy, *Leucanthemum maximum*
speedwell, *Veronica* spp.
spike gayfeather, *Liatris spicata*
Stokes aster, *Stokesia laevis*
stonecrop, *Sedum* spp., tall
tickseed, *Coreopsis grandiflora*
wormwood, *Artemisia stellerana*
yarrow, *Achillea millefolium*

For the Background

These taller-growing perennials are ideal to use toward the back of landscape beds. They make attractive companion plants with the low-growing and midbed perennials that are grown in front of them. Here are twelve popular ones to use:

artemisia, *A. lactiflora* 'Guilho'
bee balm, *Monarda didyma*
cone flower, *Echinacea purpurea*
delphinium, *Delphinium elatum*
foxglove, *Digitalis purpurea*
garden phlox, *Phlox paniculata*
goatsbeard, *Aruncus dioicus*
Japanese anemone, *Anemone hupehensis japonica*
ligularia, *Ligularia* spp.
mallow, *Malva* spp.
Michaelmas daisy, *Aster novae-belgii*
Russian sage, *Perovskia atriplicifolia*

Perennials Encyclopedia

Anemone *(Anemone hupehensis japonica).* These are very attractive late-summer and early-autumn flowering plants. They grow about 3–4 feet high, making them excellent background plants in perennial or landscape borders. Single or semi-double 1- to 2-inch flowers are ideal for cutting. Mine put on quite a display at a time when not many perennials are in bloom. They spread like crazy in our garden, so thin them once or twice a year. Plant them in partial shade, in fertile, well-drained soil.

Artemisia (*A. lactiflora* 'Guilho'). This tall perennial (4–5½ feet) has late-summer sprays of fragrant creamy-white flowers. Foliage is also aromatic. Use as cut flower in fresh or dried in arrangements. Brown stems, rich green leaves. Plant in sun, in ordinary, well-drained garden soil. See also Chapter 14, Herbs.

Silver brocade (*Artemisia stellerana* 'Silver Brocade'). Brilliant silver-gray leaves on a dense, compact plant. Plants in our garden only grow about 4–6 inches high, but will spread to 2–3 feet. Growth will trail downward in baskets or containers. Ideal rock-garden or border plant. We use them a lot in containers because of the attractive silver leaves. Yellow flowers are usually cut off because they distract from the foliage. They die in our garden if they are pruned too severely or if temperatures drop below 20 degrees Fahrenheit, so avoid severe pruning and provide protection during cold winter weather. Plant in a sunny spot, in well-drained, rich garden soil.

Wormwood *(A. stellerana).* This one is best known for its silver-gray foliage. Broader in leaf and hardier than most dusty millers (see also dusty miller). Plants grow up to 2½ feet, but look better if lightly sheared in early spring. Keep yellow flowers picked, as they distract from bright silver foliage. Use in containers, in borders, or for spot color anywhere in the sunny garden. Plant in ordinary, well-drained garden soil.

Astilbe *(A.* x *arendsii).* Also called false spirea. This is one of Myrna's favorite perennials. She uses both flowers and foliage (as filler in arrangements). I think it is one of the best shade perennials. The soft plumes of flowers stand above the delicate leaves. They range in shades of pink, rose, red, or white. Leaf color varies from light green to bronze. Dwarf varieties only grow 12 inches, but the larger-growing, more popular varieties grow 18–30 inches. This shade perennial grows best in rich, well-drained soil.

Aubrieta *(A. deltoidea).* A wonderful rock-garden perennial. The 3- to 6-inch plants will cascade down over rocks or can be used as a perennial ground cover. Single and double flowering varieties in shades of purple, lavender, dark blue,

Above: Eye-catching leaves and fragrant blooms make hostas an ideal perennial for shade gardens.

Left: Peonies come in a wide variety of flower colors and shapes, and deserve a place in the Northwest garden.

and rose-red. Spring (April to May) flowers cover the plants. Shear after bloom and they will often flower again in the summer. Plant in full or filtered sun in average, well-drained garden soil.

Autumn joy (*Sedum telephium* 'Autumn Joy'). This is a very attractive late-summer, early-fall flowering perennial. The clusters of tiny flowers open pink on stems that are 18–24 inches high. They provide a bright spot of color in borders or midbed plantings. This one is a must in our garden. Excellent cut flowers, or leave so the birds can enjoy the seeds. Plants die back and disappear during the winter. See also sedums and succulents. Plant in full sun, in typical, well-drained soil.

Avens. See geum.

Baby's breath *(Gypsophila paniculata).* This is one of the most popular cut flowers to use as a filler in floral arrangements. The delicate, white-flowering 'Bristol Fairy' (3–4 feet) is probably still the most popular variety. However, there are lower-growing, 12- to 15-inch, double pink-flowering varieties. In addition there are dwarf, 4- to 6-inch ground-cover varieties. The taller ones are ideal to use in perennial borders or landscape beds. Attractive in the garden, or use the cut flowers fresh or dried. Plant in full sun, in rich, well-drained soil.

Baby's tears *(Soleirolia soleirolii).* This low-growing 2- to 4-inch perennial is a great ground cover. See Chapter 12, Ground Covers.

Balloon flower *(Platycodon grandiflorus).* Commonly called Chinese bellflower. As the flower matures, the five petals separate into 2-inch-wide blue stars. This is one of those old-time perennials that is once again gaining popularity. Pick off individual flowers as they die to keep plant flowering. New double varieties are available, but I don't think they are as nice as the single ones. Plants grow 24–36 inches high, so are ideal to use as midbed or background plants in borders. Leaves die back and disappear over winter. Plant in a mostly sunny permanent location that will remain undisturbed. Planting soil should be fertile and well drained.

Basket-of-gold *(Aurinia saxatilis).* Here's one of the great spring-flowering rock-garden plants. The dainty clusters of bright yellow flowers cover the 6- to 12-inch-high bushy plants. With age, the plants cascade down over the rocks. I cut mine back after the spring flowering and it flowers again during the summer. Grows best in full sun or filtered sunlight. Plants grow in any ordinary, well-drained soil.

Beard tongue. See penstemon.

Bee balm *(Monarda didyma).* Probably best known because it attracts butterflies and hummingbirds. This herb is often used in the vegetable garden to attract bees for pollination. The showy tufts of fluffy flowers come in shades of pink, red, purple, and white. Most grow 3–4 feet high and make excellent background perennials in borders. They grow well in full or part sun, in even moist, heavy clay soil.

Bellflower (*Campanula* sp.). This is a big family of perennials. Some have low, 4- to 8-inch, spreading growth habits; others are upright, 18- to 36-inch plants. Flower colors range in shades of pink, rose, blue, or white. We really like the low-spreading 'Birch Hybrid' and the upright 'Cup and Saucer' varieties. There are hundreds of species. They grow really well in full or part sun, in fertile, well-drained soil.

Black-eyed susan *(Rudbeckia fulgida* and *R. hirta).* Also known as gloriosa daisy. These plants put on a nice display during the summer and early fall. Varieties range from 1–6 feet high. *R. f.* 'Goldsturm' (24–30 inches) was the 1999 Perennial of the Year. Bright yellow, 2- to 3-inch flower petals with black center. We have *R. h.* 'Goldilocks', a low, 8- to 10-inch variety with semi-double and double flowers that last a long time. All varieties make excellent cut flowers. Use the low ones toward the front of flowerbeds and the taller ones in midbed plantings. Plant in full or partial sun, in moist, well-drained soil.

Blanket flower *(Gaillardia grandiflora).* This perennial is beautiful in the garden and great for cut flowers. We have 'Goblin', which has showy, 2- to 4-inch flowers with yellow edges and bright red centers. It grows about 12–15 inches high. 'Burgundy' has deep red flowers and grows just a little bit taller. Keep spent flowers picked and they will flower all summer and into the fall. Plant in full sun, in ordinary garden soil.

Bleeding heart *(Dicentra).* This is another "must" perennial for the shady garden. They bear showy, drooping flowers that hang from an arching stem. Pick spent flowers for possible rebloom. Plant in fertile, well-drained soil.

D. formosa. The western native is great to use in naturalizing.

D. spectabilis. The common bleeding heart is the showier of the two. It grows 24–30 inches high with spring flowers that are white or pink.

Blue star creeper *(Pratia pedunculata).* See Chapter 12, Ground Covers.

Candytuft *(Iberis sempervirens).* Dark green leaves are the perfect background for the pure white, 2- to 3-inch flowers. This spring-flowering perennial is extremely popular as a rock-garden plant, but I find it also an excellent ground cover in small areas. Dwarf varieties only grow 6–8 inches, taller ones 10–12 inches high. Shear lightly after blooming to encourage bushiness and more bloom the next year. Plant in full to part sun, in well-drained, ordinary garden soil.

Cardinal flower *(Lobelia cardinalis).* When we think of lobelia, we think of the purple, blue, or white summer annuals, but these are perennial. We have 'Compliment Deep Red' in our garden. It has the most beautiful scarlet red flowers, and for a short period the foliage is also a brilliant plum red, turning bright green.

'Blue Cardinal' has bright blue flowers. Plus there are several others, including 'Queen Victoria', all of which merit consideration for use in the summer garden. Most grow 2–3 feet in full to part sun, in fertile, well-drained soil.

Carnation/clove pink *(Dianthus caryophyllus).* The carnations are noted for their fragrant 2- to 2½-inch double flowers. They need staking in the garden, as the plants will grow 18–24 inches high. Ideal for cutting and attractive in midbed plantings. The pinks come in a wide range of growing habits, 4–18 inches high. The fragrance of varieties varies considerably, so choose them when they are in bloom so you can pick the most fragrant. Single or double flowers range in shades of pink, rose, red, violet, lavender, or white. Pinks can be used as border or edging plants or in rock gardens; the taller varieties can be planted in midbed plantings. Plant in full sun, in rich, well-drained soil.

Catnip *(Nepeta cataria).* The gray-green leaves are quite nice as a contrast to the greens of most perennials. See Chapter 14, Herbs.

Champion *(Lychnis coronaria).* This one grows almost wild in many old home gardens. The leaves are a very attractive silvery gray, and the 1-inch flowers are a brilliant magenta. The plant grows about 18–24 inches or more. This plant thrives on a certain amount of neglect, and likes full to part sun, in any ordinary garden soil.

L. arkwrightii. Showy orange-red flowers. The variety 'Molten Lava' also fits this description. Both plants grow about 18 inches tall. Bronze leaves make a nice show in the perennial garden.

Chinese bellflower. See balloon flower.

Chrysanthemum. See garden mum.

Cinquefoil (*Potentilla neumanniana* 'Nana'). This low-growing, 2- to 4-inch variety has brilliant yellow flowers in spring. Plant in a location where it will be protected from the hot midday sun. Variety will tolerate moist soil.

Columbine (*Aquilegia* hybrids). There are many different species, but the hybrids are probably the most popular home garden plants. Myrna and I particularly like the 24- to 30-inch McKana hybrids and the dwarf 10- to 15-inch Biedermeier mix. Both come in a wide variety of colors and color combinations. The spur-shaped flowers stand above the medium-sized, divided, grayish green leaves. Plant in full to part shade in most any garden soil.

A. vulgaris plena. Many varieties with single or double flowers. Range in height from 12 to 24 inches or more. Predominant shades are blue, lavender, and violet.

Coneflower *(Echinacea purpurea).* Large daisylike flowers on 1- to 4-foot plants. There is a large crown in the center of the flower, with petals extending outward from its base. They are very showy in the garden and make excellent, long-lasting cut flowers. This summer-flowering perennial will continue to bloom if spent flowers are picked. An excellent plant for midbed plantings, or use a dwarf variety as a border plant. Varieties with pink, soft rosy purple, or white flowers. Plant in full or part sun, in rich, well-drained soil.

Coral bells (*Heuchera americana* and others). I think the evergreen foliage of some varieties is much prettier than the flowers. Leaf color varies from shades of green and bronze to crimson, some with contrasting markings. The dainty bell-shaped summer flowers appear on wiry stems. Flowers in shades of pink, rose, red, and white and make excellent cut flowers. Keep spent flowers picked. There are several varieties that range from 12 to 30 inches in height. Plant in full sun (part sun in hot climates) in rich, well-drained soil.

Cornflower *(Centaurea montana).* Sometimes called Persian cornflower. The thistlelike, late-spring flowers are blue and stand above the silvery gray leaves. Remove spent flowers to encourage additional bloom. Grows 18–24 inches high. Plant in full sun, in most any ordinary garden soil.

Corsican mint *(Mentha requienii).* This popular ½-inch-high plant is great to use as a perennial ground cover. See Chapter 12, Ground Covers.

Cranesbill *(Geranium).* These are the true perennial geraniums, not to be confused with the plant whose common name is geranium (*Pelargonium* species). They are difficult to describe because there are so many different varieties. The leaves of most varieties are small, but somewhat shaped like the annual geraniums. The flowers are mostly single with a few double varieties. The small flowers cover the plants. Most flower in late spring or early to midsummer. We have several varieties, but I particularly like *G. cinereum* 'Ballerina', a dwarf pink with red veins. Practically everyone who visits our garden asks what it is and then for its variety name. The flowers of these perennials range in shades of pink, rose, blue, lavender, purple, and white. Growing height varies from 8 to 24 inches. Plant in full to part sun, in moist, well-drained soil.

Creeping phlox *(P. stolonifera* or *P. subulata).* Very popular low-growing (4–6 inches), spring-flowering perennial that is often used in rock gardens. Flowers are in shades of pink, rose, red, lavender, or white. The dense, matlike growth is covered with flowers in early to mid-spring. Plants grow about 4–6 inches high and spread up to 24 inches wide. Plant in full sun, in moist, fertile, well-drained soil. See also Chapter 12, Ground Covers.

Crocosmia (*C.* hybrids). This is a perennial the hummingbirds love. The foliage looks like that of gladiolus, and the tops of arching stems are covered in midsummer with showy orange, red, or yellow flowers. The variety 'Lucifer' is very red. Plants grow 18–36 inches high. We grow them in sun and semi-sun, and I even have a couple of plants in full shade and they all do well, so it really isn't fussy about location. Plants do well in most any ordinary garden soil that has good drainage.

Cushion spurge *(Euphorbia polychroma).* Very showy, brilliant yellow-green flowers cover the plant in late spring. Plants grow 12–18 inches high. Green foliage may turn reddish in autumn. I saw these planted at the base of lilacs in Edmonds years ago, and the combination was really striking. Plant in full sun, in most ordinary garden soils.

Daylily (*Hemerocallis* hybrids). Entire books have been written on this outstanding summer-flowering perennial plant family. One grower I interviewed on our TV show said there are more than 7,000 varieties. Some of the new ones are rebloomers, providing color over a long period of time. The older varieties were basically yellow, orange, or reddish, but today's newer introductions come in wide range of colors and color combinations. Flowers stand above the straplike leaves and are excellent for cutting. Dwarf varieties grow 12–24 inches, while standard ones grow 30–48 inches high. We have several varieties in our garden, but one of our favorites is the yellow-flowering 'Stella d'Oro', as it flowers for a long time and only grows about 18–24 inches high. Use in perennial borders, in groups, or as a mass planting. This is another one of the perennials that thrives on a certain amount of neglect. Divide and transplant in the fall, about every 5–7 years. Plant in full to part sun, in any ordinary garden soil.

Delphinium *(D. elatum).* Gorgeous, stately, upright stalks with clusters of very showy flowers. Plants are colorful in borders, in group plantings, or when used for spot color. Flowers are excellent for cutting. Dwarf varieties grow 18–36 inches, taller ones about 3–7 feet or taller. Many named varieties flower in shades of clear pink, rose, peach, blue, lavender, purple, or white. Some varieties have centers of contrasting color, referred to as *bees.* For example, 'Percival' is white with a black (center) bee; 'King Arthur' is violet with a white bee. Tall varieties may need staking. I have mine planted behind some 3-foot-high rhododendrons; it seems they love the shade of the rhododendron foliage, but then peek above and bloom in full sun. Plant them in sun or part sun, in moist, fertile, well-drained soil.

Dusty miller *(Senecio cineraria).* There are several plants called dusty miller, but this is my favorite. The split, silvery gray leaves add a bright spot to the garden almost all year. They need to be sheared occasionally or they are apt to get a bit leggy. I also cut off the small clusters of yellow flowers, because I think they distract from the beautiful silver foliage. It's another must for our garden, because it adds light and life to the garden especially on cloudy dark days. Plants grow up to 2–3 feet in height and width. Plant in full or part sun, in average, well-drained garden soil.

English daisy *(Bellis perennis).* Biennial. See Chapter 13, Annuals.

False spirea. See astilbe.

Fleabane *(Erigeron glaucus).* Daisylike blossoms, most with yellow centers. Some are single, others are double-flowering. Pink, lavender, or white flowering varieties. Plants grow 12–24 inches high. A very attractive garden perennial. Pick off spent blossoms to keep plants flowering. Plant in full to part sun, in most any well-drained garden soil.

Flowering kale and cabbage. I have listed these as perennials when actually they are hardy annual vegetables, but we grow them as fall- and winter-flowering plants. They are showy, decorative garden plants because of their brilliant leaf colors and interesting textures. Leaf color varies in combination of colors, ranging from greenish gray to pink, rose, almost red, and white. Wonderful in fall containers, when used for spot color, in group plantings, or individually in borders. Plants grow 12–15 inches high. Start from seed in late June or earliest July. Plant in full sun or part shade.

Flowering sage. See sage, flowering.

Forget-me-not *(Myosotis sylvatica).* Biennial. See Chapter 13, Annuals.

Foxglove *(Digitalis purpurea).* This is an old-time garden favorite. The spikes of tubular flowers (24–36 inches) come in shades of pink, rose, purple, yellow, or white, sometimes with spotted centers. It is actually a biennial, but usually reseeds itself. Some hybrids may grow up to 5–7 feet. Thrives on a certain amount of neglect. Plant in full to part sun, in well-drained soil.

Fuchsias. Though in many places these are grown as annuals (see Chapter 13, Annuals), there are quite a few varieties of fuchsias that are frost hardy. We have several in our garden. My favorite is 'Santa Claus' (red and white), which grows about 12–18 inches high. Check with your garden center because new ones are being introduced on a regular basis. Some of the frost-hardy ones will need a straw or bark mulch (covering) if temperatures drop into the low 20s or colder. My mom grew *Fuchsia magellanica* (4–6 feet) in her garden. It would freeze to the ground but come back every year. The flowers are red and violet. Plants grow well in enriched, well-drained garden soil.

Garden mum *(Chrysanthemum).* There are more than 150 different species. For the home garden, I like the summer- and fall-flowering perennial garden mums. Hobbyists like to grow the big football mums, but they are a bit of challenge for the home gardener. The summer and fall mums are easy to grow. Most grow 1–3 feet, with some that will attain a height of up to 6 feet. Mums come in single and double flowering varieties, some with small flowers; others are quite large. They come in practically every color of the rainbow except blue. There are about a dozen or more flower forms, including spider, in-curves, pom-pom, spoon, and decorative, to name just a few. We have at least fifty plants in our garden. Some flower as early as late June, while others continue to flower right up to frost. Cut to 3–4 inches from the ground after a light frost. If you live in a cold area, cover with 2–3 inches of straw for winter protection. Plants can be divided in spring as soon as new growth appears. Pinch out the center growth of the plants when you set them out to encourage bushiness. Plant them in a bright sunny spot, in soil that is fertile and well drained.

Garden penstemon. See penstemon.

Garden phlox *(P. paniculata).* These tall, 3- to 4-foot-high perennials make stately background plants. Clusters of sweetly scented flowers are showy in the garden or as cut flowers. Grow them in full or part sun, in enriched, well-drained garden soil. Pick spent flowers to encourage re-blooming. Here are just a couple of my favorite varieties:

'Orange Perfection'. Flowers are not a true orange, but close to it.

'Starfire'. Bright, deep-red flowers with attractive bronze green leaves.

Garden sage. See sage, flowering.

Gaura *(G. lindheimeri).* A nice, airy, summer-flowering perennial. We have 'Siskiyou Pink' and 'Whirling Butterflies' (white) in our garden and love their dainty flower spikes and open, airy growth habit. They grow about 2–3 feet and bloom throughout the summer. If there is a light breeze, the name 'Whirling Butterflies' really describes the appearance of the flowers. Plant in sun to part sun, in most any ordinary garden soil.

Gayfeather *(Liatris spicata).* This is an unusual plant because the flower blooms from the top downward. There are several varieties with tufts of lavender, purple, or white flowers. Growing heights vary from 2–3½ feet depending upon variety. They have a long flowering period, from July to September. Ideal for cutting. Grow them in borders, groups, or individually. Plant in full sun, in rich garden soil that is well drained.

Geranium *(Pelargonium hortorum).* These are frost tender perennials that must be brought indoors before any frost touches them; many prefer to grow them as annual bedding plants. See Chapter 13, Annuals.

Geum *(G. chiloense).* Sometimes commonly called avens. One of the fine perennials. Flower colors range from yellow, orange, to red; some are single, semi-double, or fully double. Flower stems tend to be a bit sparse, but if dead flowers are removed, they will flower all summer. Plants range from 12 to 24 inches high with flowers that are 1–2 inches wide. *Geum* 'Borisii' has single flowers that are bright orange. This variety grows about 12 inches high. Grow in full to part sun, in any ordinary garden soil.

Globe thistle *(Echinops exaltatus).* Very attractive, round, 2- to 3-inch thistlelike flowers. The variety generally available is 'Taplow Blue', which has showy blue flowers. Bright green leaves are silver underneath. Plants grow 3–4 feet tall. Use in borders as midbed or background plants. Plants grow best in full sun, but will also do well in part shade. Plant in any ordinary garden soil that is well drained.

Globeflower *(Trollius).* These showy, buttercuplike, 2- to 3-inch flowers come in shades of yellow, orange, or white. Ideal perennial plants to grow in moist, shady parts of the garden. This perennial should not be confused with the invasive buttercup weed, as *Trollius* has a compact, nonspreading, bushy growth habit. Plants of popular varieties grow 2–3 feet high. Plant in moist but not continually wet soils.

Gloriosa daisy. See black-eyed susan.

Goatsbeard *(Aruncus dioicus).* Tiny white plume flowers stand out above the soft, deeply divided green leaves. The tall 4- to 4½-foot plants are excellent as background plants in borders, or use them as summer screening plants. Plant in sun or part sun, in ordinary garden soil.

Grasses. See Chapter 10, Ornamental Grasses.

Heartleaf bergenia *(B. cordifolia).* Some new varieties have been added to this old-time favorite perennial. Probably the best new addition is 'Bressingham Ruby', with bright red flowers and leaves that turn reddish bronze in fall. 'Bressingham White' has white flowers and bronze leaves in winter. Flower spikes open in April and May on both plants. Ideal in rock gardens, borders, or mixed plantings. Plants grow 12–15 inches high. Plants do well where they are protected from hot midday sun. Plant in ordinary, well-drained garden soil.

Hellebore (*Helleborus* varieties). These late-winter and early-spring flowering perennials are ideal to use in the semi-shady areas of the garden. New introductions come with single or double flowers in a wide array of colors and color combinations. The 1- to 2½-inch flowers come in various shades of pink, purple, soft green, cream, and white. This is another must in our garden because of the showy flowers and early blooming period. Plants range in size from 12 to 36 inches high. Established plants do not like to be moved. Plant in organic-rich garden soil.

Hosta (*Hosta,* hybrids and spp.). For the shade garden, this is the number-one perennial. They are primarily grown for their magnificent leaf shapes, sizes, textures, and striking foliage colors. One grower in the Northwest features more than 1,000 varieties. Leaf colors vary in all shades of green, greenish yellow, cream, white, and countless bicolors. One of the new ones even has red stems. Some have fragrant flowers. Protect them from slugs. Because of the various plant sizes (6–36 inches high and often 3 feet wide), they can effectively be planted in many places. Use the low varieties in borders or as edging plants, the intermediate varieties in borders or as midbed plants, and the taller varieties as background plants. They are excellent companion plants with rhododendrons, azaleas, and camellias. Plant them in full or part shade in moist, organic-rich, well-drained garden soil.

Iceland poppy *(Papaver nudicaule).* There are many new strains with 3- to 4-inch, paperlike, fragrant flowers in shades of orange, salmon, gold, yellow, pink, or white. Fuzzy base leaves are bluish green. Plants grow 12–18 inches high. Plants do not transplant well, so select a permanent place for them. Plant them in borders, groups, or mass plantings. One of the prettiest plantings I have seen of Iceland poppies was at Lake Louise in the Canadian Rockies. There they were planted on a low bank, where they got good drainage and partial sun. In my garden they grow in ordinary garden soil.

Irish moss *(Sagina subulata).* Forms a dense, mossylike carpet only 1–2 inches high; ideal to use as a low ground cover. See also Chapter 12, Ground Covers.

Scotch moss (*S. s.* 'Aurea'). See Chapter 12, Ground Covers.

Jacob's ladder *(Polemonium caeruleum).* Clusters of 1-inch, blue, fragrant, spike flowers. The attractive foliage is soft and fine textured, almost like some ferns. Very showy in the semi-shade. We have the new variety 'Brise d'Anjou', which has elegant, creamy-white and green variegated leaves. Myrna loves to dry and press the leaves. It has violet flowers. Plants grow 24–36 inches high. Plant in part shade in moist, well-drained soil.

Japanese anemone. See anemone.

Japanese iris *(Iris kaempferi).* Gorgeous flat iris flowers up to 6–8 inches across. It likes a moist, boggy type soil and is often used near ponds or in Japanese landscapes by water features. Showy June and July flowers stand up on stems above the graceful, swordlike, bright green leaves. Flowers range in shades of blue, lavender, purple, pink, and white. Plants are 3–6 feet high when in bloom. Plant in acid, organic-rich, moist soil. Plants prefer full sun to partial sun and shade.

Lamb's ear *(Stachys byzantina).* See Chapter 14, Herbs.

Lavender *(Lavandula* species). See Chapter 14, Herbs.

Lavender cotton *(Santolina chameacyparissus).* See Chapter 14, Herbs.

Lavender mist (*Thalictrum* sp.). Commonly called meadow rue. Delicate, fluffy flowers stand out above attractive leaves that somewhat resemble those of the maidenhair fern. Plants grow 3–4 feet high. *T. aquilegifolium* has lavender flowers in May and June. The variety *T. delavayi* 'Hewitt's Double' has double white flowers from July to September. They are attractive plants to use in borders as midbed or background perennials. Plant them in full or part sun in moist, organic-rich soil.

Left: Primroses provide gorgeous spring color and will often flower again in the fall.

Below: These *Primula* varieties are hardy enough to thrive in this Juneau, Alaska, garden.

Leopard's bane *(Doronicum cordatum).* Bright yellow spring flowers. The bright green leaves and yellow daisy flowers look great with the spring-flowering bulbs, azaleas, and rhododendrons. 'Little Leo' grows about 12 inches high and 'Magnificum' grows up to 24 inches high. Plant them in part shade, in moist, fertile, well-drained garden soil.

Ligularia (several spp.). Very showy summer-flowering plants. The large 12-inch leaves of *L. dentata* have a purplish tint, which really shows off the 3-foot stalks of orange-yellow flowers. When in bloom, the overall height of this plant ranges from 4 to 6 feet. Use them in borders, in midbed, or as background plants. This is an excellent plant for partial to full shade spots. Plant in moist, organic-rich garden soil.

Lithodora *(Lithospermum diffusum).* One of the best bright-blue flowering perennials. Often used as a ground-cover plant because of its low 6- to 12-inch growth habit. We used it as a ground cover around our rosebushes with great success. Plants may spread 2 feet or more. If they become leggy, just shear lightly, as they do not like severe pruning. Plant in full or part sun, in rich, well-drained soil.

Lobelia. For perennial varieties, see cardinal flower. See also Chapter 13, Annuals.

Lungwort *(Pulmonaria saccharata).* Variegated leaves and pink, blue, or white flowers combine to make this a nice early spring-flowering perennial. Showy green leaves are spotted silver, making a nice background for the pink flower buds, which turn blue as they open. Ideal border plants, or they can be used as ground-cover plants in small areas. Plants grow 10–15 inches high. Plant in part or full shade in moist, organic-rich, well-drained soil.

Mallow *(Malva).* This is the perennial type. (*Lavatera* is the annual mallow; see Chapter 13, Annuals). We have an unnamed pink variety that is absolutely beautiful. The pink 2- to 3-inch saucer-shaped flowers cover the plant from early summer to frost. Ours is now about 6 feet tall, even after rather severe winter pruning. Named varieties range in shades of pink, lavender, and magenta to white. Most varieties grow about 2–4 feet high. Plant in full sun, in warm, rich, well-drained soil.

Marsh marigold *(Caltha palustris).* Bright yellow 1-inch single or double spring flowers stand out above the round, dark glossy green leaves. Plants grow about 12–15 inches high. As the name implies, it likes a moist marsh or soggy soil in which to grow. Plant in either sun or shade, as long as the area is wet.

Meadow rue. See lavender mist.

Michaelmas daisy *(Aster novae-belgii).* One of the best fall-flowering perennials. Hundreds of named varieties that range in height from 1–5 feet. Dwarf, intermediate, and tall-growing varieties too. Most bloom during the months of August, September, and October. Small clusters of 1- to 1½-inch, daisylike flowers cover the plants in shades of blue, lavender, purple, pink, rose, or white. These are a must in our fall garden. Easy to grow in ordinary garden soil.

Moss saxifrage *(Saxifraga decipiens).* This ground-hugging plant is quite showy during its midspring flowering time. Flowers stand on short stems about 4–8 inches above the foliage. Flower colors include pink, red, or white. The green, scalloped foliage stands only 2–4 inches tall. This plant is ideal to use along the edge of borders or in rock gardens. If the plants die out in the center, it's time to dig and divide them. Grows best when placed in a spot protected from hot sun, so filtered sun or part shade are best. Plant in moist, well-drained soil.

Mother of thyme *(Thymus serpyllum).* See creeping thyme in Chapter 12, Ground Covers.

Mum. See garden mum.

New England aster *(Aster novae-angliae).* Somewhat similar to the Michaelmas daisies. They are native to many parts of the Northeast and central United States. Plants grow 3–6 feet high. Flowers range in shades of pink, deep rose, purple, and blue to white. Daisylike 2-inch flowers cover the plants from late summer into the fall. Ideal plants to use in fall landscape borders as midbed or background plants. Plant in fertile garden soil. Adaptable to well-drained or even moist soils. Plants grow and flower best in full sun or part sun and shade.

Obedience plant *(Physostegia virginiana).* The kids love this one; just move the individual flowers and they stay put. Stalks of 1-inch funnel-shaped pink or white flowers rise above the green pointed leaves. Ideal plant for a perennial border in midbed or background plantings. Plants tend to spread, so you need to keep them in check by dividing every two or three years. Plants grow 2–3 feet high. The best spot for them is in full to part sun, in rich, moist, well-drained soil.

Oriental poppy *(Papaver orientale).* Beautiful, large, 4- to 6-inch poppy flowers are a delight in any garden. Large green or gray leaves make an excellent background for the spectacular flowers. Plants grow 1½–3 feet high. Flowers range in shades of scarlet, pink, salmon, or white, most with dark centers. Use them among other plants, so as the foliage dies back in summer, the nearby plants will cover the brown leaves. Plant in full or part sun, in most ordinary, well-drained garden soils.

Ornamental grasses. See Chapter 10, Ornamental Grasses.

Painted daisy *(Tanacetum coccineum, Pyrethrum roseum,* or *Chrysanthemum coccineum).* This old-time perennial is often overlooked. Single or double 2- to 2½-inch daisylike flowers stand above the attractive fernlike foliage. Excellent cut flower. Use in borders or midbed plantings. Two-foot-tall plants are effective individually or in groups. They flower in June and July. Plant in full sun, in fertile, moist, well-drained soil.

Pansy. See viola/pansy.

Pasque flower *(Anemone pulsatilla)*. Fluffy seedheads follow single cup-shaped spring flowers. Flowers 2–3 inches come in shades of pink, violet, purple, or white. The seedheads are almost as attractive as the flowers. Plants grow 6–12 inches high and are ideal to use in foreground plantings or rock gardens. Lacy leaves are covered with hairs, giving them a green-gray cast. Plant in full sun or partial shade, in ordinary, well-drained garden soil.

Penstemon *(P.* x *gloxinioides)*. Commonly called beard tongue. These garden varieties provide color all summer if spent flowers are picked. Showy spikes of tubular 1- to 2-inch flowers are available in practically every color of the rainbow except yellow and blue, many with white centers. Most grow 2–3 feet high. Use in borders, midbed plantings, in groups, or individually. We love them in our garden because they provide nice cut flowers all summer long. Plant in full sun or part shade. Plants grow in fertile soil that is well drained.

Peony *(Paeonia lactiflora)*. An old-time favorite in any perennial garden. The single- and double-flowering bush varieties come in a wide range of colors from pink through rose, red, deep almost brownish reds, and white, some with pleasant fragrances. Most of the bush varieties only grow 30–36 inches high. Tree peonies (4–7 feet) come in shades of pink, red, yellow, and white. Best time to divide or plant peonies is during the spring or autumn, when the plants are dormant. Nursery-grown plants in containers can be planted at any time. The best-known peonies are doubles, semi-doubles, Japanese form, anemone form, and the singles. Plant peonies 1–2 inches deep in well drained, fertile soil. Peonies flower best when grown in full sun, although they will tolerate part sun and shade. If planted too deeply, they will grow, but will not flower.

Persian cornflower. See cornflower.

Pincushion flower *(Scabiosa caucasica* and *S. columbaria)*. A great plant for attracting bees and butterflies. If you keep the dead flowers picked, these plants will flower from late spring to frost. Two varieties in our garden are 'Butterfly Blue' and 'Pink Mist'. Both grow 15–18 inches high. Flowers are 1–2 inches (pincushion-like) in blue and pink as the names imply. Plant in full sun, in most any fertile, well-drained garden soil.

Pink *(Dianthus)*. See carnation/double pink.

Plantain lily. See hosta.

Primrose (*Primula,* various species). A wonderful plant for the shade, semi-shade, or filtered sun garden. There are hundreds of species, hybrids, and named varieties. Along with hostas, they are one of my favorite shade plants. Some species grow 6 inches or less, while others grow up to 3 feet, so they have a wide range of uses, from edging plants to background plants. Most make excellent container plants, especially when mixed with other spring-flowering or foliage plants. The

English primrose (*Primula polyantha;* 8–12 inches high) plants are the most popular. They flower on individual stems. Juliana hybrids (*P. juliae;* 3–5 inches high) are most often used in borders. *P. auricula* (6–9 inches high) has broad, coarse leaves and clusters of flowers. *P. denticulata* (12–15 inches high) has unusual ball-shaped clusters of flowers. In recent years, the double-flowering varieties have also gained in popularity. All like moist, organic-rich, well drained soil.

Rockcress *(Arabis caucasica).* Showy spring-flowering rock-garden plants. White or pink 4-to 6-inch flowering varieties. 'Variegata' has green leaves with white edges. An ideal plant for the rock garden, because the plants will naturally cascade down over rocks. Can also be used as perennial ground-cover plants. 'Spring Charm' is an upright-growing 6-inch form with rosy purple flowers. Plant in sun to part sun and shade in ordinary, well-drained garden soil.

Rockrose. See sunrose/rockrose.

Russian sage *(Perovskia atriplicifolia).* Bright blue flowers and fine gray leaves combine to make this a very attractive late-summer to early-autumn favorite. Plants grow 3½–4 feet and flower from late July to September. Excellent to use in borders as midbed to background plants. Shear to 6–10 inches in late fall. Plant in ordinary, well-drained garden soil.

Sage, flowering (*Salvia,* several species). 'Silver Mound', 'Silver King', 'Dusty Miller', 'Icterina', 'Purple', 'Tricolor', and many others are very attractive perennial plants. They are generally grown as herbs, but many varieties are also attractive garden plants. Some are selected for their flowers, others for their attractive foliage. We like to use the *S. officinalis* 'Tricolor' and 'Icterina' varieties because of their foliage color, mixed with other plants in containers on the patio. Bees, butterflies, and hummingbirds love these plants. Most thrive on a certain amount of neglect. Plant in a bright sunny spot, in ordinary, well-drained garden soil.

Flowering sage *(Salvia nemorosa).* These are some of the best blue, violet, purple, rose, and white summer-flowering perennials. *S. n.* 'Purple Rain', 'May Night', and 'Rose Queen' are great flowering varieties. 'May Night' with its deep indigo flowers was the 1997 Perennial Plant of the Year. We have several in our garden, and if you keep the spent flowers picked, they will bloom most of the summer. Mine thrive on neglect. Attractive flowers are on spikes about 12–24 inches high and attract bees, butterflies, and hummingbirds. Excellent cut flowers. Plant in sunny locations, in soil that is well drained.

Scotch moss. See Irish moss *(Sagina subulata).* See also Chapter 12, Ground Covers.

Sea thrift *(Armeria maritima).* Showy low-growing plants ideal to use in rock gardens, as foreground plants in borders, or in seaside gardens. The 6- to 10-inch plants have grasslike foliage, often grayish green, and in April to July are covered with pink, rosy red, or white flowers. Keep the spent flowers picked and they will flower for a longer time. This plant thrives on a certain amount of neglect. Plant in full sun, in any ordinary garden soil.

Sedums and succulents. I group the genus *Sedum* (also called stonecrop) together with succulents in general because they have the same cultural requirements. The low-growing varieties, some with contrasting leaf color, can be used as ground covers, in rock gardens, or as container plants. The succulent varieties of Hens and Chickens *(Sempervivum tectorum)* can be used in the same way. The taller-growing varieties are ideal to use in borders, or individually for spot color in the garden. The taller-growing 18- to 24-inch variety *Sedum telephium* 'Autumn Joy' provides a spectacular floral display in August and September (see autumn joy). Plants grow in full sun, in well-drained, ordinary garden soil.

Shasta daisy *(Leucanthemum maximum* or *Chrysanthemum superbum).* White-flowering perennials from May to October. Popular cut flowers and showy garden plants. 'Alaska' (2–3 feet) is the most popular large single-flowering variety. 'Esther Read' (2–3 feet) is probably the most popular fully double flowering variety. 'Marconi' (24–30 inch) is a popular variety with semi-double frilled flower petals. 'Little Princess' grows bushy and only 12–16 inches high. Use the taller varieties as midbed plants in borders. The semi-dwarf and dwarf varieties are attractive near the edge of borders. Taller varieties may need staking. Keep spent flowers picked to keep the plant flowering. Plant in mostly sunny spots, in fertile, well drained garden soil.

Silver brocade *(Artemisia stellerana).* See artemisia.

Speedwell/spike speedwell (*Veronica* species). Many varieties that range in height from 8 to 36 inches. Most are in shades of blue, lavender, rose-red, and white. Taller ones are excellent for cutting. Plant low ones in rock gardens or at the edge of landscape borders. Tall ones can be used effectively in midbed plantings. Grow in full to part sun. Plant in ordinary, well-drained garden soil.

Spike gayfeather. See gayfeather.

Stokes aster *(Stokesia laevis).* One of the most overlooked garden perennials. The blossoms are somewhat like an aster, but larger and showier. The July to September flowers come in soft blue, rosy purple, and lavender. Plants grow 12–18 inches high. Great cut flowers. We stake ours for protection from wind and rain. Plant in midbed borders. Place in full sun, in moist, well-drained garden soil. Plants will not tolerate wet feet.

Stonecrop. See sedums and succulents.

Sunrose/rockrose *(Helianthemum nummularium).* Nice plants for the rock garden, borders, or as a ground cover. Most grow 6–12 inches high with a mounded growth habit. They cascade over rocks, become compact and bushy when planted on the level. Flower colors range in shades of light pink, salmon, orange, and red.

Round 1-inch flowers are single or double. Cut back after flowering to encourage additional bloom and to keep the plants looking nice. Plant in full sun, in ordinary, well-drained soil.

Sweet william *(Dianthus barbatus)*. Actually a biennial, but often reseeds itself. The spicy, fragrant flower clusters are showy in the garden and make excellent cut flowers. Dwarf and standard varieties range in height from 8 to 18 inches. Plants come in a wide range of colors and color combinations from pink, rose, red, crimson, and white. Pick spent flowers to keep plants blooming longer. Great plants to use in landscape borders. Plant in full sun or partial shade, in moist, fertile, well-drained soil.

Swiss chard 'Bright Lights'. Actually a vegetable, this one is a very attractive fall and winter garden plant too! What's so outstanding about this plant are the colorful leaves and stems. The 12- to 15-inch leaves range in shades of green through reddish purple. The stems and ribs are yellow, gold, orange, pink, red, and white. A great plant for use in fall containers, borders, or groups. Plant in full or part sun, in fertile garden soil.

Thrift. See sea thrift *(Armeria)*.

Below: Low-growing creeping phlox is a great spring-flowering perennial to use in rockeries.

Thyme (*Thymus* spp.). Creeping thyme (see Chapter 12, Ground Covers) is the one most frequently used in the landscape. However woolly thyme, lemon thyme, and common thyme *(T. vulgaris)* are also often used. (For the latter, see Chapter 14, Herbs.) Thyme is often grown in containers, in the herb garden, or in borders. Small leaves are scented and flowers attract bees. Shear lightly if plants get leggy. Plant in sun or part shade, in well-drained, ordinary garden soil.

Lemon thyme *(T.* x *citriodorus).* Very attractive, lemon-scented, variegated yellow and green foliage. Plants grow 6–8 inches high. July and August flowers are pale lavender.

Mother of thyme *(T. serpyllum).* Often used between stepping stones, at the base of rock gardens, or wherever a low ground cover is needed. See Chapter 12, Ground Covers.

Silver thyme *(T.* x *citriodorus).* This one has an upright habit of growth, 8–12 inches high. Leaves are silvery, with pale lavender flowers in July and August.

Woolly thyme *(T. pseudolanuginosus).* Has bright silvery gray foliage, pinkish-white flowers, and a dense, matlike growth. The plants grow about 4–6 inches high and spread up to 24 inches wide. Plant in full sun, in ordinary, well-drained soil.

Tickseed *(Coreopsis grandiflora).* This species has attractive single or double 2- to 3-inch flowers. Although the 12- to 24-inch plants are sturdy, in our garden the plants tend to lose their shape, so we stake them. Flowers range in shades of pink, bright yellow, and golden yellow, and some have red center markings. Cut off spent flowers to keep plants blooming longer. Plant in full or part sun, in fertile, well-drained soil.

Veronica. See speedwell/spike speedwell.

Viola/pansy. Violas tend to have a very bushy, compact growth and are prolific flowering. Keep the spent flowers picked and they will flower all season. They range in shades of blue through purple, yellow, apricot, orange, red, and white. Plant them in an area where they are protected from the hot midday sun, in moist, fertile, well-drained soil. One of the most popular new varieties is 'Etain'. The showy cream-colored flowers are edged in lavender, with a yellow center. Flowers have a slight fragrance.

Winter pansy *(Viola hiemalis).* Today many different varieties and species of pansies are grown as "winter pansies." Growers tell me it is a matter of timing. Many species started in early to mid summer will flower during the winter months, and are referred to as "winter pansies." Most flower whenever winter temperature are moderate, stop flowering during cold snaps, and rebloom when weather warms again. This species produces small to medium-sized flowers. Plants grow 6 to 10 inches high. Plant in enriched garden soil, spacing the plants about 6 to 8 inches apart. These winter plants grow and flower best in part sun and shade.

Wormwood *(Artemisia stellerana).* See artemisia. See also Chapter 14, Herbs.

Yarrow *(Achillea millefolium).* Many new beautiful varieties have been developed in recent years. Rather flat flower clusters come in shades of pink, red, lavender, salmon, yellow, and creamy white. The stems tend to be a little weak, but can be wired and used as cut flowers or used as dried flowers. Plants grow 24–36 inches high. They are ideal to use in borders in midbed plantings. The plants in our garden thrive on neglect, as long as they get some water during the warmer summer months. Plant them in ordinary, well-drained garden soil.

10 ❊ Ornamental Grasses

Ornamental grasses add a pleasing, soft texture that blends nicely with evergreens, perennials, and annuals. Then as a bonus, the slightest wind wisps the grass blades, creating movement in the garden and often providing a pleasant rustling sound. Some varieties have contrasting colors in their grass blades, which adds yet another dimension when they are included in the landscape.

Facing page: Ornamental grasses add color, interest, and texture to the landscape.

GRASSES

Choosing a Location

Easy to grow, these grasses are very versatile garden plants, because there are types and varieties that grow in varying planting locations, under wet or dry conditions. Ornamental grasses are wonderful accent plants, useful in containers or group plantings; some of the low-growing varieties can be effectively used as ground-cover plants.

Most varieties require minimal care in the landscape, which also makes them very useful in areas where low maintenance is a must. Ornamental grasses have gained a great amount of interest in recent years because of their drought tolerance. Although we think of grasses as being a plant for the bright sun, there are a few varieties that actually prefer a shady, protected garden spot. Be certain to read the plant identification label, so you choose the right variety for the place you're going to plant.

Below: The bright, red-and-green blades of Japanese blood grass provide a striking accent in the garden.

Using Grasses in the Landscape

Grasses can be used very effectively both individually and in groups. The size of one's garden will determine how best to use them. In large expanses, groupings of three, five, or more plants, all of the same variety, will create a pleasing effect. In a small garden, a single clump may be all that is needed to provide a pleasant contrast of texture or color in a landscape border.

Buying Grasses

Grasses are so popular in today's landscape that most garden outlets carry them in 4-inch pots, and in 1- and 2-gallon containers. Of course, the larger plants will fill in faster, but the smaller plants can certainly be used, especially if one is on a limited budget. Choose healthy plants, with good color and a bushy growth habit.

Planting Ornamental Grasses

Prepare and plant ornamental grasses the same as you would any shrub or perennial.

When to Plant

The plants that you buy at garden stores will be in containers, so they can be planted into the garden any time of the year, providing the soil is not frozen. Established plants can be transplanted during the fall, winter, or earliest spring months.

Prepare the Soil

Mix in peat moss and organic humus with the existing soil. Provide good drainage, except for those few varieties that thrive in moist or wet soils.

Dividing Grass Plants

When your plants develop into oversize clumps and have outgrown their planting location, simply dig, divide, and replant. The best time to do this is in the autumn as the grasses begin to go dormant. Dividing at that time gives the new divisions a chance to reestablished new roots over winter. However, it can also be done in early spring.

Shearing Ornamental Grasses

As mentioned above, ornamental grasses are low-maintenance plants, but should they begin to look a little ragged or out of sorts, shear them back just before the new growth starts in springtime. In other words, if they need shearing, the months of February, March, or early April are the ideal time to cut them back. Cut them back severely, to about 2 to 4 inches above ground level. They can also be cut in the fall, but be careful or you are apt to cut off the showy grass plumes or seedheads that develop on some varieties.

Feeding Ornamental Grasses

I must admit, I have mixed feelings about the following recommendation. Most growers and specialists recommend that grasses be fertilized frequently, several times, much like you would your lawn. But we have one planting of five different grasses and over the past four years I have never fertilized them—and they look great. I am convinced that if you prepare the soil properly and give them the water they need, they are not heavy feeders. In fact, my recommendation is to feed them only when they show any signs of poor color or stunted growth.

Choosing Grasses

Needless to say, there are countless varieties of ornamental grasses, many of which may be superior to the ones I highlight here. There have been so many new introductions, and many old ones are again coming to the forefront, due in great part to their textures, growing habits, color, interest, and drought tolerance. The ones I feature here are varieties that I have had experience growing in our garden or have seen used in other home landscapes. If you intend to use ornamental grasses in your garden, take a good look at what's new and now available.

> The cut plumes of many ornamental grass varieties dry easily and are excellent for winter arrangements. To dry the grasses for arranging, my wife, Myrna, simply cuts the plumes before they go to seed and stands them up in a vase that does not contain water. Or just hang the plumes upside down in a cool, well-ventilated place to dry.

Invasive Grasses to Avoid

There are a few varieties of grasses that have no bounds and just take off in every direction, so you may want to avoid using them in many parts of the landscape. I made the mistake of purchasing one of the variegated ribbon grasses and it did just that. What a mistake! It grew into the lawn and into the roots of adjoining plants and was just impossible to eliminate. It got so bad, I moved! Well, it was almost that bad! It is important to read the label and know that you are purchasing a variety that is nonspreading and will remain in a clump.

By Size

Ground Covers

If you're looking for a low-maintenance ground cover with fine leaf texture, ornamental grasses may be just the answer for you. Ease of care, a certain amount of drought tolerance, and attractive foliage combine to make these four grasses worth considering as ground covers in small areas:

blue fescue, *Festuca ovina glauca* "Elijah Blue'
silver grass, *Miscanthus sinensis*
variegated moor grass, *Molinia caerulea* 'Variegata'
variegated velvet grass, *Holcus mollis* 'Albovariegatus'

Low-Growing (Less Than 3 Feet)

The lower-growing varieties of ornamental grasses are ideal to use in border plantings, in groups, or individually for spot color in the landscape. Here are six varieties that I am familiar with, and would include or have included in my own garden:

blue oat grass, *Helictotrichon sempervirens*
dwarf fountain grass, *Pennisetum alopecuroides* 'Hameln'
fountain grass ('Little Bunny'), *Pennisetum alopecuroides* 'Little Bunny'
golden Japanese forest grass, *Hakonechloa macra* 'Aureola'
ivory feathers, *Cortaderia selloana* 'Pumila'
Japanese blood grass, *Imperata cylindrica* 'Rubra'

Medium-Growing

Here's four varieties of ornamental grasses that will grow up to 3 feet or more. These are ideal to use in midborders, in groups, or individually in the garden:

dwarf maiden grass, *Miscanthus sinensis* 'Yakushima'
Japanese silver grass, *Miscanthus sinensis* 'Variegatus'
porcupine grass, *Miscanthus sinensis* 'Strictus'
purple fountain grass, *Pennisetum setaceum* 'Rubrum'

Tall-Growing

Looking for tall-growing grasses that will provide privacy? Here are six varieties that will grow more than 5 feet tall. These are also excellent varieties to use as background foliage in flower and shrub beds. In large areas, these plants can be used in groups or even in a row for privacy, or use them individually for spot color and interest:

fountain grass, *Pennisetum alopecuroides*
maiden grass, *Miscanthus sinensis* 'Gracillimus'
pampas grass, *Cortaderia selloana*
ravenna grass, *Erianthus ravennae*

variegated Japanese silver grass, *Miscanthus sinensis* 'Variegatus'
zebra grass, *Miscanthus sinensis* 'Zebrinus'

For Specific Sites

In Containers

If you're looking for an accent plant in a container, consider one of the attractive, fine-textured ornamental grasses. These four varieties are my favorites to use in large containers:

blue fescue, *Festuca ovina glauca* 'Elijah Blue'
pampas grass, *Cortaderia selloana* 'Ivory Feathers'
purple fountain grass, *Pennisetum setaceum* 'Rubrum'
ribbon grass, *Phalaris arundinacea* 'Fersey's Form'

In Shade

These four ornamental grasses do not do well in full shade, but will tolerate a somewhat shady location in the garden. In fact, they prefer a bit of protection from the hot midday sun:

golden foxtail grass, *Alopecurus pratensis* 'Aureus'
Japanese forest grass, *Hakonechloa macra*
ribbon grass, *Phalaris arundinacea* 'Fersey's Form'
tufted hair grass, *Deschampsia caespitosa vivipara*

In Wet Areas

Rushes, reeds, and sedges, with their grasslike foliage, are the plants we usually think of for wet areas. However, there are a few grasses that will tolerate soil that is quite moist. Here are four varieties that I have found will take moist but not continually wet soils:

northern sea oats, *Chasmanthium latifolium*
ribbon grass, *Phalaris arundinacea picta*
variegated manna grass, *Glyceria maxim* 'Variegata'
variegated moor grass, *Molinia caerulea* 'Variegata'

In Dry Soil

Almost every garden has one spot where the soil is quite dry or a spot that is difficult to reach with the garden hose. Here are four of my favorite grasses that will tolerate soil that tends to be dry at times:

blue fescue, *Festuca ovina glauca* 'Elijah Blue'
fountain grass, *Pennisetum alopecuroides* and species
maiden grass, *Miscanthus sinensis* 'Gracillimus'
zebra grass, *Miscanthus sinensis* 'Zebrinus'

Ornamental Grasses Encyclopedia

Bamboo grass. See northern sea oats.

Blue fescue *(Festuca ovina glauca* 'Elijah Blue'). A really nice, low, bushy, icy-blue 6- to 10-inch-high clump-type evergreen grass. The late-summer plumes are whitish. Spreads about 12 inches. Makes a very attractive ground cover where low, bright foliage color is needed. Plant in full or part sun, in ordinary, well-drained garden soil.

Blue oat grass *(Helictotrichon sempervirens).* Showy silvery-blue grass blades are about 1–2 feet high, with 2- to 3-foot pale blue plumes that become straw colored. A good variety to use in mid-shrub borders or wherever silver blue foliage is desired. Plant in full sun, in well-drained, average garden soil.

Dwarf pampas grass. See ivory feathers.

Fountain grass (*Pennisetum alopecuroides* and species). Plant in full or part sun in well-drained garden soil.

Dwarf fountain grass (*P. a.* 'Hameln'). This ornamental, low-growing grass has green grass blades and white 2- to 3-foot plumes. Ideal to use in borders or large rockeries.

Fountain grass ('Little Bunny') (*P. a.* 'Little Bunny'). Here is a neat little dwarf grass that forms a 10- to 12-inch mound. Showy white plumes mature creamy tan and stand just above the grass blades. It is a deciduous variety. Nice to use in borders, containers, or rock gardens.

Purple fountain grass (*P. setaceum* 'Rubrum') grows about 2–4 feet high with very showy rose-red-tipped flowering spikes. It's a great plant to use in mid to background landscape borders.

Golden foxtail grass (*Alopecurus pratensis* 'Aureus'). This is an attractive, low-growing, variegated, bright yellow-green grass. I have one in the shade and the grass blades are almost chartreuse. Mine does not form plumes, but if they did, I would cut them off to enjoy the foliage. These perennial grasses will die back in a severe winter. Plant in part shade, in moist, well-drained garden soil.

Golden Japanese forest grass. See Japanese forest grass.

Ivory feathers. See pampas grass.

Japanese blood grass (*Imperata cylindrica* 'Rubra'). A very popular variety with red grass blades. It grows slowly by underground shoots. Ours only grows about 12 inches high, but is supposed to get about twice that height. Best in full sun, but will take a little shade. It dies back during the winter. Plant in full or part sun, in ordinary, well-drained soil.

Left and below: There are countless ways to use ornamental grasses in the garden, singly or in groups: as accents, ground covers, or in the background; in containers or borders.

Japanese forest grass *(Hakonechloa macra).* Grows 1–3 feet high with all-green grass blades. Spreads slowly by underground shoots. Not nearly as popular as the variegated varieties. Arching habit of growth. Use in midborder plantings. Plant in sun or partial shade, in organic-enriched, well-drained garden soil.

Golden Japanese forest grass (*H. m.* 'Aureola'). A nice, colorful, bushy, 12- to 18-inch-high plant. The foliage is variegated bright yellow with green lines extending the length of the grass blades. It spreads slowly by underground runners. Excellent ground cover or accent plant for a shady spot in the landscape. Mine often gets streaks of pink to reddish in some of the blades. Plant in shade, in well-drained, organic-enriched garden soil.

Japanese silver grass. See silver grass.

Maiden grass. See silver grass.

Northern sea oats *(Chasmanthium latifolium).* This one gets its name from the silvery-green flowering stems that look like clusters of oats. Foliage appears somewhat like bamboo; common name is bamboo grass. Clumps 18–24 inches with flowering stems 2–4 feet or more. Straw-colored stems can be dried and used in winter arrangements. Plant in partial shade, in moist, well drained, organic-enriched garden soil.

Pampas grass *(Cortaderia selloana).* This is the common pampas grass that grows about 6–10 feet high. The grass blades are gray-green with an arching growth habit. Large, fluffy, white plumes in autumn stand 3–4 feet above the foliage. Pampas grass thrives on a certain amount of neglect. If grass blades become yellow and unattractive, cut to the ground in the autumn. Plant in well-drained, ordinary garden soil.

Ivory feathers (*C. s.* 'Pumila'). This is a very showy, low-growing 3-foot grass variety with large grass plumes up to 6 feet high. It is often called the dwarf pampas grass. The foliage on ours remains evergreen. Thrives on a certain amount of neglect. Plant in full sun, in well-drained, ordinary garden soil.

Porcupine grass. See silver grass.

Purple fountain grass. See fountain grass.

Ravenna grass *(Erianthus ravennae).* Highly rated, this variety grows 8–10 feet high, with autumn plumes standing about 2 feet above the foliage. It is said that the plumes take on brown tones mixed with orange and purple tones. Plant in well-drained, ordinary garden soil.

Ribbon grass (*Phalaris arundinacea* 'Fersey's Form'). Ribbon grasses are known for their aggressive growth, but the low varieties like 'Fersey's Form' are not as aggressive. Nevertheless, I would put a barrier around the area in which you want to confine their growth. We have this variety in our garden and so far it has

Left: The light colors and interesting shapes of variegated grasses combine nicely with other garden plants. *Below:* Here the icy-blue color and tidy shape of blue fescue provide a striking accent to a landscape planting.

maintained a clump growth habit. We're keeping our fingers crossed. Late in the season, some of the green and white variegated blades take on a pinkish tinge. The 1½- to 2-foot plants tend to fall over if planted in too much shade. Plant in full sun, in well-drained, ordinary garden soil.

P. a. picta. This is a very aggressive type of green and white variegated grass. It needs to be confined or it will wander quickly. The foliage (2–3 feet) is really pretty, so you might want to use it in a container planting. Believe me, I made the mistake of planting it in a raised bed without a barrier. It ended up in the roots of surrounding plants and even in the lawn. You have no idea how difficult it was to finally get rid of it. Plant (if you dare) in well-drained, ordinary garden soil.

Silver grass *(Miscanthus sinensis).* Grass blades are about 1 inch wide, with a showy creamy-white stripe. Plants have a nice graceful, vase-shaped growth habit. Fall plumes are silvery-white. Clumps are about 5 feet tall.

Japanese silver grass (*M. s.* 'Variegatus'). Also called variegated Japanese silver grass or just silver grass. Wide 1-inch green grass blades have a creamy-white stripe, providing an attractive foliage color. Vase-shaped plants to 5 feet high. Plumes in fall are whitish. Plant in full sun or partial shade, in well-drained, ordinary garden soil.

Maiden grass (*M. s.* 'Gracillimus'). This tall-growing, 6- to 8-foot grass has silvery-green foliage. Blades turn golden bronze in fall. Plumes are silvery-white. Use toward the back of landscape borders or as a seasonal privacy screen. Plant in full sun or partial shade, in well-drained, ordinary garden soil.

Maiden grass (dwarf) (*M. s.* 'Yakushima'). This is the dwarf 3- to 4-foot form of the standard silvery-green maiden grass. It grows about half the size, with silvery-white plumes in the fall. Plants often gain a bit of golden yellow autumn leaf color. Plant is full or partial shade, in well-drained, ordinary garden soil.

Porcupine grass (*M. s.* 'Strictus'). This grass has an interesting 1-inch stripe of cream yellow down each grass blade. These leaf markings are said to look like a porcupine's quill. Plants stand 4–5 feet and are quite upright. Autumn plumes are creamy brown, 5–6 feet tall, with a medium width. I cut mine to the ground last year, and it looks great this season. Plant in full or part sun, in ordinary, well-drained soil.

Zebra grass (*M. s.* 'Zebrinus'). Stripes of pale yellow add a pleasant contrast to the green grass blades. Our plants are 6–8 feet high with silvery-white plumes that stand 3–4 feet above the foliage. Tall enough to use as a privacy screen, hedge, or specimen plant. Plant in full or part sun, in ordinary, well-drained soil.

Tufted hair grass *(Deschampsia caespitosa vivipara).* Evergreen, mounded, 3-foot-high clumps of dark green grass. The tufted, silvery flowers are 10–12 inches long, gracefully nodding in the slightest breeze. Plant in full or part sun, in ordinary, well-drained soil.

Variegated Japanese silver grass. See silver grass.

Variegated manna grass (*Glyceria maxim* 'Variegata'). New grass blades are striped white, cream, and green with a pink tinge, and the blades will often regain some of the pink tint in the fall. Grows 3–4 feet in wet locations. Plant in wet/moist soil, in organic-rich soil.

Variegated moor grass (*Molinia caerulea* 'Variegata'). Low-growing, 12- to 18-inch variety with green and creamy-white variegated blades. Summer, creamy-white flower spikes stand 6–12 inches above the attractive foliage. Grows well in moist to wet areas. Plant in organic-rich soil.

Variegated velvet grass (*Holcus mollis* 'Albovariegatus'). Leaves broadly edged white with a narrow green center stripe. Low-growing 6- to 9-inch plants are used in borders. Small seedheads move with a light breeze. Plant in full or part sun, in ordinary garden soil.

Zebra grass. See silver grass.

Below: The striking red color of Japanese blood grass makes it a popular ornamental planting. Though best in full sun, it can tolerate a little shade.

11 • Bulbs

A bonus in any garden are bright, cheery, spring-, summer-, and autumn-flowering bulbs. Easy to plant and grow, bulbs can be a never-ending source of garden color, year after year. But how do you keep bulbs growing and flowering every year with a minimum of care? It's easy, and here are a few very common-sense ideas that no one ever tells you!

Planting Location

Some bulbs need sun, others shade, so it's important that you select the right type of bulbs for each exposure in the garden. For example, tuberous begonias are definite shade plants, while canna tubers must be planted in a sunny spot. On the other hand, many of the spring, summer, and fall bulbs will tolerate part sun and shade. So select the right exposure for whichever bulb you are planting, then be certain to provide proper drainage in the planting area.

Facing page: The unusual flowers of fritillaria crown imperial make a bold, eye-catching statement in the garden.

Above: Begonias are wonderful garden plants. Tuberous types flourish in shady areas; fibrous types are showy in sunny areas.

Buying Bulbs

Check each bulb to be certain that it is firm. Soft bulbs often indicate the early stages of disease or rot. Likewise, look for mold, and if you find a grayish powdery substance on the bulbs, avoid buying them. On some bulbs, like begonia tubers, you want to look for small new growth buds. Some folks think all bulbs have to be clean, but that's not true, as locally grown bulbs sometimes have a light dusting of soil on them. And, if you find are confused about the quality of any bulbs, ask for an honest opinion from the certified nursery person on staff.

Planting Bulbs

This is the critical time in the life of bulbs, because it is the only time you can get nutrients and organic humus directly into the root zone of your favorite bulbs. Take a few minutes to properly prepare the soil; you will be rewarded many times over with nice foliage and beautiful flowers.

When to Plant Bulbs

Spring-Flowering

Plant tulips, daffodils, crocus, hyacinths, etc., in the autumn during the months of September through early November. If you don't get them planted by November, you should still plant them in soil. (The best storage area for bulbs is in the ground.)

Summer-Flowering

Plant gladiolus, dahlias, lilies, begonias, etc., outdoors after all danger of frost has past. In most regions of the West, this is in late March, April, or earliest May.

Fall-Flowering

Most are planted in spring or early summer. The late-summer-flowering autumn crocus can be planted as late as August. The late-fall hardy cyclamen is usually container grown and can even be planted when it is in bloom. (The bulbs are often sold in the early autumn.)

We are often told that it is necessary to dig our dahlia tubers each autumn, store them over winter, and replant them in the spring. Not me! I think that's hogwash! Plant them in well-drained soil, mulch them in the fall and leave the tubers in the ground. Yes, you should dig them every three or four years, divide the tubers, and replant. But don't be a slave to your dahlias! At the same time, if you have soil that has poor drainage you may still need to dig your dahlias every year, or, better yet, plant them in a raised bed.

Dig the Planting Hole

I have an easy method for planting bulbs. Use a shovel to dig a round planting hole 12 to 18 inches in diameter. In that planting hole, place 12 to 18 bulbs. Be certain they do not touch each other, so there is no chance of disease spreading from one bulb to another. I suggest that the bulbs be all of the same color and variety. Then when they come up and flower, it's like a big bouquet, and if you want to cut a few as cut flowers, it doesn't ruin the display in the garden. Using this method, you should be able to plant about 50 to 100 bulbs in fifteen to twenty minutes or less. Believe me, it works great, looks fabulous, and is so easy to do. Most folks plant bulbs in a row, and they look so formal and not natural at all. They look like little soldiers in the garden.

Prepare the Soil for Planting

Prepare the soil 9 to 12 inches in depth. In the bottom of the planting hole, mix generous quantities of peat moss, compost (if available), and the correct amount of bulb fertilizer. It is that simple. Then, of course, plant the bulbs at the correct planting depth.

Set the Bulbs at the Proper Depth

As a general rule, bulbs should be planted three times deeper than the greatest diameter of the bulb. In recent years, the Dutch have said the planting depth should be two times the head of the bulb. Let me explain what these two terms mean: the *diameter* means the width of the bulb, side to side; the *head* means from the bottom of the bulb to the top. If a bulb is 1 inch across, plant it 3 inches deep. If it is 1½ inches high, plant it 3 inches deep.

There are exceptions to this rule. For example, tubers of tuberous begonias are set barely below the surface of the soil.

How to Start Tubers of Begonias

One of the easiest ways to start tuberous begonias is to fill a box, tray, or flat with peat moss or a seed-starting mix of soil. Scoop out a tablespoon of the mix and simply place the tuber in the hole that remains. The room temperature should be about 65 to 70 degrees Fahrenheit for starting tubers. Once the sprouts begin to develop and the new growth is 2 to 3 inches tall, replant the tubers into pots or hanging baskets. Begin feeding them immediately with a weak solution of liquid fertilizer, applying it to the soil, not directly onto the leaves. (Use the fertilizer at half strength.) By starting early, the plants should be ready to bloom when it is time to set them outdoors, after all danger of frost is over.

How to Divide Bulbs

The first question should always be, "Do the bulbs need to be divided or transplanted?" Most bulbs can remain in the ground for three to seven years without the need for dividing. If you dig and divide them each year, you are only creating extra work for yourself. Of course, there are always exceptions, such as the tender cannas or dahlias, which most home gardeners dig and store indoors over winter. Why not divide them? It's easy and only takes a couple more minutes to divide them after they are dug. Here are guidelines for the best time to dig and divide most common types of bulbs:

Right: The fragrance and beauy of the lily 'Stargazer' make it a must for every garden.
Below: Autumn crocus *(Colchicum)* bring a touch of spring to the fall garden.

Spring-Flowering

This group includes tulips, hyacinths, daffodils, and crocus. Divide them in the summer after the leaves have been cut back or have died back.

Summer-Flowering

This group includes gladiolus, dahlias, lilies, and cannas. Separate or divide these in the autumn after they finish flowering or begin to go dormant. I dig and divide my lilies about once every four to six years.

Autumn-Flowering

This group includes autumn crocus, hardy cyclamen, and crocosmia. These are easiest to divide in the spring. Mark their location in the garden so that you can find them when it is time to divide or transplant.

Bearded Iris

Divide them in early summer right after their normal flowering period. Cut back the top foliage to about 6 to 10 inches. I cut mine in the shape of a tepee. This cutting makes them easier to move, with less transplanting shock. We divide ours about every four to six years.

Feeding Bulbs

Bulbs need yearly feeding. That's right; can you imagine how much energy it takes for bulbs to produce foliage, stem, and those magnificent flowers? If they're given help, with proper nutrients provided at the right time of the year, they will flower beautifully for many years.

Here's my suggestion, given to me by a commercial bulb grower more than forty years ago, and it works. He said when the foliage of bulbs, particularly tulips, hyacinths, and daffodils (it works on all the others too) is about 2 to 4 inches high, in late winter or earliest spring, feed the foliage with a liquid fertilizer. Pour or spray fertilizer right onto the leaves. Use the recommended solution (following label directions) of liquid fertilizers such as Miracle-Gro, Rapid-Gro, fish fertilizer, or whatever type of liquid plant food you have around the house. By applying the fertilizer to the leaves, it carries it back (the direct route) to the bulb, building strength in the bulb for next year's flowers.

Then fertilize again as the bulb's flowers begin to fade. Again, use a liquid food. I recommend that you use one with a formula of 0-10-10 for this feeding (see Chapter 16, Composting and Fertilizing).

Improper Feeding of Bulbs

Don't waste your time fertilizing bulbs at the wrong time of the year. Most specialists and fertilizer companies recommend feeding the bulbs in the fall. That's fine if you are planting new bulbs and mix the fertilizer into the planting hole as you plant. But to put it on the soil of existing plantings is a waste of time and money. Tulips, daffodils, hyacinths, and crocus already have next year's flower in the bulb by autumn, so feeding is of little or no value for the next spring. Plus applying fertilizer on the soil surface in the fall isn't necessary, simply because not much of it soaks deep enough to get down to the root system, and even if it did, it is at the wrong time of the year.

Cutting Back Foliage on Bulbs

One of the most frequent questions I am asked is, "When can I cut back the leaves of my tulips, daffodils, or hyacinths?" Research done in Holland has determined that twenty-one days after flowering, the leaves and stems of tulips and daffodils can be safely cut to the ground. Apparently, after the twenty-one days no further nutrients pass from the leaves to the bulbs. As of the writing of this book, they have not determined how many days to wait before removing the leaves of the other species of bulbs.

Most of us still wait for the leaves of the other bulb species to die back naturally, then remove that ugly brown foliage. That waiting period is usually six to eight weeks. Some people tie up or braid the leaves as they die back, but that's not recommended; they should die back naturally.

Wintering Begonias

The large flowering tuberous begonias are easy to winter. Frost will ruin the tubers, so they must be brought indoors before any chance of frost. Enjoy the last of the flowers, then simply set them on a shelf or warm floor and neglect them. The stems will die back and at that point the tubers can be removed from the soil and stored in vermiculite or dry peat moss. Then in early March, they can be started again.

Left: Tuberous begonias are one of the best shade-loving summer-flowering bulbs.

Below: Tulips and other spring bulbs combine well with spring-flowering perennials.

Forcing Bulbs

Forcing bulbs for indoor color in the winter is one way to brighten things up in your home. They will take two to three months from planting, depending upon exposure and temperatures. When the bulbs are through flowering, plant them outdoors in the garden. Do not try to force them again the following year, because they will be worn out and not suitable for forcing again.

In Water

Hyacinths can be forced into bloom in a hyacinth glass or a glass filled with water. (A hyacinth glass has a cup at the top that holds the bulb, so it is not necessary to use toothpicks.) This is a great project for kids, because when the hyacinth comes into flower, the beauty and fragrance of the bulb draw attention, thus recognition. Plus it is a great lesson, because the children see all parts of plant life: the roots, bulb, stem, leaves, and flower. Here's how to do it:

- Simply fill a drinking glass with water up to 1 inch from the top.
- Place four toothpicks in a hyacinth bulb, one into each side. Stick them into the bulb approximately 1 inch from the bottom of the bulb.
- Next, rest the four toothpicks (bulb sitting upright) on the top of the drinking glass. The bottom of the bulb should be just above water level. It's that easy.

In Water and Gravel

Crocus, narcissus, colchicum, and hyacinths can easily be forced in this manner. Simply fill a saucer, bowl, or any waterproof container with gravel. (White or colored gravel looks better than just plain gravel.) Next, firm the bulbs into the gravel. Only about ¼ to ½ inch will actually settle into the gravel. Then as the final step, pour water into the gravel up to just below the base of the bulbs. When using water, the bulbs should not come into direct contact with the water.

In Soil

All bulbs that can be forced may be started in soil. Of course, it goes without saying, the bulbs need to be watered throughout all stages of growth except during the time they are outside, where rain should be sufficient. Here's the easiest process:

Plant in a Container

Using a 6-inch pot (clay or plastic) fill it three-fourths full of a store-purchased potting mix. Place the bulbs upright in the mix and cover with additional soil. A 6-inch pot will hold about three to five average-size tulips, hyacinths, or narcissus, twelve crocuses, but only one amaryllis.

Heel in Outdoors

Bulbs in soil need a dark period to develop roots. Take the container outside and either bury it in the ground or simply cover pot and all with bark or sawdust. If you live in an apartment, put the pots in a cool storage room. Cover them with newspaper, but water weekly. Leave them covered for eight to ten weeks.

Keep Cool Indoors

After the resting cycle, bring the bulbs indoors and keep them in a cool, bright room where the temperatures range between 50 and 60 degrees Fahrenheit. (Avoid 70-degree temperatures, which would cause long, leggy, unsightly foliage growth.) At this point, the new growth showing above the soil may be white or yellow. Do not worry; this is the result of no light having reached the new growth, and it will turn green in a few days of exposure to light.

Warm Up to Bloom Indoors

Once the flower buds begin to develop, the pots can be brought into the warmer rooms of the house. Enjoy, enjoy!

Choosing Bulbs

I will not attempt to mention my favorite varieties of bulbs. There are so many new ones being introduced that any mention here would be outdated even before this book is published. In fact, today as I write this chapter, I came across ten brand-new, exciting varieties being offered by just one firm. The best way to choose varieties is to actually go to a garden center and select them by the pictures on the displays. Needless to say, below are only a few of my favorites. Check with your local garden center or favorite bulb catalog for other top-notch choices.

By Particular Features

For Forcing

For forcing bulbs for indoor color, try these:

autumn crocus, *Colchicum*

crocus, all species
cyclamen, all species
Dutch amaryllis, *Hippeastrum*
dwarf beardless iris, *Iris reticulata*
glory-of-the-snow, *Chionodoxa*
hyacinth, *Hyacinthus,* all species
narcissus, 'Tete-a-Tete' and the form called paper-whites
shamrock, *Oxalis acetosella*
snowdrops (*Galanthus* spp.)
tulip, *Tulipa* (double early and single early)

For Cut Flowers in Spring

corn lily, *Ixia*
harlequin flower, *Sparaxis*
hyacinth, *Hyacinthus* spp.
narcissus
tulip, *Tulipa* varieties

> Dig one big hole and plant a lot of bulbs. That's right, if you dig a 1- or 2-foot-wide hole, you can plant up to eighteen bulbs of tulips, daffodils, hyacinths, or gladiolus. However, in that same size hole you would only want to plant about three lilies or one or two dahlias.

For Cut Flowers in Summer

calla lily, *Zantedeschia* spp.
dahlia, many varieties
flowering onion, *Allium* spp.
gladiolus, many species
iris, several species
lily, *Lilium* hybrids

Spring Bulbs for Naturalizing

When you want to create a natural look in the garden, a few bulbs poking up here and there, or in drifts, will give the appearance of them growing naturally. Here are a few of the types that are best suited for naturalizing:

anemone, *Anemone blanda*
grape hyacinth, *Muscari* spp.
narcissus
snowdrop, *Galanthus* spp.
wake robin, *Trillium ovatum*

Summer Bulbs for Naturalizing

lily, *Lilium* species
shamrock, *Oxalis acetosella*

For Shady Areas

Spring-Flowering

dog-tooth violet, *Erythronium dens-canis*

narcissus
snowdrop, *Galanthus* spp.
wake robin, *Trillium ovatum*
winter aconite, *Eranthis hyemalis*

Summer-Flowering
lily, *Lilium* hybrids
tuberous begonia

Fall-Flowering
hardy cyclamen

By Size

For Edging/Borders in Spring
anemone, *Anemone blanda*
dog-tooth violet, *Erythronium dens-canis*
Dutch crocus, *Crocus vernus*
ranunculus, *R. asiatica*
snowdrop, *Galanthus* spp.

For Edging/Borders in Summer
dahlia, dwarf varieties

For Edging/Borders in Fall
hardy cyclamen

Taller-Growing Background Spring Bulbs
daffodils
fritillaria
iris species (spring and summer)
tulips

Taller-Growing Background Summer Bulbs
canna varieties
dahlia varieties
flowering onion, *Allium* spp.
gladiolus species
lily, *Lilium* hybrids

Bulbs Encyclopedia

❶ planting depth
❷ flowering time
❸ height
❹ remarks

Allium. See flowering onion (*Allium* spp.).

Amaryllis *(Hippeastrum hybrida).* ❶ Only about one-half of the bulb is covered with soil in the pot. ❷ Flowering time varies by planting time, but usually occurs between mid December and early February. ❸ Height usually ranges from 2 to 3 feet. ❹ Usually two or more large, trumpet-shaped flowers form at the top of each stalk. It is not unusual for the bulbs to produce four flowers per stalk and sometimes more than one flowering stalk. Each flower may reach 6–8 inches across. One of the showiest of all bulbs for forcing. Bulbs are usually potted in the fall and bloom during early to late winter. If started in September, they often flower by Christmas time. The biggest problem one experiences with these bulbs is trying to get them to bloom the next year. However, it's easy; it is simply a matter of feeding them every two weeks during the growing and flowering season. The bulbs use up so much strength in producing the blossoms and foliage that it must be replenished, and the only way to do this is by feeding them.

Anemone. ❶ 3–4 inches. ❷ Late winter or late spring. ❸ 5–12 inches. ❹ Two types are particularly popular.

Anemone blanda. The early-flowering one, with daisylike flowers, about 5 inches tall. It comes in shades of blue, pink, rose, and white. It is ideal for naturalizing or for spot color in semi-shady locations.

A. coronaria. The larger-flowering one, which grows up to 10 inches or more. The newer hybrid varieties have attractive flowers up to 3–4 inches across. The flowers are single, in shades of red, blue, purple, or white, often with centers of a contrasting color.

Autumn crocus *(Colchicum).* ❶ 3–4 inches. ❷ Early fall. ❸ 5–8 inches. ❹ Here's one that flowers in the autumn and looks like a spring-flowering crocus. The 4- to 8-inch flowers come in shades of pink, lavender, violet, lilac, and white. Some varieties have single flowers, others are double. They produce bold, foot-high foliage in the spring, which dies back in early summer; then the flowers appear in late summer and early autumn on leafless stems. The best time to plant or transplant the corms is right before or immediately after they have flowered. The only drawback about autumn crocus is that the foliage is unattractive when it dies back, so plant the bulbs among other plants to hide the unattractive dying

Left: I call the fritillaria crown imperial lily a conversation piece. Its unusual shape draws attention immediately. *Below:* I recommend planting tulips and other bulbs in groups of 3, 6, 9, or 12, using the same color.

leaves. Let the plants develop into clusters for best effect in the garden. In August, corms can also be forced in pots for indoor color. Plant in full sun or part sun and shade. Plant the corms in rich, well-drained soil.

Avalanche lily. See dog-tooth violet *(Erythronium dens-canis).*

Begonia (tuberous types). See also fibrous types of begonias in Chapter 13, Annuals. ❶ ½–1 inch. ❷ All summer to frost. ❸ 12–18 inches or more. ❹ Extremely popular summer-flowering tuber for a shady spot in the garden. Bold leaves with double and/or single flowers up to 6 inches across. New strain 'Non-stop' begonias are very popular. They often form a tuber as they grow. Generally grown in containers, so they are easy to move and care for. There are both upright and trailing varieties. The trailing type is most often used in hanging baskets. They are not hardy, so must be brought indoors before the first frost in fall. Feed monthly during the summer. Start tubers in pots indoors in February, but do not set outdoors until all danger of frost has passed. A few new varieties are fragrant. Pot in well-drained soil mixed with peat moss. Plant tuber at slight angle so water does not gather in the concave top portion of the tuber, otherwise it could cause rotting.

Calla lily (*Zantedeschia* sp.). ❶ 4–6 inches. ❷ Early spring to early summer. ❸ 18–48 inches. ❹ Several new outstanding varieties. The combination of variegated (spotted) leaves, large or small flowers, and ease of growing make these popular bulbs (rhizomes). Flowers range in shades of yellow, bronze, pink, and white. Plant in semi-sunny areas. Ideal for spot color or borders.

Canna. ❶ 3–4 inches. ❷ Early to late summer. ❸ 1½–6 feet. ❹ Once again becoming popular because of many new showy varieties. My favorite is a new one, 'Tropicanna', with beautiful variegated green, cream, and orange leaves and attractive orange flowers. Cannas come in shades of red, pink, coral, yellow, apricot, and white. There are both dwarf and standard-growing varieties. These colorful rhizomes are ideal for borders, for spot color, or as background plants (the taller varieties are excellent for this last). Plant them in full sun for best flowering. Do not plant them outdoors until after all danger of frost has passed and the soil has warmed up. Plant in sandy, well-drained soil.

Chionodoxa. See glory-of-the-snow.

Colchicum. See autumn crocus.

Corn lily *(Ixia).* ❶ 4–5 inches. ❷ Late spring to early summer. ❸ 18–24 inches. ❹ Many hybrid varieties are available in a wide range of colors. Flowers appear in clusters, reminding one of miniature glads. Some are fragrant; all are long lasting in the garden or as cut flowers. Usually sold in mixed shades of cream, yellow, pink, red, and orange. Mulch for winter protection. Must be planted in full sun, in well-drained soil.

Crocus. This is one of the first bulbs to flower at the beginning of the year. The small-flowering species crocus is the first, usually appearing in January, followed in February by the larger-flowering common Dutch crocus.

Dutch crocus *(C. vernus).* ❶ 3–4 inches. ❷ Late February–April. ❸ 3–4 inches. ❹ Larger flowering, these crocus are ideal for borders, edging, spot color, or in small groups. Colors include white, yellow, purple, or striped.

Species crocus *(C. speciosus).* ❶ 2–4 inches. ❷ January-February. ❸ 1–3 inches. ❹ In my book, these are a must for low planting areas, like a rockery or in border plantings. They come in some really unusual colors, including orange, pink, and baby blue, plus the typical white, purple, and yellow.

Cyclamen. See hardy cyclamen.

Daffodil. See narcissus.

Dahlia (many varieties). ❶ 6–8 inches. ❷ All summer into the fall. ❸ 6 inches to 6–8 feet or more. ❹ One of the most dependable, continually summer-flowering tubers. There is a variety for practically any planting spot in the sunny garden, from low-growing, small-flowering varieties to ones that have flowers as large as a dinner plate. Single or double flowers range in practically every color of the rainbow. There are several distinctive flower types, including ball, cactus-flowering, collarette, formal decorative, informal, miniature, pom-pom, peony, and others. I think dahlias deserve a place in every garden. They also make excellent cut flowers. Use the low ones for borders, the midsized ones are excellent massed or used for midbed planting, and the taller ones are ideal to use in background plantings. The more you pick the flowers, the more they bloom! In cold climates, the tubers can be potted up indoors in late winter then set outdoors after all danger of frost is over. Plant new tubers outdoors in late March or April. Slugs love the new tender sprouts, so be certain to provide protection from the slugs. One way is to remove the bottom of a coffee can and place it over the new growth. This method keeps the slugs away, and the interior of the tin can reflects the heat from the sun and the plants will develop quicker. Plant in full sun, in soil that is well-drained.

Dog-tooth violet *(Erythronium).* ❶ 4–5 inches. ❷ Spring flowering. ❸ 4–15 inches. ❹ Several varieties native to the West. Specialty growers list more than twelve varieties. American species are also known as trout lilies or avalanche lilies. Naturalize well or can be used for spot color in the shady garden. Corms grow best in semi- to full shade.

Dutch crocus. See crocus.

Easter lily (*Lilium longiflorum* plus other species). ❶ 3–5 inches. ❷ Summer flowering. ❸ These lilies usually grow about 18–24 inches tall. ❹ Plant in a semi-sunny spot. Easter lilies will flower again in the fall. See also lily.

Eranthis. See winter aconite *(E. hyemalis).*

Erythronium. See dog-tooth violet *(E. dens-canis).*

Flowering onion *(Allium).* ❶ 4–6 inches. ❷ May, June, and later. ❸ 8–36 inches. ❹ Maybe one of the most overlooked bulbs of all. My wife loves these as cut flowers, and dries some of them for winter arrangements. Some flower heads up to 12 inches wide. A huge family with flowers in shades of pink to purple, yellow, and white. I know one grower who lists more than six dozen varieties. Plant in full sun to part sun and shade.

Fritillaria *(Fritillaria imperialis)* ❶ 4–7 inches. ❷ Mid- to late April. ❸ 3–4 feet. ❹ I refer to this spring bulb, also known as fritillaria crown imperial, as a conversation piece in the garden because it has leaves at ground level; then, on the top of the stem, hanging bell-shaped flowers capped off with a tuft of more foliage above. When anyone visits our garden, they are immediately drawn to this unusual-looking plant. The bulb and flowers have an odor that repels deer, squirrels, raccoons, and even moles. The primary flower colors are yellow, orange, or crimson. Plant in full sun in soil that is well drained.

Gladiolus. ❶ 5–6 inches. ❷ Late spring to late summer. ❸ 1½–6 feet or taller. ❹ It's hard to beat the upright, stately flower spikes of the colorful glads. Plant the corms ten weeks before you want them to bloom, then stagger the planting times at two-week intervals and you will have them flowering all season. Very showy in the garden, and top-notch cut flowers. Be sure to check out the Butterfly *(G. primulinus)* and baby *(G. colvillei)* glads. Tall varieties are great for background color, while the baby glads are nice in midbed plantings. They tend to be rather stiff and formal, so I like to plant them in groups of five or six in my garden. I think that eases their formality. Then, if Myrna cuts one or two to use as cut flowers, it doesn't ruin the garden display. Plant in full sun, in soil that is well drained.

Glory-of-the-snow *(Chionodoxa).* ❶ 2–3 inches. ❷ Late winter to early spring. ❸ 5–6 inches. ❹ Often overlooked, this bulb offers attractive early flowers in shades of pink, blue, or white. Up to six to ten blooms per 6-inch stem. Ideal for underplanting with other bulbs, in groups, naturalized, or in containers with other bulbs. Plant in part sun and shade.

Grape hyacinth *(Muscari).* ❶ 2–3 inches. ❷ Late March and early April. ❸ 6–8 inches. ❹ These bright-blue flowering bulbs are terrific when planted near the bright flowering tulips, daffodils, and hyacinths. Often used for edging, in containers, or as a foreground to other bulbs. Naturalize with yellow or white daffodils. Plant in part sun and shade to full sun.

Hardy cyclamen. ❶ ½–1 inch. ❷ Mid-October to November. ❸ 3–6 inches ❹ Attractive flowers are often described as shooting star–like. The foliage, which is often marked in lighter tones, makes an excellent background for the unusual flowers. Flowers range in shades of pink, rose, red, crimson, or white. They grow exceptionally well under trees or in an area where they get some overhead protection. Over several years, the tubers will get large enough to cut and divide. After bloom, mulch lightly with small leaves or pine needles. Plant in rich peat soil that is well drained.

Harlequin flower *(Sparaxis).* ❶ 3–4 inches. ❷ Late spring to early summer. ❸ 6–24 inches. ❹ Very attractive flowers on a stem (like glads) with flower centers of a contrasting color. The species *S. tricolor* is the most popular and showiest. Showy in the garden and they make excellent cut flowers. Ideal for extending the spring-flowering bulb season. Plant in fall, in a sunny spot, where the soil is well drained.

Hyacinth (*Hyacinthus* spp.). ❶ 4–6 inches. ❷ March and April. ❸ 8–10 inches. ❹ The combination of beauty and intense fragrance make these bulbs a must for any spring garden. They have an upright stiff, formal growth habit, making them ideal for borders, formal plantings, or containers. In my garden I like to use them in group plantings, as that takes away their formality. Always plant them near the entry area, driveway, or walkways where foot traffic is heavy, so their fragrance and beauty can be enjoyed the most. Save a few bulbs for forcing indoors, as this is one of the best for that purpose. To save yourself some money, use the smaller bulbs for outdoor planting and the larger ones for forcing. It only makes "cents" because the large bulbs produce large flowers that are more apt to break outdoors during heavy spring rains or strong windstorms.

Iris (several species). ❶ 1–6 inches. ❷ Spring and summer. ❸ 6–48 inches. ❹ Dutch and Spanish iris are grown from bulbs. They are the ones most often used as cut flowers in floral arrangements. Flower colors range primarily in shades of blue, purple, yellow, and white. They flower in late spring and early summer. Plant them 4 to 6 inches deep, in a sunny spot with good drainage.

Bearded iris hybrids. Grown from rhizomes that are planted right at ground level. Miniatures only grow 8 inches high, while the tall bearded may attain a height of up to 48 inches. Flower colors span the color spectrum, with many very attractive bicolor varieties. Plant them in full sun, in rich, well-drained soil.

Dwarf beardless iris *(Iris reticulata).* Another group that merits attention in the garden and is readily available. These are ideal for rockeries, low borders, and spot color in landscape beds. Most grow only 5–8 inches high. In our garden, they bloom in early spring in shades of purple, lavender, blue, and yellow. Plant the rhizomes in the fall.

Japanese iris. Very popular for pond gardening or in marshy soils. The 6- to 9-inch flat flowers on 24-inch stems are quite attractive. June flowers are available in a wide range of colors. Ideal for low moist areas and along streams, pools, and lakes. Divide rhizomes in spring or fall if needed.

Siberian iris. A beardless flower; plants develop into a nice clump in the garden. Flowers are purple, blue, red, or white. Excellent for borders, grouping, or for spot color in the sunny garden. They generally produce several flowers on 2- to 3-foot stems. Divide rhizomes every five to seven years in spring or fall.

Ixia. See corn lily.

Jonquil. See narcissus.

Lily (*Lilium* hybrids). See also calla lily, corn lily, easter lily. ❶ 6–8 inches. ❷ Varies; May to October. ❸ 2–8 feet. ❹ Undoubtedly one of the most beautiful of all bulbs. There are eight divisions, from the early-flowering Asiatic hybrids to the late-flowering species lilies. Among the best known are the Asiatic hybrids (2–5 feet; spring), American hybrids (4–8 feet; early summer), trumpet hybrids (4–6 feet; summer), and Oriental hybrids (2–8 feet; late summer). Hybridization over the past fifty years has resulted in some magnificent new varieties of outstanding beauty, some with tremendous fragrance. If you have space for only one, try 'Stargazer' (Oriental hybrid); its beauty and fragrance are overwhelming. The flowers are beautiful in the garden and will last up to eight to ten days as cut flowers. A must in the Hume garden. I suggest that you plant the bulb on its side, as it has a hole in the middle that is apt to collect water, which could cause rotting of the bulb if the soil is too wet. Lilies like it cool at the base, so place them among other plants. They will grow in full sun to part sun and shade, and I have a few planted in rather deep shade. Plant them in deep, rich, well-drained soil.

Muscari. See grape hyacinth.

Narcissus (daffodils and jonquils). ❶ 4–6 inches. ❷ Late February to April. ❸ 4–24 inches. ❹ These are some of the first of the large-flowering spring bulbs to bloom. The new varieties are unbelievably beautiful, with many new introductions yearly. 'King Alfred' (trumpet daffodil) is the all-time favorite, with its huge bright-yellow flowers. Many new introductions are also really striking, in shades of orange, pink, white, and various shades of cream, yellows, and combinations of colors. Paper-whites (a Tazetta hybrid), 'Tete-a-Tete', and 'Bridal Crown' are among the best varieties for forcing. The dwarf varieties are ideal for borders, rockeries, and container plantings. The taller varieties are ideal for naturalizing, group plantings, midbed plantings, and large containers. Daffodils make excellent, early cut flowers. They will tolerate filtered shade, but grow best in full sun or part sun and shade.

Oxalis. See shamrock *(O. acetosella).*

Ranunculus *(R. asiatica).* ❶ 3–4 inches. ❷ Late spring. ❸ 12–18 inches. ❹ These prolific-flowering bulbs (roots) are a nice addition to the spring garden because they flower after the tulips, daffodils, and other spring bulbs have finished. The large, double, 3- to 5-inch flowers are attractive in the garden or as cut flowers. Some excellent new hybrid strains are now available. Broad range of flower colors

Far left: Anemones bloom in the late spring, bringing vivid color to the garden.

Left: Amaryllis are wonderful bulbs to force for indoor color.

Below: Bishop dahlia provides bright color in the sunny summer garden.

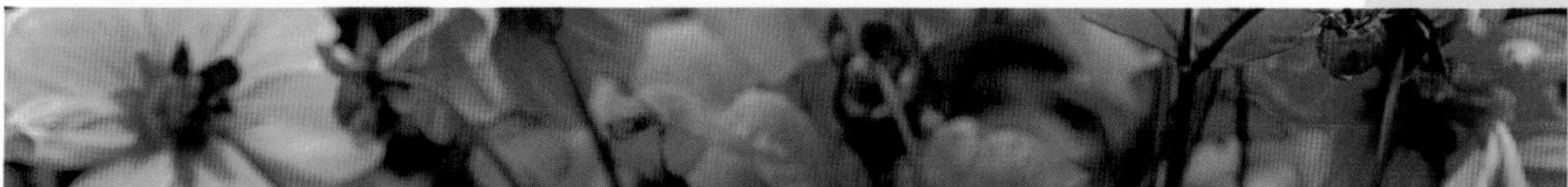

including white, yellow, pink, red, and orange. Plant in fall or late winter. Plant them in full sun or part sun and shade, in well-drained soil.

Shamrock *(Oxalis).* ❶ 1–3 inches. ❷Varies; spring or summer. ❸6–10 inches. ❹These are really prolific-growing and spread rapidly, so should be planted in containers or in a spot where they can grow unchecked. Many varieties make excellent houseplants. Most are white-, pink-, or red- to violet-flowering. Cloverlike leaves and open, five-petal flowers make nice displays inside or outdoors. Sometimes used as deciduous naturalized ground cover. Plant in semi-shady spots.

Snowdrop (*Galanthus* spp.). ❶ 2–4 inches deep. ❷Late winter to early spring. ❸6–12 inches tall. ❹These are a wonderful, early-flowering bulbs, for a moist, shady, naturalized garden spot. There are several varieties, most with single flowers, but one, *G.* 'Flore Pleno', has double flowers. Bulbs can be forced for early winter color indoors.

Sparaxis. See harlequin flower.

Trillium *(T. ovatum).* Also called wake robin. ❶ 2–4 inches. ❷Midspring. ❸12–30 inches. ❹This is a rhizome, not a bulb, but is generally included with bulbs. Attractive three-petal flowers, with showy dark green leaves. Native varieties are white fading with a pink tinge. New introductions vary in shade of purple, pink, maroon, and chartreuse. Ideal for naturalizing; ideal in shade borders or in shrub beds with rhododendrons, camellias, and azaleas. Plant in a shady spot in well-drained soil.

Trout lily. See dog-tooth violet.

Tuberous begonia. See begonia.

Tulip (*Tulipa* varieties). They are undoubtedly one of the most beautiful of all the spring-flowering bulbs. From the low-growing species type to the large Darwin and Cottage varieties, it's hard to beat the beauty of tulips in the spring garden. Because of the varying growing heights, shapes, and forms, there is a type for practically any sunny or partly shady location in the garden. Here are a few of my favorite (types) species:

Bouquet tulips. ❶ 4–6 inches. ❷Mid- to late April. ❸9–20 inches. ❹Each stem has several small flowers, like a little bouquet. These have become extremely popular in recent years, providing a nice garden display and pretty cut flowers. Multiflowered tulips combine well with other tulips, and the lower-growing varieties are ideal in containers. Orange, pink, and red are the most popular colors.

Double flowering. ❶ 4–6 inches. ❷Late March and late April. ❸10–18 inches. ❹Very attractive double flowers that look like miniature peonies. There are two types: the early-flowering in March and the late April–flowering type. There is a broad range of individual flower colors and combinations. The lower-growing varieties are ideal for edging, grouping, or using in containers.

Fringed tulips. ❶ 4–6 inches. ❷ Mid- to late April. ❸ 15–24 inches. ❹ Flower petals are lacy at the tip, hence the name "fringed." These late-flowering bulbs provide a beautiful garden display. Flowers are large and very showy. Many new attractive varieties in a range of colors.

Lily-flowered tulips. ❶ 4–6 inches. ❷ Mid-April. ❸ 15–24 inches. ❹ Attractive flower shape and long lasting in the garden and as cut flowers. Without question one of my favorite types of tulips. Use them in midbed plantings, in groups, or large containers. These are a must in my garden. They have long pointed buds and flowers with petals that curve outward, giving them a distinctive flared appearance. They come in a wide selection of colors.

Other classified tulips. Triumph hybrids, Rembrandt tulips, *T. greigii, T. kaufmanniana,* and *T. fosterana* are some of the other classifications of tulips that merit a place in the spring garden. When you are selecting your bulbs in the fall, take a minute to look over all the possible choices, as each of them has its advantages.

Parrot tulips. ❶ 4–6 inches. ❷ Late April. ❸ 18–20 inches. ❹ Unusual flowers; feathery, ruffled petals that are serrated and slightly curled. Again, this is one of my favorites because the spectacular flowers create a lot of interest. Use them in a high-traffic focal spot.

Single, early, and late. ❶ 4–6 inches. ❷ Late March and mid-April. ❸ 15–24 inches. ❹ These include the popular Cottage and Darwin type tulips. Large-flowering varieties are ideal for midbed planting, massing, and group plantings. Varieties available in practically every color of the rainbow. Popular as cut flowers.

Species tulips. ❶ 4–6 inches. ❷ Early March to late April. ❸ 5–10 inches. ❹ Some have very attractive leaf markings. Flowers are small to medium-size, some with more than one flower. Ideal for rockeries, low borders, or along the edge of spring containers. I like to use a few in a grouping in front of the taller types. Color range is a bit limited compared to the other types of tulips, but reds, yellows, whites, and combination colors are very showy.

Wake robin. See trillium.

Winter aconite *(Eranthis).* ❶ 2–3 inches. ❷ February to early March. ❸ 2–3 inches ❹ Early, bright-yellow 1-inch, buttercup-like flowers. Ideal for rockeries, borders, or at the edge of a container. Prefers a partially shady location. Will tolerate moist but not wet soils.

12 Ground Covers

Want to cut down on the amount of time you spend weeding and maintaining the garden? Ground covers may be just the answer for you. Used properly, ground covers enhance the overall appearance of the garden, help eliminate continual weeding, and reduce the number of annual flowers you use each year.

Facing page: Bearberry 'Victoria Creeper' is a fast-growing evergreen ground cover with attractive fall and winter berries.

Choosing the Location

In this region we are fortunate to be able to grow a wide range of groundcover plants suitable for practically any planting situation: on hillsides, in rockeries, between stepping stones, and in narrow areas. Some varieties are even suitable as grass substitutes in small areas. There are ground covers for just about any planting situation: wet, dry, sun, or shade. Here are a few things you need to consider before choosing a ground cover for any part of the garden:

- What is the size of the area? How many plants will you need?
- What height plants do you need? Do they need to be very low? Do you need to walk on them?
- How much time do you want to devote to maintaining the planting?
- Do you want the plants to flower? Should they have berries? Do you want green or variegated leaves?
- Should the plants have evergreen foliage or is it all right if they are deciduous?

Use Several Ground Covers

You can create a much more attractive landscape by using several different types of ground covers instead of just one. In my garden I use ground covers in groups of three, five, seven, or more. Then I'll plant a grouping of another type of plant in the adjoining area. By doing this, you can create different textures, leaf colors, and varying flowering times.

Below: Bunchberry, the Canadian dogwood, is a colorful deciduous ground cover for use in the shady garden.

Use More Ground Covers to Minimize Maintenance

How much area you devote to ground covers depends upon the time you have to garden and your actual interest in gardening. If you enjoy annual and perennial flowers, roses, and flowering shrubs, you probably will decide to give yourself more open space so you can include more of them in the garden. Conversely, if you don't have a lot of time to spend maintaining the garden, when it comes to using ground covers, I say "the more the merrier!"

Planting Ground Covers

Dig the Planting Hole

Prepare a planting hole twice the width and depth of the root ball of the plant.

Prepare the Soil for Planting

As I emphasize so often, it is very important to prepare the soil properly for planting. Remember that planting time is the only time you can get organic matter and nutrients directly into the root zone. The addition of compost, peat moss, or processed manure with your existing soil is certainly beneficial.

> It's tough to mow grass between stepping stones, so why not use low-growing thyme or sagina moss to fill in those areas? These plants look great, you can walk on them, and they require minimal care. One of our neighbors planted thyme in their parking strip. This is a great alternative to grass because it does not require mowing or much water, and it can be walked on just like a lawn.

Set the Plant at the Proper Depth

Be certain to set the plant at the same depth as it was previously planted.

Use a Triangular Planting Pattern

The plants will grow together faster and look better if they are planted in a triangular pattern. Simply place one plant at each point of a triangle, spacing them according to label directions.

Mulch New Plantings

When you first plant out ground covers, the spacing between plants leaves a considerable amount of open bare ground. Weeds and unwanted grasses can soon encroach into these areas if you do not mulch or apply preemergence weed killers. Mulching looks nice and at the same time helps control unwanted weed and grass growth. An inch or two of bark or sawdust is usually used as mulch.

Fertilizing Ground Covers

When to Feed

The best times to fertilize are in late spring and earliest summer. Avoid late summer feeding, which encourages new growth at a time when you want the plants to begin hardening for winter.

What and How to Feed

Because ground-cover plantings are so dense, it is difficult to apply standard fertilizers to them. The simple answer is to feed them overhead with a liquid fertilizer. Fish fertilizer, Mir-Acid, or similar type liquid fertilizers can be used for this type of feeding. Applying liquid fertilizer is an especially effective way of feeding ground covers as well as plants situated under trees.

Pruning Ground Covers

Late winter, spring, and early summer are the best times to prune ground covers if they need it. Shearing the tops of ground covers is the best method, because this encourages bushiness and a much denser growth habit.

Choosing Ground Covers

Where do you get ideas on which plants to use? It's easy! As you drive through your neighborhood, just observe what other people are using as ground covers and where and how they are using them. You can also get ideas from commercial landscape plantings, which generally use ground covers extensively to cut down on maintenance. In addition, your local park probably has a few. Or you can see which ones your local nursery features—and don't be shy in asking for their recommendations. To make this job even easier, read on for a few of my favorites.

Ground Covers That Can Get Out of Control

Although these make nice ground-cover plants, you must take steps to be certain that they do not take over the garden. Unchecked, these plants can become invasive. Also, watch vines such as honeysuckle and silver lace vine, because they can take off if left unattended. To confine the growth of these species to a designated space, submerge into the soil a 6- to 12-inch plastic or concrete barrier.

bishop's weed, *Aegopodium podagraria*
English ivy, *Hedera helix*
mint, *Mentha,* all species
salal, *Gaultheria shallon*
St. Johnswort, *Hypericum calycinum*
sweet woodruff, *Galium odoratum*

By Size

Low-Growing (Less Than 6 Inches High)

Use low-growing plants near the front of flower and shrub beds. Here are a few that will do a nice job with a minimum amount of care:

bearberry, *Cotoneaster dammeri*
carpet bugle, *Ajuga reptans*
Ceanothus gloriosus
Cotula squalida
creeping phlox, *Phlox subulata*
kinnikinnick, *Arctostaphylos uva-ursi*
myrtle, *Vinca minor*
winter creeper, *Euonymus fortunei radicans*
wintergreen, *Gaultheria procumbens*

Medium-Growing (Less Than 1 Foot High)

In large planting areas or in the middle of flower and shrub beds, a higher-growing ground cover is often more suitable. Here are a few that are fairly easy to maintain in the landscape:

blue fescue, *Festuca glauca*
heather, many genera
Japanese spurge, *Pachysandra terminalis*
lingonberry, *Vaccinium vitis-idaea minus*
mother of thyme, *Thymus serphyllum*
St. Johnswort, *Hypericum calycinum*

Taller (1 Foot or Taller)

In the background of shrub beds, taller-growing ground covers are often used to provide foliage and flower color. Here are a few to consider:

alpine laurel, *Kalmia polifolia*
bog rosemary, *Andromeda polifolia nana*
rockrose, *Cistus corbariensis*
rockspray cotoneaster, *Cotoneaster microphyllus*
rosemary, *Rosmarinus officinalis*
sarcococca, *Sarcococca hookerana humilis*

For Specific Sites

On Hillsides

One of the biggest problems to solve is steep hillsides or areas where soil retention may be a problem. Often these areas are difficult to maintain, so here are a few of the best ground covers to plant in such locations:

Ceanothus gloriosus
English ivy, *Hedera helix* varieties
Euonymus fortunei varieties
heather, many species
Japanese spurge, *Pachysandra terminalis*
juniper, *Juniperus horizontalis,* various varieties
kinnikinnick, *Arctostaphylos uva-ursi*
rockrose, *Cistus corbariensis*
St. Johnswort, *Hypericum calycinum*
Victoria creeper, *Cotoneaster dammeri* 'Victoria Creeper'

In Full Sun

Need a ground cover to grow in a bright, sunny part of the garden? Here are a few of the most dependable ones:

bishop's weed, *Aegopodium podagraria*
blue fescue, *Festuca glauca*
broom, *Genista pilosa* 'Vancouver Gold'
carpet bugle, *Ajuga reptans*

Below: Moss can be a great ground cover in the shady parts of the landscape.

Ceanothus gloriosus
Cotoneaster dammeri, several varieties
English ivy, *Hedera helix,* small leaf varieties particularly
Euonymus fortunei varieties
juniper, *Juniperus horizontalis,* many spreading varieties
kinnikinnick, *Arctostaphylos uva-ursi*
myrtle, *Vinca minor*
rosemary, *Rosmarinus officinalis* varieties

In Shade

Believe it or not, there are plenty of ground covers to choose from for shady areas in the garden. Here are a few of my suggestions for ground covers that thrive in the shade:

bishop's weed, *Aegopodium podograria*
blue star creeper, *Pratia pedunculata*
bunchberry, *Cornus canadensis*
carpet bugle, *Ajuga reptans*
Japanese spurge, *Pachysandra terminalis*
lingonberry, *Vaccinium vitis-idaea minus*
myrtle, *Vinca minor*
sarcococca, *S. hookerana humilis*
St. Johnswort, *Hypericum calycinum*
sweet woodruff, *Galium odoratum*
wintergreen, *Gaultheria procumbens*

In Part Sun and Shade

Trees, buildings, fences, and other structures often create portions within the garden that are partly sunny and partly shady, so here are some low-growing ground covers that will do well in such locations:

bearberry, *Cotoneaster dammeri,* several spreading varieties
bog rosemary, *Andromeda polifolia nana*
English ivy, *Hedera helix* and varieties
kinnikinnick, *Arctostaphylos uva-ursi*
myrtle, *Vinca minor* or *V. major*
Rubus pentalobus
salal, *Gaultheria shallon*
winter creeper, *Euonymus fortunei radicans*

In Areas You Can Walk On

How often do we have a small spot in the garden where we need a very low-growing plant? Maybe it's a narrow area to the water spigot, a small area between stepping stones, or a spot between the base of the rockery and the sidewalk. Wondering what to plant in the cracks between stepping stones or in place of a small lawn? Here are some low-growing ground covers that will tolerate limited foot traffic:

- baby's tears, *Soleirolia soleirolii*
- blue star creeper, *Pratia pedunculata*
- Corsican mint, *Mentha requienii*
- creeping thyme, *Thymus serphyllum* (pink, lavender, or white)
- Irish moss, *Sagina subulata*
- Scotch moss, *Sagina subulata* 'Aurea'
- white star creeper, *Pratia angulata*

In Wet Soil

Spots where the soil does not drain well, remaining moist or even wet for extended periods of time, can be a problem in the garden. These ground covers will do well with moderate amounts of wet feet:

- alpine laurel, *Kalmia polifolia*
- blue star creeper, *Pratia pedunculata*
- bog rosemary, *Andromeda polifolia nana*
- cranberry, *Vaccinium macrocarpon*
- dwarf bamboo, *Sasa ramosa,* several varieties
- pennyroyal, *Mentha pulegium*

In Rather Dry Soils (and Can Thrive on Some Neglect)

Practically every garden has one spot that is hard to reach, so it doesn't get the watering, feeding, or general care that the rest of the garden gets. In such spots, these are the ground covers that seem to thrive:

- broom, *Genista pilosa* 'Vancouver Gold'
- cinquefoil, *Potentilla,* several evergreen varieties
- kinnikinnick, *Arctostaphylos uva-ursi*
- lavender cotton, *Santolina chamaecyparissus*
- rockrose, *Cistus corbariensis*
- rosemary, *Rosmarinus officinalis*
- St. Johnswort, *Hypericum calycinum*
- stonecrop, *Sedum,* several varieties

Under Trees

In this region, with all the beautiful evergreen and deciduous trees, many landscapes end up with those difficult-to-maintain areas under trees. The trees are so big and dominant that they grab all the moisture and nutrients before the plants underneath get any. It takes special plants to be able to survive under those conditions. Here are a few I have in my garden that seem to do the job exceptionally well:

English ivy, *Hedera helix*
Rubus pentalobus
salal, *Gaultheria shallon*
St. Johnswort, *Hypericum calycinum*

Over Walls and Rockeries

Do you have an ugly wall, unattractive old rockery, or similar spot that you want to cover? These cascading ground covers are ideal to help hide or soften unattractive areas. Plant them at the top of the area and let their cascading growth cover. Here are just six of my favorites:

creeping jenny, *Lysimachia nummularia*
English ivy, *Hedera helix*
myrtle, *Vinca minor*
thyme, *Thymus* spp.
Victoria creeper, *Cotoneaster dammeri* 'Victoria Creeper'
winter creeper, *Euonymus fortunei radicans*

By Particular Features

With Interesting Leaf Color

There's no reason not to include some showy leaf colors in your ground-cover plantings. Here are a few of my favorites:

Algerian ivy, *Hedera canariensis*
bishop's weed, *Aegopodium podagraria*
blue fescue, *Festuca glauca*
Euonymus fortunei, variegated varieties
myrtle, *Vinca minor,* variegated varieties
ribbon grass, *Ophiopogon planiscapus* 'Nigrescens'

With Showy Flowers

Want to add a little color to your ground-cover plantings? Here are some outstanding plants that have showy flowers. By selection of varieties, you can have something in bloom all twelve months of the year:

yellow—broom, *Genista pilosa* 'Vancouver Gold'; St. Johnswort, *Hypericum calycinum*

pink—rose daphne, *Daphne cneorum;* bog rosemary, *Andromeda polifolia nana* 'Grandiflora'

lavender/purple—alpine laurel, *Kalmia polifolia*

purple—carpet bugle, *Ajuga reptans* 'Tricolor'

blue—*Ceanothus gloriosus; Lithodora;* myrtle, *Vinca* spp.; rosemary, *Rosmarinus officinalis*

several colors—heather; creeping phlox, *P. stolonifera*

With Fragrant Flowers

Another important element in creating an interesting garden is the use of plants that have fragrance. These are six of my favorite fragrant ground-cover plants:

Corsican mint (foliage), *Mentha requienii*
creeping thyme, *Thymus serphyllum*
lavender, *Lavandula* varieties
rose daphne, *Daphne cneorum*
sarcococca, *S. hookerana humilis*
sweet woodruff (leaves), *Galium odoratum*
wintergreen (berries), *Gaultheria procumbens*

Native Plants to Use as Ground Covers

Sometimes we get our greatest ideas on how to use plants by just observing what grows naturally in our surroundings. That's certainly the case with low-growing native ground covers of this region. They thrive on natural rainfall and the care Mother Nature gives them, so in our gardens, they should do well in low-maintenance areas. Here are four that I think merit a spot in most gardens:

bunchberry, *Cornus canadensis*
dwarf Oregon grape, *Mahonia nervosa*
kinnikinnick, *Arctostaphylos uva-ursi*
salal, *Gaultheria shallon*

With Berries

Plants that flower and then produce berries add additional interest to the landscape. As an added bonus, the berried plants often attract birds. Here are four of my favorite evergreen ground covers that have attractive berries:

bearberry, *Cotoneaster dammeri* 'Lowfast'
cranberry, *Vaccinium macrocarpon*
kinnikinnick, *Arctostaphylos uva-ursi*
lingonberry, *Vaccinium vitis-idaea*

Ground Covers Encyclopedia

Ajuga. See carpet bugle *(A. reptans).*

Alpine laurel *(Kalmia polifolia).* The first time I saw this plant was in the peat bogs just south of Vancouver, B.C., and was really impressed with the growth habit and summer rosy-lavender flowers. It is a Northwest native plant. The small flowers are in clusters and look nice along with the small, dark green leaves. Small ground cover–type plants only grow about 1 foot high and almost as wide. Plant in part shade or filtered sun, in organic-enriched, well-drained garden soil.

Andromeda. See bog rosemary *(A. polifolia nana).*

Baby's tears *(Soleirolia soleirolii).* This low-growing 2- to 4-inch perennial is a great ground cover at the base of ferns and other shade-loving plants. It is tender, but can survive limited walking-on. Plants might turn black if severe cold weather touches the foliage, but they usually rebound quickly. Plant in the shade in moist, fertile soil.

Bearberry *(Cotoneaster dammeri).* This is an excellent low-growing evergreen with clusters of spring flowers and fall and winter red berries. In my opinion, the varieties of 'Lowfast' and 'Victoria Creeper' (see below) are two of the best. Low-growing, 10- to 12-inch-high branches may grow up to 6–9 feet, rooting along the way. Plant them in full sun or partial shade, in organic-rich, well-drained soil.

Rockspray cotoneaster *(C. microphyllus).* Small, dark gray-green leaves on 2- to 3-foot plants. Spreads to 6 feet. Berries are rose-red. Shear to keep lower.

Victoria creeper (*C. d.* 'Victoria Creeper'). One of the best. We have a planting at our home that does a super job of retaining soil on a slight slope and hangs over some rocks at the base of the slope. 'Lowfast' has the same growth habit.

Bishop's weed *(Aegopodium podagraria).* Robust, invasive plant that needs to be confined. Variegated green and white leaves. Grows 6–8 inches high. Spreads by underground roots. Likes part to full shade. Grows in ordinary, well-drained soil.

Blue fescue (*Festuca ovina glauca* 'Elijah Blue'). A really nice, low, icy-blue, clump-type evergreen grass. See also Chapter 10, Ornamental Grasses.

Blue star creeper *(Pratia pedunculata).* This is one of those low-growing perennials that is often planted between stepping stones. The tiny, blue, star-shaped spring flowers stand just above the 1-inch foliage. This plant is often used as a ground cover and will tolerate limited walking-on. We have it growing in part sun and shade, but it will tolerate full sun in the cool Northwest garden. Plant in rich, well-drained soil.

Left: Blue-flowering carpet bugle provides brilliant spring color.

Below: Woolly thyme is one of the best and most versatile low-growing ground covers.

Right: Yellow-flowering creeping jenny is a showy ground cover for shade.

Below: It took only three plants of bearberry 'Victoria Creeper' to cover this 6 x 12–foot planting area in five years.

White star creeper *(P. angulata)*. A very low-growing 1- to 2-inch perennial ground cover. Ideal to use between stepping stones, in rock gardens, or in small areas. The white summer flowers are often tinged light blue. Can be walked on occasionally, but will not take a lot of abuse. Will grow in full to part sun, in enriched, well-drained garden soil.

Bog rosemary *(Andromeda polifolia nana)*. The variety most readily used is 'Grandiflora' because of its attractive, bluish green leaves and soft pink flowers. The plant grows about 12–15 inches high and will spread in a clump about 2–3 feet. As the name implies, it will tolerate moist or boglike soils. Plant it in full or partial sun. Mix peat moss and organic matter into the planting soil.

Broom (*Genista pilosa* 'Vancouver Gold'). A fast- and low-growing deciduous shrub. Completely covered with bright golden-yellow spring flowers. Plants only grow 12–18 inches high, but spread 5–7 feet over time. Plants have a dense branching habit and are covered with tiny leaves. Grows best in full sun, in ordinary garden soil.

Bunchberry *(Cornus canadensis)*. This low- growing, 4–8 inch, deciduous ground cover is ideal to use in cool shady parts of the garden. Pure-white leaf bracts surround the green center flower. The whorl of green leaves makes an attractive background for the late spring to early summer 1–2 inch dogwood flowers. Clusters of red berries follow in late summer. Plants grow best in natural, woodsy, organic-rich soil.

Carpet bugle *(Ajuga reptans)*. This popular, low-growing, perennial ground cover spreads rapidly by runners. Bright-blue 5- to 6-inch flower spikes put on a nice show in late spring and early summer. Oval leaves are green to bronze on the common variety, but vary considerably by named varieties. Myrna and I really like the variety 'Burgundy Lace'. The leaves of this variety are variegated in reddish bronze, pink, and white. 'Rosea' is a variety with pink blossoms. The variety 'Alba' has white flowers. 'Variegata' leaves are edged in light yellow. Plus there are several others. Plants only grow about 4–6 inches high in the sun and 6–8 inches in the shade. Watch for slugs; they like to nest under the low-growing foliage. Plant in full sun or partial shade in organic-rich, well-drained garden soil.

Ceanothus *(C. gloriosus)*. Low growing, 8–12 inches high. Mid to late spring flowers are brilliant deep blue to purplish blue. Leaves are medium to dark green and oval in shape. Plants may eventually spread 4–6 feet.

Cinquefoil (*Potentilla neumanniana* 'Nana'). A 2- to 4-inch high perennial with brilliant yellow flowers in spring. See also Chapter 9, Perennials.

Corsican mint. See mint.

Cotula *(C. squalida).* Fernlike foliage on a 2- to 3-inch creeping perennial. Can be used between stepping stones or as a very low ground-cover plant. Plant in partial shade to full sun. Grows well in ordinary, well-drained garden soil.

Cranberry *(Vaccinium macrocarpon).* Low-growing 4- to 6-inch plants flower and bear edible cranberries. Red berries follow white (tinged pink) flowers. Small dark green leaves make an attractive, dense foliage mat, covering the ground nicely. Leaves turn bronze in autumn. Plant in moist to wet, organic-enriched garden soil.

Creeping jenny *(Lysimachia nummularia).* Often used as an annual in hanging baskets or containers, it is actually a perennial. The previous owners of our home planted it as a ground cover and it got completely out of control at our house, rooting and seeding as it grew. The chartreuse-green leaves of the variety 'Aurea' are quite attractive with its small (1-inch) yellow early-summer flowers. At our place, it only grows 4–6 inches high, but will spread up to 2 feet or more a year. *L. n.* 'Aurea' is an excellent ground cover for the shade. Plant in organic-enriched garden soil.

Creeping phlox *(P. stolonifera* or *P. subulata).* Very popular low-growing, spring-flowering perennial that is often used in rock gardens or as a ground cover in small areas. Phloxlike flowers are in shades of pink, rose, red, lavender, or white. The dense, matlike growth is covered by flowers in early to midspring. Plants grow about 4–6 inches high and spread up to 24 inches wide. Plant in full sun, in moist, fertile, well-drained soil.

Creeping thyme *(Thymus serphyllum).* Super low-growing, 3-inch-high creeping thyme (also called mother of thyme) is the one most frequently used as a ground cover in the landscape. However, woolly *(T. pseudolanuginosus),* lemon *(T. citriodorus),* and common thyme *(T. vulgaris)* are also used (for woolly thyme, see Chapter 9, Perennials; for lemon and common thyme, see Chapter 14, Herbs). The low-growing creeping varieties come in shades of pink, lavender, red, and white. They are often used between stepping stones, as low ground covers, or in rock gardens. Plants will tolerate some walking-on. In fact, one of our neighbors uses creeping thyme on the parking strip instead of grass. It works out great: no mowing, beautiful summer flowers, and it withstands the foot traffic. Shear lightly if plants tend to get leggy. Plant in full sun or part shade, in well-drained, ordinary soil.

Dwarf bamboo (*Sasa ramosa* 'Ella'). Although it is listed as a taller-growing bamboo, I am told it is used as a ground cover. May need to be cut back to the ground if it tends to get too straggly. Confine the root system with 32-mil polyethylene, so roots do not extend into unwanted areas. Plant in semi- to shady areas in moist, well-drained soil.

Dwarf fernleaf bamboo *(Pleioblastus distichus).* Sometimes a bit taller (1–2 feet); is another running dwarf bamboo, and a good choice as a ground cover in the shade. Cultivation is same as for dwarf bamboo.

Left: Fast growth and attractive leaves make myrtle *(Vinca major)* a popular ground cover.

Below: Many low-growing perennials also make excellent ground covers. Candytuft and aubrieta are two of the best.

Dwarf Oregon grape *(Mahonia nervosa).* This is the low-growing Northwest native. The 10- to 15-inch-long, divided leaves are pointed and coarse in texture. Early-spring 3- to 5-inch clusters of yellow flowers stand above the leaves and are followed by blue berries. Plants grow 18–24 inches high and about 2½–3 feet wide. In our garden this plant grows best in the shade. Excellent ground cover for a woodland setting or a shady spot in the garden. Plant in organic-enriched, well-drained garden soil.

Dwarf rosemary. See rosemary *(Rosmarinus officinalis).*

English ivy (*Hedera helix* and other species). Though this is the variety that is most frequently used as a ground cover, this is one ground cover that is on the "unwanted" list in Oregon because it is running rampant in some areas of the Northwest. It's been used as a ground cover and to help control soil erosion. If the vining growth is kept under control and the vines sheared occasionally, it can make a nice-looking, confined ground-cover plant. In addition, there are many slower-growing, finer-leafed varieties (some variegated) that make even better and easier-to-control ground covers. Check them out at your local nursery or garden center. Vines should be cut away if they start to climb trees, as it cuts off air to the trees. Grows in sun, part sun, or shade, in most any ordinary garden soil.

Euonymus (*E. fortunei* varieties). Many low-growing varieties make excellent ground covers. Check to see which low-growing varieties your nursery features, as some have attractive leaf variegations. Plant in full sun or shade in organic-rich, well-drained soil.

> **Winter creeper** *(E. f. radicans).* Probably the most popular ground-cover variety. Has green leaves, grows about 12 inches high, and can spread up to 20 feet over time.

Garland daphne. See rose daphne.

Gaultheria. See wintergreen *(G. procumbens).*

Genista. See broom (*G. pilosa* 'Vancouver Gold').

Heather/heath. (*Erica, Calluna,* and other genera). I really do not know where to begin with these plants because there are so many (see several listed in Chapter 4, Shrubs). Check with your local nursery or garden center to see which varieties they feature. Hundreds of varieties are commercially grown and available in this region. Dorothy Metheny wrote a whole book on the subject, which is a classic. About all I can say in the limited space I have here is that these should be a must in your garden. By selection of variety, you can have at least a dozen different varieties flowering at any time throughout the year. Flowers come in a wide range of colors, and some plants have outstanding foliage colors in all shades of green, gray, pink, and gorgeous golden variegations. I think we have at least a dozen different varieties in our garden. Most bloom for a month or more, some 3–6 months. Heights vary by varieties from 6 inches to 6 feet or more. Most are low-growing (1–2 feet) and they make ideal ground covers. Plant them in full or part sun for best flowering and growth. It is important to plant them right at ground level, so the top of the root ball is sitting right on the surface of the soil. They require an acid-type soil, so mix a little peat moss and compost into the planting soil. Provide good drainage for them.

Irish moss *(Sagina subulata).* Irish moss is green and forms a dense, mossylike carpet. Plants only grow 1–2 inches high but will spread up to 12 inches or more. Little white flowers in April and May. This is an ideal plant to use between stepping stones, as a low ground cover, in rock gardens, or as a low border plant. Plants will tolerate a certain amount of foot traffic and are sometimes used in place of grass in small areas. I have grown it in full shade, but find the plants tend to stretch a little and lose a bit of their form. You can cut new plants into 2-inch squares and plant 6–8 inches apart as a means of saving money, because they will pretty well fill in the very first year. Grows well in full sun to part shade, in organic-enriched, well-drained soil.

Scotch moss (*S. s.* 'Aurea'). Scotch moss is yellow. Growth and care is the same as for Irish moss.

Ivy (*Hedera helix* and varieties). See English ivy.

Japanese spurge *(Pachysandra terminalis).* A great ground cover for the shade. Dark green foliage with small spikes of spring white flowers. The 8- to 12-inch-high plants spread by underground runners. There is a variegated variety called 'Silver Edge', which has green leaves with white margins. Leaves are apt to turn yellowish if the plants get too much sunlight. Plant in a shady location with moist, enriched organic humus mixed with ordinary garden soil.

Juniper (*Juniperus horizontalis,* many varieties). The low-growing types make great evergreen ground covers. 'Wiltonii' is a very low 6-inch variety with bluish-silver foliage. This variety may spread up to 5–7 feet in width over time. 'Blue Chip' grows up to 12 inches high and 6–8 feet wide; very bright silvery-blue foliage. 'Bar Harbor' (12 inches high and 6–9 feet wide) has grayish-blue foliage that takes on a bit of a purple tinge during the winter. Needless to say, these are only a few of the most popular ground-cover varieties. They grow best in full or partial sun and shade. Plant them in ordinary, well-drained garden soil.

Kalmia. See alpine laurel *(K. polifolia).*

Kinnikinnick *(Arctostaphylos uva-ursi).* One of the best native ground covers. Runners hug the ground, rooting some as they grow. 'Point Reyes', 'Radiant', 'Vancouver Jade', and 'Wood's Compact' are probably four of the most popular varieties. Spring flowers are white to pink, often followed by fall and winter red berries.

Excellent as a hillside ground cover, although it can be used in any part of the garden. Plant in full or part sun in ordinary, well-drained garden soil.

Lavender (Lavandula spp.). See Chapter 14, Herbs.

Lavender cotton *(Santolina chamaecyparissus).* The silver-gray foliage is fragrant and very attractive. The 18- to 24-inch plants are often used as ground covers in small areas. It is believed that the plants are a bit fireproof and also repel deer. Yellow flowers can be dried. Plant in ordinary, well-drained garden soil.

Lingonberry *(Vaccinium vitis-idaea minus).* Here is a nice, low-growing evergreen ground cover for part or full shade. The plants only grow about 8–12 inches high. Flowers are white to pinkish and are followed by large berries. The new growth is only about ½ inch wide and often has a reddish tinge. It's an excellent ground cover for rock gardens or small, low, shady areas of the garden. Plant in moist, peaty, well-drained soil.

Lithodora (Lithospermum diffusum). See Chapter 9, Perennials.

Mint (*Mentha,* several species). These perennial herbs spread rapidly by underground roots, so be careful where you use them as ground covers or they're apt to take over. The taller-growing (1½–3 feet) peppermints *(M. piperita),* spearmints *(M. spicata),* apple mints *(M. suaveolens),* and others can be used as ground covers in open areas. Plant in full to part sun, in moist, rich garden soil.

Corsican mint *(M. requienii).* This is a popular plant to use between stepping stones. It only grows about ½ inch high in a dense, matlike growth habit. It will take limited walking-on. Tiny, round leaves emit a pleasant minty fragrance when touched. Small purplish summer flowers are quite insignificant. A great plant to use as a perennial ground cover.

Pennyroyal *(M. pulegium).* Another of the mints that makes a fine ground cover. Low, mat-type growth (6–16 inches) with round, bright green leaves. Small lavender flowers. Aromatic mint fragrance especially noticeable when foliage is bruised or crushed. Plant in shade or filtered sun in moist, ordinary garden soil.

Mother of thyme *(Thymus serphyllum).* See creeping thyme.

Myrtle *(Vinca major* and *V. minor).* Often goes by two common names: periwinkle and myrtle. The large-growing *V. major* species comes in green and variegated varieties. The leaves, flowers, and growth habit are all larger than *Vinca minor.* The lower-growing *Vinca minor* also comes in green and variegated leaf varieties. This one is the most popular ground-cover type because it is not as rampant; has smaller 1- to 1½-inch leaves and 1-inch flowers. There are varieties with blue, purple, or white flowers. Low-growing stems often root along the way. Plants have a mounding growth habit to about 6–12 inches high. The variegated leaf varieties are nice to use for added foliage color in the shade. Plants grow in full or part sun or light shade in organic-enriched, well-drained garden soil.

Left: Rubus is a wonderful, low-maintenance ground cover.

Below: I think heathers make very attractive year-round evergreen ground covers.

Pennyroyal. See mint.

Periwinkle. See myrtle.

Ribbon grass (*Phalaris arundinacea* 'Fersey's Form'). Ribbon grasses are known for their aggressive growth, but the low varieties like 'Fersey's Form' are not as aggressive. Nevertheless, I would put a barrier around the area in which you want to confine their growth. We have this variety in our garden and so far it has maintained a clump growth habit. We're keeping our fingers crossed. Late in the season, some of the green and white variegated blades take on a pinkish tinge. The 1½- to 2-foot plants tend to fall over if planted in too much shade. Plant in full sun, in well-drained, ordinary garden soil.

P. a. picta. This is a very aggressive type of green and white variegated grass. It needs to be confined or it will wander quickly. The foliage (2–3 feet) is really pretty, so you might want to use it in a container planting. Believe me, I made the mistake of planting it in a raised bed without a barrier. It ended up in the roots of surrounding plants and even in the lawn. You have no idea how difficult it was to finally get rid of it. Plant (if you dare) in well-drained, ordinary garden soil.

Rockrose *(Cistus corbariensis).* This hybrid variety grows about 2–3 feet high with about twice the width. Attractive 1- to 1½-inch white flowers with yellow centers. Small leaves are a dull green. Landscapers use this as a ground cover in large areas. These plants flower best in full sun in ordinary, well-drained garden soil.

Rose daphne *(D. cneorum).* Also called the garland or rock daphne. Plants grow less than 12 inches high and about 3–4 feet wide. In rock gardens it will cascade over the rocks. Plants are covered with highly fragrant pink flowers in springtime. The variety 'Ruby Glow' will often rebloom again in late summer. Small evergreen leaves cover the plant, creating an attractive, compact plant. However, occasional shearing after bloom will keep the plant from becoming bare in the center. Expensive to use in large areas, but a nice choice where only one to three ground-cover plants are needed. Plant in full sun, in enriched, cool, well-drained soil.

Rosemary *(Rosmarinus officinalis).* Nice gray leaves and showy blue flowers. See Chapter 14, Herbs, for information on other varieties. Plant in full sun, in ordinary, well-drained garden soil.

Rubus *(R. pentalobus).* We have this ground cover on a hillside and it clings to the ground, rooting as it grows. It's in a no-maintenance area and does really well for the little care it gets. Ours has spread about 3 feet in three years. The variety most often used as a ground cover plant is 'Emerald Carpet'. The 1- to 1½-inch leaves are medium green, three lobed (somewhat like miniature maple leaves). The surface of the leaf is rough textured and the underside is whitish. Ours thrive on neglect. I have never seen the small white flowers they are supposed to have. Plant in full or part sun in ordinary, well-drained garden soil.

Salal *(Gaultheria shallon).* In the right place, this is an easy-to-grow native ground cover. It grows naturally in our garden under six huge Douglas firs. In fact, I have difficulty keeping it out of my adjoining planting areas. The leaves are dark green and rather leathery. May flowers are pale pink, followed by small purple berries. It spreads by underground shoots. Mine vary from 1½ feet in full sun to 5 feet in the shade. They can be severely pruned in early spring if they get too straggly, and they come right back. Plant them with any exposure, in ordinary, well-drained garden soil.

Sarcococca *(S. hookerana humilis).* This is a great low-growing, fragrant ground cover for shady spots in the garden. Evergreen plants grow 6–18 inches high and 4–6 feet wide over time. Narrow, 3-inch-long, dark green leaves. Small, white, fragrant flowers appear in late January or February. Wonderful plants to use near the entry where everyone can enjoy the intense fragrance. Plant spreads by underground shoots. Plant in shade, in enriched, well-drained garden soil.

Scotch moss (*Sagina subulata* 'Aurea'). See Irish moss.

St. Johnswort *(Hypericum calycinum).* Robust-growing 12-inch evergreen with bright yellow 3-inch flowers with showy sunburst centers. Plants flower in our garden in June and July. If foliage is ruined in a severe winter, just cut it to the ground the following spring. It may be necessary to make a barrier to keep it under control. Plant in full or part sun in ordinary, well-drained garden soil.

Stonecrop (*Sedum* and other succulents). There are so many varieties that it is impossible to even start mentioning them. I group these together because they have the same cultural requirements. The low-growing varieties, some with contrasting leaf color, can be used as ground covers, in rock gardens, or as container plants. The succulent varieties of hens and chickens *(Sempervivum tectorum)* can be used in the same way. The taller-growing varieties are ideal to use in borders or individually for spot color in the garden. Plants grow in full sun, in well-drained, ordinary soil.

Sweet woodruff *(Galium odoratum).* The early-summer white flowers cover the delicate green leaves. Plants grow up to 10–12 inches in the shade, a bit lower in part sun and shade. A great ground cover for the woodland garden. See also Chapter 14, Herbs. Plant in rich, well-drained soil.

Thyme (Thymus spp.). See creeping thyme.

White star creeper *(Pratia angulata).* See blue star creeper.

Winter creeper *(Euonymus fortunei radicans).* See euonymus.

Wintergreen *(Gaultheria procumbens).* Underground stems grow to 6 inches with pinkish early-summer flowers, followed by bright red berries. Leaves and berries have fragrance of wintergreen. One of my friends uses it very effectively as a ground cover at the base of his blueberries. Wonderful ground covers in part shade. Plant in organic-rich, well-drained garden.

13 · Annuals

It's hard to beat the beauty of the summer-flowering annuals. Many of them flower all summer and some even into the fall, until the first hard frost. If there is one drawback, it is that they are not hardy plants, so they last for only one season.

Choosing a Location

The various growing habits and long flowering season of annuals make them excellent plants to use for spot color in the garden and as mass plantings. Many can be used for container plantings and some as cut or dried flowers.

Facing page: The multi-colored leaves of a coleus plant create dazzling effects in the summer garden.

Below: It's hard to believe, but the colorful Livingstone daisy can actually thrive in the hot, neglected parts of the garden.

Display Plants Formally

Formal planting is simply laying out the rows in lines, one right behind the other. Unless you have a formal garden, this is probably not the best way to arrange summer annual flower displays.

Plant Flowers Informally

This is my favorite way, one I refer to as the old English or cottage garden method, in which you plant three, five, or seven plants all the same color in a triangular or circular grouping. These small group plantings, if properly planned, can create a riot of color in your garden.

Plant in Borders

Borders are generally planted in single rows. However, many homeowners are finding it more effective to plant two borders instead of just one. When this method is used, the front border is generally of one type of plant and the second border of another; for example, white alyssum in front and purple lobelia behind, then a third border of bright yellow dwarf marigolds makes a striking contrast. I do not recommend planting just one plant of a variety unless you are planting perennials, which bush out and provide multiple flowers and a much larger display.

Buying Bedding Plants

When choosing the small starter plants (called *bedding plants*), look for bushy, well-branched, compact plants. Avoid tall, spindly plants. Also, avoid those plants that are skimpy but flowering, because they generally suffer some transplanting shock and take too long to reestablish and flower again. Of course, you will also want to select those plants with the healthiest-looking foliage.

Growing sunflowers? To enjoy the edible seeds, hang the seed heads upside-down in a spot that has good air circulation. If the seeds tend to drop as they dry, cover the seed head with netting. You can eat the seeds fresh or roasted. Toast them for added flavor by putting the hulled seeds in an oven at 350 degrees Fahrenheit. Spread them on a pan or baking sheet and bake for approximately ten minutes. Stir the seeds occasionally. The hulled seeds can also be toasted for ten minutes in a dry frying pan over medium-low heat. Again, be certain to stir them, as scorched seeds are apt to have a bitter flavor.

Planting Annuals

Starting Seeds Indoors

You can start annuals indoors to get a jump on the gardening season, then set out the seedling starter plants as the weather warms up. Start the seeds in late February or early March indoors.

Choosing a Location for Starting Seeds Indoors

A sunny windowsill, greenhouse window, sun porch, or greenhouse are the best places to start your seeds. However, they can be started in any bright-light part of the home or garage. If possible, place them in a spot where there is warmth from below, such as over a heating duct. Bottom heat or a heating cable really helps the seeds in the germination process. (Heating cables are available at most garden outlets.)

Most seeds germinate best in a warm location. Select a spot where the temperatures will range between 65 and 72 degrees Fahrenheit, unless the seed packet recommends otherwise.

Containers

You can use flats, pots, trays, egg cartons, eggshells, paper cups, or peat pots as containers. Just be sure they have a drainage hole in the bottom, so the new young seedling plants do not sit in water.

Soil Mix

Store-bought seedling mixes are the best to use. However, a regular potting soil, vermiculite, perlite, sponge rock, or a combination of sand and peat moss are all suitable mixes to start seeds.

In fact, they can be started in soil from the garden if it is sterilized and porous. One way to sterilize your outdoor soil is to bake it in the oven (in a baking tray) for approximately two hours at 170 to 180 degrees Fahrenheit.

Sowing the Seeds

Read and follow sowing (planting) directions on the back of the seed packet. This is a very important step because some need to be covered with soil; others need to be uncovered and exposed to light in order to germinate. There is a tendency to cover the seeds with too much soil or peat, so be certain to barely cover the seed.

Next, water in thoroughly. Use a fine spray (atomizer type) to water the seeds until the plants are at least an inch tall. Otherwise the water tends to wash all the seeds to the edges of the pots or trays.

Preparing Starts for Transplanting

Once the new young seedlings have developed one set of true leaves, or are about 1 to 1½ inches high, they can be individually potted or spaced in a flat or tray. It's best to transplant them in individual containers, so when the time comes they can be easily transplanted with a minimum of shock. Then, of course, do not plant them outdoors until the proper planting time. See below.

Sowing Seeds Outdoors

The seeds of many annuals can be sown directly into the garden after all danger of frost has passed—in most areas, late April or May.

Prepare the Soil for Planting

Whether you start your annuals from seed or buy the plants, you need to take time to properly prepare the soil for planting. Mix a little peat moss, compost (if you have it), and processed manure with your existing soil. The reason for this is that annuals are fast growing and prolific flowering, so they need rich soil in which to get established.

Set the Plant at the Proper Depth

Next, set the seedlings/bedding plants right at the same level as they are in the container they came in. Pull the soil in around them. Water in thoroughly with a light application of fertilizer. Use it at about one-third of the recommended dilution. It's that easy!

When to Plant Annuals

Since most annuals are tender plants, you need to wait until all danger of frost has passed before planting them outdoors. Then you need to know which can be planted early, which need to wait for warmer weather, and which ones need even warmer June weather before planting takes place.

Wonder why your seeds are not growing? Chances are they were sown too deeply or planted too early; birds or soil insects ate them; fertilizer burned them; or the soil was keep wet or too dry. The first thing to do is check and see if the seeds are still there. If they are gone, it's soil insects or birds. If you can find them, see if they are soggy or mushy, as that indicates they were too wet. If the seeds are dried up, they were kept too dry or were burned up by fertilizer. Now you know what to do to correct the situation so it doesn't happen again!

Early Spring (March/April)

Annual flowers that will tolerate some cool weather (usually March/April) include:

calendula, *C. officinalis*
mimulus hybrids
pansy, *Viola* x *wittrockiana*
schizanthus, *S. pinnatus*
snapdragon, *Antirrhinum majus*
stock, *Matthiola incana*
sweet pea, *Lathyrus odoratus*
viola, *V. tricolor*

Spring (April/May)

These annuals need a little warmer weather (usually April/May), before they are planted/seeded outdoors:

alyssum, *Lobularia maritima*
baby's breath (annual), *Gypsophila elegans*
candytuft (annual), *Iberis amara*
clarkia species
cleome, *C. hasslerana*
coleus, *C. hybridus*
cosmos, *C. bipinnatus*
dahlia (annual)
four o'clock, *Mirabilis jalapa*
fuchsia, *F. hybrida* varieties
geranium, *Pelargonium hortorum*
godetia, *Clarkia amoena*
gourds
heliotrope, *Heliotropium arborescens*
larkspur, *Consolida ambigua*
linaria, *L. maroccana*
livingston daisy, *Mesembryanthemum crystallinum*
lobelia, *L. erinus*
marigold, *Tagetes erecta*
morning glory, *Ipomoea nil*

nasturtium, *Tropaeolum majus*
nemesia, *N. strumosa*
nicotiana, *N. alata*
petunia, *P. hybrida*
phlox (annual), *P. drummondii*
poppy (annual), *Papaver rhoeas* and *Eschscholzia californica*
portulaca, *P. grandiflora*
salpiglossis, *S. sinuata*
salvia, *S. splendens*
statice, *Limonium sinuatum*
strawflower, *Helichrysum bracteatum*
sunflower, *Helianthus annuus*
Swan River daisy, *Brachycome iberidifolia*
viscaria, *Silene coeli-rosa*

Late Spring (Late May/June)

These plants need warmer late-spring weather (usually late May to June) to do well:

aster (annual), *Callistephus chinensis*
convolvulus, *C. tricolor*
impatiens, *I. wallerana*
wax begonia (annual), *B.* x *semperflorens-cultorum*
zinnia, *Z. elegans*

Feeding Annuals

When to Feed

Because annuals are fast growing and prolific flowering, they certainly benefit from monthly feedings. Apply fertilizer monthly according to label instructions. You can apply weaker solutions more frequently, but why bother? It only makes more work for you. Morning is by far the best time to feed plants. Avoid feeding late in the day, which creates wet soil and the possibility of disease problems.

What to Feed

Plants that lose their leaves over winter are called *deciduous.* A rose or all-purpose garden fertilizer (vegetable fertilizer too) can be used to feed deciduous plants; for example, annual plants can be fed with these same types of fertilizers.

Watering Annuals

Whenever possible water before 2 p.m., so the surface soil has a chance to dry a little before the cooler evening hours set in. Again, this is done to lessen the chances of disease problems. It's best to keep the sprinkler water off the leaves and flowers, but I always water my annuals overhead with a sprinkler because I simply do not have the time to irrigate the beds individually. It doesn't seem to affect them in any negative way. So do what works for you!

Protecting Annuals from Cold Weather

Mulch Half-Hardy Summer Annuals Outdoors

Stock and snapdragons are two prime examples of annuals that will sometime become perennials and winter over if given a little mulching attention. Use 1 inch of straw, bark, or sawdust for mulching around these plants.

Winter Some Annuals Indoors

There are a few summer annuals, such as New Guinea impatiens, wax (fibrous) begonias, abutilon (flowering maple), and coleus, that can be dug directly from the garden, potted in soil, brought indoors, and treated like houseplants over winter. Then late the following spring, after all danger of frost is over, plant them outdoors again.

Choosing Annuals

By Color

Yellow

This is an ideal color because of its brilliance, due to the reflection from the sun:

bidens, *B. ferulifolia*
calendula, *C. officinalis*
coleus (foliage color), *C. hybridus*
cosmos, *C. bipinnatus* 'Bright Lights'
marigold, *Tagetes erecta* spp. (dwarf, midsize, tall)
mimulus, *M. hybridus*
nasturtium, *Tropaeolum majus*

pansy, *Viola* x *wittrockiana*
snapdragon, *Antirrhinum majus*
stock, *Matthiola incana*
sunflower, *Helianthus annuus*
viola, *V. tricolor*
zinnia, *Z. elegans*

Orange

A bright, warm color to use with whites, yellows, and blues:

calendula, *C. officinalis*
cosmos, *C. bipinnatus* 'Bright Lights' (other shades with it)
geranium, *Pelargonium hortorum*
marigold, *Tagetes erecta*
nasturtium, *Tropaeolum majus*
pansy, *Viola x. wittrockiana*
zinnia, *Z. elegans*

Red

Bright red draws the eye to any part of the garden:

aster (annual), *Callistephus chinensis*
carnation/double pink, *Dianthus chinensis*
coleus, *C. hybridus* (red leaf varieties)
cosmos, *C. bipinnatus*
dahlia (annual)
geranium, *Pelargonium hortorum*
impatiens, *I. wallerana*
nasturtium, *Tropaeolum majus*
nicotiana, *N. alata*
petunia, *P. hybrida*
salvia, *S. splendens*
snapdragon, *Antirrhinum majus*
stock, *Matthiola incana*
wax begonia, *B.* x *semperflorens-cultorum*
zinnia, *Z. elegans*

Pink

Soft pinks blend well with the brighter colors:

ageratum, *A. houstonianum* 'Pink Mist'
aster (annual), *Callistephus chinensis*
baby's breath, *Gypsophila elegans* 'Rosea'
carnation/double pink, *Dianthus chinensis*
cosmos, *C. pinnatus*
centradenia, *C. grandiflora*

If you're starting plants from seed, be careful not to cover the seeds with too much soil. Seeds should never be covered with soil that is more then twice the greatest diameter of the seed. And some seeds should not be covered with soil at all, because they need light to germinate. That's why it is so essential to follow the planting instructions on the seed packet of each type of flower, vegetable, or herb you are growing.

cuphea, *C. hyssopifolia*
forget-me-not (pink), *Myosotis sylvatica*
geranium, *Pelargonium hortorum*
impatiens, *I. wallerana*
mallow, *Lavatera trimestris*—pink
petunia, *P. hybrida*
snapdragon, *Antirrhinum majus*
stock, *Matthiola incana*
wax begonia, *B.* x *semperflorens-cultorum*
zinnia, *Z. elegans*

Blue/Purple

A difficult color to find in plants, yet so effective with whites and yellows:

ageratum, *A. houstonianum*
aster (annual), *Callistephus chinensis*
bachelor's button, *Centaurea cyanus*
bacopa, *B.* 'Sutera cordata'
convolvulus, *C. tricolor* 'Ensign Tricolor'
felicia, *F. amelloides*
forget-me-not, *Myosotis sylvatica*
heliotrope, *Heliotropium arborescens*
larkspur, *Consolida ambigua*
lamium, *L. maculatum*
lobelia, *L. erinus*
pansy, *Viola* x *wittrockiana*
salvia, *S. farinacea* 'Blue Bedder'
scaevola, *S. aemula*
viola, *V. tricolor*

White

White flowers bring out the vibrant colors of all other annuals:

alyssum (annual), *Lobularia maritima*
aster (annual), *Callistephus chinensis*
baby's breath (annual), *Gypsophila elegans*
cleome, *C. hasslerana*
dahlia hybrids
geranium, *Pelargonium hortorum*
lobelia, *L. erinus*
nicotiana, *N. alata*
pansy, *Viola* x *wittrockiana*
petunia, *P. hybrida*
snapdragon, *Antirrhinum majus*
stock, *Matthiola incana*

wax begonia, *B.* x *semperflorens-cultorum*
zinnia, *Z. elegans*

Mixed Colors

Some annuals are most effective when used in mixed colors, and others are only available in a mixture. Here are some of the best and easiest to grow:

aster (annual), *Callistephus chinensis*
California poppy, *Eschscholzia californica*
candytuft (annual), *Iberis umbellata* 'Dwarf Fairy'
carnation/double pink, *Dianthus chinensis*
cigar plant, *Cuphea ignea*
clarkia species
cosmos, *C. bipinnatus*
dahlia (annual)
English daisy, *Bellis perennis*
flowering maple, *Abutilon hybridum*
four o'clock, *Mirabilis jalapa*
fuchsia, *F. hybrida*
godetia, *Clarkia amoena*
lantana hybrids
larkspur, *Consolida ambigua*
linaria, *L. maroccana*
livingstone daisy, *Mesembryanthemum crystallinum*
nemesia, *N. strumosa*
painted daisy, *Chrysanthemum coccineum*
phlox (annual), *P. drummondii,* dwarf varieties
portulaca, *P. grandiflora*
shirley poppy, *Papaver rhoeas*
salpiglossis, *S. sinuata*
scabiosa, *S. atropurpurea*
schizanthus, *S. pinnatus*
statice, *Limonium sinuatum*
strawflower, *Helichrysum bracteatum*
Swan River daisy, *Brachycome iberidifolia*
sweet pea, *Lathyrus odoratus*
sweet sultan, *Centaurea moschata*
verbena, *V. hortensis*—broad range of colors
viscaria, *Silene coeli-rosa*

For Hanging Baskets

These are plants that trail (hang), have interesting foliage or attractive flowers, or lend themselves to hanging basket culture. Many plants are even more attractive when you can look up at the flowers, so some of the ones mentioned are selected for that reason alone:

From Seed

alyssum (annual), *Lobularia maritima*
black-eyed susan vine, *Thunbergia alata*
coleus, *C. hybridus*
convolvulus, *C. tricolor* 'Ensign Tricolor'
impatiens, *I. wallerana*
livingstone daisy, *Mesembryanthemum crystallinum*
lobelia, *L. erinus*
marigold, *Tagetes erecta* (dwarf varieties)
mimulus, *M. hybridus*
nasturtium, *Tropaeolum majus*
petunia, *P. hybrida*
portulaca, *P. grandiflora*
schizanthus, *S. pinnatus*
Swan River daisy, *Brachycome iberidifolia*

From Bedding Plants

Here are just a few of the best one-season plants that are very effective and attractive as hanging basket plants:

bacopa, *B. sutera*
begonia (hanging basket; bulb)
bidens, *B. feruifolia*
creeping charlie, *Glechoma hederacea*
creeping jenny, *Lysimachia nummularia*
creeping zinnia, *Sanvitalia procumbens*
felicia, *F. amelloides*
fuchsia, *F. hybrida*
geranium, ivy, *Pelargonium hortorum*
helichrysum, *H. bracteatum*
impatiens, New Guinea hybrids
lantana (dwarf varieties)
lotus vine, *L. berthelotii*
million bells, *Calibrachoa*
petunia, P. hybrida 'Wave' and 'Cascade'
potato vine, *Solanum jasminoides*
scaevola, *S. aemula*
snapdragon (trailing), *Antirrhinum majus* 'Clownerie'
verbena (trailing), *V. hortensis* 'Tapien'

For Baskets and Containers

In Sun

If you're looking for hanging basket or container annuals that will thrive in a bright, hot, sunny spot in the garden, here are a few of my favorites:

bacopa, *B. sutera*
bidens, *B. feruifolia*
creeping charlie, *Glechoma hederacea*
creeping zinnia, *Sanvitalia procumbens*
cuphea, *C. hyssopifolia*
felicia, *F. amelloides*
geranium (ivy type), *Pelargonium hortorum*
helichrysum, *H. bracteatum*
lantana, dwarf varieties
lotus vine, *L. berthelotii*
million bells, *Calibrachoa*
petunia, *P. hybrida*
potato vine, *Solanum jasminoides*
scaevola, *S. aemula*
snapdragon (trailing), *Antirrhinum majus*
verbena, *V. hortensis*

In Shade

One of the most popular areas to use hanging baskets or containers during the summer is in the shady, more protected part of the garden. Here are a few of my favorite shade annuals to use in containers or hanging baskets:

coleus, *C. hybridus*
creeping jenny
fuchsia, *F. hybrida*
impatiens, New Guinea hybrids
impatiens, *I. wallerana*
mimulus, *M. hybridus*
wax begonia, *B.* x *semperflorens-cultorum,* hanging basket type

By Particular Features

With Fragrance

If you're looking for annuals for the patio, deck, lanai, or any area where foot traffic is heavy, don't forget to use a few of the ones with fragrance. These are some of my favorite fragrant annuals:

alyssum, *Lobularia maritima*
carnation/double pink, *Dianthus chinensis,* many varieties
cleome, *C. hasslerana*
heliotrope, *H. arborescens*

nicotiana, *N. alata*
petunia, *P. hybrida,* few varieties—smell blossoms
sweet pea, *Lathyrus odoratus*
verbena, *V. hortensis*
wax begonia (uprights), *B.* x *semperflorens-cultorum,* some varieties

With Attractive Leaves

The leaves of some plants are as beautiful, or in some cases even more beautiful, than the flowers. To add some plants with attractive leaves is really a bonus and a showy addition to the summer garden:

alternanthera, *A. houstonianum*
artemisia, *A. stellerana* 'Silver Brocade'
centradenia, *C. grandiflora*
coleus, *C. hybrida*
creeping charlie, *Glechoma hederacea*
dusty miller, *Senecio cineraria*
flowering maple, *Abutilon hybridum*
geranium, *Pelargonium hortorum,* variegated varieties
impatiens, New Guinea hybrids
lamium spp.
licorice vine, *Helichrysum*
lotus vine, *L. berthelotii*
Persian shield, *Strobilanthes acanthaceae*
plectranthus, variegated variety

Best Annual Vines

See Chapter 7, Vines, for a list of some great single-season vines that will provide an abundance of color and interest during the summer and fall growing seasons.

By Size and Site

For Borders in Sun

Looking for a plant to use for edging your flower or shrub beds? Here are a few of my favorites that flower prolifically in sun:

ageratum, *A. houstonianum*
alyssum, *Lobularia maritima*
lobelia, *L. erinus*
marigold, *Tagetes erecta,* dwarf varieties
nasturtium, *Tropaeolum majus,* dwarf varieties
petunia, *P. hybrida*
salvia, *S. splendens,* dwarf varieties

verbena, *V. hortensis*
wax begonia, *B.* x *semperflorens-cultorum*

For Borders in Shade

Prolifically flowering annuals for edging flower or shrub beds in shade:

impatiens, *I. wallerana*
impatiens, New Guinea hybrids
pansy, *Viola* x *wittrockiana*
viola, *V. tricolor*
wax begonia, *B.* x *semperflorens-cultorum*

For Midbed Planting in Sun

It seems as though it's easy to find plants for along the border of beds or as background plants, but what about plants for the middle of your flower beds? Here are some of my favorite annuals for midbed planting in sunny spots:

California poppy, *Eschscholzia californica*
candytuft, *Iberis amara*
clarkia spp.
cosmos, *C. bipinnatus*
dahlia (annual)
four o'clock, *Mirabilis jalapa*
geranium, *Pelargonium hortorum*
godetia, *Clarkia amoena*
heliotrope, *Heliotropium arborescens*
larkspur, *Consolida ambigua*
linaria, *L. maroccana*
marigold, *Tagetes erecta,* mid-African type
mimulus, *M. hybridus*
nemesia (part sun too), *N. strumosa*
nicotiana, *N. alata*
phlox (annual), *P. drummondii*
salpiglossis, *S. sinuata*
salvia, *S. splendens*
schizanthus, *S. pinnatus*
shirley poppy, *Papaver rhoeas*
snapdragon, *Antirrhinum majus*
statice, *Limonium sinuatum*
stock, *Matthiola incana*
strawflower, *Helichrysum bracteatum*
sunflower, *Helianthus annuus*

For Midbed Planting in Shade

Here are some of my favorite annuals for midbed planting in shady spots:

begonia, *B.* x *semperflorens-cultorum* 'Nonstop'
coleus, *C. hybridus*
fuchsia, *F. hybrida*
impatiens, *I. wallerana*
impatiens, New Guinea hybrids

In the Background in Sun

Taller-growing summer flowers are needed toward the back of flower beds. Here are some that will grow several feet high in the sun and provide a backdrop for the lower-growing annuals, perennials, and shrubs:

baby's breath, *Gypsophila elegans*
cleome, *C. hasslerana*
mallow, *Lavatera trimestris*
marigold, *Tagetes erecta,* American (tall) varieties
salvia, *S. splendens,* tall varieties
sunflower, *Helianthus annuus*
sweet pea, *Lathyrus odoratus*
sweet sultan, *Centaurea moschata*
zinnia, *Z. elegans,* tall varieties

In the Background in Part Sun and Shade

Toward the back of flower beds, you need taller-growing summer flowers that grow best in part sun and part shade to provide a backdrop for the lower-growing annuals:

aster, *Callistephus chinensis,* tall varieties
bachelor's button, *Centaurea cyanus*
cosmos, *C. bipinnatus*
larkspur, *Consolida ambigua*
painted daisy, *Chrysanthemum coccineum*
salvia, *S. farinacea* 'Blue Bedder'
snapdragon, *Antirrhinum majus,* tall varieties
sweet pea, *Lathyrus odoratus*

In the Background in Shade

Fuchsias are taller-growing summer flowers that will grow several feet high in the shade:

fuchsia, *F. hybrida,* trees or standards

Annuals Encyclopedia

Abutilon. See flowering maple *(A. hybridum).*

Ageratum *(A. houstonianum).* Flowers range in shades of lavender, rose ('Pink Mist'), and white. Compact clusters of powder-puff-like flowers cover the plant from May to cool fall weather. Bushy 8-inch plants are ideal for borders or group plantings. Plant in full sun or part sun, in enriched, well-drained soil.

Alternanthera *(A. ficoidea).* Often used because of the colorful foliage, sometimes striped in contrasting color. Excellent for borders or group planting. Upright 8- to 12-inch plants benefit from pinching or shearing. Needs full sun, well-drained soil.

Alyssum *(Lobularia maritima).* Also called sweet alyssum. Prolific-flowering, low-growing, fragrant annual in shades of pink, lavender, and white; 2- to 6-inch-high plants spread to about 9 inches in width. Does best in full or part sun, in soil that is well drained.

Artemisia (*A. stellerana* 'Silver Brocade'). See silver brocade in Chapter 9, Perennials.

Aster *(Callistephus chinensis).* Annual varieties come in shades of pink, red, purple, blue, lavender, and white. Single or double flowers. Double flowers are pom-pom shaped. Dwarf and tall varieties, so they range in height from 6 to 36 inches. Nice cut flowers, showy garden plants. Plant in full to part sun in moist, fertile soil.

Baby's breath *(Gypsophila elegans).* Annual varieties come in white or pink. Ideal to cut and use as a filler in flower arrangements. Plants grow up to 2 feet or more. Delicate flowers are also showy when combined with other annuals and perennials. Plant in full sun in fertile soil.

Bachelor's button *(Centaurea cyanus).* This old-time favorite blue flower now comes in pink, red, or white flowering varieties. Grows 24–30 inches and is ideal for cutting. Plant in full or part sun in fertile soil.

> **Sweet sultan** *(C. moschata).* Attractive, fluffy, 1-inch thistlelike flowers in shades of pink, rose, yellow, and white. Plants grow 2–3 feet high, so they are ideal to use in borders or toward the back of landscape beds. They also make nice cut flowers. The long-stem flowers have a light fragrance. Plant in a hot, sunny area where the soil is fertile but well-drained.

Bacopa *(B. sutera).* A recent introduction to the United States, this attractive, prolific-flowering, vine-type plant comes with white, pink, or violet flowers. The small, delicate flowers cover the plant. Has wintered over in my garden during a mild winter. Ideal in containers or planters. Plants grow very low, and spread up to 24 inches or more in a single season. The white flowering one is the most popular one. The new variety with variegated green and cream leaves is a real winner too! Must have good drainage. Grows very well in full sun or part sun and shade. Variegated variety: 'Gold 'N Pearls'.

Begonia. See wax begonia *(B.* x *semperflorens-cultorum).* See also tuberous begonia in Chapter 11, Bulbs.

Bidens *(B. ferulifolia).* This is a relatively new introduction to the United States and is a very showy, prolific-flowering trailing plant. The small yellow flowers cover the plant all summer long. Ideal for mixed hanging baskets, containers, and rockeries. Provide a spot in full or part sun with fertilized, well-drained soil.

Black-eyed susan vine *(Thunbergia alata).* See Chapter 7, Vines.

Busy-lizzie. See impatiens.

Butterfly bush. See schizanthus.

Calendula *(C. officinalis).* Commonly called the pot marigold. Fully double 3- to 5-inch flowers in shades of yellow, orange, or cream. Bushy plants grow to 12–24 inches in height. Keep spent flowers picked so plant will flower longer. Easy to grow, in even poor soil.

California poppy *(Eschscholzia californica).* Another favorite. Now comes in a mix of single and double flowers in shades of yellow, gold, orange, white, pink, and orange-red. They grow about 12–18 inches high. Easy to grow. They thrive with a certain amount of neglect. Plant in full sun, with well-drained soil.

Candytuft *(Iberis amara).* The one I like the best is *I. umbellata* 'Dwarf Fairy' mix. It is a compact-growing plant with flowers in dazzling pastel shades. Ideal for borders, bedding, or rock gardens. However, there are other varieties that grow up to 18 inches high. Easy to grow, providing soil is well drained. Plant in full or part sun.

Carnation/double pink *(Dianthus chinensis).* Most dianthus are perennials except for a few newer ones, such as these, commonly called annual carnations or double pinks. They range in height from 6 to 18 inches, with grasslike, usually silver-green foliage. Flowers range in shades of pink, salmon, rose, red, and white. Taller varieties are excellent for cutting. Telstar is an extra dwarf strain; 'Wee Willie' variety grows about 8–12 inches high with a 8- to 10-inch spread and clusters of single flowers. Generally not as fragrant as the perennials. Excellent for bedding, massing, and borders. Needs good drainage, but only moderate fertility. Plant in full sun or partial shade.

Centradenia *(C. grandiflora).* A nice trailing annual with greenish-bronze leaves and deep-rose flowers. Grows about 12 inches high and about the same width. Grown primarily for its attractive foliage. Provide good drainage and fertile soil. Grows in part sun or shade.

Cigar plant. See cuphea.

Left: Unusual markings and varying flower colors make painted tongue *(Salpiglossis sinuata)* a distinctive annual.

Below: Groupings of mixed annuals create a beautiful summer border.

Clarkia *(C. unguiculata).* There are several species, some with single, others with double flowers. One of the easiest of all annuals to grow. Plants range in height from 18 to 24 inches. Flowers range in shades of pink, red, purple, and white. Excellent for cutting. Provide excellent drainage and go light on feeding. Plant in full or part sun.

Cleome *(C. hasslerana).* Commonly called the spider flower. The attractive clusters of flowers come in pink, lavender, or white. The plants grow 3–6 feet in height. This is a superb annual to use toward the back of flower and shrub beds. Plant in full sun, in average garden soil.

Coleus *(C. hybridus).* These are extremely popular foliage plants for the shady garden. However, it should be noted that recent hybridization has resulted in some varieties that will tolerate sun. The leaves range from solid colors to dazzling combinations of pink, red, maroon, copper, yellow, light orange, and chartreuse. Height ranges from about 12 to 36 inches, depending upon variety. These also make excellent houseplants. Plant in shade or part sun. Grows best in organic-enriched, well-drained soil.

Convolvulus (*C. tricolor,* 'Ensign Tricolor'). Commonly called dwarf morning glory, though it does not vine; see morning glory *(Ipomea tricolor)* in Chapter 7, Vines. The brightly colored flowers have unusual markings and come in a wide range of mixed colors. Grows best in full sun in ordinary garden soil. Go light on feeding.

Cosmos *(C. bipinnatus).* All the varieties of cosmos deserve a spot in the garden. However, I prefer the new variety 'Bright Lights' because of its smaller flowers and brilliant colors; it grows 2½–3 feet high. The Seashell strain is also worth noting because of its exotic tubular flowers on plants 4–5 feet. 'Sonata' only grows 24 inches high. The Sensation strain grows 3–4 feet. They are all quick and easy to grow. Seed them in full sun in ordinary garden soil.

Creeping charlie *(Glechoma hederacea).* Sometimes called ground ivy. The green scalloped leaves with white margins are very attractive hanging plants. Most often used in hanging baskets or container plantings. Plants may hang 18 inches or more in a single year. During a mild winter the plants may winter over. Grows in sun or shade, with minimal care. Grows well in ordinary, well-drained soil.

Creeping jenny *(Lysimachia nummularia).* See Chapter 7, Vines.

Creeping zinnia *(Sanvitalia procumbens).* Looks a lot like a zinnia, even though it isn't. We have grown the variety 'Mandarin Orange' in a bright sunny spot, and the orange flowers with dark brown centers are quite showy. The spreading plants grow only about 6 inches high and spread about 18–24 inches. Plant in ordinary, well-drained garden soil.

Cuphea *(C. hyssopifolia).* Sometimes called Mexican heather. Showy tiny pink or lavender flowering plant. Compact growth to about 1 feet high. Ideal for borders or at the edge of a hanging basket. Plant in enriched, well-drained soil. Grows well in full sun or partial sun and shade.

Cigar plant *(C. ignea).* Also an attractive annual. Its flowers are shaped like miniature cigars. This plant also grows about 1 foot high, with orange, red, and white coloring. I have both, and think the Mexican heather is much showier. This one has survived two mild winters.

Dahlia. The summer annual type are very attractive with their 2- to 3-inch flowers in many different colors. Plants grow about 12–18 inches high and they will usually form tubers. These make excellent border annuals. Like the tuberous type (see Chapter 11, Bulbs), the more you pick them, the more they will flower. Protect them from slugs, snails, and earwigs. Plant in rich, fertile, well-drained soil. They love a bright sunny spot in the garden.

Dianthus. See carnation/double pink.

Double pink. See carnation/double pink.

Dusty miller *(Senecio cineraria).* This is really a semi-tender perennial, but is generally sold as a bedding plant. Varieties like 'Silver Lace' are not hardy in my garden; others will make it some winters and die to the ground others. See dusty miller in Chapter 9, Perennials.

Dwarf morning glory. See convolvulus.

English daisy *(Bellis perennis).* These are actually a biennial, but generally reseed themselves. The old, small, single or double flowers are not used much anymore. The large-flowering varieties on low-growing 4- to 6-inch plants are used in borders, for edging, and for spot color. Flowers are white, pink, or red. Flower from March to June. Easy to grow. Plant in most any ordinary garden soil. Grow in practically any exposure, sun to shade.

Felicia *(F. amelloides).* Showy daisylike flowers in light blue, medium blue, or white. Bright green leaves. Keep spent flowers picked and plant continues to flower all summer. Grows 15–18 inches high and 18 inches wide. Use in containers, hanging baskets, and borders. Plant in a sunny spot with good drainage.

Flowering maple (*Abutilon hybridum* and others). Flowering maple hybrids have hanging 1- to 3-inch flowers ranging in shades of yellow, orange, pink, and red. Maplelike leaves green or some variegated. Use outside during summer, or inside as houseplant. Grows up to 8–10 feet, seldom over 2–3 feet in a single summer. Grows best in sun to part sun. Requires good drainage.

Flowering tobacco. See nicotiana.

Forget-me-not *(Myosotis sylvatica).* This biennial reseeds itself. Blue-flowering variety is the most popular, but there are also pink and white varieties. Average height is 6–12 inches. They make excellent border plants and are often used along with the spring-flowering bulbs because bloom periods overlap. They make a colorful spring display for massing or spot color. Grows best in filtered sunlight or part shade, in ordinary garden soil.

Four o'clock *(Mirabilis jalapa).* A fragrant, old-fashioned flower so named because the single clusters of trumpet-shaped flowers usually don't open until 4 p.m. Showy flowers come in shades of pink, red, yellow, and white and are often bicolor. It's not unusual for the flowers to come in different shades of color on the same plant. Plants often reseed or grow back from their tuberous roots. Bushy plants grow up to 24 inches in most any ordinary garden soil. Plant in bright sunlight.

Fuchsia (*F. hybrida,* many varieties). The majority of the varieties are frost tender and are either grown as annuals or must be given winter protection. See Wintering Fuchsias in Chapter 9, Perennials. Many new, hardier varieties have been introduced in recent years. The outer flower petals (corolla) and the inner petals (corona) are often of gorgeous contrasting colors. These exotic-looking plants come with either upright or trailing growth habits. The trailing varieties are ideal for hanging baskets in shade (a few will even grow in part sun), and the uprights are used in containers in shade or as bedding plants. Flower size ranges from about the size of a nickel to a few that are almost cup size. They are often trained into 5- to 6-foot trees. Pinch tips to encourage bushiness, but do it early in the season. Flowers appear on the new tip growth, and late-season tip pinching would result in removal of the flowers. Remove spent flowers before they go to seed. Plants need twice-monthly feeding during the summer growing season. Check watering needs of hanging baskets daily during hot weather. Most varieties require protection from the hot midday sun. One of the most popular plants to grow in the shade. Plant them in organic-rich soil or use a commercial potting soil.

Geranium *(Pelargonium hortorum).* They are frost tender, so if you want to keep them from year to year, they must be brought indoors before any frost touches them (they also can be treated as annual bedding plants). Many types provide excellent summer color in the sunny to part sun garden. Geranium flower colors just about span the color spectrum. Clusters of prolific, showy flowers cover the plants most of the summer, up to frost. Pick off spent flower stems to keep plants flowering. Many new introductions; check to see which you like the best. The common upright geranium, trailing ivy geranium *(P. peltatum),* and upright Martha Washington geraniums *(P. domesticum)* are the most popular. Ivy geraniums are used in hanging baskets and along the edge of containers because of their hanging growth habit. Uprights are used in containers, bedding, mass plantings and for spot color. Marthas (pansy geraniums), with their interesting colors and color combinations, are ideal in containers or when used for spot color. Scented leaf types (*Pelargonium* spp.) have leaf fragrance, which is evident when you brush against the plants. Some types are grown in 5- to 6-foot tree forms. Plants range in size from 6 to 24 inches or more. Some have very attractive variegated leaves that are almost more showy than the flowers. Feed monthly during the growing season. Plant in sunny spots in moist, fertile, well-drained soil.

Godetia *(Clarkia amoena).* Dwarf and tall, single and double, the flowers are slightly fluted. Flower colors range in shades of pink, rose, red, or white. Dwarf varieties grow 8–12 inches, taller ones 15–18 inches high. The new strain of 'Satin' has larger single flowers. This is one annual flower that thrives on a certain amount of neglect. It is not unusual for godetia to reseed itself. Plant in any ordinary garden soil. Plant in full to part sun.

Ground ivy. See creeping charlie.

Helichrysum. See strawflower *(H. bracteatum).*

Heliotrope *(Heliotropium arborescens).* For fragrance, this one is hard to beat, plus the clusters of large purple flowers put on quite a show in the summer garden. There are several varieties in shades of purple, lavender, and white, but the purple-flowering ones are the favorites. We keep a hanging basket of them right in the entry area all summer, just for their tremendous fragrance. Our plants grow 14–18 inches high and quite bushy. Keep the spent flowers picked. Plant in full sun, in fairly rich soil, and avoid overwatering.

Hyacinth bean *(Dolichos lablab).* See Chapter 7, Vines.

Impatiens *(I. wallerana).* Commonly referred to as busy-lizzie. It gets its common name rightfully because this plant flowers prolifically all summer. There are numerous new strains and varieties, most of which range in height from 6 to 12 inches, with a 8- to 14-inch spread. Ideal plants to use in groups for spot color, massing, borders, containers, or even hanging baskets. Flowers range from single to fully double in shades of pink, rose, red, orange, salmon, lavender, purple, or white and many in-between shades. Impatiens are a must in the shade garden. This is one plant that grows especially well in part to full shade; however, there are a few that will tolerate considerable sun. Grow in fertile, well-drained soil.

New Guinea hybrids. The variegated leaves of some of these varieties are almost as pretty as the flowers. Other varieties have light to dark green, bronze, or red leaves. The flowers are larger than the regular impatiens, standing above the foliage nicely, but not as prolific. Leaves are larger and plants tend to grow tall, up to 12 inches in my garden. They will take more sun than the regular impatiens. These are tender perennials grown as summer annuals, but you can pot them up in the fall, before the first frost, and take them inside to grow as houseplants over the winter.

Ipomoea *(I. batatas).* Commonly called the sweet potato vine. The attractive foliage makes this a great accent plant. The large, 4- to 6-inch, deeply lobed leaves come in chartreuse, purplish black, or variegated, providing bright color and a wonderful texture. They are frost tender, so do not plant them until late spring. Often used in hanging baskets, the plants will also do well in the open ground in full sun, providing they get good drainage.

Morning glory *(I. nil).* Annual vines, not to be confused with the nuisance perennial bindweed. See Chapter 7, Vines.

Lamium *(L. galeobdolon* and *L. maculatum).* Both are grown for their attractive foliage and flowers. The *galeobdolon* varieties have a vining growth habit and are often used in hanging baskets. Vines can be invasive, so keep them under control. The *maculatum* varieties are bushy plants and used more in container plantings. Their flowers range in shades of orchid, lavender, pink, or white. They grow in most any ordinary garden soil, in sun, part sun, and even shade.

Lantana. There are many hybrid varieties that have attractive clusters of verbenalike flowers. Plants range to 4 feet high, often shorter here, because of our short growing season. They range in brilliant shades of orange, yellow, lavender, pink, or red, many with contrasting colors. Dark green foliage is excellent background for showy flowers. They are not frost hardy, but I have had one or two live over in a mild winter. Plant them in full sun, in well-drained soil.

Larkspur *(Consolida ambigua/Delphinium ajacis).* Often called the annual delphinium. This showy annual grows up to 4 feet tall and is excellent as a backdrop to other flowers. They come in a broad range of colors, including pink, rose, salmon, lilac, purple, white, or blue. They make excellent cut flowers. Plant in full sun, in fertile, well-drained soil.

Licorice vine *(Helichrysum petiolare).* There are several varieties with outstanding leaf color. My favorites are 'Limelight' with its lime-green leaves and 'Silver Licorice Vine' with its silver-gray foliage. Excellent plants for mixed hanging baskets and container plantings. Vines grow 24–36 inches in a season. Leaves color best in full to part sun, in well-drained soil.

Linaria *(L. maroccana).* Sometimes called toadflax. A couple of different species are grown for their summer flowers. 'Fantasy' (hybrids) mix grows 12–18 inches and 'Dwarf' mix of the Fairy Bouquet strain grows only 8–10 inches high. These colorful plants have miniature snapdragon-like flowers. The pastel flower colors are showy in group or mass plantings. Although they like a mostly sunny spot, avoid planting them in hot spots. Prepare a fertile, well-drained soil planting area.

Livingston daisy *(Mesembryanthemum crystallinum).* For the hottest, driest, most neglected area in the garden, you may want to consider this plant. Succulent leaves and brilliant daisylike flowers on low-spreading plants. Mixed luminous colors and bicolor in shades of pink, red, orange, cream, or white. Does especially well in sand at the ocean. Plant in bright, hot sun. Grows in any ordinary garden soil.

Lobelia *(L. erinus).* See also cardinal flower in Chapter 9, Perennials. The trailing types are used for hanging basket and containers and the bush types for borders or at the edge of containers. For years, the dark purple varieties were the most popular, but today the light blues and whites are also gaining favor. The trailing varieties now come in red, rose, lilac, blue, and white. The bush type grows to only 4–8 inches, while the trailing type will spread up to 12 inches or more. They grow in full or part sun, and even do well in shade. Plant in well-drained soil.

Lotus vine *(L. berthelotii).* Common name is parrot's beak. Delicate gray foliage and small, 1-inch, bright red flowers combine to make this a great vining plant for hanging baskets and containers. *L. maculatus* 'Gold Flash' is the yellow-flowering variety. Vines may grow 2–3 feet a season. Need full sun to flower at their full potential. Provide fertile, well-drained soil.

Mallow *(Lavatera trimestris).* Large 3- to 4-inch satiny flowers on plants 3–4 feet high. Pick spent flowers and plants will flower all summer. Excellent background plants ideal for seasonal summer hedge. Feed monthly with rose type fertilizer. Plant in full or part sun, in rich, well-drained soil.

Marigold (*Tagetes erecta* and ssp.). The large-flowering, taller-growing American strains now come in plants that range in size from 1 to 4 feet high. The fully double 3- to 4-inch orange or yellow flowers are long lasting and very showy. The tallest ones are used as background annuals, while the shorter varieties are often used in borders. Marigolds grow well in full or part sun, in well-drained, fertile soil.

> **French marigolds** *(T. patula).* These lower-growing marigolds come in a wide range of 2- to 2½-inch flowers in yellow, orange, red, brown, and combinations of colors. These low-growing ones are ideal for borders, groupings, or mass plantings.

Mexican heather. See cuphea.

Million bells (*Calibrachoa).* A wonderful plant for hanging baskets, with great trailing habit and small, petunia-like flowers. See the Tip on page 14.

Mimulus *(M. hybridus).* Commonly called the monkey flower. This is a colorful, low-growing, early-flowering annual. The multicolored flowers are said to resemble the face of a grinning monkey. An easy-to-grow summer annual. Do not let the plants dry out. Feed monthly during the blooming period. Plant in rich, moist soil in a cool, partially shady spot.

Morning glory. See ipomoea.

Moss rose. See portulaca.

Nasturtium *(Tropaeolum majus).* One of the most popular old-time annual flowers. There are two types: the trailing/climbing (3–6 feet) one and the low-growing dwarf (18 inches) plants. Showy flowers are available in either single or double, and come in shades of yellow, orange, creamy white, red, and reddish brown. Cut flowers are excellent for small bouquets. 2- to 2½-inch flowers stand out above the bright green leaves. Easy, quick-growing annual from seed. Thrives on considerable neglect. Plant in full or part sun, in ordinary garden soil.

Nemesia *(N. strumosa).* This is one plant that the Canadians grow to perfection, due in part to their cooler summers. The small clusters of bright mixed colors cover the compact plants. They grow about 12 feet wide and up to 12–18 inches high. Very showy in mass bed plantings, as well as for edging and container planting. Plant in a mostly sunny spot with fairly rich, somewhat moist, but well-drained soil.

New Guinea impatiens. See impatiens, New Guinea hybrids.

Nicotiana *(N. alata).* Commonly called flowering tobacco. The fragrance at dusk is very pleasant, with white-flowering varieties having the best fragrance. There are dwarf, semi-dwarf, and tall varieties. Plants range in size from 2 to 6 feet. Tubular, flaring flowers appear at the top of the stems. Use low varieties in borders and taller ones as background flowers. Use near the entry area where fragrance can best be enjoyed. Plant in full sun or part sun and shade. Prefers rich, moist, well-drained soil.

Painted daisy *(Chrysanthemum coccineum).* An old-time favorite that is once again becoming popular. The extremely showy 2-inch daisy flowers come in striking combinations of colors. Plants grow up to 2 feet. Starts easily from seed when planted in full to part sun. Keep soil somewhat moist during the summer. Plant in fertile garden soil.

Painted tongue. See salpiglossis.

Pansy *(Viola* x *wittrockiana).* One of the first annuals to flower in the spring. Some are winter-hardy. Many flowers have markings that somewhat resemble faces. The 2- to 4-inch flowers come in a wide range of colors and color combinations, including yellow, bronze, blue, purple, pink, red, orange, and white. Bushy plants grow 4–8 inches high. Ideal for borders, mass plantings, edging, rock gardens, and along the edge of containers. Pinch back leggy growth to encourage bushiness. Also pick off spent flowers to keep the plants blooming. Plant in rich, well-drained, cool soil. Although they will grow in full sun, pansies flower for a longer period of time in cooler, shady parts of the garden.

Persian shield *(Strobilanthes acanthaceae).* Often grown as a houseplant, this is also a great foliage plant to use in containers. The pointed 6-inch oval leaves have a bluish, metallic sheen that is extremely attractive when combined with other plants. It occasionally has pale blue flowers, but it's the foliage that counts. Keep plants about 12–18 inches high. Can be potted up and brought indoors before the first fall frost, then grown as a houseplant over winter. Grows in filtered sun, in fertile, well-drained soil.

Petunia *(P. hybrida).* Many different strains are featured in today's garden. One of my favorites is the new trailing 'Wave' petunia, which is ideal for hanging baskets or mass plantings. They are rapid-growing and prolific-flowering. However, many others merit a place in the garden. Petunias come in single and double flowering varieties. I think the smaller multiflora (floribunda) varieties are the best for marine climates like the Pacific Northwest. Rains and overhead watering do not spoil the flowers as quickly as they do for the larger-flowering hybrids. Flower colors practically span the color spectrum. Smell the flowers, as some varieties have a very pleasant fragrance, especially the purple ones. Flowers are open-funnel-shaped and about 2 inches across on the multifloras. Petunias are ideal to use in borders, edgings, mass plantings, rock gardens, or containers and hanging baskets. Feed monthly during the growing season. Plant them in well-drained, ordinary garden soil.

Phlox *(P. drummondii).* My favorites are the dwarf bushy varieties that grow only 8–10 inches high. Typical phlox flowers in shades of pink, salmon, scarlet, crimson, blue, lilac, yellow, and white. Some varieties have star-shaped flowers. Ideal for mass plantings, borders, and container plantings. Removal of spent flowers will keep the plants flowering for a longer period. Plant in full sun in fairly rich, well-drained soil.

Pincushion flower. See scabiosa.

Plectranthus. The variety I have in my garden is 'Troy's Gold'; it has leaves that are creamy yellow along the margins and dark green in the center. It's great foliage color for a hanging basket or container in shade. Often grown as a houseplant; you can bring it inside in the autumn and grow it as an indoor plant. Plant in the shade, in rich, fertile, well-drained soil.

Poor man's orchid. See schizanthus.

Poppy. See California poppy, shirley poppy.

Portulaca *(P. grandiflora).* Commonly called moss rose. These low-growing succulent plants have bright flowers that resemble tiny roses. Some come in individual colors of named varieties, but most are grown in mixed colors of yellow, white, orange, pink, and red. Plants grow only 4–6 inches high, bushing out to 10–12 inches. Excellent plants for a bright, hot, sunny spot. Use as a summer ground cover, as a rock garden annual, or for borders. Plants survive on a certain amount of neglect. Plant in a sunny spot, in ordinary garden soil.

Potato vine *(Solanum jasminoides).* Often used in hanging baskets, the plant may have an unruly growth habit and need a bit of pinching. Clusters of 1-inch white flowers. Solid-green leaf variety and one with variegated green and cream foliage. Grows rapidly in full sun, in fertile soil that is well drained.

Pot marigold. See calendula.

Salpiglossis *(S. sinuata).* Common name is painted tongue. This is a plant you saw in grandma's garden, and it merits a place in today's garden too! I call this annual a conversation piece when planted in the garden. The unusual markings on the 2- to 2½-inch trumpet-shaped flowers are brilliantly bicolor and veined in contrasting colors. Plants grow 2–2½ feet in full sun. Plant in fertile, well-drained soil.

Salvia *(S. splendens).* Do not confuse these annuals with the many perennial varieties. For years the annual varieties, dwarf to tall, came only in red. Today, the flower colors range from purple, lilac, salmon, red, to white. The dwarf 8- to 12-inch varieties are the most popular. Some varieties grow up to 2 feet or more. Dwarf salvia are ideal for mass planting, borders, and spot color. Grow in a mostly sunny location, in ordinary, well-drained garden soil.

S. farinacea 'Victoria' or 'Blue Bedder'. Another of the annual salvias that has become popular (and my favorite). These have blue or white flowers and grayish-green leaves. They sometimes winter over in our garden. These varieties grow up to 1½–2 feet in our garden. Spike-type flowers stand above the sage-scented foliage. Bees are attracted to these salvias.

Scabiosa *(S. atropurpurea).* Commonly called the pincushion flower. The 2- to 2½-inch ball-shaped flowers come in shades of deep crimson, lavender, rose, pink, and white. Plants grow up to 2½ feet high. Keep the spent flowers picked and they will flower all summer. Showy in borders, in group plantings, or in the cut flower garden. Grows best in full sun, in fertile, well-drained soil.

Scaevola *(S. aemula).* This is a rather new introduction to the Northwest. The lavender-blue, fan-shaped flowers are like half flowers. It flowers all summer, nicely shedding the spent flowers on its own. We have used it in combination planters and by itself in hanging baskets, and have been really pleased with its performance. The plant tends to trail unless planted with other plants; then it will have some branches that hang and others that will work their way upward through the other plants, creating quite a show. Especially effective in hanging baskets and containers. Branches grow 18–30 inches long. Plant in full to part sun, in fertile soil that is well drained.

Schizanthus *(S. pinnatus).* Commonly called poor man's orchid or butterfly bush. This is an annual the Canadians grow to perfection, because it likes their cool spring and summer weather. Clusters of orchidlike flowers cover the upright stems, which stand above attractive fernlike foliage. The showy flowers have colorful contrasting markings. Ideal to grow under trees, in mass plantings, or for spot color. Plants grow 12–18 inches high. Plant in filtered sunlight, in moist, fertile soil.

Shirley poppy *(Papaver rhoeas).* One of my favorite annual poppies. The shirley poppies have single and double flowers in shades of pink, rose, or red. They grow up to 2½ feet high. They are easy to grow and thrive with a certain amount of neglect. Plant in full sun, with well-drained soil.

Snapdragon *(Antirrhinum majus).* Many new varieties with varying growing habits make them even more popular. These plants sometimes winter over in our garden. Dwarf, medium, tall, and 'Luminaire Series' trailing varieties have unlimited uses in the garden. The low ones are ideal for borders or massing, while medium and tall varieties make excellent cut flowers and are nice plants to use in borders, as background plants, or for spot color. Colors of the single- and double-flowering varieties range in shades of pink, rose, red, peach, yellow, and white. Cut back spent flower stocks and plants will rebranch and continue to flower. A whole host of fascinating varieties and growing habits. In fact, you might want to consider growing the new trailing variety in hanging baskets or containers. Plant in a sunny to part sun location, in fertile soil that is well drained.

Spider flower. See cleome.

Statice *(Limonium sinuatum).* One of the most popular flowers to use in dried arrangements. New strains come in a wide variety of mixed colors. Spike flower clusters are papery and are excellent for fresh as well as dried arrangements. Plants grow 24–30 inches tall. They thrive with a certain amount of neglect. Grow in full sun in ordinary garden soil.

Stock *(Matthiola incana).* Possibly the most fragrant of all annual flowers. The attractive flower spikes can be either single or double. Very showy in the garden, they also make excellent cut flowers. Growing heights vary by variety from 12 to 24 inches, with the Giant strain growing up to 3 feet. Especially colorful in borders, massing, or group plantings. Plant them in an area where you can best enjoy their intense fragrance. They have wintered over in our garden on occasion. They must have good drainage. Plant them in full sun, in a light, fertile soil.

Strawflower *(Helichrysum bracteatum).* Not only attractive in the garden, it is outstanding to use as a dried flower. Papery 2-inch flowers range in shades of pink, red, yellow, orange, or white. Excellent for cutting fresh or drying. Grows 2–2½ feet high. Plant in full sun, in light, well-drained soil.

Sunflower *(Helianthus annuus).* One of today's most popular annual garden plants. This is one the adults and kids both love to grow. The huge mammoth variety, with its large flowers, grows up to 10–12 feet but some of the newer varieties are fast becoming popular because of their attractive single or double flowers, many with growth heights of only 1½–6 feet. Flower colors of the new ones vary from yellows through orange, reds, bronze, to mahogany. Plant in full sun, in deep, fertile soil, in order to grow largest flowers and tallest plants.

Swan River daisy *(Brachycome iberidifolia).* Very attractive 1- to 1½-inch daisy flowers on bushy, compact plants. New varieties range in color from blue, mauve, and pink to white. Most grow about 10–16 inches high, but some will spread up to 2–3 feet in a season. Ideal for containers, combination hanging baskets, or rock gardens. Plant in semi-shade to sun, in rich, moist soil.

Sweet alyssum. See alyssum.

Sweet pea *(Lathyrus odoratus).* Probably the all-time favorite fragrant flowering vine. However, today there are low 12-inch plants like the Little Sweetheart strain, medium-sized 24-inch vines like 'Supersnoop', and then the climbing varieties that grow 6 feet or taller. Fragrance varies between varieties, so if it's fragrance you want, you may need to grow a collection like 'Old Spice'. You will find them in individual flower colors or mixed collections. They are beautiful, fragrant cut flowers. In the garden, trellis the taller-growing varieties. Grow the vines in a north-south direction for best air circulation and sun exposure. Sweet peas like it cool, so plant them in a sunny spot, but early in the season. Seeds should be sown in about mid-February in most areas. Plant in fertile, well-drained soil.

Sweet potato vine. See ipomoea.

Sweet sultan. See bachelor's button.

Toadflax. See linaria.

Verbena *(V. hortensis/hybrida).* Very colorful clusters of attractive tiny flowers. The bush varieties make compact, free-flowering plants that are ideal for edging, borders, spot color, or mass plantings. The new trailing-type verbenas are especially attractive in hanging baskets and container plantings. They often spread 18–24 inches. I have had these winter over a couple of times in my garden. I think these are a must for summer garden color. Plant them in full sun, in fertile, well-drained soil.

Viola *(V. tricolor).* Often called the faceless pansy; however, some varieties of violas do actually have markings. Violas tend to have a very bushy, compact growth and are prolific flowering. Keep the spent flowers picked and they will flower all season. They range in shades of blue through purple, yellow, apricot, orange, red, and white. Plant them in an area where they are protected from the hot midday sun, in moist, fertile, well-drained soil.

Viscaria *(Silene/Lychnis coeli-rosa).* Old-time favorite annual. The open, airy stems bear single 1-inch sprays of flowers in shades of lavender, rose, pink, and white.

Plant in groups in borders or containers. Plants grow 12–15 inches high. They grow best in full sun in ordinary garden soil.

Wax begonia *(B.* x *semperflorens-cultorum).* These fibrous begonias grow 6–12 inches high in a dense ball shape. Flowers range in shades of pink, red, and white. Foliage ranges in shades of green, bronze, reddish, to variegated green and white. Very popular for edging or small group planting. See also tuberous begonia in Chapter 11, Bulbs. Plant in shade, part sun, or even full sun. Plants will grow and flower best in well-drained, organic-enriched soil.

'Nonstop'. These begonias are a strain started from seed. Their flowers are not as large as the tuberous-type begonias (for those, see Chapter 11, Bulbs), but very showy. Plants flower all season long, hence the name. Plants grow 12–18 inches high. May form tuber by the end of the season.

Zinnia *(Z. elegans).* The common single- or double-flowering zinnias are top-notch summer plants. Gorgeous in the garden or as cut flowers. There are dwarf (8–15 inches), medium (15–24 inches), and tall (24–36 inches) varieties, plus the low single-flowering varieties (8–10 inches) that spread into bushy plants. These are ideal for low borders, bedding, containers, and mass plantings, while the medium ones are excellent for midbed planting and the tall ones are excellent background annuals. The flowers on mine seem to last for the longest time and are in shades of gold, orange, or white. I think they are real winners! See also creeping zinnia. Plant in a warm, sunny spot. They do best in rich, fertile, well-drained soil.

14 Herbs

In recent years, the popularity of herbs has simply skyrocketed. It's no wonder, because most are so easy to grow, can be grown in many different ways, and have many culinary uses; some also make very attractive landscape plants. Just consider their uses alone: in cooking, in teas, for fragrance, and in cosmetics, medicine, dyes, wreaths, and arrangements. Herbs are so useful and showy that I seem to add at least one new herb to our garden every year. From the landscape point of view, the bright foliage colors, various textures, flowers, and interesting growing habits make them ideal plants to include in the garden.

Facing page: Chives are wonderful herbs to grow outdoors in the summer or indoors, in pots, over the winter.

Below: Sage is a great seasoning herb and an attractive garden or container plant.

Choosing the Location

In Containers

I like to see herbs planted in a window box, just outside the kitchen window. My second favorite place is in a container on the patio, deck, or lanai just outside the kitchen door. Of course, the idea is to plant them in a place that is really convenient, so they will be used for culinary purposes, beauty, and fragrance.

For years, Myrna and I have enjoyed herbs planted in a strawberry barrel. The pockets along the sides of the barrel hold about half a dozen different herbs. The first time we planted a strawberry barrel of herbs, I planted a catnip plant in the top soil area. Our cat, Tiki, thought it was a terrific treat, a super place to roll and sleep—great for the cat, but not a good idea for the herb grower: the other three surrounding herb plants were crushed. The moral of this story is to plant catnip in a special place where the cat will not disturb other plants.

In the Vegetable Garden

Herbs are often grown in the vegetable garden, and this is fine but sometimes not the most convenient place for picking and using them.

Throughout the Landscape

Some herbs are so attractive that they merit a place in the landscape. In fact, for centuries the herb garden has been a prominent feature within the world's most celebrated gardens. They may appear in formal, semiformal, or informal plantings. Today, many homeowners are incorporating scaled-down versions of the old-fashioned herb gardens in their modern landscapes. In our garden we have herbs mixed with our evergreen shrubs, perennials, and annual plantings, and find the textures, foliage color, and flowers make a very pleasing combination. *Note:* Never use pesticides in or near the herb plants or near any edible crop.

Indoors

Chives, parsley, sage, lavender, thyme, and rosemary are a few herbs that are quite easy to grow in pots indoors during the winter, on a north- or east-facing windowsill or in a greenhouse window. They may tend to stretch and get a little leggy, but continual shearing and use of the greens will help keep them looking nice. Many other herbs can be grown indoors in winter if placed under fluorescent lights. The lights should be placed about 2 inches above the tops of the plants and turned on for fourteen to sixteen hours a day.

Planting Herbs

There are five ways in which you can get started with herbs:

- Start them from seed.
- Buy the already started plants.
- Start most from cuttings.
- Start a few by layering.
- Start some from divisions.

From Seed

Starting Seeds Indoors

You can start the seeds indoors during the late winter. Read and follow seeding directions on the package, or if you have collected your own seed, see my seed starting recommendations in Chapter 9, Perennials. Sow the seeds of annual herbs indoors in early to midspring so the seedling plants will be ready to plant outdoors as soon as all danger of frost has passed.

Sowing Seeds Outdoors
The perennial herbs can be seeded outdoors anytime during the spring and summer months.

From Bedding Plants

Many garden centers offer herb starts in pots. Most are available in 4-, 6-, or 8-inch pots. Some of the ground cover–type herbs are often available in flats, so they can be divided to cover larger areas; for example, thyme, Corsican mint, and sweet woodruff. See Chapter 12, Ground Covers.

From Cuttings

Most perennial herbs can also be started from cuttings. The best time to take most cuttings is during the months of July and August. Winter cuttings can also be taken from the evergreen (perennial) herbs. Take short cuttings (from tip growth) only about 2 to 4 inches long. Start the cuttings in a 50 percent sand and 50 percent peat moss mix, or light potting soil. Keep the cuttings in a warm room with bright light until they have rooted. Pot them into individual pots and set outside as soon as danger of frost is over.

Dig the Planting Hole

Prepare a planting hole as you would for any plant, about two times larger in width and depth than the root ball of the plant you are planting.

Prepare the Soil for Planting

Most herbs are not very fussy about soil. The majority of them seem to grow well in most any semi-sandy soil. The addition of organic humus in the form of compost, processed manure (the bagged kind), or peat moss is also beneficial in getting the plants off to a good start.

> The herb stevia is a natural sweetener, sometimes called the "sugar bush." It is 150 to 400 times as sweet as sugar, with just a few calories. It needs full sun in well-drained soil. I like to see it planted on raised soil. The plant will grow up to 3 to 4 feet tall. Starter plants are generally available in the spring at nurseries and garden centers.

Set the Plant at the Proper Depth

Set the plant in the prepared soil so the top of the root ball is level with the soil surface. Make a small well around the plant to collect water, and stand back and watch the plant double in size the first year.

How far apart should herbs be spaced? Answer: depends upon the variety. On average, about 12 to 15 inches. If you have ample room, space them a bit farther apart.

By Layering

Herbs that have stems lying on the ground or close to the soil can be *layered.* This is the process of gently making a cut on the underside of a stem, then lightly covering the stem with soil and weighting it down with a rock to keep it in place until roots develop. Some herbs, such as thyme, rosemary, and lavender, will sometimes develop layering roots on their own.

From Divisions

The best time to dig and transplant large established herbs or perennial herbs that develop more than one underground stem is during the months of September and October, or during the spring months of March or early April. Actually, small plants can be replanted on any cool day throughout the spring and summer.

Dig a clump of dirt with the roots attached (commonly referred to as a root ball). Replant into a new planting area immediately so the roots do not dry out. If desired, this is a good time to also divide larger herb plants, providing they have multiple stems coming from roots. If you try to divide the clumps, you will find it easier to do and there will be less root breakage if you wash or shake off some of the soil from around the roots.

Pruning or Shearing Herbs

A certain amount of pruning or shearing is done as you actually use the herbs. In some cases, no further shaping is needed. However, if your plants get out of shape, lightly prune them anytime during the growing season. If severe pruning is needed, it is best to do it in early spring. You can prune in the fall, but then the plant will look pruned all winter, and the heartwood (main stem) of the plant will be exposed to severe winter weather.

Harvesting and Preserving Herbs

When is the best time? That's easy! Early morning on a dry day, when oil content is at its peak: Just cut the few inches of tip growth on the leafy type herbs. Cutting back too far will restrict new growth, thus reducing the frequency of harvesting, so try to confine your tip cutting to 2 to 4 inches.

Drying Herbs

Leafy Herbs

Cut stems several inches long, bundle a few stems together, tie with string, and hang the bundle upside down in a warm, well-ventilated room. A basement or semi-heated garage is ideal for drying herbs. It's a good idea to label each one so you know which herb it is, because their appearance will change a little as they dry. Once they have dried, the leaves can be stripped from the stems. Short-stemmed herbs can be dried over a screen if it's more convenient.

Seed Herbs

Be certain to harvest the seedheads before they become ripe, burst, and fall to the ground. They can be dried in the same way as the leafy herbs, providing you make sure the seedheads are intact throughout the drying period. Some herbs will dry in seven to ten days. Separate the seed from the chaff, then let the seeds dry for another week.

Microwave Drying

A much quicker way to dry herbs is in the microwave. Wait two to three days after harvest before using this method. Place a paper towel in the microwave, spread one layer of herb leaves, then cover with one thickness of paper towel. Set the microwave on low heat for two minutes. If they have not dried sufficiently, turn them over and set the microwave for another one or two minutes.

Storing Dried Herbs

Once the herbs are dry, store them in an airtight container. Keep the dried herbs in a cool, dark place. Use glass jars, resealable plastic bags, or similar containers to store herbs. Avoid using paper or cardboard containers, which tend to absorb the oils.

Freezing Herbs

I had never heard of this method until recently, but it really makes sense; it is ideal for leafy herbs such as basil, chives, parsley, etc. Simply wash the fresh leaves, pat them dry, remove them from the stems, place them in a plastic freezer bag, and put it in the freezer.

I think this is a better idea: place a few leaves in each section of a water-filled ice-cube tray and freeze. Once frozen, place the frozen cubes in a freezer bag. When you're ready to use them, simply take out a cube and add it for seasoning.

Protecting Herbs from Cold Weather

Many of the most common perennial and evergreen herbs are quite winter hardy and really do not need winter protection in this region. However, if you are concerned about the winter hardiness of a particular herb plant, simply mulch over the surrounding soil with an inch or two of bark, sawdust, or straw. Then in early spring, after all danger of frost has past, simply pull the mulch away from the base of the plant.

Choosing Herbs

By Particular Features

Our Favorite Culinary Herbs

Since I grow them but don't use them in everyday cooking, I've asked my wife, Myrna, and our daughter-in-law, Ann, for their suggestions of which thirteen herbs they use the most. Keep in mind there are countless others, some of which you might like even better, but these are their choices:

basil
chives
coriander
dill
fennel
garlic
marjoram
oregano
parsley
rosemary
sage
tarragon
thyme

Best Herbs to Begin With

If you're growing herbs for the first time, start with these six:

chives
peppermint
parsley
rosemary
sage
thyme

Ed's Favorite Landscape Herbs

Many herbs deserve a prominent spot in the landscape. Over the years, I have grown many different ones in our garden and I think the following have been the most rewarding for ease of growth, texture, and leaf color. Next time you're in a garden center or nursery, take a look at these herbs and if you agree, give them a try in your garden:

artemisia species
basil, *Ocimum basilicum*
bay, *Laurus nobilis*
catnip, *Nepeta cataria*
feverfew, *Chrysanthemum parthenium*
lavender, *Lavandula* spp.
lavender cotton, *Santolina chamaecyparissus*
rosemary, *Rosmarinus officinalis*
sage, *Salvia officinalis*
scented-leaf geranium, *Pelargonium* spp.
thyme, *Thymus vulgaris*
yarrow, *Achilles millefolium*

Herbs to Attract Hummingbirds

This is a question I am often asked about herbs. Answer: here are three of the best:

bee balm, *Monarda*
catnip, *Nepeta cataria*
sage, *Salvia officinalis*

Below: Parsley has many uses in the kitchen and also looks beautiful planted among summer-flowering annuals.

For Specific Sites

Indoors

Twelve of the most popular herbs to grow indoors over the winter are:

bay, *Laurus nobilis*
chives, *Allium schoenoprasum*
coriander, *Coriandrum sativum*
garlic chives, *Allium tuberosum*
ginger, *Zingiber officinalis*
lavender, *Lavandula* spp.
mint, *Mentha* spp.
oregano, *Origanum heracleoticum*
parsley, *Petroselinum crispum*
sage, *Salvia officinalis*
savory, *Satureja hortensis*
thyme, *Thymus vulgaris*

In a Shady Spot

Here are six herbs that will do well in the shade:

borage, *Borago officinalis*
lemon balm, *Melissa officinalis*
mint, *Mentha* spp.
parsley, *Petroselinum crispum*
sweet woodruff, *Galium odoratum*
tarragon, *Artemisia dracunculus*

By Size

Low-Growing

Six ground cover–type herbs:

lamb's ear, *Stachys byzantina*
lavender cotton, *Santolina chamaecyparissus*
creeping thyme, Thymus *serpyllum*
dwarf rosemary, *Rosmarinus officinalis* 'Prostratus'
sweet woodruff, *Galium odoratum*
woolly thyme, *Thymus pseudolanuginosus*

Medium-sized

Six popular medium-sized herbs that are ideal in size for planting in borders, containers, or in the vegetable garden:

basil, *Ocimum basilicum*
coriander (cilantro), *Coriandrum sativum*
lavender cotton, *Santolina chamaecyparissus*
rosemary, *Rosmarinus officinalis*

sage, *Salvia officinalis*
yarrow, *Achillea millefolium*

Tall-growing Herbs

Here are two of the most common taller-growing herbs. These would be ideal plants to use as background herbs in landscape borders, or on the north side of the vegetable garden, where they would not shade your other crops.

bay laurel
dill

Fragrant Herbs

Although almost all herbs are noted for their fragrances, these six are among the best of the herbs commonly grown in Northwest gardens.

bay laurel (leaves)
geraniums, scented leaf (leaves)
lavender (leaves and flowers)
mints (leaves, all varieties)
rosemary (leaves)
thyme (leaves, all varieties)

Herbs That Grow in Moist Soil

Of the more than two dozen herbs I have listed in this chapter, here are the two that will tolerate moist soils. These two will also tolerate shade, so they become versatile herbs in many gardens.

mints (all varieties except catnip)
parsley (all varieties)

Herbs That Grow in Dry Soil

Although many herbs are noted for their ability to grow with a certain amount of neglect, these eight are among the easiest to grow, even in dry soil.

borage
chives
feverfew
lavender
rosemary
sage
thyme
yarrow

Herbs Encyclopedia

Artemisia (*A. frigida* and other species). Commonly called wormwood. This is a very attractive landscape plant because of its colorful silvery-gray leaves. There are several species; *A. stellerana* is probably the most popular (see silver brocade in Chapter 9, Perennials). *A. frigida* is also very popular because of its delicate soft gray foliage. It grows about 18 inches or less. In the landscape, plant them in borders or along with other herbs. Shear in springtime to keep plants bushy. Mugwort is also an artemisia *(A. vulgaris);* it grows up to 5 feet. Artemisia grows best in full to part sun, in any ordinary, well-drained garden soil.

Tarragon *(A. dracunculus).* Commonly called French tarragon; is considered the true tarragon. Plant in borders, window boxes, or the vegetable garden. A "must" herb for gourmet cooks. Popular to use with poultry, veal, fish, salads, and soups. Leaves can be used fresh before the inconspicuous, sterile summer flowers bloom. Leaves can also be frozen or dried. Plant in fertile, well-drained garden soil.

Basil *(Ocimum basilicum).* There are many varieties that merit a place in the home garden and kitchen. Probably the most popular landscape subject is 'Purple Ruffles' basil. Others range in size from 1 to 6 feet. This is one of the most popular annual kitchen herbs. Its fresh or dried leaves are used in soups, with vegetables, and in Italian cuisine. The variety 'Italian Large Leaf', as the name implies, has larger leaves. Be certain to pick off flowers, or the plant goes to seed and leaves begin to drop off. They are ideal to grow in containers, the herb or vegetable garden, or landscape borders. Must be planted in a sunny spot, with warm soil, moist but well drained.

Bay *(Laurus nobilis).* Often called "Sweet Bay." The attractive 3- to 4-inch dark-green leaves have numerous seasoning uses in soups, stews, sauces, etc. The plants are a bit on the tender side and may need winter protection when temperatures dip below 25 degrees. This evergreen tree may grow up to 25–30 feet tall here in the Northwest. However, pruning and shaping can control its height. If you live in a cold area, grow it in a container so the plant can be taken in during cold spells. Plant in full sun, in rich, well-drained soil.

Bee balm *(Monarda didyma).* Attracts butterflies and hummingbirds. See Chapter 9, Perennials.

Borage *(Borago officinalis).* The gray-green leaves are ornamental and young leaves are used in teas or as fresh or cooked greens. This herb can be quite invasive, so it's best grown in a container, in a confined area, where it cannot self-seed. Eventual height up to 2½ feet. It thrives on a certain amount of neglect. Plant in full sun in most any ordinary garden soil.

Catnip *(Nepeta cataria).* A great plant for the cats, as they love the smell of the leaves. Grow it in a container or area of the garden where they can roll on the plant. Dried leaves can be used in cat toys and in teas. The plants usually grow 18–30 inches high. Attractive gray-green leaves and lavender or white flowers. Plant in full sun, in ordinary, well-drained soil.

Catmint *(N.* x *faassenii).* The other plant that cats love is of the same family. It grows about 12 inches high and about 1½ feet wide. Flowers are lavender.

Chives *(Allium schoenoprasum).* Foliage has delicate onionlike flavor. Used for flavoring salads, soups, or stews. Foliage is also used in dips, in sauces, and with cottage cheese. Plants grow 6–12 inches. Leaves that are cut will grow again. Grow year-round outdoors during the spring, summer, and fall, then pot up and bring indoors and place on a windowsill during the winter. Grows best in full sun, in fertile, well-drained soil.

Garlic chives *(A. tuberosum).* Have flattened leaves, unlike ordinary chives, and have a garlic flavor.

Garlic *(A. sativum).* Grow from garlic sets (bulbs) planted in the fall, at about the same time as you plant tulips and daffodils. Harvest bulbs when tops die back in midsummer. Use fresh or braid stems and air-dry, then store in a cool, well-ventilated place. It has just about unlimited seasoning uses. Grow garlic cloves in a sunny place, with fertile, well-drained soil.

Giant elephant garlic *(A. scorodoprasum).* Has much larger, mild-flavored bulbs.

Left: Lavender not only makes a lovely garden plant, but also can be used in fragrances, sachets, potpourris, or in dried arrangements.

Coriander *(Coriandrum sativum).* Commonly called cilantro. Flavorful leaves and seeds are both used in a wide variety of different ethnic recipes. Uses for the leaves include flavoring meats, soups, and spicy dishes; the seeds are used in pastries, pickles, and sausage. Annual plants grow 24–30 inches high. Plant in a sunny spot, in rich, fertile, well-drained soil.

Dill *(Anethum graveolens).* Dill is, of course, used for making pickles, but is also used in salads, in sauces, and with fish. Plants grow 3–5 feet tall. Use as a background plant in borders or in the vegetable garden. Plant in a sunny location, in fertile, moist, well-drained soil.

Feverfew *(Chrysanthemum parthenium).* This is a free-seeding, prolific-flowering herb. Small daisylike flowers are a colorful addition to the herb garden. Plants grow 1–3 feet. Strongly scented leaves are used for medicinal purposes. Use as a border plant or for spot color in the garden. Grow in full sun, in most any ordinary garden soil.

Garlic. See chives.

Garlic chives. See chives.

Geranium. See scented-leaf geranium (*Pelargonium* species).

Ginger. *(Zingiber officinale).* The rhizome (root) is an important seasoning in curries, baked goods, beverages (tea), and candies. Currently it is being used as a treatment for motion sickness. Grows about 2 feet high. Take indoors or into a greenhouse over winter. Since is tropical, it should be grown in pots in a bright, sunny area. Plant in potting soil or organic-enriched, well-drained garden soil.

Lamb's ear *(Stachys byzantina).* This is an ornamental perennial herb, used primarily for its woolly, silver-gray foliage. The plants grow 12–18 inches with whorls of small purple flowers. Excellent for borders, edging, or group planting. Flowers can be used in dried arrangements. Grow in full or part sun, in ordinary, well-drained soil.

Lavender *(Lavandula angustifolia).* This is the English lavender. Most English lavenders grow 2 feet or less and make excellent bushy ground covers. Many have grayish green, aromatic foliage. Flowers range from pink, lavender-blue, violet, to white depending upon variety. There are several other species as well; most make very attractive, fragrant garden plants. We have the Spanish lavender *(L. stoechas)* in our garden and find it an excellent flowering perennial. Flower colors range from white, lavender, pink, to purple. These herbs are grown primarily as ornamental plants; however, the dried flowers and seeds are used in arrangements, sachets, and potpourris. Oils are also used in soaps and perfumes. Most varieties range from 18–24 inches. Plants are bushy and grow best in full sun. Plant in ordinary soil that is well drained.

French lavender *(L. dentata).* I particularly like the grayish-green foliage and summer fragrance. The lavender flower spikes provide additional color and make nice cut flowers.

Lavender cotton *(Santolina chamaecyparissus).* It is used primarily as an insect (moth) repellent or for dried flowers. The 18- to 24-inch perennial plants have attractive silver-gray, fragrant foliage. For best garden display, remove spent yellow flowers. Plants are showy in borders, as edging plants, or when used individually. It is believed that the plants are a bit fireproof and also repel deer. Grows best in full sun, in ordinary garden soil.

Lemon balm *(Melissa officinalis).* Nettlelike leaves have a strong lemon scent. Leaves are used in place of lemon peel to add a lemon flavor to drinks, salads, and fish. Leaves can be dried and used in potpourri. Small white summer flowers attract bees. Perennial; plants grow 2–3 feet in full to part sun. Plant in rich, well-drained soil.

Marjoram *(Origanum majorana).* This tender perennial attracts bees. Its leaves are used for flavoring soups, meat dishes, poultry, vegetables, salads, and jellies. Use it fresh or dried. Plant grows about 12–24 inches high. Plant in a sunny spot where soil is well drained.

Oregano *(O. heracleoticum).* There are several varieties of oregano and marjoram in this *Origanum* genus.This perennial herb is excellent to use with Greek, Mexican, Spanish, and Italian dishes. Use fresh or dried in soups, sauces, salads, and with meat, fish, and poultry dishes. Plants grow 12–18 inches high and can be planted in perennial borders or the vegetable garden. Cut back flowers to encourage new leaf growth. Leaves should be picked for drying just before flowers open. See Harvesting and Preserving Herbs, page 312. Plant in well-drained soil in a sunny spot.

Mint (*Mentha* species). These perennial herbs spread rapidly by underground roots, so be careful where you plant them, as they're apt to take over. The taller-growing (1½–3 feet) peppermints *(M. piperita),* spearmints *(M. spicata),* apple mints *(M. suaveolens),* and others can be used in teas. The peppermint and spearmint varieties are by far the most popular home garden varieties. I recommend planting them in containers, as it is much easier to keep them from becoming invasive. The bright green leaves have numerous uses and are especially popular to use in teas, for seasoning, as a garnish, and so forth. Plant mint in full to part sun, in moist, rich garden soil.

Corsican mint *(M. requienii).* See Chapter 12, Ground Covers.

Pennyroyal *(M. pulegium).* Low, mat-type growth (6–16 inches) with round, bright green leaves. Small lavender flowers. Aromatic mint fragrance especially noticeable when foliage is bruised or crushed. Plant in shade or filtered sun in moist, ordinary garden soil.

Mugwort. See artemisia.

Nepeta. See catnip *(N. cataria)*.

Oregano. See marjoram.

Parsley *(Petroselinum crispum)*. There are several types and varieties. 'Forest Green' has fine-textured curly leaves. Used for a wide variety of dishes, including salads, soups, and sauces. Also excellent for drying and to use as a garnish. The 'Italian Dark Green' has flat, plain leaves. The leaves are a rich source of vitamins. It too is used as a garnish and in stews, soups, salads, and even stuffing. Both grow about 12 inches high. They are attractive plants in containers, borders, or herb pots. Pot up a plant and bring it indoors in the autumn so you can enjoy fresh greens over winter. Plant in sun or part sun and shade, in rich, moist, well-drained soil.

Rosemary *(Rosmarinus officinalis)*. Rosemary is used for medicinal purposes and the leaves are used with pork and veal. It is also used in stews, herbal butter, bread, jam, and vinegar. Oil from the leaves is used in perfumes. Nice gray-green leaves and showy blue or white flowers. Plant in full sun, in ordinary, well-drained garden soil.

'Arp'. Grows 1½–3 feet with lavender flowers. Use the intermediate varieties in borders or midbed plantings.

'Prostratus'. Another dwarf rosemary. Use the dwarf varieties in rock gardens, as ground covers, or along the edge of borders. Pale blue flowers at various times during the fall, winter, and early spring. We had this one at our place at the ocean and it was wonderful for seasonal color. Plants grow about 18–24 inches tall and will spread up to 4–6 feet. Tip pinch occasionally to keep plants bushy.

'Renzel's Irene'. Dwarf ground cover–type rosemary. It has blue flowers and grows about 12 inches high, spreading to about 18 inches. Use the dwarf varieties in rock gardens, as ground covers, or along the edge of borders.

'Tuscan Blue' grows up to 6 feet. Use the tall varieties like this in border background plantings.

Sage *(Salvia officinalis)*. There are several species of this attractive herb. Common sage (perennial) grows 18–24 inches and has violet blue flowers and grayish green leaves. Leaves are used for seasoning pork, lamb, veal, poultry, meatloaf, stew, stuffing, and chowders. Use leaves fresh, dried, or frozen. A pretty ornamental plant that can be used in containers, in borders, or in the vegetable garden. Plant sage in a sunny location in light, well-drained garden soil.

Santolina. See lavender cotton.

Savory *(Satureja hortensis).* Commonly called summer savory. It is an annual that grows up to 18 inches high. Tiny soft pink flowers during the summer. Use leaves fresh or dried for seasoning fish, meats, soups, and vegetables. Use as a border plant or for edging. Plant in full sun, in enriched, well-drained soil.

Winter savory *(S. montana).* Perennial. Grows 12–15 inches high. Summer flowers are deeper in color. Leaves can be harvested all year. Shear it occasionally to maintain an attractive shape.

Scented-leaf geranium (*Pelargonium* species). There are dozens of species (see also geranium in Chapter 9, Perennials). The fragrances and aromas vary by species and varieties. Flower size and significance varies by variety. Fragrances include lemon, peppermint, chocolate, lime, ginger, and several others. These are nice plants to use in a perennial border or containers. Average growing height varies from 1 to 4 feet. Fragrant leaves are often dried for sachets and potpourris. Leaves are sometimes used in jellies and cakes. Oils from leaves are used in perfumes. Plant in full sun for best fragrance and growth, in ordinary, well-drained garden soil.

Sweet woodruff *(Galium odoratum).* This plant is used more as a ground cover than as an herb, and it is great for the woodland garden. The early summer white flowers cover the delicate green leaves. The leaves are used in teas, perfumes, sachets, and potpourris. Plants grow up to 10–12 inches in the shade, a bit lower in part sun and shade. Plant in rich, well-drained soil.

Tarragon. See artemisia.

Thyme *(Thymus vulgaris).* In the landscape, this perennial herb is often used at the edge of borders, in containers, or as a ground-cover plant. Creeping thyme *(T. serpyllum),* woolly thyme *(T. pseudolanuginosus),* and most of the other species make great ground cover plants as well (see Chapter 12, Ground Covers; see also Chapter 9, Perennials). The aromatic odor of the leaves makes this herb popular in meat dishes, soups, and stews. Leaves can be used fresh or dried. Harvest when flowers first begin to open. Plant in full or part sun, in average, well-drained garden soil.

Lemon thyme *(T. citriodorus).* Also used in cooking. The variegated green and yellow foliage makes this a very attractive plant. Lemon scented leaves. July to August flowers are pale lavender. Plants grow 6 to 8 inches high, and spread up to 12 inches or more.

Winter savory. See savory.

Wormwood. See artemisia, and Chapter 9, Perennials.

Yarrow *(Achillea millefolium).* See Chapter 9, Perennials.

15 · Vegetables

Growing fresh vegetables in your own garden is so gratifying. The fresh taste and the added nutritional value are unbeatable. In addition, you know what has been used (if anything) on your crop to control insects and diseases. And you have the advantage of growing your favorite varieties and types of veggies.

Keep in mind that some vegetables are just as pretty as flowers; for example, Swiss chard 'Bright Lights', artichokes, flowering kale and cabbage, etc. The foliage of many veggies is also attractive in flower and shrub beds, including rhubarb, asparagus, artichokes, carrots, etc. Don't hesitate to include some vegetables right along with your flowers and shrubs. This chapter provides some important pointers in helping you successfully grow vegetables.

Facing page: Clusters of cherry-sized tomatoes grow in abundance on two of my favorite varieties, 'Sweetie' and 'Sweet Million'. *Above:* Snowball cauliflower produces early, solid heads of top quality.

Choosing a Location

Vegetables can be grown in a space set aside for vegetables, in containers, in among your flowers, or even in hanging baskets. At the very first home Myrna and I purchased, our neighbor was a farmer who loved to garden. One day he invited us down to his place to see his vegetable garden. Upon entering his small back garden, which was full of flowers, I asked him, "What vegetables"? He walked over to the flowers and pulled them aside to reveal carrots, radishes, lettuce, and several other vegetables neatly planted among his wife's flowers. If you're limited in space, you can do exactly the same thing.

Try to select the sunniest spot in the yard for your vegetable garden. The combination of bright sun, good air circulation, proper drainage, and rich soil is the key to having a garden that will produce a bountiful harvest. The vegetable garden should receive a minimum of six to eight hours of bright summer sunlight. More sun is better! If you have only low-light areas, plant leaf crops such as lettuce, chard, and spinach.

Layout of the Vegetable Garden

I recommend, when possible, designing the garden so the rows run in a north to south direction. Winds in this region tend to be from the southwest or northwest, so with this configuration there is better air circulation down the crop rows. The sun plays a major part also, because it rises in the east and sets in the west. Rows running north to south get better sun exposure for a longer period of time than those that run east to west. It is also very important to plant the tall-growing crops (this includes peas, beans, and corn) to the north of the garden, so they do not shade the lower-growing vegetables. Next, in the center of the garden plant the medium-sized crops. Plant the lowest-growing crops on the south end of the garden.

Raised Beds

Have you ever noticed that farmers and commercial growers always grow their crops on raised rows in the fields? Whether they are growing vegetables, bulbs, berries, or other crops, if you look closely you will find they are planted on raised soil. This is done primarily for better drainage and warmer soil and is particularly beneficial in a wet spring. It's estimated that soil temperatures can be increased by 8 to 13 degrees Fahrenheit by simply planting on raised soil. Warmer soil means you can plant earlier and harvest later into the season. Raised beds are one of the keys to successful vegetable gardening.

One of the most popular ways to raise the soil is to make a frame 8 to 10 inches deep, 3 to 4 feet wide, and usually 10 to 12 feet long. Wood, cement blocks, concrete hardscape blocks, and even some plastic products are used for raised beds. Never use railroad ties for this job; they contain creosote. If a preserved wood is used, check to be sure that the particular brand is safe for use in the vegetable garden. I would not rely on the clerk's answer; check the company brochure. Peter Chan, the famous garden author, simply mounds the soil in his garden; he doesn't use any type of frame around the raised soil, and his garden is spectacular.

Wide Row Method

This is the second most important point in raising vegetables in the home garden: conserve space by growing your crops close together. Don't waste garden space with aisles between each row. In the average-size home garden, you can make beds of vegetables or at least place several rows together. For example, if you are growing beets, grow four to six equally spaced rows together. In a raised bed, if you space the beets 4 inches apart (in all directions) in an area 3 feet wide and 2 feet in length, you would have the equivalent of a single row 54 feet long; that's about a year's supply for a family of four. Even corn can be grown in a wide row by simply planting it 1 foot apart in all directions. In a raised bed 4 feet wide by 4 feet in length, you have the equivalent of a single row of corn 16 feet long. Here are some of the greatest advantages of wide row gardening:

> One of the best ways to tell whether your soil is ready for planting (in springtime) is to grab a handful of soil and squeeze it in your fist. If water runs out, it's still too wet and cold for planting. Simply wait until the soil is drier. Planting in raised soil beds will help the ground dry out more quickly, so you can plant earlier and harvest later into the fall.

- *Conserves water:* Less water is needed due to closeness of plants.
- *Controls weeds:* Plants tend to crowd out many weeds.
- *Improves feeding:* Less fertilizer is used because of closeness of plants.
- *Conserves space:* Prepared soil is used by plants rather than being wasted in aisle space.
- *Improves yield:* Maximum yield is obtained in a very small space.

Planting Vegetables

Should you begin with plant seedlings or seeds? Both have their advantages. Seeds are relatively inexpensive, and many vegetables (such as root crops) must be started directly in the garden by seed; they will not transplant satisfactorily as young plants. Others, such as pumpkins, squash, and cucumbers, are sometimes set back by being transplanted, so direct seeding is often easier and more successful for these vegetables.

On the other hand, tomatoes, peppers, and many leaf crops are easily transplanted as young plants. Both tomatoes and peppers are often started indoors from seed because a specific variety is not available as seedlings. By planting started plants, the home gardener can often get a jump of two or three weeks (or more) on the growing season.

When to Plant Vegetables

The planting chart on the next page gives you an idea of the best time to begin your vegetable garden. It also gives you some ideas on when to start seeds indoors or outdoors, and how many plants are needed for the average family. Of course, you may need to adjust the number of plants to suit your family's preferences.

Moon Gardening

Gardening by the phases of the moon is certainly nothing new. It has been passed down through many generations. Just as the moon's gravitational pull influences the ocean's tides, it is theorized that it also influences the movement of fluids within plants. Moon gardening is based on this belief. It has not been scientifically proven or disproved, but countless home gardeners and professionals report continued success from this method of gardening.

However, actual planting tasks or gardening jobs to be undertaken depend upon both the phase (quarter) and the actual moon sign. You can obtain additional information on this fascinating method of gardening from my yearly Moon Sign Garden Almanac. Here are the basic phases of the moon:

Light of the Moon (Increasing Light). This is the first and second quarters, when the moon goes from new to full. Generally used for planting crops that produce aboveground.

Dark of the Moon (Decreasing Light). This is the third and fourth quarters, when the moon goes from full to new. Generally used for planting crops that produce vegetables below the ground.

Starting Seeds Indoors

You can start seeds indoors to get a jump on the gardening season, then set out the seedling starter plants as the weather warms up. Start the seeds in late February or early March indoors.

Choosing a Location for Starting Seeds

A sunny windowsill, greenhouse window, sun porch, or greenhouse are the best places to start your seeds. However, they can be started in any bright-light part of the home or garage. If possible, place them in a spot where there is warmth from below, such as over a heating duct. Bottom heat or a heating cable really helps the seeds in the germination process. (Heating cables are available at most garden outlets.)

Most seeds germinate best in a warm location. Select a spot where the

Vegetable Planting Chart

	Start indoors	Plant outside	Spacing	Depth	Plant per 4 persons	Comments
Asparagus	N/A	2/1 to 4/1	9" to 12"	14" to 2"	32 plants	Attractive foliage
Beans (Bush)	N/A	4/15 to 7/1	4" to 6"	1" to 1½"	80-120 ft. row	Plant in intensified rows
Beets	N/A	3/1 to 7/15	4"	½"	60 ft. row	Add lime to soil
Broccoli	FEB	3/15 to 7/1	24" to 30"	⅛"	12-15 plants	Great for stir fry & salads
Cabbage	FEB	3/15 to 7/1	24" to 36"	⅛"	12-15 plants	Protect from cabbage moth
Carrots	N/A	3/15 to 7/15	2" to 4"	⅛"	40 ft. row	High vitamin content
Cauliflower	FEB	3/15 to 7/1	18" to 24"	⅛"	12-15 plants	Keep moderately moist
Corn	N/A	4/15 to 6/1	8" to 12"	1"	140 ft. row	Eat within 5 hrs. of picking
Cucumbers	APR	5/1 to 6/15	8" to 36"	¼"	6-8 plants	Plant in hills 3 ft. apart
Kohlrabi	N/A	4/1 to 7/15	6" to 8"	⅛"	12-15 ft. row	Excellent with dips
Lettuce (Leaf)	FEB 15	3/15 to 9/1	12"	⅛"	20-30 ft. row	Plant every 2 weeks
Mustard	FEB 15	3/15 to 8/15	6"	⅛"	3-4 plants	Grow during cool weather
Onions (Green)	N/A	3/15 to 8/1	1" to 2"	⅛"	10 ft. row	Plant every 3 to 4 weeks
Peas	N/A	2/1 to 6/15	2"	1" to 1½"	120-160 ft. row	Plant in late winter
Peppers	APR	5/1 to 6/15	18" to 24"	⅛" to ¼"	6-10 plants	Need full bright sun
Pumpkins	APR	5/1 to 6/15	36" to 48"	½"	3 plants	Ideal Halloween crop
Radishes	N/A	4/1 to 9/1	2"	¼"	20 ft. row	Sow every 2 to 3 weeks
Spinach	MAR	4/1 to 8/15	12"	¼"	10-20 ft. row	Very nutritious
Squash	APR	5/1 to 6/15	36" to 48"	½"	3 plants	Harvest before frost
Tomatoes	FEB/MAR	5/1 to 6/15	24" to 36"	⅛"	10-15 plants	Need full, bright sun
Turnips	N/A	4/1 to 7/15	4" to 6"	¼"	10-15 ft. row	No manure in planting area

Planting dates based on April 1 as last frost. (Adjust dates for the last frost in your area.)

Vegetables

temperatures will range between 65 and 72 degrees Fahrenheit, unless the seed packet recommends otherwise.

Containers

You can use flats, pots, trays, egg cartons, eggshells, paper cups, or peat pots as containers. Just be sure they have a drainage hole in the bottom so the new young seedling plants do not sit in water.

Soil Mix

Store-bought seedling mixes are the best to use. However, a regular potting soil, vermiculite, perlite, sponge rock, or a combination of sand and peat moss are all suitable mixes to start seeds.

In fact, they can be started in soil from the garden if it is sterilized and porous. One way to sterilize your outdoor soil is to bake it in the oven (in a baking tray) for approximately two hours at 170 to 180 degrees Fahrenheit.

Inoculating Pea and Bean Seeds

Inoculating is simply a process of coating the seed with nitrogen bacteria, which enables the seeds to get nitrogen from air and use it in root development. Inoculant powder is generally available in packets, which you can easily mix with water to coat the seeds. Although most soils have enough of the bacteria already present, avid gardeners like to assure success by treating the seed.

Pre-Sprouting Seeds

You can pre-sprout vegetable seeds. This is generally done for one of several reasons:

- to speed up germination
- to determine the germination rate of a seed (this is especially helpful if you have seed left over from year to year)
- to start seeds that are difficult to germinate

Pre-sprouting seeds is easy. Here's how:

- Just take a couple of paper towels, soak them in water, then ring out the excess water.
- Place ten to twenty seeds on the moist paper towel.
- Roll up the towel or fold it over so the seeds are covered by toweling on all sides.
- Place the towel in a warm spot; the kitchen drain board is ideal.
- The seeds should germinate in four to six days. Plant the seeds as soon as they have germinated.

Sowing the Seeds

Read and follow sowing (planting) directions on the back of the seed packet. This is a very important step because some need to be covered with soil; others need to be uncovered and exposed to light in order to germinate. There is a tendency to cover the seeds with too much soil or peat, so be certain to barely cover the seed.

Next, water in thoroughly. Use a fine spray (atomizer type) to water the seeds until the plants are at least an inch tall. Otherwise the water tends to wash all the seeds to the edges of the pots or trays.

Thinning Starts

If you seed too close, the young seedlings will grow but they will not have enough space to develop a strong root system or to fully develop the crop. It is then necessary to thin out the weakest plants so that the strongest seedlings have space to develop. You can replant the thinned seedling plants or discard them. If you plan to replant the thinned seedlings, be certain to moisten the soil thoroughly before thinning so the soil clings to the roots, improving the likelihood that they will survive. Seedlings of root crops like carrots, radishes, and beets cannot be transplanted, so they must be seeded directly into the garden.

Transplanting Starts

Once the young new seedlings have developed one set of true leaves or are about 1 to 1½ inches high, they can be individually potted or spaced in a flat or tray. It's best to transplant them into individual containers so when the time comes, they can be easily transplanted with a minimum of shock. Then, of course, do not plant them outdoors until the proper planting time.

Prepare the Soil for Planting

Soil preparation should always be done when the soil is workable. Test the soil by taking a handful and squeezing it in your hand; if water oozes out, it is still too wet (not yet workable) to spade or till.

Once you have spaded or tilled the area, rake it smooth to prevent water from collecting in the low areas. It's best to add organic humus to your existing soil. Compost, well-rotted manure (or processed bagged manure), and peat moss are among the best forms of organic humus to use in preparing vegetable garden soils. Add about an inch or two of one or more of these sources of organic matter to your existing soil. Fresh manure can be added in the late fall, because the winter rains and exposure to weather will break it down by spring planting time. Mix the organic humus with your existing soil.

Sowing Seeds Outdoors

The seeds of many vegetables can be sown directly into the garden after all danger of frost has passed—in most areas, late April or May. When seeding vegetables directly into the garden, be certain to follow seeding directions on the back of the seed packet, observing seeding depth and spacing as indicated. The biggest problem that occurs is sowing the seeds too deeply. As a general rule, seeds should barely be covered with soil, but remember that the actual seeding depth is stated on the seed packet.

Very Small Seeds

Some vegetable seeds are very small and difficult to sow without getting them too thick. If you sow seeds by hand, you will get a better distribution by holding your hand a foot or two above the row or garden bed. This doesn't work if the wind is blowing. There are a couple of things you can do to make seeding a little easier.

- Mix a little sand or fine soil with the small seeds.
- Cut a small hole in the end of the seed packet and scatter the seeds directly from the packet.
- Broadcast the very small seeds from a salt shaker.

Biggest Problems

These are the biggest problems in sowing seeds directly outdoors:

- covering the seeds with too much soil
- sowing seeds too early, when soil is still too wet or cold
- burning up the seeds with high-nitrogen fertilizers or fresh (hot) manure
- having birds or insects eat the seeds before they germinate
- letting the soil get too dry after seeding
- failing to protect small seedlings from slugs

Set the Plant at the Proper Depth

If you are setting out greenhouse or nursery-grown plants, follow planting instructions on the plastic label in each container. Always moisten the soil in a container before removing the plant, so the soil will cling to the roots. Vegetables should be planted at the same depth as they are in the containers. However, there is an exception with tomatoes; they can be planted deeper in the soil if desired. Sometimes tomato plants are planted at an angle so as to encourage a more prolific root system or to bury a long, leggy stem. Refer to the planting chart on page 329 for detailed spacing, depth, etc.

Protect Early Plantings

If you want to get a jump on the growing season, there are several aids you can use to provide protection and warmth to your plants during cool spring weather: Here are a few of the most popular ones:

Aqua Dome

This is a plastic product with an interior wall that holds water. It can be placed over tomato, pepper, or other tender plants for protection from cold weather.

Wall of Water

This is a polyethylene liner that holds water in the walls of the poly. The water warms during the day, then radiates warmth during the evening hours.

Reemay

This is a fabric product that is used to cover plants for protection from the cold and can also be used as an insect barrier.

My Own Idea

Take a tomato cage, turn it upside down, and firm it in the soil with pieces of wire. Next, cover the top with a plastic dry-cleaners bag. This provides a windbreak and warm cover over tender plants. It acts like a miniature greenhouse.

Cold Frames—Hot Beds

Did I get your attention? It's not what you think! A cold frame is simply a box built into the soil, with a glass, clear poly, or plastic cover. It can be as simple as taking an old window frame, then constructing a box of the same size in the soil. Use 2-by-10 or 2-by-12 boards, and for height, you may want to stack them two high. Place the window frame over the box and install a couple of door hinges on the north end of the window frame, so you can open and close it. Face the cold frame to the south, with the north end being a little higher; this provides the best light exposure for winter crops. Now you've got a cold frame.

To make it a hot bed, all you have to do is add a soil heating cable, or during slightly cold evenings, even an electric light bulb will offer some heat. Leave the heat source on when temperatures are freezing or below. On warm days, you may want to prop up the cover for ventilation. Over winter, you can grow leaf lettuce, green onions, spinach, chard, radishes,

Hints for Growing Tomatoes

Here are a few simple hints on how to best grow tomatoes:

Use protection devices: See Protect Early Plantings, page 333.

Provide support for the plants: Tomato cages are one of the most popular ways to support plants. Vase-shaped wire supports fit down over and around the plants, supporting their upright growth. Unfortunately, most are too small to be of much help.

Stakes, wooden or plastic, can also be used to support tomato plants. Again, use soft material such as panty hose to tie up the tomato stems.

Water: See Watering the Vegetable Garden, page 335.

Prune: Grandma and grandpa told us that tomatoes had to be pruned. Not so! They take very little pruning. Prune lower foliage so it doesn't touch the ground. Limit growth to two or three main stems. Do not bother cutting off suckers that develop on stems; it only slows down (shocks) development. Also, we were told to remove leaves so the sun would ripen the fruit. That's also incorrect. Sun on the fruit scalds it. The fruit needs the shade from the leaves to ripen.

Help to set fruit: Once the flowers begin to develop, there are a couple of ways you can encourage proper pollination. (1) Gently tap (or shake) the plant to dislodge the pollen. (2) Use a "blossom set" product. This is sprayed on the flower clusters (only once) and only for a split second. Too much spray will result in the fruit being misformed.

Change planting locations: Do not plant in the same location next year. If it is the only sunny spot you have in the entire garden, then be sure you completely reprepare the soil for planting each season.

Diagnose possible problems:

Early or late blight (blights turn the vines, leaves, and fruit black) is most often caused by rains from mid-July to September. The easiest way to protect against this problem is to cover above the plants with clear polyethylene. I recommend that a frame with the poly cover be put in place when you first set out your plants. It acts like a greenhouse, warming the plants from the beginning and brings them on quicker, plus protects against the blights.

Tomatoes do not develop fruit. If the plant has flowers but no fruit, it can be one of several things: (1) too much water, (2) too much fertilizer, or (3) nighttime temperatures too cold. Most tomato varieties need nighttime temperatures above 55 to 57 degrees Fahrenheit in order to set fruit.

Blossom-end rot (bottom of tomato is black) can be caused by irregular watering, lack of calcium (that's why I recommend adding dolomite lime), or exceptionally hot weather and not enough water.

Leaf curl is natural on some varieties, particularly along the stem.

and many other crops. During the rest of the year, you can use the frame for rooting cuttings, starting seeds, or storing plants.

Watering the Vegetable Garden

The best time to water the vegetable garden is during the morning hours, so the soil has a chance to warm up before evening. Avoid evening watering because the soil then remains cold and wet overnight, which tends to slow growth and make plants more susceptible to mildew or other disease—and cool, wet conditions are an invitation to slugs.

Avoid watering for short periods of time. It's best to moisten the soil thoroughly; then it's not necessary to water as often. I apply water down to a depth of 6 inches in the soil. Using this method, during average summer weather my vegetable garden only needs to be watered about once a week. If you can, it's best to water at soil level (irrigate), keeping the water off the leaves of your vegetables. If you must use a sprinkler, then morning watering is a must!

Feeding Vegetables

What to Feed

Plants that lose their leaves over winter are called *deciduous.* A rose or all-purpose garden fertilizer can be used to feed deciduous plants; for example, vegetable plants can be fed with these same types of fertilizers if they do not contain insecticides. Or use a vegetable garden–type fertilizer. They are available in both commercial and organic formulas. In my garden, I like to use one that contains the micronutrients such as iron, boron, magnesium, and sulfur because soils in this maritime climate are often lacking in these elements.

When to Feed

If you correctly prepare the soil before planting, only limited feeding should be necessary during the growing season. Fertilize about once every four to six weeks as needed. If you are getting too much leaf growth, it usually indicates excessive water or nitrogen, so check to see whether you are overfeeding. On the other hand, if the plants are yellowing or stunted, that's an indication that additional feeding may be necessary.

Harvesting Vegetable Crops

I touch on this subject in more detail in the listing of each vegetable in the Vegetables Encyclopedia. However, the simple rule is to harvest your vegetables when they have reached the proper size and color. Or, better yet, when they have passed your taste test!

Planting Fall and Winter Crops

The greatest advantage of growing fall and winter vegetables is that they extend the harvest season, providing you with fresh vegetables directly from your own garden during winter. Plus the cooler fall weather tends to intensify the flavor of many vegetables. As a bonus, you are able to harvest your own vegetables at a time when supermarket prices skyrocket.

Most of the winter crops should be seeded or planted from starter plants in the garden in late June, July, or August. Slow-maturing crops such as the cole crops (cabbage family) are seeded into the garden in June, while the quicker carrots, beets, onions, and spinach can be seeded in July or August. Parsnips and rutabagas are other suitable winter vegetables; sow seeds of these two crops in July. Radishes and leaf lettuce can be seeded in August through early September. Cover with Reemay or cloth (burlap or old sheets) if the weather gets exceptionally cold (near freezing), removing the cover as soon as the weather moderates.

Cover Crops

Cover crops (also known as green manure) are a natural way to replenish the nutrients in your vegetable garden soil. In the autumn (September or October) after the vegetables have been harvested, you can cultivate the soil and seed a cover crop. This is a great way to rebuild the soil over winter. Cover crops fix the nitrogen in the soil, replenish nutrients, add organic matter to the soil, and help suppress weeds over winter.

All you need to do is clean up the vegetable garden, cultivate, and broadcast the cover crop seed by hand or spreader. Most cover crop seeds are quite large and easy to distribute. However, if you use small seed varieties, simply mix a little sand or fine soil to make it easier to sow the seed evenly. Rake in the seed to an average depth of about ¼ inch. Water as needed to ensure germination, then let the fall rains take over. In late winter or early spring, cut the greens and till (or spade) them into the soil.

Wait a couple of weeks to allow decomposition of the cover crop before planting your spring vegetable crops.

There are quite a few different plants that can be used as cover crops. In my garden I use a combination of Austrian winter field peas, hairy vetch, winter cereal rye, and crimson clover. Cover crops are a great way to naturally grow your own fertilizer over winter.

Controlling Weeds in the Vegetable Garden

Weeds rob valuable nutrients from the soil and are competition to the growing vegetables. Plus they are often hosts to various insects and diseases, so it is important to eliminate them. In the vegetable garden, it is probably best to cultivate using a hoe (I like the Winged Weeder) or pull the weeds by hand.

The natural (organic) preemergent weed control called *gluten of cornmeal* can be used between rows, but you must be careful not to use it in places where you plan to seed your crops, because it will kill your vegetable seeds as well.

Mulch to Reduce Weed Growth

By putting down an inch or two of mulch between the rows in your vegetable garden, you can slow down, or in some cases prevent, the regrowth of weeds. Bark, sawdust, straw, newspapers, and grass clippings are the most common materials used for mulching in the vegetable garden. The black-and-white pages of the newspaper are often spread on the soil, then covered with one of the mulches. If you use grass clippings, be certain that they are not from a lawn that has been treated with Weed & Feed, because the weed killer (herbicide) can remain active for up to one year. Black plastic is sometimes used for mulch. It's not the most attractive material to use, and it tends to wrinkle up and hold puddles of water. If you do use it, be certain to weight it down with stones so it doesn't blow away.

Controlling Insects and Diseases

I am not an entomologist or pathologist, so I try to keep insect and disease problems under control using simple means. Because most combination vegetable garden dusts and sprays are formulated with botanic (natural plant) derivatives, I use them in my vegetable garden. Insects that belong to the caterpillar family can be controlled with products containing BT *(Bacillus thuringiensis)*, which is a biological control. Neem oil, from the neem tree, is also being used extensively as a natural insecticide, fungicide, and miticide. Of course, you must read and follow application directions on the label before using any type of pesticide in your garden.

I do not recommend planting marigolds or nasturtiums as a means of controlling insects in the vegetable garden. It is believed that nasturtiums host black bean aphid, so they will keep the aphid away from the beans . . . not so! Likewise, it is believed that marigolds will repel aphids and other insects. Not so! In fact, you will find spider mites, slugs, and even aphids on marigold plants. Instead, plant onions, garlic, and herbs that do discourage harmful insects.

Controlling Nuisance Creatures in the Vegetable Garden

Additional information for coping with these creatures and others can be found in Chapter 18, Protecting Plants from Cold and Creatures.

Slugs

Baits (gels, powders, meals, pellets), iron phosphate, copper strips, beer, diatomaceous earth, and salt are methods often used to control slugs in the vegetable garden. Whatever you use, apply at the perimeter of the garden, so you attract the slugs out of the garden or control them before they enter. Apply materials that specify they can be safely used in the vegetable garden, then apply only as directed on the label.

Deer

Bloodmeal, solutions made from eggshells, deodorant soaps, pepper spray, and several other repellents are used to try to control deer. I think fencing or a motion-sensor sprinkler is the most effective means of control.

Rabbits

Several rabbit repellents are available, but low 2-foot-high fencing is probably the most effective means of controlling them.

Moles, Voles, and Shrews

Trapping is the most effective means of controlling these creatures in the vegetable garden, but this has been outlawed in the state of Washington.

Raccoons, Possums, Etc.

Live traps are effective. Contact the Washington State Department of Fish and Wildlife for information on where they can be released, etc. Pepper sprays and other deterrents are sometimes effective.

Choosing Vegetables

For Mixed Plantings

If you want to really conserve space, simply grow several vegetables together. For example, lettuce and radishes can be grown in the same row or bed together. The radishes reach maturity first and leave space for the lettuce to develop. Other excellent combinations are beets and onions; radishes and beets; carrots and lettuce; carrots and onions; and radishes and spinach. They can all be seeded at the same time. Radishes grow very quickly, so they do a good job of marking the row or bed.

Companion Plants

Here are a dozen of the most popular vegetables and a list of the best companions to plant near them:

beans—celery, cucumbers
beets—beans, cabbage, lettuce, onions
cabbage family—beets, celery, onions, potatoes
carrots—lettuce, onions, radishes, tomatoes
corn—beans, cucumbers, peas, potatoes, pumpkins
cucumbers—beans, corn, peas, radishes
lettuce—carrots, cucumbers, onions, radishes
onions—beets, lettuce, tomatoes
peas—beans, carrots, corn, cucumbers, potatoes, radishes, turnips
radishes—beans, beets, carrots, cucumbers, lettuce, spinach
squash—corn, cucumbers, radishes
tomatoes—carrots, onions, parsley

For Specific Sites

In Containers

If you're limited in space, or if the only sunny spot is the patio, lanai, or similar spot, then growing a few vegetables in a container may be just the answer for you. Actually, you can grow any vegetable if the container is large enough. Use an organic soil mix in the container. I have friends who even grow corn, beans, and peas in large containers. You can conserve space by growing several types of vegetables together in containers. For example, to create a "salad bowl," plant a tomato plant in the center, next leaf lettuce, green onions, and beets; then spinach and, along the edge of the pot, radishes. The new 'Spacemaster' (bush type) squash and/or cucumbers could also be planted along the edge to trail over the side of the container. Use your imagination, and you'll end up with a spectacular container of veggies! The following are a few of the best vegetables to grow in containers:

beets
bush squash: 'Black Beauty', 'Gold Rush', 'Jackpot', 'Round', 'Scallop', 'Table King'
carrots
cucumbers
green onions: 'Evergreen White Bunching'
leaf lettuce: 'Grand Rapids', 'Salad Bowl'
peppers
radishes
spinach
tomatoes

In Hanging Baskets

The small cherry tomatoes are the most popular plants to grow in hanging baskets. The new variety 'Tumbler' is one of the most popular for baskets. Cucumber 'Salad Bush Hybrid' is an all-American variety that can be grown in baskets. Of course, any of the other vegetables that grow in containers can also be grown in hanging baskets. Use an organic potting soil or soil from your vegetable garden when planting vegetables in hanging baskets.

On Fences

Peas and beans are often grown on fences, trellises, or poles, but did you ever think of growing cucumbers, gourds, or small squash and miniature pumpkins on fences or trellises? This is a great way to conserve space, keep the fruit clean, and harvest a bountiful crop. If you have any kind of wire or cyclone fencing, spray-paint it gray first; otherwise the wire might burn the vines and cause crop failure. Larger fruit may need support as it matures, so simply tie a nylon sock or mesh bag to the fence and place the fruit inside; as it develops, its weight won't tear or break the vine.

Vegetables Encyclopedia

❶ propagation
❷ spacing requirements
❸ planting information
❹ feeding
❺ harvesting suggestions
❻ remarks

Artichoke. ❶ Seed or root division. ❷ 3–5 feet apart. ❸ A bit on the tender side. May need protection in severe winters (mulch crown of plant with 2 inches of straw). Otherwise, an easy crop to grow in full bright sun. This is a perennial vegetable so plant it off to the side of the garden where it will not interfere with cultivation. The plants are so attractive, you may want to use them in the landscape. (Bold, serrated leaves are grayish green.) Dig and divide root divisions every three to five years. ❹ Vegetable garden fertilizer in March or April. ❺ Harvest buds when they are 3–4 inches across and before they open. Cut the buds off and leave about 1 inch of the stem attached. ❻ A top-notch perennial vegetable. Buds are tasty when steamed or boiled.

'Improved Green Globe'. The variety generally grown here.

Asparagus. ❶ Two- or three-year-old roots, available in spring, or seeds sown outdoors in early spring. Plants started from seed are not ready to harvest until the third year. ❷ 12–15 inches apart. ❸ Do not plant them too deep. Unfortunately, it is sometimes recommended that they be planted 6–10 inches deep. In this region they will not make it if they are planted deep. Plant asparagus roots only about 2 inches deep, with the long roots spread out just a little bit. They need a sunny location with well-drained soil. It is very important to take time to prepare the soil with organic matter such as compost and/or well-rotted manure because these perennial plants will remain in the same spot for up to fifteen years. Likewise, I suggest that the plants be situated off to the side of the garden, so they do not interfere with fall spading or tilling. To grow tender white stems, hill soil up gradually around the base of the stalks so they are covered to a depth of 3–4 inches. ❹ February and again in late June with a vegetable garden fertilizer. ❺ Start harvesting when roots are three years old. Harvest season lasts for approximately four to six weeks. Slender, weaker stalks indicate time to stop harvesting. ❻ Easy to grow. A very popular vegetable to use raw or cooked. Ideal in salads, for dips, or as a cooked vegetable.

'Jersey Giant'. An all-male variety that is up to five times more productive than old standard varieties.

'Martha Washington'. Has been a very popular and dependable variety. Easy to grow. Excellent flavor.

Bean. ❶ Seed. A bit difficult to transplant. ❷ Pole type in hills of four to six seeds per hill; thin to strongest three when plants are 4 inches tall. Bush type seeded 2 inches apart in rows or beds; thin to 4 inches apart when seedlings are 4 inches tall. ❸ Bean seeds also benefit from being treated with an inoculant (see Inoculating Pea and Bean Seeds, page 330). Seed directly into the garden in April, or as soon as all danger of frost has passed. Bush type can be grown in rows or beds. Plant in a sunny location, in rich, well-drained soil. Cover the seeds with 1–1½ inches of soil. The rows of pole beans should be planted at the north end of the garden, so the tall plants do not shade the rest of the garden. Seed later crops in May and June for longer harvest. Do not cultivate around plants or water overhead when plants are in bloom. ❹ Organic or nonburning vegetable garden fertilizer before planting. ❺ Pick when pods are young for best flavor and texture. Snip ends from beans prior to cooking. ❻ Easy to grow. This is a great low-calorie vegetable that is high in fiber and a source of calcium, phosphorus, and moderate amounts of vitamins A and B. There are approximately 3,500 varieties of beans, too many to begin to cover here. Below are a few of the bush and poles types that I particularly like.

'Blue Lake' (bush). Excellent variety for home gardens. Vigorous, heavy bearing with pods 5–6 inches long. An All-American winner. (58 days)

'Blue Lake' (pole). Our favorite green pole bean. Early maturing, produces abundantly, with pods 5–6 inches long. The stringless white-seeded pods are an even, deep green color. (64 days)

'Cascade Giant' (pole). A descendent of the old favorite 'Oregon Giant', this one was developed by Oregon State University (use green or dry and shell). Bicolor pods grow to 10 inches. Taste and color similar to Oregon Giant. (80 days)

'Contender' (bush). Especially good for cool climates. Heavy yielding with dark green pods over 6 inches long. (51 days)

'Fava' (broad). A popular bean that does not fit the pole-type or bush-type groups. English broad bean. Plant it in February.

'French Marseilles' (bush). Gourmet quality. Round pods are 4–5 inches long, dark green and delicious. A tasty variety. (52 days.)

'Goldkist Wax' (bush). Bright golden yellow, stringless wax bean with excellent flavor. Heavy producer. (60 days)

'Kentucky Blue' (pole). An all-American variety, a cross between 'Blue Lake' and 'Kentucky Wonder'. It produces earlier than its parents, combining the best characteristics of each. Prolific, sweet-flavored round pods are 6–7 inches long. (60 days)

Left: Colorful stalks of 'Bright Lights' Swiss chard are a nice addition to the flower garden too!

Below: As this photo from the VanDusen Botanical Gardens in Vancouver, B.C., demonstrates, a vegetable garden can be a place of beauty and still provide a bountiful harvest.

'Kentucky Wonder' (pole). Popular variety with 7- to 9-inch pods in clusters. Heavy producer of light-brown beans noted for their distinctive flavor fresh or dried. Stringless when young.

'Purple Queen' (bush). A glossy purple-green bean. Round pods up to 6 inches long turn green when cooked. (52 days)

'Roma II' (bush). Wide, light green, smooth, flat pods are borne at top of plants, making them easy to pick. Flavorful pods are slow to develop fiber and seeds, which gives its pods better texture. Longer than other romano beans. (59 days)

'Scarlet Runner Bean' (climber). Another popular bean that does not fit the pole-type or bush-type groups. Scarlet flowers (ornamental). Harvest when pods are young or use later as shell beans.

'Tendercrop' (bush). Developed by the U.S. Department of Agriculture, it has slender, uniform pods over 5 inches long and dark green in color. Fine flavor, tenderness, and compact growth. (56 days)

Beet. ❶ Seed. Plants do not transplant very well. ❷ Sow seeds 2–4 inches apart. Cover seeds with ½ inch soil. Thin to 4 inches apart when plants are a few inches high and enjoy the greens in salads. ❸ Plant them in part to full sun in soil that is well drained. If soil tends to be acid, add a little lime. Beets do not like competition so be sure to keep them thinned and eliminate weeds. They grow continuously, so do not let them completely dry out at any time. ❹ Vegetable garden fertilizer at seeding time. Plants benefit from feeding with liquid fertilizer once or twice during growing season. ❺ Begin harvesting when beets are 1–3 inches in size, and before they become woody. Harvest greens anytime. ❻ A very popular vegetable because beets can be grown year-round. Rich in iron, calcium, potassium, phosphorus, and many vitamins. This is one vegetable all of whose parts can be eaten—leaves and roots. In fact, the beet greens are almost as popular as the edible root.

'Cylindra'. Roots are long (like a fat carrot) instead of round. 8-inch-long cylindrical beets are excellent for eating fresh, canning, freezing, or pickling. Greens are delicious. (60 days)

'Improved Detroit Supreme'. New improved variety of an old standard. Smoother globe-type roots and better color. Excellent flavor. Young leaves make delicious greens. July-seeded crops ideal for winter use. (59 days)

'Lutz'. The greenleaf 'Winter Keeper'. A very popular variety for late-season growing and winter storage. Deep red roots are sweet, become sweeter during storage. Tasty greens. (63 days)

'Red Ace Hybrid'. Fast-growing hybrid with uniform roots that size up faster than most strains. Good, even red color. A very delicious and sweet flavored variety. Tops are bright green and erect. One of the best home garden varieties. (54 days)

Broccoli. ❶ Seed or starter plants. Start seeds indoors in late winter or sow seeds directly into the garden after all danger of frost and again in midsummer. Cover seeds with ⅛ inch of fine soil. ❷ Space plants 18–24 inches apart. Sow seeds about 12 inches apart, then thin and replant when seedlings are about 3–5 inches tall. ❸ If soil tends to be acid, apply lime because these crops are apt to suffer from club root if the soil is too acid. Plant early for summer crop and again in late June or July for fall and winter crop. Plant in full sun in moist, well-drained soil. Do not plant in the same location two years in a row. ❹ Prepare soil by adding organic humus with existing soil, then fertilize with vegetable garden fertilizer at seeding or planting time. Plants benefit from liquid feeding six weeks after planting. ❺ Harvest while buds are still firm and before yellow flowers appear. ❻ This is part of the brassica family, often referred to as cole crops. They are cool-season crops, growing and producing at their best when temperatures range between 65 and 80 degrees Fahrenheit during summer. They will generally tolerate winter temperatures up to 10 degrees below freezing. All are tasty vegetables containing many vitamins.

'Raab (Rapini) Sorrento'. Grown for its zesty, mustardlike flavor; used in Italian and other ethnic cuisine. Small flower heads and leaves spice up salads. Also used as greens. (50 days)

'Super Blend Hybrids'. This is my favorite because it is a mix of three varieties that provides early, midseason, and late harvesting. 'Packman' is very early, 'Mariner' matures in midseason, and 'Pirate' comes on later. (55–70 days)

'Waltham 29'. An old-time favorite variety that is very dependable. Head size varies from small to large. Delicious when eaten raw, steamed, or stir-fried. (74 days)

Brussels sprout. ❶ – ❹ See broccoli. ❺ Harvest from below, as soon as the lowest sprouts begin to touch each other. ❻ See broccoli.

'Long Island Improved'. Miniature cabbagelike heads are tasty and nutritious. Although they are slow to develop, they produce over an extended period of time.

Cabbage. ❶ – ❹ See broccoli. ❺ Begin harvesting when heads have sized and are firm and glossy. ❻ See broccoli.

'Danish Ballhead'. A late-season variety. Heads are 7–8 inches in diameter. Excellent flavor, ideal for sauerkraut or winter storage. (110 days)

'Early Jersey Wakefield'. Dark green conical heads about 7 inches long. Easy to grow; popular home garden variety. (70 days)

'Golden Acre'. Early round-head cabbage is easily grown. Heads are about 6–7 inches in diameter on compact plants about 1 foot high. Heads are firm, medium green in color. (65 days)

'Red Acre'. Top-notch red variety. Heads are deep red, globe-shaped, 6–7 inches in diameter. Stores better than most early cabbages. (77 Days)

Carrot. ❶ Seed. Carrots do not transplant well. ❷ Sow seeds approximately 1 inch apart. This is difficult because seeds are so fine. Be careful not to cover the seed with too much soil; ⅛ inch is enough. Then when young plants are 2–5 inches tall, thin them to 2–3 inches apart. Young thinned plants are great to eat fresh or in salads. ❸ Plant carrots every two to three weeks for continuous harvest. They produce best in full sun, but will tolerate some shade. Plant them in a rich, well-drained, deep soil. ❹ Do not use manure where carrots are to be planted. Mix a vegetable garden-type fertilizer into the soil prior to planting. Additional feeding is usually not required, unless planting soil is of poor quality, then use a liquid plant food six weeks after sowing the seed. ❺ Begin harvesting, first by using thinned plants, then continuing as carrots gain orange color and when they are finger size to fully grown. ❻ Carrots are delicious, sweet flavored, and easy to grow. They are rich in potassium and vitamin A and a good source of fiber. Some varieties are also high in beta-carotene. A super crop to grow in raised beds and wide rows.

'Danvers Half Long'. Great variety for shallow soils. Excellent flavor and ideal for overwintering. (75 days)

'Imperator'. One of the standards and a popular home garden variety. Long, tapered carrots. (75 days)

'Ingot Hybrid'. This one is sweet, a national taste test winner. Deep orange in color, smooth in texture with long cylindrical roots. Very high in beta-carotene. (70 days)

'Little Fingers'. Probably the most popular of the baby carrots. These tender, sweet miniature carrots are ideal for eating fresh, canning, or cooking. (65 days)

'Parisian Market Thumbelina'. This has been a popular European variety for many years. Short, round carrots are a novelty. They grow well in shallow soil. (60 days)

'Royal Chantenay'. Uniform deep orange, coreless roots are smooth, moderately tapered, 5–7 inches long. The staff at our seed company really likes this one. (70 days)

'Scarlet Nantes'. Sweet and tender with cylindrical shape and blunt tip with bright orange-red color throughout. A very popular home garden variety. (68 days)

Cauliflower. ❶ – ❹ See broccoli. ❺ As soon as the cauliflower heads are about 2–3 inches across, tie the outer leaves over them to keep the heads white. Harvest when fully developed. ❻ See broccoli.

'Early Snowball'. Large, white, delicious, solid heads of excellent quality. This early variety is about ten days ahead of most varieties normally grown here. (75 days)

Chinese mustard. ❶ Seed sown in spring or fall. ❷ Thin seedlings to 4–6 inches apart, using greens in salads. ❸ Sow seeds in early to midspring and again in the fall. Cover seeds with ⅛ inch fine soil. Grow in cool area, where soil is well drained but moderately moist. ❹ Feed three to four weeks after plants are up, with nitrogen. ❺ Harvest outer leaves when young for best flavor, leaving inner leaves to grow out. ❻ Also called pak-choi; non-heading Chinese cabbage. Crisp, sweet, with mild flavor. Growth is somewhat similar to Swiss chard. Large, dark green leaves with thick white stems. Leaves and stalks have endless uses in cooking and are the main ingredient in chow mein. 'Tendergreen' is one of the most popular varieties.

Celery. ❶ Seed started indoors or starter plants. ❷ Thin to about 12 inches apart. ❸ Plant them outdoors in late May or early June. Keep them well watered during warm summer weather. Prepare soil as you would for other vegetables. ❹ Fertilize monthly with vegetable garden fertilizer. ❺ Begin harvesting the outer stalks when they are big enough to eat. ❻ Just a brief word about growing this popular vegetable: this is one crop you may want to try on a very limited basis. The benefits of celery are that it is rich in vitamins, minerals, and fiber.

'Utah 52-70 Improved'. My favorite variety for this climate. Long, crisp stalks. (120 days)

Corn. ❶ Seed; plants do not transplant very well. Starter plants you purchase are often slow to take hold, so you are generally better off to direct sow the seeds. ❷ Sow seeds 4–6 inches apart, covering them with 1 inch of garden soil. Seeds germinate in seven to ten days. When seedlings are 2–3 inches tall, thin them to 8–12 inches apart. Space rows 24–30 inches apart. In wide beds, space plants 12 inches in all directions. ❸ Full sun. Plant on north side of the vegetable garden so this tall crop does not shade your other vegetables. This crop needs good air circulation. ❹ Corn is fast growing so it benefits from rich, well-drained soil. Fertilize before planting with all-purpose vegetable garden-type fertilizer. Apply nitrogen to rows around the Fourth of July to give them a boost for better growth and yield. ❺ When the ear begins to pull away from the stalk, you should pull back just a bit of the top husk and check the color of the kernels. Or, you can take a bite of a few kernels to evaluate whether they are ripe. ❻ This is the favorite at the Hume household. We always make sure to grow enough corn for eating fresh and freezing. You may want to plant one early variety and a late one to extend the harvest season. High in vitamin A, phosphorus, and potassium. Pick it fresh and cook within five hours for peak flavor.

'Alpine SE White Hybrid'. A superior sugar enhanced–type white sweet corn. Ears are tender and flavorful, 8 inches long with 16 rows of kernels. Vigorous and early maturing. (79 days)

'Arrowhead Hybrid'. This is another early sugar–enhanced variety. The bicolor ears have yellow and white kernels, and average 7 inches in length. Flavor is quite sweet. (64 days)

'Early Sunglow'. A top-notch hybrid variety. Home gardeneers rate this as one of the best varieties of sweet corn. It has relatively shorter stalks than other varieties. Sweetness, flavor, and tenderness are excellent. (63 days)

'Golden Cross Bantam'. This hybrid is one of the older garden varieties. You may remember it in dad or mom's garden. Sweet, tender ears are 7–8 inches long. (85 days)

'Golden Jubilee'. Highly rated hybrid variety that is also popular with commercial corn growers. Large ears up to 9 inches long. Good flavor and lasting quality. (85 days)

'Kandy Korn'. This is one of the favorites at the Hume household. We love it fresh, and Myrna freezes it for winter use. Superhigh natural-sugar content. 14–16 rows of kernels. Pick it when the kernels are a light yellow. (90 days)

'Peaches and Cream'. This is another variety that we really like. It is a hybrid sugar-enhanced variety with yellow and white kernels. Ears average 8 inches in length. Flavor is quite sweet. We like it fresh or frozen for later use. (82 days)

'Sugar Buns'. Reports on this one have been very good. I have not tried it, but it is a sugar-enhanced sweet corn of gourmet quality. (72 days)

Cucumber. ❶ Seed or prestarted bedding plants. Starter plants often go into shock after they are set out, so I prefer to sow the seeds directly into the garden after all frost has passed. (My suggestion is late May.) Starter plants can also be planted at the same time. ❷ Plant on raised soil (hills) or in containers. Cover seeds with only ¼ inch of soil. In rows, leave about 8–12 inches between plants and space rows 3 feet apart. Space hills 3–5 feet apart, depending upon variety. ❸ Vines need bright sun exposure. Plant in rich, well-drained soil. Water deeply twice weekly during warm weather, keeping the water off the leaves, if possible. Most varieties grow very well in ordinary garden soil. ❹ Mix all-purpose vegetable garden fertilizer into the soil at planting time. Then feed monthly during the growing season with a liquid fertilizer. ❺ When you harvest is up to you. Leave some to get larger for pickles and salads. ❻ This is a wonderful low-calorie salad vegetable containing several vitamins and minerals. Easy to grow, cucumbers can be grown on a hill, in beds, or trained upward on a fence or trellis.

'Fanfare Hybrid Slicer' (semi-dwarf). An early-maturing All-American winner with an extended harvest season. Semi-dwarf plants produce flavorful 8- to 10-inch-long cucumbers. A superior, disease-resistant, nonbitter variety. (63 days)

'Lemon' (novelty). An exceptionally nice variety for cool, short-season climates. The fruit looks like a round lemon instead of a cucumber. A sweet-flavored variety that is ideal to use in salads or relishes. Myrna loves these. (70 days)

'Marketmore 76' (slicing). This has been a home garden favorite for years. Dark green cukes are 8–9 inches at maturity. Resistant to many cucumber diseases. An excellent slicer in salads and for other fresh uses. (66 days)

'Salad Bush Hybrid' (slicing). A new, All-American winner. This bush variety produces cucumbers about 7–8 inches long, on compact plants. Highly resistant to disease. High yield over a long season. (57 days)

'SMR-58' (pickling variety). This variety produces uniform, prolific small cucumbers that are ideal for pickling. (56 days)

'Spacemaster' (semi-dwarf). Another compact bush, ideal for small growing areas. Excellent for pickling when small, or use for slicing when larger. (62 days)

'Sweet Slice' (slicing). A long burpless slicing cucumber. 10–12 inches long, crisp and sweet. Resistant to a wide range of cucumber diseases. (63 days)

Eggplant. ❶ Seed sown indoors in mid-March, about 8–10 weeks before planting seedling transplants outdoors. ❷ Space plants about 2 feet apart or grow individually in containers. ❸ This is a warm-weather vegetable and should not be planted outdoors until mid- to late May at the earliest. ❹ Fertilize with liquid plant food monthly during growing season. ❺ Harvest when fruit is 6–8 inches long. When mature, the skin should not spring back when pressure is applied with your thumb. ❻ Eggplant is very popular when baked, fried, in casseroles, or

Left: It's hard to beat the flavor of tomatoes picked fresh from your own garden. Check out my selection of the best ones for this region.

in Italian and other ethnic dishes. Plants are attractive enough to use in the flower garden or landscape as an ornamental.

'Twilight'. I like this variety because it does well in short-season climates. (65 days)

Kale. ❶ – ❺ See broccoli. ❻ This is a hardy, nutritious, easy-to-grow vegetable. It has a high content of vitamins A and C. Grow it in sun during the cooler early or late season.

'Blue Curled Scotch'. My favorite variety. It grows only 12–14 inches high, but up to 3 feet wide. Bluish green, finely curled, tender and crunchy leaves. (75 days)

Kohlrabi. ❶ Seed sown outdoors in early spring, after danger of severe frost has passed. Cover seeds with ⅛ inch of fine soil. Seed several times from April to August for long harvest period. ❷ When seedlings are 2–3 inches high, thin to 6–8 inches apart. ❸ Likes a sunny location. Ordinary garden soil will do, as long as plants are watered regularly. Seed germinates in about two weeks or less. ❹ Fertilize at planting time and once again about 30 days after seeding. ❺ Harvest when bulbs are about 2–2½ inches across, cutting stems at soil level. ❻ This tasty vegetable is often overlooked for the home garden, despite being very easy to grow. Its bulblike growth develops aboveground and has a distinctive nutlike flavor. Kohlrabi seems to be insect and disease free. Myrna uses slices for summer dips.

'Purple Vienna'. Popular variety. Excellent in salads, in dips, or as a cooked vegetable. (60 days)

'White Vienna'. Popular variety. Excellent in salads, in dips, or as a cooked vegetable. (60 days)

Leek. ❶ Seed sown in early spring as soon as soil is workable. When sowing seeds, cover with just ⅛ inch of fine garden soil. ❷ Space 2–4 inches apart, thinning as needed. ❸ Plant in full sun in soil that is well drained. As the plants begin to grow, hill soil up gradually to a depth of 3–4 inches around the base of plants to create tender white stems. ❹ Light monthly feeding at half strength will aid in producing larger sized plants. ❺ Harvest as needed from pencil size to mature plants. Sometimes grown a second year before being harvested. ❻ This is one member of the onion family that is often overlooked. It's easy to grow and quite tasty. Excellent for flavoring soups, salads, and stews.

'American Flag'. Our seed company features this variety because of its mild flavor and vigor. (130 days)

Lettuce. ❶ Seed sown directly into the garden after last frost, or starter plants. Cover seeds with ⅛ inch of fine soil. Sow seeds from early to midspring and again in late summer and early fall. ❷ Leaf lettuce should be spaced about 8–12 inches apart. Space head lettuce about 15–18 inches apart. ❸ They will have the best flavor if grown in a cool, moist part of the vegetable garden. Ideal crop to grow in cold frames for winter harvest. Keep moderately moist throughout growing season. ❹ Prepare the soil by adding a complete vegetable garden–type fertilizer prior to seeding. Feed them nitrogen two or three weeks after they are up for more flavor and better growth. ❺ Begin harvesting as you thin the plants. Outer leaves can be picked at any time. Don't let the plants get too old. Replant frequently for most flavorful leaves. ❻ The crisp, flavorful lettuce leaves fresh from the garden are hard to beat. Lettuce greens are ideal for salads. They are a great source of fiber, rich in potassium and moderate amounts of vitamin A.

'All Year Round' (bibb type). A cool-season, hardy, easy-to-grow lettuce. Heads are fairly compact and light green in color. Great for early and late plantings. Can be grown in containers or ideal for winter cold frames. Excellent flavor and texture for salads. (50 days)

'Buttercrunch' (bibb type). Tender, delicious, and vigorous, compact heads. Considered one of the top-quality varieties. Easy to grow. (65 days)

'Corn Salad'. Dark green full-heart winter lettuce. Also known as lambs lettuce. It has a somewhat nutty flavor and mixes well with spinach, lettuce, and other greens in salads. It grows best during cooler weather and is ideal for fall-winter crops. (60 days)

'Grand Rapids' (leaf lettuce). Crisp, tender, and tasty variety. Ideal variety to grow in the garden, cold frames, or greenhouse. (55 days)

'Great Lakes' (head lettuce). Crisp, tender, fresh heads are tasty in salads. A popular home garden variety. Does well in cool climates. (88 days)

'Mesclun' (mixed salad greens). The 'Gourmet Blend' is a mix of various types of leaf lettuce and greens. Long popular in Europe, mesclun or mixed greens are now being used widely here. They are healthy and flavorful salad greens. (30–50 days)

'Parris Island' (romaine). Tender, crisp, and sweet flavored. It is tolerant to many lettuce diseases and is slow bolting. Upright growth to 10 inches. (65 days)

'Red Sails' (leaf lettuce). An All-American winner. A truly superior lettuce. It is long-standing with red and light green rumpled leaves. Very attractive when mixed in salads. (45 days)

'Salad Bowl' (leaf lettuce). An excellent home garden variety. Flavorful, tender, medium green, deeply notched, frilled leaves are tasty in salads. (45 days)

Melon. ❶ Seed started indoors in mid-March. ❷ Space hills about 4 feet apart. ❸ Set plants outdoors in mid-May under a *cloche* (individual protective cover) until late June. Grow plants in hills or on raised soil, with black plastic covering the soil for added warmth. ❹ Feed sparingly during growing season or you are apt to encourage too much foliage growth. ❺ You will know when the melons are ripe, because they will separate from the vine with a slight pull. ❻ Cantaloupe and watermelons can be grown very successfully in areas where summer weather is hot. And with a little special care, it's fun to try to grow them in cool climates.

'Crimson Sweet' (watermelon). Growers are focusing on developing new quick-maturing varieties, so there may be many new selections in the near future.

'Hale's Best' (cantaloupe). I like this variety for this region.

Mustard. See Chinese mustard.

Onion. ❶ Seed or small, young starter plants. Cover the seeds with ¼ inch of fine soil. This is one crop that can be planted early, as soon as the last frost has passed in spring. ❷ Sow seeds of globe types about 3 inches apart, then thin to 6 inches apart when plants are 4 inches high. Sow seeds of the bunching type (green onions) about 1 inch apart and thin to 1–2 inches apart. ❸ They grow in a fertile, well-drained soil. Do not let the plants go to seed. ❹ Prepare the soil with well-rotted manure or vegetable garden fertilizer, because onions benefit from a generous amount of fertilizer. Feed again when plants are 4–6 inches high, using a vegetable garden–type food. ❺ Bunching types (green onions) can be harvested as soon as desired; small to medium-sized plants generally have the best taste. Bend over the tops of the globe type onions to hasten ripening and to form the globe before harvesting. ❻ An extremely popular vegetable to use in salads, sandwiches, soups, and stews. They are part of the allium family, which includes leeks, garlic (see separate listings in this chapter), and shallots. Here we discuss both the globe type and the bunching ones (green onions). Both are easy to grow. Onions are an excellent fall and early winter crop too.

'Early Yellow Globe'. Excellent variety for eating fresh or storing. Ideal for slicing, cooking, or for use in salads, stews, and soups. (110 days)

'Evergreen White Bunching' (green onion). Small bunching type that is ideal in salads, soups, stews, and as a garnish. Plant several times for extended harvest. (75 days)

'Red Globe'. Medium-sweet variety. Stores well. Ideal for slicing and just as colorful as it is delicious. Great in salads, soups, and stews. (110 days)

'Walla Walla Sweet'. This is one of the sweetest globe-type onions. Large size is ideal for slicing, cooking, and frying, in salads, soups, and stews. It's an award-winning sweet onion. (110 days)

Pea. ❶ Seed sown directly into the garden. Fix seed by treating it with nitrogen inoculant. Sow seeds as soon as soil is workable in the late winter or earliest spring. Usually seeding is done from late February to late April. Sow in late July or early August for fall crops. Cover with 1–1½ inches of soil. Seed germinates in one to two weeks depending upon weather. ❷ Space seeds in furrows 2 inches apart. When growing pole-type peas, plant a row on each side of the trellis. For wide-row gardening, plant seeds of bush type 2 inches apart in all directions. ❸ Soil should be somewhat moist, rich in organic humus. Plant peas in the cooler part of the garden. When possible, plant rows in north/south direction for best sunlight and air exposure. Water by irrigation method; never water with an overhead sprinkler. ❹ Prepare planting soil with organic-rich compost or well-rotted manure. Feed lightly with liquid nonburning plant food when vines are 1 foot high. ❺ Pick peas when firm and before pods begin to yellow or shrivel. It's easiest to taste-test the edible pod–type peas. ❻ Here's one of the most popular of the early vegetables. Peas and early potatoes are a must for many home gardeners. Peas are a delicious source of many vitamins and minerals. There are several types, with the edible pod, shelling, and newer sugar snap types being the most popular here. Varieties feature both pole and bush types.

'Alaska' (bush). One of the earliest maturing peas. It will grow 2–3 feet tall, depending upon weather and time planted. A good pea for eating fresh, freezing, canning, or dried. (56 days)

'Dwarf Gray Sugar' (edible pod). A favorite bush-pod pea with attractive purple blossoms. Sweet, tender pods are ideal for steaming, stir-frying, or eating fresh. (66 days)

'Eclipse' (tall bush). New extra-sweet variety; 3-inch pod on 36-inch vines. Grow on raised soil. A real winner. A must in our garden. (63 days)

'Green Arrow' (bush). An old-time favorite. Slender 4- to 4½-inch pods contain nine to eleven tender, sweet garden peas. It is a good yielder and is resistant to many diseases. Vine height is 2–2½ feet. Ideal for shelling and eating fresh. (68 days)

'Little Marvel' (bush). Popular shelling variety. Early producing. Eight peas in a 3-inch pod. Excellent for eating fresh, canning, or freezing. (62 days)

'Olympia' (bush). A new high-yielding bush pea. Large peas grow in slender 4½- to 5-inch pods in pairs with eight to ten peas per pod. A truly superior variety with resistance to many diseases. An excellent shelling pea for eating fresh, cooked, or frozen. (61 days)

'Oregon Sugar Pod II' (edible pod). Oregon State University developed this bush variety. Edible pods are ideal for stir-fry dishes. Pods 4–4½ inches long. Snow peas are crisp, tender, full of flavor. (60 days)

'Sugar Ann' (edible pod). All-American winner. An outstanding variety of bush edible-pod, snap-type pea. (56 days)

'Sugar Lace' (afila-type bush). Stringless, self-supporting bush pea. *Afila* means a plant with few leaves. Interlocking tendrils take the place of staking. Pods are at the ends of the vines for easy picking. (68 days)

'Super Sugar Snap' (edible pod). An improved selection of the popular sugar snap (pole) pea. It's earlier with more numerous and more plump pods. It is also more disease resistant. Delicious eaten fresh, in salads, for dips, steamed, or stir-fried. (65 days)

'Tacoma' (afila-type bush). This is an ideal variety for cool, short-season climates, and great for wide-row intensive plantings. It is resistant to many diseases and earlier than other peas of this type. (63 days)

'Tall Telephone/Alderman' (pole). Considered one of the finest pole varieties for cool, short-season climates. Excellent yield, robust growth, and fine quality. 4½- to 5-inch pods. (74 days)

Pepper. ❶ Seed or starter plants. Sow seeds indoors in March or April. Seeds of most varieties germinate in two to three weeks. Do not plant outside until late May or early June. ❷ Space about 18–24 inches apart. ❸ Contrary to popular belief, sweet peppers do not require temperatures as warm as the hot peppers. Plant both types in full sun, in rich soil that is well drained. During a cool summer, place black plastic under hot pepper varieties for added warmth. ❹ Peppers are heavy feeders, so be sure to mix into the soil a vegetable garden–type fertilizer prior to planting. Then feed monthly during the growing season with the same food. When the plants come into bloom, feed them lightly with Epsom salts, using 1 tablespoon Epsom salts to 1 gallon water. ❺ Color is usually the best indicator that the peppers are ready for harvesting. Cut off a short piece of stem with fruit to avoid damaging the plant. ❻ The sweet and hot peppers are popular vegetables for a bright, sunny part of the garden. This is one of the most attractive vegetable plants not only for the colorful peppers, but also because of the bright, dark, glossy green leaves. Taste varies from mild to strong depending upon types and varieties. Numerous varieties are available, so here are just four of my favorites:

'Chili Peppers' (mixed varieties). This is a spicy collection of mixed chili peppers. Included are cayenne, Hungarian wax, serrano, habanero, hot cherry, and other hot chilies. This mix provides a real adventure in hot pepper growing as the different varieties come into maturity at different times. (70–100 days)

'Jalapa' (early hybrid). A very early-maturing hot jalapeño pepper. Compact plants produce many small green peppers that slowly turn red at maturity. Eat fresh, cooked, pickled, dried, or in salsa. (70 days)

'North Star' (early hybrid bell). Here's a sweet bell pepper that will mature in short-season climates. Its crisp, blocky fruit will turn from medium green to red if left on the plant longer. Excellent to use as stuffed pepper, in tempura recipes, and with dips. (75 days)

'Yellow Banana Sweet'. Ideal variety for cool, short-season climates. Excellent flavor for eating raw or cooked, flavoring sauces, stuffing, or pickling. Attractive, long, pointed fruit. (75 days)

Potato. ❶ Certified seed potatoes (potatoes that are disease free); available in springtime, at garden outlets. Do not use potatoes from the produce counter; most have been treated with a growth retardant that slows growth. Each potato has "eyes" (new growth buds). The potatoes can be planted individually, or cut in half or quarters and planted, as long as each piece has at least one "eye." If you cut the potatoes in half or quarters, the cut pieces can be planted right away; you do not have to wait for them to develop a scab over the cut. Cover pieces with 3–4 inches of soil. New growth will often appear within ten days to two weeks depending upon temperatures. ❷ On hills, place three or four pieces (per hill) about 8 inches apart. In rows, plant pieces about 12 inches apart. Space rows about 24–36 inches apart. ❸ Here's where you can have a lot of fun because potato tubers can be grown in the ground, in tires, in garbage cans (with drainage holes in the bottom), and in straw. Often grown on hills of soil, one or two cut potatoes are all you need per hill. Be certain the potato tubers are covered with soil at all times. Green tubers, which result if the tubers are not covered, are poisonous. The seed that develops after the flower looks somewhat like a small green tomato; it is not, and is not edible. Potatoes will grow in just about any soil, as long as it is well drained. They like cool summer nighttime temperatures and acid soil (4.6–5.6 pH) conditions. ❹ This crop benefits from organic matter mixed into the soil. Also add a vegetable garden-type fertilizer when preparing the soil. It's best not to use lime or fresh manure of any kind in soils where potatoes are to be planted. ❺ The first new potatoes will be ready about the time the first peas are harvested. To harvest them, simply reach in with your hands or gently use a garden fork to lift a few. The main crop is harvested after the tops die down. Potatoes are easy to dig with a garden fork. If you damage any, eat them right away. If your soil is well drained, you can leave some in the ground until you are ready to use them. We grow ours in tires and harvest them as we need them. ❻ It's estimated that the average person eats more than 100 pounds of potatoes a year. Potatoes are easy to grow and high in vitamins B1 and B2, phosphorus, and potassium. They can be stored for year-round use.

'Kennebec' (midseason). A favorite among Northwest home gardeners. Produces large potatoes that are good keepers. Excellent for boiling or mashing. (110 days)

'Nooksack' (late). Very large, round potatoes excellent for baking. Well adapted to the marine climate west of the Cascade Mountains. Good keeper. (130 days)

'Norgold' (early). A russet type, long white potato. Excellent for baking and mashed potatoes. Not the best for storage. (100 days)

'Norland M' (early). A popular red, oblong-shaped potato. Has many cooking uses; especially popular for boiling. Good keeper. (90 days)

'Russet Burbank' (midseason). Commonly called the Idaho potato. This is the ever-popular baker variety. (110 days)

'White Rose' (midseason). Popular all-round potato. Tubers are long and rather flat. (110 days)

'Yellow Finn' (late). A good-keeping yellow potato. Pear-shaped tubers are excellent for baking, boiling, and frying. (130 days)

'Yukon Gold' (early). An excellent yellow variety for steaming and potato salad. (100 days)

Pumpkin. ❶ Seed sown directly into the garden in early to mid-May, or a bit later if soil or temperatures are still cool. Cover seeds with ½ inch of fine soil. Starter plants are often available, but I find they go through a bit of shock in being transplanted, so you are better off to start from seed. ❷ Plant in rows or hills. In rows, space about 4–6 feet apart. Leave about 4 feet between rows. Sow six to eight seeds per hill, then thin to two plants. ❸ Plant them in a bright, sunny part of the garden. They grow best in fairly rich, well-drained soil. To conserve space, the vines can be planted between rows of corn. ❹ Fertilize prior to planting with vegetable garden–type fertilizer. Then feed monthly with the same type fertilizer. ❺ Pumpkins will change color when they are ready to be harvested. The stem will also begin to yellow. Cut an inch or two of the stem with the pumpkin. ❻ Pumpkins are fun to grow and popular with kids and adults. The medium-sized varieties are the most popular to use as Halloween pumpkins. All varieties (except the miniatures) are excellent for pies and breads. Have kids write their name on a baseball-size pumpkin with a ballpoint pen, and they can watch their name grow as the pumpkin grows.

'Connecticut Field'. This is a popular variety for commercial growers. Excellent for carving and baking. Fruit is medium orange in color, 8–10 inches in height, and 12 inches in diameter. The average weight is 12 pounds. (110 days)

'Dill's Atlantic Giant'. This is the one that has produced the world's largest pumpkins. Color is pinkish to medium orange. This variety takes a lot of space, but it's fun to grow. The world's record is more than 1,000 pounds. Competitors start seed indoors in March. (125 days)

'Howden'. This is an ideal jack-o'-lantern type that kids love to grow. Ideal 10- to 12-inch pumpkins are just right for carving or painting. The average weight is 10–15 pounds. (115 days)

'Jack Be Little'. This is a new miniature pumpkin that's ideal for table decorations, painting, or really small jack-o'-lanterns. Easy to grow, plants bear several 2- to 3-inch pumpkins. They are edible, but more highly valued for their decorative use. (95 days)

'Small Sugar'. This is one of the best varieties for baking. Pumpkins are sweet and dark orange in color. Small in size, only 6–8 inches and weight about 6 pounds. Fine for carving or painting too. (115 days)

Radicchio. ❶ Seed sown directly into the garden from late spring through late summer. Barely cover seeds with soil. ❷ Space plants 6 inches apart. ❸ Plant in a sunny location, in fertile, well-drained soil. ❹ Requires little if any feeding if soil is fertile at planting time. ❺ Outer leaves can be harvested as they grow. The flavor increases with cool weather. ❻ This leaf crop is popular in Italy, and is fast becoming popular here; also known as red leaf chicory.

'Red Verona'. I like this variety. Its somewhat bitter flavor is enjoyed both raw in salads or cooked. Plants form a compact head as weather turns colder. Usually grown as a fall crop, because the flavor improves as the weather gets cooler.

Radish. ❶ Seed sown directly into the garden (like all root crops). Sow directly into the garden anytime the soil is workable from March through September. Plant every two to three weeks for continual harvest. Cover seeds with ¼ inch fine soil. Seeds germinate in a week or less. ❷ Sow seeds 1½ inches apart. Once seedlings are established, thin to 1½–2 inches apart. ❸ Protect from insects by covering planting area with cheesecloth or agricultural netting strung above the plants. Plant in moderately rich soil. Plant in a mostly sunny spot, and keep moderately moist. ❹ Mix some vegetable garden fertilizer into the soil prior to seeding. Then do the same as you prepare the soil for subsequent plantings. ❺ They taste best when they're young. Some varieties grow larger than others, so harvest by variety. ❻ This is one of the most popular root crops. It's a tasty, versatile vegetable that is ideal to use in salads and dips, or to eat fresh from the garden. They are easy to grow, fun for kids to grow, and quick maturing. Save space by interplanting them with other vegetables. A good source of several vitamins and minerals.

'Champion'. A favorite in our seed company test gardens. A bright red, crisp, round radish with large tops. Popular for eating fresh, in salads, and as garnishes. (28 days)

'Cherry Belle'. A small round variety with bright red roots and short tops. A top-notch variety for home gardens. (22 days)

'Early Scarlet Globe'. Popular home garden variety for eating fresh, using in salads, and for garnishes. Early yield. (24 days.)

'Easter Egg II'. A colorful, tasty mixture of red, purple, and white globe type radishes. Firm, crisp quality. Brighten your salad and vegetable tray with this showy mix of radishes. (28 days)

'French Breakfast'. Roots are elongated with red tops and white tips. Good flavor, excellent for dips or as a garnish. (26 days)

'Gourmet Blend'. A delicious mixture of firm, crisp radishes in a wide range of colors and shapes. Children love this colorful mixture. Excellent for relish trays, in salads, or as a garnish. (25 days)

'Icicle'. My favorite long, white radish. Quick maturing with roots 5–5½ inches long. Tender, rich flavor. Excellent garnish for salads. (27 days)

Rutabaga. ❶ Seed sown in midsummer. Cover with ¼ inch fine soil. ❷ Sow seeds 24 inches apart, thin to 6–8 inches apart. ❸ Easy to grow. ❹ Seldom require additional feeding if soil is fertile at seeding time. ❺ Harvest when roots are 3–4 inches wide. Roots can be harvested up to the first freeze, then stored for winter use. ❻ Both tops and root are edible. High in vitamin A and C. This is an excellent fall crop.

'American Purple Top'. This old favorite is sweet and fine grained with yellow flesh that cooks to bright orange. (90 days)

Spinach. ❶ Seed. Put seeds in refrigerator for one week prior to sowing. Starter plants are also available in springtime but often are slow to take hold. Cover seeds with ¼ inch soil. ❷ Sow seeds 3–4 inches apart, then thin to 6–8 inches apart. Either transplant thinned plants, or enjoy them in salads. Leave 18–24 inches between rows. ❸ Plants grow best in fairly rich soil kept somewhat moist. Some varieties tend to *bolt* (go to seed) during hot weather, so plant in early spring and in the fall. ❹ Like all leaf crops, spinach benefits from regular feeding. Start by mixing vegetable garden type fertilizer into the planting soil. Then feed once or twice during the growing season with the same type of food. ❺ Begin picking outer leaves when plants are 2–4 inches high. ❻ Greens of spinach are very popular in salads, as cooked greens, and in soufflés. This is one leaf crop that grows best during the cooler spring and fall months. However, some of the new long-standing varieties will even produce during warmer summer weather. High in vitamin A and C, potassium, and calcium.

'New Zealand'. Not a true spinach, but very popular for growing during warm summer weather. Use as you would regular spinach. High in vitamin content. Heavy yield. Seed germination rate tends to be rather low. (70 days)

'Olympia'. This Northwest variety is a top-notch, smooth-leaf (long-standing) hybrid. Leaves are thick and dark green. Highly recommended for spring, summer, and fall. Provides winter harvest most seasons. (48 days)

'Perpetual Spinach' (green leaf Swiss chard). This is a long-standing type, meaning it is slower to bolt than other types. It is quite hardy and prolific, supplying a "perpetual" harvest of succulent leaves from spring through fall. (50 days +)

'Tyee'. Semi-savoy (long-standing) hybrid developed in the Northwest. Slightly rumpled leaves are ideal for salads, cooked greens, and soufflés. Fast growing; excellent for spring, fall, and overwintering crops. (46 days)

Squash. ❶ Seed or starter plants. I prefer seeds to starter plants because the plants seem to develop more quickly. Cover seeds with ½ inch of fine soil. Seeds of most varieties germinate in about one to two weeks. ❷ Easiest to plant in hills. Sow seeds 4 inches apart, six to eight seeds per hill. Thin to three healthiest per hill. Space hills 3–4 feet apart. Squash can be planted between corn, spacing hills about 10 feet apart. ❸ This is a warm-weather crop, so sow seeds in mid- to late May. Soil should be kept moderately moist throughout the growing season. Plant in full sun. Vines can be trimmed back as long as sufficient foliage is left to support fruit. If first (small) squash do not develop and rot on vine, it is because male flowers have not yet developed. Simply pick off decaying fruit. ❹ Mix vegetable garden-type fertilizer into planting soil prior to planting. No additional feeding should be required, unless leaves show signs of yellowing. ❺ Harvest summer squash when fruit is correct size and skin is still soft enough to penetrate with your fingernail. Pick summer squash when it is immature. Harvest winter squash when it is mature. Winter squash has its best flavor if picked just before the first frost. (The big leaves will usually protect it if a frost occurs.) Another good sign that winter squash is ready to be harvested is when the stem begins to turn brown and shrivel. ❻ Summer and winter types of squash can be used steamed, boiled, baked, or fried. The summer types can also be eaten raw or used for dips. Winter varieties store well. Squash takes quite a bit of space, unless the vines can be trellised. It's easy to grow, and the various varieties offer an assortment of delicious tastes.

'Black Beauty' (zucchini; bush). Compact plants produce abundantly throughout the summer. Fruit is dark green and glossy, and tapers toward each end. Delicious when baked, fried, steamed, and raw in a variety of recipes. (50 days)

'Blue Hubbard' (winter keeper). This is an old-time favorite. Outside is gray-green, inside bright orange. Fine textured and quite sweet. Delicious in pies or cut and used baked or steamed. Excellent storing quality through the winter. (110 days)

'Crookneck Bush' (summer). Early, delicious, tender butter-yellow fruits. Fruits continuously when regularly harvested at 5–6 inches long. Use steamed, raw, boiled, baked, or fried. (45 days)

'Delicata' (winter keeper). This is my granddaughter's favorite. Sometimes called sweet potato squash because of its flavor and shape. Very productive and stores well throughout the winter and into the spring. Enjoy this fine-grained, light orange squash steamed or baked. Semi-bush vines do not take over the garden. (100 days)

'Gold Rush' (zucchini; hybrid bush). Outstanding early variety of zucchini. Produces a high yield of bright yellow fruit on open, compact plants. Colorful in salads and delicious in breads, baked, or stir-fried. (50 days)

'Jackpot' (zucchini; hybrid bush). A very popular high-yielding variety. Long, smooth, cylindrical fruit is very popular in zucchini bread, salads, cooked, baked, or fried. (50 days)

'Round' (zucchini; bush). An unusually shaped zucchini variety. This round type can be used in salads, baked, stir-fried, or in zucchini bread and works especially well for stuffed zucchini recipes because of its shape. (45 days)

'Scallop' (summer; early white bush). Also known as pattypan. This tasty summer squash is delicious fresh, steamed, or baked. Best flavor is obtained when fruit is picked at 2–3 inches in diameter. (47 days)

'Sweet Dumpling' (winter). A mini-sized winter squash. Round in shape and 3–4 inches across. Very sweet in flavor with tender, light orange flesh. Produces prolifically on fairly short vines and stores well. (75 days)

'Sweet Meat' (winter keeper). Many a home gardener raves about this one. The thick flesh is deep yellow, quite sweet, and smooth in texture. Plant is vining in nature, bearing up to several 9- to 5-inch fruits averaging 10 pounds when mature. Delicious baked or steamed. (105 days)

'Table King' (winter; bush acorn). This is an excellent bush variety of the popular acorn squash. Provides a heavy yield in a limited space. Ideal for baking, pies, and storage. (82 days)

'Vegetable Spaghetti' (winter keeper). A real conversation piece because of its spaghetti-like appearance inside. Unusual and delicious. Becoming very popular for use in salads or with butter and cheese sauces. Enjoy baked, steamed, boiled, or microwaved. (100 days)

'Waltham Butternut' (winter keeper). Fruit is 8–10 inches long with sweet, fine-grained yellow-orange flesh. Ideal to use steamed, boiled, or baked. (95 days)

Swiss chard. ❶ Seed. Starter plants do not transplant well. Sow seeds in early spring and again in mid- to late summer. Cover seeds with ¼–½ inch fine soil.

❷ Sow seeds 4–6 inches apart, then thin to 8–12 inches when seedlings are 3–4 inches high. Use the leaves of the thinned plants in salads. ❸ Very easy to grow. Full sun to part sun and shade. Grow in rich soil that is moderately moist. ❹ Add vegetable garden–type fertilizer at seeding time. Then, like all leaf crops, feed at least once during the growing season, using the same type of fertilizer. ❺ Begin picking outer leaves when plants are about 8 inches high. However, chard is not fussy. If all of the leaves are cut 1–2 inches aboveground, new leaves will form. ❻ This colorful vegetable is a member of the beet family. The slightly rumpled leaves are used much the same as spinach leaves or beet greens. The biggest advantage of chard is that it will tolerate cool or hot growing weather, when most other greens tend to bolt if temperatures get too hot. I think one of the greatest advantages is that these are attractive plants that can be used in the landscape as well as in the vegetable garden. They are easy to grow.

'Bright Lights'. A new award-winning multicolor Swiss chard. Stalks grow in a rainbow of colors, with some variation of leaf color. A very showy outdoor foliage plant for the autumn and winter garden. Use the young leaves to brighten salads. Leaves and stems can be used raw, steamed, or stir-fried. (55 days)

'Rhubarb' chard. The crimson-colored stalks resemble rhubarb in color and shape. Use much the same as spinach. High in vitamin content. (60 days)

'White Rib Chard'. Large, fairly smooth, thick leaves with white rib. White ribs can be sliced and used in salads and stir-fries or steamed like asparagus. Use leaves much the same as spinach. (60 days).

Tomato. ❶ Seed sown indoors about six weeks before setting the plants outside. As a rule, sow seeds in late March or early April. Barely cover the seeds with ⅛ inch of fine soil or peat moss. Transplant starter plants into individual 4-inch pots when they are about 2–3 inches tall. If you start them earlier, repot into 8-inch or gallon pots when the seedlings are 8–12 inches tall. ❷ Leave about 2 feet between plants. If they are the tall *indeterminate* (final height undetermined) types, they will need more space, so plant them 3 feet apart. ❸ Plant them in the sunniest spot in the garden. In cold climates, plant them on the sunny side of a fence or against the house, where they get additional reflected sun and heat. In the test garden we grow our tomatoes in tires. The raised soil and warmth of the tires help bring on the tomatoes earlier. At home, I grow our plants in a raised bed for earlier fruiting. Any of the varieties can also be grown in containers, where warmer soil and limited growing area help encourage earlier ripening. In cool climates, mid-May is usually the right time to set the plants outdoors. However, if temperatures are still cool, wait until the first of June. (Nighttime temperatures should average over 55 degrees Fahrenheit.) Leaves that turn purplish or yellowing lower leaves are a sign that it's still too cold for tomatoes. Tall, spindly plants can be planted lying down, with the top above the ground. Roots will form all along the buried stem. (Never plant with leaves on the underground stem, and be certain the lower leaves of the plant never touch the soil.) Bushy, sturdy plants should be planted deep, so part of the stem is underground. ❹ Prepare the soil well, mixing in organic humus in the form of compost, well-rotted manure (don't use fresh manure), processed manure that you buy in bags and peat moss. Also, add a complete vegetable garden fertilizer such as 5-10-10 or an organic brand. Prepare the soil to a depth of at least 1 foot. Add a half cup of dolomite lime in each planting hole, mixing it thoroughly with the planting soil. Also, mix 1 tablespoonful of Epsom salts to 1 gallon of water and add it. Do this a week or two before planting. Contrary to popular belief, tomatoes are not really heavy feeders. In fact, if they are overfed or overwatered, the plants will get a lot of leaves but few flowers and tomatoes. If soil preparation is done right, little if any feeding should be necessary. However, once the tomatoes begin to form, a light application of 0-10-10 will aid in the development of the fruit. ❺ Warmer temperatures encourage quicker ripening. At the end of the season, as frost dates approach, green tomatoes can be picked and ripened indoors. If you have quite a few green tomatoes, place them in a cool, dark room and bring out a few at a time. Keep those that you bring out in a dark spot, but expose them to 65- to 70-degree temperatures. Do not put ripening tomatoes on the windowsill; they will not ripen as fast and may sun-scald. Another way to ripen green tomatoes is to dig up the entire plant, strip off the leaves, and hang the plant upside-down in a garage or utility room where temperatures will remain above freezing. (Watch the tomatoes closely and pick them as they ripen, otherwise they will fall to the floor and create quite a mess.) ❻ Tomatoes seem to be such a challenge for so many folks, yet I think they are fun and easy to grow if you simply observe a few cultural requirements. They are actually the most popular of all crops that home gardeners grow. It's easy to understand because of their value for slicing, salads, relishes, pasta, freezing, and canning. Below are a dozen of the most dependable and popular varieties for this area.

'Early Girl'. Outstanding early variety that's dependable and tasty, and produces uniform 4- to 5-ounce tomatoes. (75 days)

'Fantastic'. A Northwest favorite with meaty, bright-red fruit and beefsteak flavor. (85 days)

'Gold Nugget'. An early golden cherry tomato with sweet fruit on a compact plant. (60 days)

'IPB'. Early, dependable, firm, juicy, and small to medium-size fruit. Another Northwest favorite. (60 days)

'Legend'. Extra-early 4- to 5-inch fruit. Quite resistant to late blight. Developed at Oregon State University.

'Oregon Spring'. Developed at Oregon State University. Combines early fruiting with large size and good flavor. (65 days)

'Pik Red'/'Pik Rite'. Excellent large tomato that ripens in short-season climates. Firm, juicy, solid red fruit. A favorite with all Hume families. (70 days)

'Siberia'. Cool-weather variety that can set fruit during low nighttime temperatures. Small to medium-size tomatoes. (48 days after flowering)

'Siletz'. Very large, early maturing tomato. Fruit size is 10–12 ounces. Another outstanding variety introduced by Oregon State University. (65 days)

'Sweet Million'. Disease-resistant cherry tomato. Flavorful tomatoes set grapelike clusters and are 1–1½ inches in diameter. (70 days)

'Sweetie'. Outstanding cherry tomato with sweet taste; a prolific producer. (70 days)

'Tumbler'. This is considered one of the best varieties to grow in hanging baskets. Sweet, 1-inch, bright-red fruit hangs in clusters. (49 days)

'Viva Italia'. A terrific roma tomato with blocky, plum-shaped fruit. (75 days)

'Yellow Pear'. A very tasty, pear-shaped yellow tomato. Tall growth needs staking. (75 days)

Turnip. ❶–❺ See rutabaga for growing suggestions; they are grown in the same way. ❻ Give this versatile, easy-to-grow vegetable a try. It has a large, sweet, fine-grained root that is excellent for storing, canning, and freezing. Tops are an enjoyable green with rich vitamin content.

'Purple Top.' I like this old favorite variety.

16 · Composting & Fertilizing

Whether you make your own or purchase recycled garden waste that has been made into compost, you are adding the best organic soil amendment you can possibly add to your garden. And good, rich soil is the key to having a really great garden. Then to keep your plants healthy and in tip-top shape, they need to be fertilized at the right time and with the correct fertilizer. So in this chapter, let's take the mystery out of composting and feeding, and see how easily they can be done!

Composting

For years, composting has been portrayed as a tedious task, but the process is really quite simple and very rewarding, building rich, organic humus for use in the garden and providing a wonderful way of recycling garden and kitchen waste.

Compost humus results from the thorough decaying of leaves, grass clippings, coffee grounds, vegetable parts, weeds, and other garden and kitchen waste. This material, once decomposed, becomes a loose, rich, friable source of organic humus, adding some valuable nutrients to the soil, and has value for retaining moisture and conditioning garden soils. Compost is living soil, containing billions of microorganisms, so it is undoubtedly the best soil amendment there is.

Facing page: Compost made from garden waste is one of the best sources of organic humus.

Above: Here a simple container made with wire and wood scraps is used as a compost bin.

Choosing a Location

In most gardens, there are several possible sites in which to construct a compost pile or place a commercially made compost bin. Choose a permanent site that is easily accessible, in bright sun, out of sight for appearance's sake, and close to a water source. Often the composting site can be hidden behind a few shrubs or you can screen it with a low fence.

Homemade Compost Piles

Compost piles can consist of simply a heap of refuse, a bottomless barrel filled with garden refuse, a hole in the ground, or a specially constructed bin made of wood, plastic, or concrete. In some of the compost demonstration gardens, they show how to make a compost bin with pallet boards, or by using various types of wire (chicken wire or hog wire). The wire bins are often made using wood frames or can be made by simply making a round wire cage in which you can make compost. It can be as simple or as elaborate as you want.

You can construct a compost pile of any size. The general shape is usually oblong and seldom is more than 4 or 5 feet wide, but often stretches much longer. The top of the pile is generally kept at a convenient height of approximately 3 or 4 feet. For example, my compost pile is a heap above the ground, about 8 feet long and 3 feet wide. Those dimensions are a result of the only available space I have in our whole garden.

Commercial Compost Units

In recent years, many new commercially made composting bins have been introduced. Probably the most popular ones are the tumblers, an adjustable type, slatted bins, and various bins made from plastics, recycled plastics, wood, and wire. Most are efficient and are considered more attractive than most homemade compost piles. These are available through garden centers, mail-order catalog firms, and sometimes even through local government agencies.

How to Start Making Compost

The key to making great compost is the addition of equal parts of "brown" and "green" material. (Both are listed in detail below.) The browns are rich in carbons and increase aeration, while the greens are rich in nitrogen and encourage the reproduction of microorganisms to help break down the compost material.

It's best to build the compost in layers. Start by using a layer of 4 to 6 inches of mixed brown and green refuse. It is not necessary, but if you want to enhance quicker composting, add a composting agent (inoculant). Next, add a 2-inch layer of soil or manure. Then all you do is repeat these layers until the compost pile is of a convenient height. The key to making good compost is creating heat in the pile, and layering is the process that encourages the warmth. During the summer, you make the top layer concave (lower in the middle) to collect water, then in winter you mound the center so excess water runs off.

Left: Many commercially built composting units are available to the home gardener. This is one of the tumbling type.

Some Important Composting Hints

- Compost feeds the soil. That's because compost is living soil, containing billions of microorganisms, making it the best soil amendment there is. You'll find it really pays to take the time to recycle your garden waste by composting.
- Have you applied a "weed and feed" product to your lawn? Do not add those grass clippings to the compost pile, as the weed killer (herbicide) may remain active as long as nine to twelve months after application. If it is composted, that new compost could kill or damage landscape plants and seeds, and possibly contaminate food crops, too.
- Recycling or mulching lawn mowers cut the grass clippings into fine pieces that fall back into the lawn, returning moisture, nutrients, and organic matter to regenerate the turf.
- Make compost by digging green and brown materials directly into the soil. That's right, if you're limited in space or don't have the time to compost, simply collect the organic material and dig it in to the soil in the fall and/or winter. Let Mother Nature compost it naturally over winter.

"Brown" Materials to Use

Brown materials are added to the compost pile because they are rich in carbon and help to aerate the pile. Large leaves and plant parts break down quicker if they are chopped or shredded. One easy way to do this is to simply lay them on the lawn and run the lawn mower over them. When doing this, do not include branches or other hard items.

It's difficult to keep "brown" materials on hand all year, so it is a good idea to bag up some of the fall leaves; then you will have them on hand as you need them for spring and summer composting. Here are some of the best "browns" to use for composting:

- corn husks
- eggshells
- leaves (dried or fallen)
- newspaper, shredded
- pine needles (use sparingly)
- plant parts
- sawdust, bark, and/or wood chips
- small branches, shredded or chopped
- straw

"Green" Materials to Use

Green materials are added to the compost pile to add organic nitrogen and encourage reproduction of microorganisms. Again, these materials break down quicker if chopped or shredded, but it is not necessary. Young weeds can also be added to the compost. However, avoid morning glory (bindweed), horsetail, ivy, blackberries, and other nuisance weeds. Also avoid old weeds and grasses that are going to seed. Here are some of the best "green" materials for composting:

- coffee grounds
- flowers (annuals and perennials)
- green leaves
- greens from the kitchen
- lawn clippings (from pesticide-free lawns)
- manure (except from dogs, cats, and pigs)
- seaweed and/or kelp, chopped or shredded
- tea bags
- vegetables

Kitchen Materials to Use

Among the best kitchen scraps are:

- coffee grounds
- eggshells
- flowers

fruit parts (chopped) and peelings
newspaper, shredded
tea bags
vegetable parts, peelings, waste

Kitchen Materials Not to Use

Avoid using these kitchen scraps:
bones
dairy products
meat
pet food

Garden Materials to Use

In addition to the list below, wood ashes can sparingly be added to the compost pile for their potassium content, ½ to 1 inch at most. Among the best garden materials to use are:
flowers
plant greens
grass clippings
manure (not cat, dog, or pig)
pine needles (sparingly)
small pruned material (chopped)
straw
tree and plant leaves
wood chips, sawdust, and bark
young weeds (noninvasive)

Garden Materials Not to Use

Never add diseased plants or those treated with pesticides to the compost pile. Send them away with the garbage carrier. Specifically, be careful to avoid these garden materials:
charcoal
dog, cat, and pig manure
grass clippings from Weed & Feed–treated lawn
madrona or walnut leaves
old weeds going to seed
poisonous plants, all parts
pressure-treated wood scraps
rhododendron leaves or branches
rhubarb leaves

Turning (Aerating) the Compost Pile

About once every two weeks it's a good idea to turn the compost. Use a pitchfork for this job. As you turn the compost, the center should be hot enough to heat up the tines of the pitchfork (or you'll see some steam rise from the pile); that way, you know the compost pile is actively working. Turn the tumbler type compost units as per manufacturer's recommendations. Incidentally, if you are trying to create compost in a hurry (hot composting), then the pile should be turned every three to seven days.

Watering the Compost Pile

It is a good idea to occasionally provide ventilation by poking some holes in the compost pile with a shovel handle or crowbar, which will help hasten decomposition. Likewise, do not let the compost pile dry out completely, because moisture is necessary if the bacteria are to decompose the plant material properly.

Screening the Compost

The finished compost-humus from the pile should be sifted through a ½- to 1-inch wire-mesh screen. Any materials too coarse to penetrate the screen should be returned to the compost pile for additional decomposition.

Using the Compost

When Is the Compost Ready to Use?

You can probably tell by the texture of the compost or by the smell when it is ready to use. Or you can put some of the compost in a pot or flat, sow twelve radish seeds, and see how quickly and how many germinate.

How Much Compost Should Be Used?

On average, about 1 to 2 inches of compost is ideal for planting, mulching, or mixing into a new planting area. You can use up to 3 inches in areas where you plant vegetables or annual flowers. As a top-dressing on lawns, use sparingly, ½ inch at most.

Controlling Composting Problems

Bad Odors

These can be caused by fermenting food scraps, grass clippings, seaweed, or kelp. Mix and bury these materials deeper into the pile. Grass clippings tend to create an unpleasant odor if they are wet or piled too deep and not mixed with brown material.

No Decomposing

This problem could be caused by any one of several things, but aeration unquestionably is the major problem. Here are the most common problems:

- poor aeration: turn regularly
- too dry: add moisture as needed
- too wet: here in the Northwest, cover your compost during the rainy season
- not enough greens: add nitrogen

Rodents and Insects

This is generally the result of adding food scraps or manure, then not covering or mixing them deep enough into the pile. If this becomes a major problem, cover the pile with wood or heavy plastic so the critters cannot gain access to the compost.

Composting with Worm Bins

In recent years, it has become increasingly popular to make a worm box and let the worms do the composting. I have never composted in this manner, but have seen several compost demonstration sites where they have worm bins, and marvel at the end product, which is beautiful, black, worm castings–rich compost. The worms rapidly break down greens, coffee grounds, eggshells, and limited amounts of food and fruit scraps.

Start with a little soil, scraps of shredded or torn (moist) paper, and a few red worms. Worms from the garden are not effective; you need to purchase red worms. The bin will need drainage holes in the bottom and air holes in the side.

A Popular Alternative to Composting

Today, if you're a lazy gardener or simply don't have a suitable spot for composting, you can send your garden waste away on recycling yard-waste day and (in some areas) buy back the finished product. That certainly is the case where we live. Although I have a small compost pile, we have twice-monthly yard-waste pickups, then we can buy the finished compost by the yard, by the truckload, or in 1-cubic-foot bags. The dark-black finished compost is great for planting or transplanting, or makes an attractive mulch. I use it extensively, as do my neighbors.

Fertilizing

The proper feeding of garden plants is one of the least-understood garden projects. Like anything else we do in the garden, it's just a matter of using good common sense and learning to recognize when your plants need nutrients. A bright-green, healthy-growing, prolific-flowering plant probably does not need feeding. On the other hand, a yellow, stunted, or poorly flowering plant needs help, and feeding is often the answer.

Overfeeding should also be recognized and avoided, because it is apt to cause rapid and excessively tender growth. Overfed plants often become too tall and leggy, misshapen, and susceptible to freezing weather. Also, overfeeding can burn the tender new growth.

What to Feed Plants

What Do the Three Numbers Mean?

Every packaged fertilizer has three numbers; for example, 12-4-8. These numbers are often referred to as "npk." The "n" is for nitrogen (in the example, 12); the "p" is for phosphorus (in the example, 4); and the "k" is for potash (in the example, 8). Thus, the example is a formula for 12 parts nitrogen, 4 parts phosphorus, and 8 parts potash.

- Nitrogen aids in foliage growth and leaf color.
- Phosphorus aids in all forms of growth, particularly stem, seed, fruit, and root growth.
- Potash aids in all parts of growth, particularly stem, hardiness, and some disease resistance.

Are There Easy-to-Follow Fertilizer Guidelines?

As a general rule, a rhododendron or evergreen-type fertilizer is used to feed those plants that maintain green foliage year-round. A rose, all-purpose garden, or vegetable-garden fertilizer can be used for deciduous plants. In a nutshell, here are the types to use:

- Deciduous trees: deciduous/rose or vegetable garden–type fertilizer

Fertilizing Tips

- What about using the same fertilizer each time you feed your plants? How would you like a hamburger for every meal? I don't advocate having a whole shelf of different types of fertilizer, but I do suggest that you occasionally feed your plants with a different type of plant food. That gives them different minerals and often varying amounts of useful micronutrients.
- If the lower leaves of chrysanthemum or clematis plants turn yellow, and eventually brown, the plants may be trying telling you something. That's often a sign the plants need magnesium, also known as Epsom salts. Apply magnesium in mid-April at the rate of 1 tablespoon to a gallon of water.
- Plants need vitamins too! When selecting a brand of fertilizer for feeding your plants, check the ingredient part of the label to be certain it contains micronutrients (sometimes referred to as minerals or trace elements). They will be listed as iron, magnesium, boron, sulfur, zinc, etc.
- Water it in! One of the biggest mistakes people make in applying fertilizer is failing to water it in. Unless the fertilizer label specifies otherwise, water it in. Don't rely on rain. The combination of moist soil and (hot) fertilizer can burn plant roots quickly, and can result in unsightly burned leaves or in severe cases stunting or even loss of the plant.

- Evergreen trees: evergreen/rhododendron fertilizer
- Deciduous shrubs: rose/garden or vegetable garden–type foods
- Evergreen shrubs: rhododendron or evergreen fertilizer
- Roses: rose fertilizer
- Bulbs: bulb or rose type fertilizer
- Vegetables: vegetable garden–type fertilizer or rose food that does not contain an insecticide
- Houseplants: fertilizers specifically made for houseplants

Should You Use Liquid or Dry Food?

Which is better, a liquid or a dry fertilizer? I suggest that you simply choose the type that is easier for you to use. Dry or granular-type fertilizers are generally more concentrated and must be watered in after application. Liquid fertilizers are diluted and applied by sprayer, with a sprinkling can, or through an injection system.

When to Feed Plants

The big question, after we know what we should use to fertilize plants with, is when should it be done. The answer: as new growth starts in spring or just after the new growth has begun is the best time to feed plants. In the Pacific Northwest, this is the period from mid- to late March, and again if needed in late May or early June.

How to Feed Plants

Dry Fertilizers

Be certain to thoroughly water in all dry fertilizers because many types may severely burn plant parts (roots, foliage, and branches) if they are left dry on the topsoil.

Liquid Fertilizers

Apply liquid fertilizers during the morning hours. Avoid applying them in the late afternoon, as the wet foliage of plants is more susceptible to overnight disease exposure. Plants growing under tall evergreens or where they are in competition with other plants will absorb liquid fertilizers more readily and rapidly.

Read the Label

Last but certainly not least, it is very important to mix and apply all fertilizers according to label instructions. Overdoses are apt to burn or even kill plants, and weak solutions probably will not create the results you expect.

17 · Protecting Plants from Creatures

Have you awakened in the morning to find holes in the lawn, mounds in the garden, or plants half-eaten? Maybe a plant has even disappeared. Chances are, the culprit is one of a possible dozen uninvited creatures that has found your garden to be a great grazing ground. This chapter discusses some of the telltale signs that indicate the presence of these creatures, and humane ways in which they can be controlled—or at least discouraged from damaging your garden.

I have tried to recommend friendly ways of discouraging or eliminating the troublesome creatures. We have a possum and a family of raccoons in our garden, and since they are not troublesome, we gladly share our garden with them, and I hope you will too. It's when they become troublesome that you may need to discourage them, and hopefully these methods will be of assistance. If you're not into mixing your own formulas, you will find that garden outlets usually carry several types and brands of repellents. The following dozen creatures (in alphabetical order) are the ones gardeners ask me about the most.

Birds—They Love Berries, Cherries, and Some Fruit

You go to bed at night thinking you'll pick your ripe cherries the next morning, only to wake up and find that the birds have eaten or taken a bite out of practically every cherry on the tree. Or they have nibbled on fruit (even apples) or have gotten into the blueberries, etc. Yet if you're like me, you love to have the birds in the garden. Remember, birds are our friends in so many ways; they do a great job of controlling insects, eliminate some weed seeds, are beautiful, and serenade us. So what can we do to do discourage them but not harm them?

Facing page: Battery-operated devices such as this mole chaser discourage moles by emitting periodic sounds and creating minor vibrations.

Foil Strips

When I was growing up, my folks hung strips of aluminum foil in the trees and the strips' flashing movement fooled the birds for awhile.

BirdScare Flash Tape

Today, one of the most common methods is to use a BirdScare Flash Tape. This is a mylar tape that is red on one side and silver on the other. Red is like fire to birds and the silver flashes and scares them. This tape is twisted to show both sides. It's quite effective, and often used by commercial growers. Spread throughout the tree or berry bush.

Netting

Netting can do a pretty good job of keeping birds from eating your crop, and, if installed properly, can even discourage squirrels and raccoons. Spread the netting over berries or small trees, or build a frame and cover it with netting on the top and all sides, and then the plants inside are protected.

Noise

Some folks will go so far as to place a radio in the berry patch, cover it with plastic, and keep it on from sunrise to sunset. Others will make up some kind of clapper noise that sounds off every fifteen to thirty seconds.

Scare-A-Way Tape

This is a nylon tape that when strung tight, with no twists in the tape, creates a supersonic sound the birds can hear and discourages them. Again this is often used commercially by growers. (In fact, it is also quite often used over commercial fish-hatchery pens.)

Scarecrows

Scarecrows often work too!

Fake Predators

Fake snakes or owls work really well in some gardens, at least for awhile. Move them occasionally.

Cats—They Love to Mess Up the Soil

That's right; cats look for the softest dry soil and consider it the ideal place to use as their personal latrine. New plantings, a newly planted lawn, or a dry soil area under the eaves of the house can be their favorite messing spot. So what do you do to discourage them?

Water

Keeping the area wet until they change their habit and find a new spot sometimes helps.

Pepper

Dusting a little cayenne pepper in the area will often discourage them for awhile. Wear gloves and a face mask when you apply the pepper in case you are allergic to it.

Commercial Repellents

Several new commercial repellent products are on the market. When using any of them, always apply according to label instructions.

Are cats digging in your flower and shrub beds? If you check closely, you will often find the soil in that area is quite dry. Sometimes the simple solution is to keep that area moist or even wet, and they will find a new spot, hopefully in their master's yard.

Deer—Such Beautiful Creatures, but They Often Eat Their Way Through a Garden

These magnificent creatures are so beautiful, interesting, and fun to watch, but, boy, can they raise havoc with roses, evergreens, and the vegetable garden. We had a couple that visited our garden regularly at a place that we had at the ocean, so we chose to use fuzzy-leaf plants in the garden, because deer are not particularly fond of them. However, we found that if they are really hungry deer will eat just about any garden plant. So how can you enjoy the deer and your garden too?

Motion-Sensor Sprinklers

My oldest son uses a motion-sensor sprinkler in his garden. When the deer come within range of the sensor, the sprinkler goes on and the deer take off. It scares the deer but does not hurt them. Just be certain you turn the sprinkler off when you're working in the garden!

Hand Soap

A few years ago the *Gardening in America* crew and I were taping a show at a vegetable research garden in Delaware, and I noticed that the head gardener had Dial (a detergent hand soap) hanging from surrounding tree branches in mesh bags and nylon stockings. Incidentally, the bars of soap were still in their packages, with just the top of the wrapper opened. They were spaced about 10 feet apart and about 5 feet high—right at the level of a deer's nose. I asked him how it worked, and he said it hadn't worked at all the previous year. But they found that it was a matter of timing. He said they found that if they put the bars of soap in place in the fall, before the male deer rut, it worked. In fact, they had not had any deer damage so far that spring.

Fencing

Fencing also works, but some deer can jump fences up to 7 or 8 feet high. So usually one has to either build the fences higher or build two high fences about 2 to 3 feet apart. Then the deer will not try to jump them.

Pepper-Spray Recipe

Pepper spray applied to the foliage of plants will also often discourage deer. Blend three fresh hot peppers and three cloves of garlic with 1 tablespoon of liquid detergent soap (the type you use to handwash dishes in the sink). Mix into 1 gallon of water and lightly sprinkle on the area. Wear gloves and a mask if you are allergic to hot peppers.

With commercial sprays, read and follow label instructions.

Commercial Repellents

There are also a number of commercial repellents on the market. Most need to be reapplied after several rains. Apply them according to the manufacturer's instructions.

Fish Line

One gardener we interviewed on *Gardening in America* strung up fish line along the edge of the property to keep the deer out. The deer apparently can't see the fish line and it worked for that person. String several lines about 1 foot apart to a height of 6 feet.

Dogs—"Man's Best Friend" Until You Have to Clean Up the Mess

Adult dogs and puppies can be so cute and so smart, but if they're not yours and use your lawn as a bathroom, or tear and scratch holes in your lawn, then it's a different story. Fortunately these days, with dog leash laws, dog problems are not as widespread as they were a few years ago. And pet owners are generally more considerate, even going to the extent of cleaning up after dogs with poop-scoops or other devices.

Female dogs urinating on lawns can leave yellow or brown spots, ruining the appearance of the lawn. As soon as you see these spots beginning to turn dark green or dull green, soak the spots thoroughly with water. Then help neutralize those areas by spreading a dusting of gypsum over them. If your dog is the problem, check with your veterinarian, because they can often change the dog's diet and help prevent urine spots in the lawn. (I am told they add yeast and garlic to the dog's diet to mellow the urine.)

Here are a few ideas on how to discourage dogs from using your lawn and garden as their rest stop.

Plastic Jugs

Place water-filled, gallon-size plastic jugs in a row at an angle, spacing them about 5 feet apart. This spooks the dogs and they will go around the jugs. It doesn't look good, but usually does the job.

Pepper Spray

Add a little pepper spray with your dog repellents where you are having the most trouble with dog damage. See the recipe listed under Deer, above. With commercial sprays, always apply according to label instructions. Wear gloves and a mask if you are allergic to hot peppers.

Motion-Sensor Sprinklers

Motion-sensor sprinklers work pretty well. (See a description of them above, under Deer.)

Rotten-Egg Recipe

One radio show listener recommends a mixture of six cracked eggs (shells and all) and a half bottle of hot sauce; put them into a 1-gallon container, fill up halfway with water, cap it tightly, and allow it to ferment for five days. Then, she says, hold your nose and spread it around your garden. She says, "It's guaranteed to keep four-legged creatures away." Not to mention two-legged ones!

Slugs a problem in your garden? Whatever method you use to control them, start it early, in late January or early February when they first appear. The more slugs you eliminate the less you will have to contend with later in the year. I've been told that each slug reproduces up to 250 offspring, and the offspring reproduce too. So it only makes sense, the more you can eliminate early in the season, the fewer slugs you should have to contend with later in the season.

Geese—Beautiful as They Are, Their Droppings Create a Terrible Mess

We now live on a lake, and one of the beautiful sights to see is a flock of geese as they glide down and land on the water. But if they decide they want to come up out of the lake and rest or feed on the lawn, they can create the biggest mess. In fact, birders say that each bird leaves about 3 pounds of droppings per day. I guess one could look at this as manure, but don't try to walk through it! So how do we keep them off the lawn?

Commercial Repellents

Rejectit is a newly developed goose repellent made from grape seeds. Through the grapevine, I have heard it's a recycled product from wineries.

BirdScare Flash Tape

As mentioned under Birds earlier in this chapter, the BirdScare Flash Tape sometimes is effective.

Moles, Voles, and Shrews—The Ones That Like to Make Mounds

These interesting little guys are our friends in that they are primarily after insects, their source of food. Unfortunately, they also leave ugly mounds of soil, and the tunnels they make leave plants high and dry. So practically every homeowner and gardener goes after them with a vengeance. Homeowners use exhaust from the car (to gas them), water from the hose (to drown them), glass or blackberry canes placed in their tunnels (to cause them to bleed to death), and probably a hundred other home remedies, most of which do not work. So if any of these creatures are a problem in your garden, here are a few things you can do that might discourage them . . . at least temporarily.

Trapping

Trapping is considered the most effective way to catch moles. However, this method has been outlawed in some areas (such as in Washington State). Where it is legal, the Out-of-Sight trap is considered to be one of the most effective.

Castor-Oil Recipe

A combination of castor oil and detergent soap seems to do a pretty good job of discouraging them. Many gardeners claim that it remains effective for about ninety days. However, I used this mix in my garden about a year ago and the moles still have not returned. If you want to give it a try, here's the formula:

You need ¼ cup of castor oil and 2 tablespoons of liquid dishwashing detergent (the type you use at the kitchen sink). Blend them together in a blender (they will not mix by hand). Add 6 tablespoons of water and blend again. This formula should be kept in a closed container until you are ready to use it.

When you are ready, add 2 tablespoons of this formula to 1 gallon of warm water, then pour it over the area where the moles are working. (Do not pour it into the tunnels.) Here's how it works: The solution works its way into the soil, coating the insects with castor oil. Then when the moles/shrews/voles eat the insects, they get an unpleasant taste, and since that is their source of food, they move on.

Cats and Dogs

A hungry cat will wait by the hour for any one of these creatures to start digging. Then they pounce on them, play with them for awhile, and leave them on your doorstep to show you what a great job they are doing protecting your property.

Some types of dogs are also good mole catchers. My aunt had a dachshund that was one of the best mole catchers I've ever seen. He would average one a week. The only problem was, he always left a huge hole where he had gone after the mole.

Vibrations

There are several types of vibrating devices that will discourage moles. Most are battery-operated; they make periodic sounds and create a minor vibration, which seems to scare away the moles for awhile.

I installed two in my garden, because one of my radio listeners asked about them and I had no personal experience with them. The first one worked great and is still working a year later. The second one I placed in the front garden, and the very first day a mole made a mound within 1 foot of the device. But now the rest of the story: the mole never came back, and six months later, there has been no mole activity in that part of the garden. However, some home gardeners say these devices only work for awhile, and since I only have one year's experience with them, I guess the jury is still out on this one.

Rabbits—They Love Carrots, Greens, and Lots of Other Plants

They are so cute, but, boy, can they raise havoc in the garden. So what are some of the ways to try to keep them out of the garden?

Fake Snakes

Fake snakes seem to do a good job of keeping rabbits out of an area of the garden. Sometimes even a short piece of garden hose, curled a little bit, will do the job. Move them around occasionally. Do not leave them in the same spot for more than a week or so.

Fencing

Low fencing (about 2 feet high) works really well, because rabbits can't jump or climb it. But they are apt to dig under it, so if you are going to use it, submerge it 8 to 10 inches into the ground.

Onions and Garlic

Onions, garlic, shallots, and leeks are rabbit repellents, so interplant your vegetables with them if you live in an area where rabbits are a problem.

Limestone Flour or Wood Ashes

I have never tried it, but a gardener in rabbit country said it works to place limestone flour or wood ashes either on the ground or on damp leaves.

Commercial Repellents

There are several new rabbit repellents on the market, and success reports from home gardeners have been pretty good. Of course, apply according to label instructions.

Mountain Beavers—These Are Dry-Land Beavers

Don't mess with these guys; they can be mean. I had one take 3 feet out of a 6-foot-high pine tree, and it didn't like being chased by me. So the beaver won! However, I must admit the tree was better off, because it developed the most beautifully contorted shape and became a great conversation piece. Mountain beavers burrow into the ground, usually in a hillside but sometimes on the level ground. If whole branches disappear from your plants overnight, there is a good chance the culprit is a mountain beaver.

Live Trapping

The best way I know of controlling this pest is to trap it in a baited live trap. Then move it to a new location. Your State Department of Fish and Wildlife can recommend whom to contact about obtaining the live traps and where the beavers should be released. (Or they will be able to refer you to the proper authority.)

Lemon Peel

I understand mountain beavers do not like the smell of crushed lemon peels, so you might give that a try.

Electric Fence

A low-watt (6- or 12-volt) electric fence is often quite effective in keeping them out of an area.

Raccoons—Cute as Can Be, but They Can Be Destructive

Some folks refer to raccoons as bandits because of the markings on their face. They love corn and fish. So if your corn stalks are down one morning and only one bite taken out of each ear, it's probably raccoons. Likewise, if fish start disappearing from your pond, look for raccoons or herons. Be sure you or your pets never get between mother raccoon and her babies. She can turn on you in the blink of an eye. Our *Gardening in America* crew has a tape of this happening to a neighbor's pet. (Fortunately, the dog escaped with very minor scars.) Here are a few things that may help to discourage raccoons.

Lemon Peel

This is another of the creatures that does not like the smell of crushed lemon peels.

Mesh

Mesh placed over the pool or pond will help keep both raccoons and herons from getting your fish.

Electric Fencing

Low-watt (6- or 12-volt) electric fences are quite effective. Raccoons work at night, so there is no need to leave the fences on during the day when you and your pets are in the garden.

Rotten-Egg Recipe

The egg formula I mentioned earlier under Dogs is also quite effective, I understand.

Noise

Raccoons are quite noise-wary too, so a radio playing in their favorite snack area when a crop ripens will often discourage them. See Noise, under Birds, above.

Slugs and Snails—The Creepy, Slimy Guys

These small, slimy creatures can really raise havoc in the garden. Slimy trails and chewed leaves are the telltale signs that slugs are active in your garden.

I think the secret to controlling slugs is to first find their home base. Their nesting (resting) area is usually in a cool, moist, shady spot. It is from this spot that they travel each night to your seedlings and the lush leaves of vegetables and flowers. In the early morning hours, you will find them heading for home; or at about dusk in the evening, you'll find them heading out for their dinner. Once you determine these nesting/resting places, those are the areas where you should concentrate your slug control program. It is important to note that the average garden will have more than one spot where they hang out during the warm daylight hours.

Researchers say only about 5 percent of the slugs are out at any one time, so if you are spending your time trying to control them in the wrong spots, you'll never get ahead of their reproduction cycles, and they will continue to be a problem. Here are a few ideas that may help you to control slugs in your garden.

Commercial Baits

Commercial baits are often used to control slugs. To protect your pets and other friendly garden creatures, consider using one of the following methods to apply them:

- Take an average-size 16-ounce plastic pop bottle, cut it in half, place 1 teaspoonful of bait in the bottom half, then take the top and insert it upside-down into the bottom. That way the bait is completely covered, the slugs are drawn to it, and once they are inside, they are trapped and hopefully on their way to slug heaven. I first saw this homemade device at a Master Gardener's home in Redmond, Washington, and while we were taping a TV show in the garden, the first slugs were already being attracted to the slug bottle. I use these in my garden, using green-colored containers in the flower garden, then tucking them up under the green leaves of plants; you can hardly see them.
- This idea is from Peter Chan, the famous author of *Magical Landscapes* and *Better Vegetable Gardens the Chinese Way*. Peter showed me a clear plastic container about the size of a small cottage cheese or sour cream container. On the sides at the bottom, he had cut three or four small round holes about 1 inch across, spacing them an equal distance apart. Then he put about 1 tablespoon of slug bait inside the container, placed the lid on top, firmed the container in the soil, and placed a rock on top so the wind wouldn't blow it away. Again, the bait is inside, hopefully out of the reach of pets, birds, etc. I've used these very effectively in my garden. Place them about 10 feet apart. I suggest you use them at the perimeter of the garden so you get the slugs before they devour anything.

Beer Traps

Many gardeners report good success in using beer in bowls partially submerged in the soil. They say it attracts the slugs, they drink it, become intoxicated, and drown.

I've got a great story for this one: I was conducting a group of Northwesterners on a tour of England. When I was checking the group into a small hotel in the countryside, the desk clerk said, "I have a telegram for you, Mr. Hume." It read, "Tell Mom (so I knew Mom was in our group), stale beer doesn't work. Tell Mom her dogs have been drunk ever since she left." "Mom" then told me she was trying to control slugs with the beer. I haven't found this method very successful in my garden, but many find it very effective. So maybe it's worth a try.

Diatomaceous Earth

If you have only a few plants that slugs like, you can circle them with a ½-inch band of diatomaceous earth. (This is often used to filter hot tubs, terrariums, etc.) Broken bits of seashells are often used also. The sharp bits of shell cut the slugs, which they do not like.

Copper Strips

Place a 1-inch-wide strip of copper or copper wire on the top of a raised bed to keep them out. Trouble is, if they are already in the bed, they can't get out either. The copper reacts with a chemical on the snails' and slugs' bodies and actually gives them an electric shock, sometimes killing them.

Sawdust and Wood Ashes

Cedar sawdust and wood ashes spread around plants will help protect the plants (slugs do not like to crawl over these rough materials), but will not eliminate the slugs.

Hand-Picking

There are several other ideas, but probably the one most used by old-timers is collecting and destroying them, by spearing them with a stick or using a knife on them.

Commercial Barriers

There is a product made in the Pacific Northwest called Slug & Snail de Fence that is composed of low-density polyethylene plastic and vacuum-grade table salt. It's really a barrier, because most slugs will withdraw from the salt barrier; if they don't, they will meet their demise.

Iron Phosphate

There are now several products on the market containing iron phosphate that are considered environmentally friendly and seem to be fairly effective in controlling slugs.

Ducks, Geese, Toads, and Snakes

Last but not least, ducks, geese, toads, and snakes will eat slugs, so you can help eliminate the slugs by encouraging these guys to your garden. We live on a lake and we'd be happy to give you some of our wild geese (ha-ha), as they trample low plants and poop all over the lawn. It's easier to put up with the slugs than with the temperamental, messy geese.

Research Continues

As we go to press, I understand research is also being done on a compound found in dead quack grass and a compound in the rinds of oranges, both potential slug controls. I believe this is only the beginning; the continuing interest in this subject will result in even more advances and new environmentally friendly slug controls.

Snakes—A Friend to Every Garden, Unless You're Scared of Them

Snakes do a great job of insect (and slug) control, but some people are startled or even petrified when they see them. So what can you do to discourage them from some parts of the garden?

Lemon Peel and Pepper Spray

I have a friend who uses a mix of lemon peels and pepper spray. She says it works quite effectively.

Commercial Repellents

There are also a couple of commercial products on the market you might try. One is called Snake-A-Way; the other is Mr. T's repellent. Use according to the manufacturer's directions.

Squirrels—Cute, Fast, Feisty, and Sometimes a Real Nuisance

These fuzzy-tailed, tree-climbing characters are fun to watch and a challenge for all dogs and cats. They love nuts or anything that looks like a nut–crocus bulbs, for example! They dig them up, then bury them in another part of the garden. We have a nut tree, and they raise havoc in that tree before the nuts even have a chance to get mature. In one spot under some trees, our lawn is continually dug up. It seems they also like the moss for their nests. Right now as I write this chapter, two squirrels are outside my window picking off the flower buds of our camellia. They just pick and discard them, like little brats. If they are raising havoc in your garden, what can you do to keep them out of certain areas?

Pepper Spray

One reader says to mix a little hot pepper spray (see the recipe under Deer earlier in this chapter) with a dog and cat repellent. Pour it over the area where you plant your bulbs and they'll leave them alone.

Chicken Wire

Chicken wire spread over a planting spot will usually discourage squirrels. Place it right on the ground or they'll make their way under it.

Netting

Cover the top of small nut and other trees with netting, then tied at the trunk. The openings in the netting must be small so squirrels cannot climb through it, and it must be tied at the trunk so they can not get up under it.

Lemon Peel

I have heard that they don't like the smell of lemon peels.

Index

A

B

C

INDEX

D

E

F

G

H

I

J–K

L

M

N

O

P

INDEX

Q–R

S

T

U–V

W–Z

INDEX

About the Author

Ed Hume is a recognized gardening authority both in the Northwest and nationwide. For years he has been offering down-to-earth, practical advice to home gardeners—advice gleaned from a lifetime of experience. His television program, *Gardening in America,* is viewed by millions of households throughout the Northwest, and he also hosts a popular weekly radio program. Hume's gardening articles have appeared in local, regional, and national publications. He is the recipient of numerous awards and honors, including the National Garden Communicator's Award, the Fellowship Award from the Garden Writers of America, and Governor's appointee on the Washington State Landscape Architects Licensing Board. He lives with his wife, Myrna, in Kent, Washington.